Teaching Reading to the Mildly Retarded Child

PATRICIA H. GILLESPIE
Indiana University

LOWELL E. JOHNSON
Fairmont State College
Fairmont, West Virginia

CHARLES E. MERRILL PUBLISHING COMPANY
A Bell & Howell Company
Columbus, Ohio 43216

Published by
CHARLES E. MERRILL PUBLISHING COMPANY
A Bell & Howell Company
Columbus, Ohio 43216

Library of Congress Catalog Card Number: 73-88245

International Standard Book Number: 0-675-08859-3

Printed in the United States of America

Preface

Reading is one of the skills most often stressed in the special class for the educable mentally retarded child. Although much research has been conducted in order to determine what particular reading methods and materials are most effective in working with the retarded child, most studies indicate that no reading approach is superior to others. Perhaps more attention should be placed on the learning styles of each retarded child and methods and materials best suited to his abilities rather than on any one particular method for each group of retarded children. Such an approach is a concern of this book.

Teaching Reading to the Mildly Retarded Child is intended as an introduction to the field of reading and how it relates to the educable and borderline retarded child. This book should be of particular interest to the special-education teacher, the classroom teacher of heterogeneously grouped children, and others working or preparing to work in the area of special education. The teacher of the educable retarded child should have a knowledge of basic reading skills; reading characteristics and deficits of the retarded; and of diagnostic, developmental, and remedial approaches and techniques. This book deals with all of these areas. The latter part of the book deals with a diagnostic-prescriptive and problem-solving approach to teaching reading to the retarded.

The first chapter of this text contains an overview of the field of mental retardation which includes definitions, incidences, terminologies, causes, and characteristics of the retarded. Current programs and implications for the future education of the retarded are also considered. This chapter is intended as a quick overview for those in fields other than special education.

Chapter Two provides the special-education teacher with what he should know about the basic reading skills. This chapter is an overview of the psychology and components of reading. Word perception, phonics, and comprehension are discussed. Those who are not in the field of reading may benefit from this chapter.

Chapter Three contains the reading characteristics and deficits of the retarded. Many authorities have suggested that mentally handicapped children have specific learning characteristics which may affect reading performance. Both this hypothesis and opposing viewpoints are reviewed in this chapter. Characteristics such as poor quality of language and experimental status, visual and auditory perception problems, specific difficulties in comprehension, and reading interests of the retarded also are discussed.

Chapter Four contains an overview of trends in diagnosis, such as use of standardized measures, criterion-referenced tests, and modality testing.

In Chapter Five, formal reading and reading-related tests are discussed, while Chapter Six deals with informal testing procedures and the inquiry or problem-solving approach to diagnosis.

The developmental reading approaches that have been used with the retarded in the past are reviewed in Chapter Seven. Related research also is included.

The remedial or specialized approaches that have been developed for problem readers or retarded children are included in the discussion in Chapter Eight.

Chapter Nine considers reading-related programs (e.g., perceptual and language programs) that have been included within the total reading plan for the retarded.

Various learning management techniques as well as classroom application of the diagnostic-prescriptive and/or problem-solving approach to instruction are the concern in Chapter Ten. A simulated class of children is the focal point of the discussions in the latter part of this chapter.

The use of the masculine pronoun in referring to the teacher in this text is in no way intended as a slight to the many women working in the field of special education. Rather, it is used as a generic term to refer to all teachers regardless of sex and is employed only because our language does not contain a pronoun which can be applied to *either* sex.

The authors would like to express their appreciation to the many who have contributed to this book. Specifically, we express our gratitude to Bonnie Brown and Carol Steakley for their many contributions to Chapters Eight and Ten, and to Roger Newman, Becky Enright, and Mike Grella for their many suggestions concerning instructional programs for children.

We want to give special recognition to Dr. Eddie C. Kennedy and Dr. Thomas C. Hatcher of West Virginia University for their influence in our thinking concerning the field of reading and its relationship to special children.

We also express our appreciation to Debbie Martin, Dawn Crizer, Rachel Wampler, Susie Anderson, and Linda Trillman for their excellent typing of the manuscript.

We are grateful to our families for their encouragement, assistance, and patience during the time this book was being prepared.

Contents

ONE

Overview of
the Retarded

One of the greatest challenges that still faces the nation and its school systems is learning how to deal effectively with mentally retarded children. In spite of our technology, no answer has been found for the treatment, education, and training of mental retardates. In fact, much of the populace is ignorant of the basic facts regarding retardation. In addition, the authorities in special education have been unable to reach agreement on the major facets of retardation. Although perfect harmony can never be expected among all those concerned with the retarded, people can be expected to attempt to understand the ever-present problems of retardation and to deal with them in a positive fashion. To aid in attaining this goal, this chapter is organized to present the following information on the following topics:

1. Definitions of retardation
2. Causes of retardation
3. Cultural-familial retardation
4. Theories of intelligence and learning as they are related to the retarded
5. Historical development and modern concepts of special education

6. School programs for the retarded
7. Criticisms of and alternatives to present programs
8. Litigation and the retarded

DEFINITIONS OF MENTAL RETARDATION

According to Kirk (1962), the problem of finding a definition for mental retardation has been difficult because mental retardation is not a disease, like cancer or tuberculosis, but, rather, a condition which includes many criteria. In addition, many general terms which may denote the same thing have been attached to children. These terms include mentally retarded, mentally deficient, feebleminded, minimal brain dysfunction, underachiever, educationally retarded, and culturally disadvantaged. Because all of these terms may be applicable to many children with subnormal intelligence, it is possible that the children we speak of as mentally retarded may include not only those with brain damage and various easily recognizable clinical types of retardation but also the culturally disadvantaged and the cultural-familially retarded, those from families of low socioeconomic status in which mild mental retardation tends to run through the families (Dunn, 1968). Thus, it becomes necessary to determine which of these individual children are actually mentally retarded.

Definitions by Tredgold and Doll

A. F. Tredgold (1937) gave a traditional definition of mental retardation:

> . . . a state of incomplete mental development of such a kind and degree that the individual is incapable of adapting himself to the normal environment of his fellows in such a way as to maintain existence independently of supervision, control, or external support.[1]

Edgar Doll (1941) elaborated on Tredgold's definition and made mental deficiency more specific in nature. He stated six criteria which he considered essential to an adequate definition:

---

[1]A.F. Tredgold, *A Textbook of Mental Deficiency*, 6th ed. (Baltimore, Maryland: William Wood and Co., 1937), p. 4.

These are (1) social incompetence, (2) due to mental subnormality, (3) which has been developmentally arrested, (4) which obtains at maturity, (5) is of constitutional origin, and (6) is essentially incurable.[2]

Doll's idea of the incurability of retardation contained little hope for amelioration of the condition and no doubt influenced the type of programs that were established in many school systems. This definition may also account for the attitude that has prevailed in many institutions for the retarded.

Kanner's Definition

Leo Kanner (1948; 1957) recognized three kinds of mental retardation which he termed "absolute," "relative," and "apparent" feeblemindedness. Absolute feeblemindedness refers to the condition of those individuals who are defective in all areas of mentation and would not respond successfully to any type of educational or therapeutic treatment. Relative feeblemindedness describes individuals who have intellectual inadequacies related to the culture which surrounds them. These inadequacies may remain unrecognized in primitive societies, but soon come into evidence when the individuals are asked to perform scholastically in competition with others. Nonetheless, these people may become quite active in the unskilled labor force. In apparent feeblemindedness, individuals have not achieved their full potential because of such factors as lack of opportunity, physical handicaps, or inadequate instruction related to their disability. It is possible for such an individual to be diagnosed as having apparent feeblemindedness yet later become socially and/ or intellectually adequate.

School Definition

As far as the public school is concerned mental retardation has been determined consistently by means of a "normal curve" concept based upon the child's performance on an intelligence test. Special significance has been attributed to *individual* intelligence tests such as the *Wechsler Intelligence Scale for Children* (WISC) or the *Stanford Binet*.

---

[2]Edgar A. Doll, "The Essentials of an Inclusive Concept of Mental Deficiency," *American Journal of Mental Deficiency* 46 (1941): 215.

Terman (1916) introduced a rough classification of ability based upon the Stanford-Binet IQ test, which was revised in 1937. His classification attained such wide usage that it became the standard for public school use. Wechsler (1955) set up a similar classification which included as intellectually retarded the entire group which falls more than one standard deviation below the mean on such tests. Assuming a mean of 100 and a standard deviation of sixteen (The standard deviation may vary slightly with the test used), the following levels of retardation and the terms by which they are usually designated are:

Level of Retardation	IQ Range
Borderline (slow learner)	68-84
Mildly Retarded (educable)	52-68
Moderately Retarded (trainable)	36-52
Severely Retarded	20-36
Profoundly Retarded	0-20

The borderline retarded are considered to be just slightly below the "normal" child in terms of intellectual ability and are usually taught in the regular classroom. The educable retarded children are frequently from the lower socio-economic levels and are considered to have some intellectual deficiencies. Their motor coordination is slightly below that of the normal child of the same chronological age (Johnson, 1963), but they learn in much the same

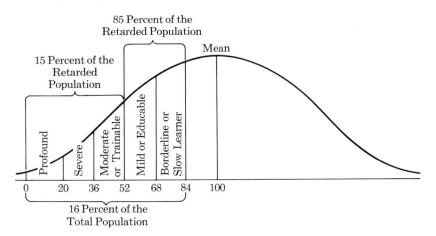

Figure 1: Degree of Mental Retardation Based on a Normal Curve Concept.

way as do normal children (Kirk, 1964); however, they may be placed in special-education classes. The moderately retarded or trainable group is usually taught in special classes. Kirk (1962) has indicated that children in this category can achieve limited success in self-help skills, social adjustment to home and neighborhood, and economic usefulness in the home or workshops, but they usually cannot succeed in the community at large. The severely retarded have serious deficiencies in language, motor, and physical integrities, as well as in intellectual ability. Although it has been found that this group can learn such simple self-help skills as toilet-training and feeding, the profoundly retarded usually are dramatically impaired in almost every respect. Language is absent and impairment is usually profound in motor and physical integrities as well as intellectual abilities. Those falling in this group must have complete care. No research currently shows possibilities for teaching or training such children in academic areas.

Figure 1 places the levels of retardation on a normal curve. An examination of this figure shows that of the total population, 16 percent have an IQ score below 84; however, only 2 to 3 percent of the total population has an IQ below 52. Eighty-five percent of the retarded population is made up of the mild and borderline retarded, while only 15 percent can be considered moderately, severely, and profoundly retarded.

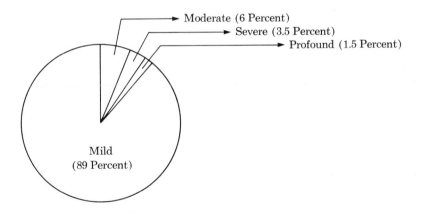

Figure 2: Classification of the Mentally Retarded Population[3]

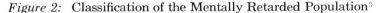

[3]President's Committee on Mental Retardation. *A First Report on the Nation's Progress and Remaining Great Needs in the Campaign to Combat Mental Retardation* (Washington: U.S. Government Printing Office, 1967), p. 1.

The President's Committee on Mental Retardation (1967) has made a similar classification. In terms of the retarded population, this classification places 89 percent in the mildly retarded, 6 percent in the moderately retarded, 3.5 percent in the severely retarded, and 1.5 percent in the profoundly retarded range (see Figure 2).

On the basis of the school's definition of retardation, many school systems place children in special classes if their IQ scores fall below 70 on an individualized intelligence test. Too often, other factors which might be related to academic failure or lack of achievement are ignored.

AAMD Definition

Recognizing that previous catagorizations may have been somewhat limited in scope, and may have ignored the fact that many who are labeled retarded can cope successfully with adult life, the American Association on Mental Deficiency (AAMD) has developed a definition which is today widely accepted by authorities in special education. R. Heber has stated this definition:

> Mental retardation refers to subaverage general intellectual functioning which originates during the developmental period and is associated with impairment in adaptive behavior.[4]

"Subaverage intellectual functioning" refers to performance which is greater than one standard deviation below the mean as assessed by the performance on one or more objectives tests of intelligence such as the Stanford-Binet or WISC. "The developmental period" is considered to include the time from prenatal development to approximately sixteen years. "Adaptive behavior" includes three aspects: the maturational self-help skills which are generally learned in the pre-school years and are basically sensory-motor in nature; the types of learning which are formally approached in the school years and which facilitate knowledge; and social-personal adjustment of the individual to his peers and his environment (Heber, 1961).

Although this definition incorporates the IQ classification utilized in the school definition as the measure of intellectual func-

---

[4]R. Heber, "A Manual on Terminology and Classification in Mental Retardation, Second Edition." Monograph of the *American Journal of Mental Deficiency* (1961): 3-4. Reprinted by permission of the American Association on Mental Deficiency and the author.

tioning, it would classify as retarded only those individuals who are inadequate in *both* intellectual functioning and adaptive behavior. Therefore, a person may be retarded in one phase of life but not another. Many children who would be considered retarded by the school may be quite able to support themselves, marry, rear families, and adjust with at least minimum adequacy to adult life.

CAUSES OF RETARDATION

The AAMD has classified eight catagories of mental retardation. The AAMD believes, at present, that mental retardation can be caused by: infection (rubella, encephalitis, syphilis, or meningitis), intoxication (maternal toxemia), trauma (forceps delivery), disorders of metabolism, growth and nutrition (PKU, galactosemia, hypoglycemia, hypothyroidism), new growths (tumors), unknown prenatal influences (cerebral defects, hydrocephaly, macrocephaly, microcephaly, mongolism), unknown causes with structural causes manifest (encephalopathy), and uncertain causes with functional reactions manifest (cultural-familial retardation). (Heber, 1961).

The President's Committee on Mental Retardation (1967) has given a similar breakdown which is presented in Figure 3. According to this report, 25 percent of cases of retardation are caused by genetics, prenatal influences, new growths, metabolic, trauma, intoxication, infection, and organic causes. However, 75 percent of

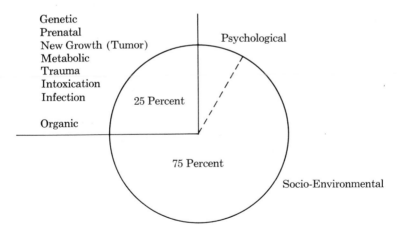

Figure 3:   Mental Retardation by Cause[5]

[5]President's Committee on Mental Retardation, p. 1.

the causes of retardation is not clearly known and are placed in the psychological and socio-environmental categories.

CULTURAL-FAMILIAL RETARDATION

Because so much retardation falls within the cultural-familial category, it is necessary to examine this type of retardation further. Sir Francis Galton (1869) first studied afflicted individuals and traced the incidence of their disorders within their family trees. Additional study built on Galton's work is found in Dugdale's study (1887) of the Jukes family and Goddard's study (1912) of the Kallikak family. Because he found many incidences of crime, immorality, pauperism, and mental retardation in the Jukes family, Dugdale concluded that heredity and environment were both involved in the Jukes' family history. Goddard traced two lines of descent from Martin Kallikak, a soldier in the Revolutionary War who had had an illicit love affair with a feebleminded tavern girl. The majority of the descendents from this relationship were socially inadequate and lacking in intelligence. However, Kallikak's marriage with a woman who was not feebleminded produced another line of descendents in which almost all were normal or outstanding members of society. Goddard concluded that in the case of the Kallikaks, heredity was an overwhelming contributor to intellectual ability and social adequacy.

Goddard's point of view has its modern adherents. Prominent among them is Jensen (1969) who has defended his viewpoint that intelligence is essentially an inherited "g" or general factor. He believes that abstract reasoning and problem-solving are largely inherited abilities and cannot be improved substantially by compensatory education or forced exposure to the culture and environment. Thus, he contends that there is a definite link between heredity and retardation.

On the other hand, intellectual retardation can be regarded with greater optimism if one believes that an early and favorable environment can produce considerable improvement in intellectual functioning. Masland, Sarason, and Gladwin (1958) do not deny that heredity is a factor in mental deficiency but they do hold that much of this view is based on speculation and bias. Sarason (1959) contends that mentally retarded individuals:

> ... of somewhat staggering numbers in our population come largely from the lowest social classes, or from culturally distinct

> minority groups, or from regions with conspicuously poor edu-
> cational facilities or standards. . . . Regardless of theoretical
> bent, no responsible investigator has denied that the level and
> quality of the functioning of the mentally retarded reflects
> social and cultural factors.[6]

This view is supported by Dunn (1968) who has reported that
in the upper range of retardation, 60 to 80 percent of the children
are from lower socioeconomic backgrounds. In addition, studies by
Kirk (1968), Davis (1940), and Skeels and Dye (1939) present
evidence that mentally retarded children may be functioning at
lower intellectual levels because of cultural deprivation.

In regard to the heredity-environment controversy, Heber has
stated:

> The exact role of genetic factors cannot be specified since the
> nature and mode of transmission of genetic aspects of intelli-
> gence is not yet understood. Similarly, there is no clear under-
> standing of the specific manner in which environmental factors
> operate to modify intellectual functioning.[7]

INTELLIGENCE AND LEARNING THEORY

Theories of Intelligence

That intellectual adequacy is basic to learning and that intellectual
retardation makes learning more difficult are not debatable points;
however, there is a difference of opinion in special education as to
what abilities — or lack of abilities — constitutes intellectual adequacy and intellectual retardation. This confusion may be due to
three major reasons: intelligence is difficult to define operationally;
the definition of intelligence frequently suits the needs, prejudices,
and philosophy of the person defining the term; and no one knows
all the factors which constitute intelligence (Garrison and Magoon,
1972). Nor can one assume that intelligence and learning are the
same thing. Thus, in order to understand retardation, one must
have an understanding of the concept of intelligence.

---

[6]S.B. Sarason, *Psychological Problems in Mental Deficiency*, 3rd ed.
(New York: Harper & Row, Publishers, 1959), p. 644.

[7]R. Heber, "A Manual on Terminology and Classification in Mental Retardation," *American Journal of Mental Deficiency* 64 (1959): 40. Reprinted
by permission of the American Association on Mental Deficiency and the
author.

Garrison and Magoon have discussed the concept of intelligence under unifactor, two-factor, and multifactor theories. Unifactor theory, advocated by Binet and Simon (1916), considers intelligence to be monogenetic or a general "g" factor. The two-factor theory, accepted by Spearman (1904), postulates that a "g" factor underlies all memory functions but that multiple factors, "s," are specific to given tasks. Thus, every mental activity involves at least one "s" factor. A person inferior in "g" would have difficulty in learning a specific task.

Multifactor theories include the ideas of such educators as Thorndike, the Thurstones, and Guilford. Thorndike (1921) saw intelligence as being composed of abstract ability, mechanical ability, and social ability. All three involved the common "g" element and were correlated highly. On the other hand, Thurstone and Thurstone (1941) conceived of intelligence as consisting of: primary mental abilities, which include verbal, number, and spatial skills; word fluency; memory; reasoning; and perception. The Thurstones also saw the "g" factor as underlying all of the above factors.

Guilford (1959) visualized intelligence as consisting of three faces — contents, operations, and products; these faces would be placed in a cube form which contained 120 small cubes. (see Figure 4). At present, eighty of the factors in Guilford's cube have been isolated. According to Guilford, the content of any mental function is either figural (objects), symbolic (letters, numbers), semantic (communications), or behavioral (overt) in nature. Operations involve cognition (ways of understanding and comprehending), memory (retention, recall), convergent thinking (bringing together known facts or associations which result in one definite, predictable outcome), divergent thinking (utilizing knowledge in new ways to produce one or more novel solutions or a variety of ideas), and evaluation (synonymous with critical thinking). Applying operations to content results in products which can be either units (discrete concepts), classes (two or more units), relations (relationships between units), systems (structuring of information), transformation (restructuring information), or implications (making predictions).

Learning Theory

Scientific learning theories basically are concerned with how a child can learn in the best way. Of interest to the field of mental retarda-

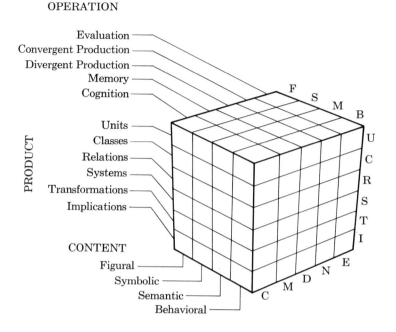

Figure 4: Cubical Model of the Intellect[8]

tion are gestalt psychology and the theories of Lewin, Piaget, Hebb, Skinner, Ellis, and Luria.

Gestalt Psychology: Wertheimer, Kohler, and Koffka were the great leaders of the Gestalt movement in psychology. The major emphasis here was on laws relating to the organization of the perceptual field; the major premise was that the whole is more than the sum of its parts. In learning, those holding the gestalt theory are interested in insight, problem-solving, recall, and transposition as an explanation of transfer. Perception is regarded as a maturational aspect of development.

Lewin (1935; 1951) was much influenced by the early Gestaltists. He devised a theory of personality called "field theory" in which he asserted that a person exists in a field of forces which comes from within the personality (vectors) and from the psycho-

---

[8]From *The Nature of Human Intelligence* by J.P. Guilford (New York: McGraw-Hill Book Co., 1967). Copyright © 1967 McGraw-Hill Book Co. Used with permission of the McGraw-Hill Book Co. and author.

logical environment (valences). How a person behaves is the result of the action of the field of vectors and valences upon his person. In addition, two environments influence the person. The phenomenal environment is the environment as the individual perceives it to be, while the physical environment represents things as they actually are. The person also is made up of two regions: perceptual-motor (which takes in information and produces action), and inner-personal (which consists of tension systems). When a need is satisfied, the tension in the system either disappears or is considerably reduced.

Lewin recognized that as an individual develops, behavioral changes occur. These changes Lewin characterized under the concepts of: differentiation (creation of a larger number of regions within the person and his phenomenal environment as he develops), permeability (permission to change and communication between regions and their boundaries), and organizational interdependence (characteristics of the older individual and reference to the complex relationships which develop between separate regions). As the child increases in chronological age, there is increased rigidity between boundaries; however, as the mental age increases, the differentiation within the personality also increases. In some people, rigidity in boundaries may result in perseveration, concreteness, and other stereotyped behaviors, but in others, it may enable them to begin new activities. Thus, differentiation in the retarded may be the same as in the normal child, although the rigidity may be greater (Robinson and Robinson, 1965).

Piaget: Piaget (1950; 1952; 1954; 1957) has promulgated a developmental approach to child learning. In his theory, adaptation is most important because it involves establishing equilibrium between the organism and the environment. Within adaptation, assimilation and accommodation are important. Assimilation describes the ability of the organism to handle new situations with its present stock of mechanisms, while accommodation describes the process of change through which the organism becomes able to handle new situations which are at first too difficult for it. Furth (1970) has described these processes in this way:

> Assimilation therefore emphasizes the direction from the particular situation to the general structure; accommodation stresses the direction from the general structure to the particular situation. By the same token, assimilation focuses on what is essential to all knowing, namely, the sameness, commonality, and generalization in a given situation; whereas

accommodation focuses on what is particular, new, and different, and by doing so it provides the basis for change and learning.[9]

Piaget has named three major periods of intellectual development: sensori-motor, concrete operations, and formal operations. The sensori-motor period covers the period from birth to approximately two years of age and deals with the formation of perceptions and overt movements; the child forms relationships between his body and his movements. The period of concrete operations (ages two to eleven) preconceptual (ages two to four), intuitive (ages four to seven), and concrete operations (ages seven to eleven). During this period, the child develops language and eventually develops thought based upon his operations with objects rather than on verbally expressed hypotheses. By the period of formal operations (age eleven and over), the child is able to abstract hypotheses and deduce possible solutions to problems presented.

Piaget has shown little interest in retarded children. However, one of his close associates, Barbel Inhelder (1944), has proposed a scheme to order adult retardates according to Piaget's stages of development. The profoundly retarded adult operates at the level of sensori-motor intelligence, while the moderately retarded adult operates in the preoperational intuitive subperiod; the mildly retarded is in the level of concrete operations, while the borderline retardate may be able to do some of the simpler forms of formal operations (Robinson and Robinson, 1965).

Five additional implications of Piaget's theory can be found in Garrison and Magoon (1972):

1. Piaget's intensive observations on the child's development are helpful.
2. The learner must be active if learning is to occur.
3. The teacher has a scale of operations for assessing the child's development in the work of Piaget.
4. The teacher can help the child to progress from existing physical entities to new levels and help him to internalize new activities.
5. The child must be guided in learning.

Hebb: D. O. Hebb's (1949) view of learning also begins with sensory stimulation and perception. However, Hebb is concerned with the transmission of impulses from one part of the nervous system to the other by means of a neural discharge.

---

[9]H.G. Furth, *Piaget for Teachers* (Englewood Cliffs, New Jersey: Prentice-Hall, Inc., 1970), p. 3.

Bugelski (1964) has shown how early learning occurs on the basis of Hebb's theory. He has stated:

> In early life an organism would start out with a more-or-less unorganized brain. There would be no particular neural reaction to any particular stimulus. With repeated specific stimulation, certain cell assemblies would include motor-neuron components and lead to some specific action. If some assemblies were excited in succession by successive stimulations, the cell assemblies would themselves become organized into successive patterns or phase sequences.[10]

Thus, early learning consists of the formation of cell assemblies or new learning associations. Later learning consists of organizing cell assemblies into more complex patterns called "phase sequences." There must be constant perceptual input in order for the central nervous system to function properly.

Benoit (1959) has presented a definition of retardation based on Hebb's neurophysiological theory. He has stated:

> Mental retardation may be viewed as a deficit of intellectual functioning resulting from varied intrapersonal and/or extrapersonal determinants but having as the common proximate cause a diminished efficiency of the nervous system . . . thus entailing a lessened general capacity for growth in perceptual and conceptual integration and consequently in environmental adjustment.[11]

According to this definition, mental retardation is caused by nervous system impairment. Hebb's theory also suggests that perceptual and conceptual integration is necessary for normal development and that a rich and stimulating environment for the retarded child will aid him in achieving his optimal level of learning.

Hebb also has indicated that early brain injury can affect the person's intellectual capacities to a greater extent than if the person has already reached maturity. The exception to this rule is in the development of sensory and motor capacities. After damage in these areas, the infant brain tends to reach higher levels than does the brain of one who receives the damage at maturity (Hebb, 1949).

---

[10]B.R. Bugelski, *The Psychology of Learning Applied to Teaching* (Indianapolis, Indiana: The Bobbs-Merrill Co., 1964), p. 135.

[11]E.P. Benoit, "Toward a New Definition of Mental Retardation," *American Journal of Mental Deficiency* (1959): 559-64.

Skinner and Ellis: Skinner (1938; 1950) has not been so much interested in a formalized theory of learning as in a functional analysis of behavior. In Skinner's view, a discrete operant is the basic unit of behavior. Because, in this case, the organism acts on the environment. It is possible to shape an individual's behavior on the basis of one of his schedules of reinforcement by using primary and secondary reinforcers. The consequence of reinforcement of an operant is to increase the rate at which the operant response is emitted. Reinforcement always increases the probability of a response. Punishment, which is not reinforcement, is either the presentation of a negative reinforcer or the removal of a positive reinforcer. Learning occurs not through punishment but through reinforcement. Thus, in working with the retardate, one can apply Skinner's concepts by placing the goals of instruction in sequential steps, thus shaping the behavior and rewarding the child through reinforcement. This is the basic concept behind teaching machines and programmed learning.

Ellis (1963) has considered the possibility that behavioral inadequacies in retardates may be caused by short-term memory deficits. When an individual receives stimuli, they are usually stored for a few seconds by means of a stimulus or reverberatory trace before they begin to decay. Yet these stimulus traces may cause structural changes in the brain which permit long-term memory to occur. If the central nervous system is damaged, the stimulus trace is shortened in duration and intensity and possible deficits in learning and retention occur, especially if the stimulus trace is defective. This is the case with the retardate. Retardates have more inadequacies in short-term memory and difficulty in making connections between one stimulus situation and another (Robinson and Robinson, 1965).

Luria: Luria (1960; 1963), a Russian psychologist, has developed a verbal dysfunction theory of retardation. Luria does not consider retardation to be inherited but rather, takes the Russian viewpoint which says that retardation is caused as the consequence of nervous system pathology. In Luria's theory, two primary signal systems exist which subserve higher nervous activity. One system gets direct signals from the environment while the other involves language. The language system regulates responses to direct signals and is preeminent over motor behavior. Higher nervous activity consists of excitation and inhibition.

Baumeister (1967), in writing about Luria, has stated:

> Stimulation reaching the cortex, spreads (irradiates) over
> the sensory area involved but with diminishing intensity from
> the point of origin. . . . However, the very process of excitation
> is said to produce an opposite effect — inhibition — in neigh-
> boring cortical regions. Learning, i.e. conditioning, occurs when
> the excitation established by a neutral stimulus temporally and
> spatially approximates that of the unconditioned stimulus.
> After the two simuli are paired a sufficient number of times, the
> excitation of the former elicits the conditioned response.[12]

The properties of the higher nervous processes are strength,
equilibrium, and mobility. Strength is the speed of conditioning;
Equilibrium, the balance between excitatory and inhibitory responses; and mobility, the rapidity of adjustment to changing
stimulus conditions.

Again, Baumeister has stated:

> Thus, the individual with a pathological weakness of the
> basic processes will acquire connections slowly, will respond
> inappropriately, and will be easily disrupted by extraneous
> stimuli and fatigue. If a disequilibrium between excitation and
> inhibition occurs, the effect depends upon which process pre-
> dominates. If it is inhibition, the subject will require many
> trials to learn and will be "sluggish" in his higher thought
> processes. Should the excitatory processes prevail, the subject
> will respond erratically, impulsively, and inappropriately. Fi-
> nally, when the faculty of mobility suffers, the subject no longer
> will adapt easily and readily to changing stimulus conditions.
> In this case the outstanding symptom is perseveration.[13]

Thus, according to Luria, the education of the retarded should
include thorough diagnosis, vocabulary development, and combining motor reactions with verbal reactions.

THE DEVELOPMENT OF MODERN CONCEPTS
OF SPECIAL EDUCATION

Today, educational programs in a democratic society are committed
to the educational training of all children regardless of their intellectual ability or socio-economic status. However, many citizens
have viewed the mentally retarded as a strange group of individuals

---

[12]Alfred A. Baumeister, *Mental Retardation* (Chicago: Aldine Publishing
Co., 1967), p. 202. Reprinted by permission of the publisher.
[13]*Ibid.*, p. 202.

having little in common with other human beings. In past history, retarded children have been considered to be demon-possessed, cursed by God, tolerated for amusement, or the blessed of God who were to be protected.

Although society today has entered a scientific age in its regard for all phases of exceptionality, there are still opposing and conflicting views concerning the education of the retarded. One way of gaining an understanding of the differing concepts used in teaching the educably retarded is to examine the contributions of outstanding individuals and their learning approaches.

Education for the retarded began in the early nineteenth century when Jean Itard took charge of a twelve-year-old boy captured in the forest of Aveyron, France. His method of teaching emphasized sensori-motor exercises to teach fundamental academic skills.

One of Itard's students, Edward Seguin (1866), refined Itard's ideas and established a "physiological method of education." As did Itard, Seguin (1866) believed in training the senses in a formal way. In addition, however, he advocated muscular activities that satisfied the child's needs, and thus placed emphasis upon the whole child and his need for individualized teaching.

Maria Montessori (1912) believed that mental deficiency was an educational problem. She held that an individual posseses a level of intellectual functioning closely related to the stimuli provided in his environment. The greater the intensity and the quantity of the stimuli in the environment, the greater the chances for mental development (Kolstoe, 1956). Thus, Montessori developed auto-education (self-teaching) techniques to train each sense, except for taste and smell, separately. In the Montessori system, the child uses twenty-six different items, under a teacher's supervision, to train the senses.

In the 1920s, two additional approaches were advocated by Annie Inskeep and Alice Descoeudres. Inskeep (1926) placed emphasis on "watering down" the regular curriculum. Thus, traditional school subjects were presented at a slower pace for retarded children. Descoeudres (1928), on the other hand, believed that "idiots and low grade imbeciles" should be excluded from the public schools, while higher-grade mental defectives could be educated in special classes within the public schools. Her teaching approach was based on Dewey's theory of "learning by doing" and emphasized perceptual training through concrete activities.

The 1930s and 1940s saw the implementation of additional learning approaches. John Duncan (1943) developed a project method in which the academic subjects were correlated with shop work, crafts, and home economics. Ingram (1935; 1960) advocated the unit method based on real life experiences and the developmental characteristics of children. Hungerford (1948) and Douglas (1944) proposed occupational education classes which emphasized preparation for employment. Thus, during this period, occupational information and academic materials were correlated.

Strauss and Lehtinen (1947) concerned themselves with a particular type of mentally handicapped child, the brain injured, and based their educational process on two basic ideas. First, "the undamaged portions of the brain hold resources from which the organism may substitute, compensate for, or restitute the disbilities resulting from injury."[14] Second, certain adjustments are necessary to minimize such specific problems as perseveration, hyperactivity, perceptual disturbances, and distractability. In order to make these adjustments, the brain-damaged child must be in an environment which is as nonstimulating as possible. Instruction for these children includes motor activity, perceptual training, and the use of cues.

Since 1950 most recognized authorities in special education have gone to an eclectic approach. Martens (1950), Kirk and Johnson (1951), and, more recently, Goldstein and Seigle (1958) have indicated that units of work should be based on the life situations, developmental needs, and characteristics of the retarded children. No one curriculum plan is to be preferred over another. In other words, diversification rather than standardization is considered important today.

Rothstein (1961) has noted that Flora Daly, Leo Cain, and Ivan Garrison place emphasis on the secondary-education program for the retarded. Personal occupational judgment is the major goal of such education and should draw upon experiences from the home, society, and guidance. The program should include prevocational testing and exploration, in-school vocational training, and a supervised school-work period with job placement as the major goal.

SCHOOL PROGRAMS FOR THE RETARDED

In most cases, educable and slow-learning children are taught in the regular classroom; however, several special types of programs

---

[14]Alfred A. Strauss and Laura E. Lehtinen, *Psychopathology and Education of the Brain-Injured Child* (New York: Grune & Stratton, 1947), p. 129.

are sometimes provided for the educable. These include: regular classroom placement with help and materials being provided by a specialist; tutoring sessions for which the child is taken out of class; special classes which the child attends part of the day, while being involved in the regular program the rest of the day; and full programs in which the child's entire day is spent in a special program in a room or building separate from the other children.

School programs for the educable retarded child have been worked out at five levels. The *preschool level* (chronological ages four to six; mental ages two to four) generally emphasizes language, perceptual, and conceptual development, and spending time on self-help skills. The *primary level* (chronological ages six to nine; mental ages three to seven) stresses manners and work habits. The *intermediate level* (chronological ages ten to twelve; mental ages five to nine) strives to develop skills in basic subjects by using such approaches as learning by doing, the unit approach, a watered-down curriculum approach, or Duncan's idea of a concrete curriculum. The *advanced program* (chronological ages thirteen to eighteen; mental ages seven to twelve) gives a utilitarian program based on a core plan. The *post-school program* (chronological age sixteen and over) tries to provide job training, job placement, and counseling (Kirk, 1962).

Methods of Instruction

Besides the organization of specific objectives and special classes, Kirk (1962) also advocates certain principles of instruction in special-education classes for the educable mentally retarded. These include: assessment in the form of medical, social, psychological and educational evaluations with periodic reassessment; special instructional materials geared to the development of the retarded child, plus supplementary and instructional materials to be used in a variety of situations; special remediation of areas of specific disabilities that go beyond developmental retardation (e.g., communication, arithmetic, relating abstract concepts); learning special principles by using the best practices in learning; systematic or planned instruction in sequence with little reliance on incidental learning; individualizing instruction by adapting instruction and materials to the child's achievement level, plus clinical educational teaching for specific disabilities; success experiences to develop a positive attitude toward learning and a positive self-concept.

✓ CRITICISM OF PRESENT PROGRAMS

According to the President's Committee on Mental Retardation (1967), there are 677,000 students in special-education classes at the present time, and 400,000 others have the benefit of residential and community services. Only 4 percent of the six million retardates in this country are cared for in institutions while 96 percent are cared for outside institutional walls (see Tables 1-4).

Table 1:   Training Programs in the Field of Mental Retardation.[15]

Year	Mentally Retarded Persons Trained	Persons Trained to Work with Mentally Retarded
1963	160	12
1964	90	90
1965	2,727	664
1966	1,740	281
1967	2,777	250

Table 2:   Diagnostic Clinics for the Mentally Retarded[16]

Year	Number of Clinics	Number of Children Served
1950	00	0
1955	33	10,000 (est.)
1959	70	20,000 (est.)
1963	110	42,000
1964	139	45,000
1965	147	47,000 (est.)
1966	191	58,000

Table 3:   Special-Education Classes for the Educable Mentally Retarded[17]

Year	Number of Classes	Number of Children
1953	—	108,903
1958	—	201,443
1963	22,500	363,000
1964	26,415	406,000
1965	31,277	459,442
1966	36,851	519,422
1967	43,525	587,722

---

[15]President's Committee on Mental Retardation, p. 4.
[16]*Ibid.*, p. 13.
[17]*Ibid.*, p. 5.

Table 4: Special-Education Classes for the Trainable Mentally Retarded[18]

Year	Number of Classes	Number of Children
1953	—	4,659
1958	—	16,779
1963	2,500	30,000
1964	3,490	40,035
1965	4,678	52,341
1966	6,329	68,322
1967	8,522	89,252

In addition over 400 million dollars a year are now appropriated for federal programs benefiting the retarded. However, there are major needs still facing special education, including the following problems:

1. Half of the nation's 25,000 school districts offer no classes for pupils having special learning problems or needs. Many of the existing special-education classes do not offer an opportunity for retarded students to learn and achieve to their full capacity.
2. Three quarters of the nation's 201,000 institutionalized mentally retarded live in buildings fifty or more years old; many of these buildings are "hand-me-down" mental or tuberculosis hospitals.
3. The 81,000 full-time staff in public facilities for the mentally retarded must be almost doubled to reach minimum adequacy.
4. The mentally retarded who live in disadvantaged neighborhoods often receive significantly less service from public and private agencies.
5. An estimated two million retarded persons capable of learning to support themselves need job-training and placement services.
6. The cause of three in every four cases of retardation remains unknown.

A number of authorities in special education are responding to unfavorable research results on current programs by viewing those programs negatively. Kirk (1962), for example, has cited

---

[18]*Ibid.*, p. 5.

research indicating that the educable child who has remained in the classroom is academically superior to the child in special-education classes. He has also indicated, however, that children in special classes are somewhat better adjusted than those in regular classes, perhaps because they do not have to bear the continual criticism or ridicule of classmates functioning at a higher level.

Lloyd M. Dunn (1968), a past president of the Council for Exceptional Children, is very outspoken in his criticism of present programs. He has indicated that something better than special-class placement is needed for children with mild learning problems. In addition, placing the child in special classes is discriminatory to those in the lower socio-economic segments of our society. In fact, special-class placement may be unconstitutional, as it represents a "track system" of education. Special-class placement is also debilitating to the child's self-concept, for he needs the contact and stimulation of being with "normal" children. There is also the fact teachers in special classes have a tendency not to push the child to "progress" too much; in the regular classroom, the teacher will make more effort to see that the child reaches his optimum level of success. Finally the placement of a child in a special class gives him a "disability level" that goes with him and leads to a pre-judgment on the part of teachers and all who work with him.

On a more positive note, Dunn has suggested departures in both diagnosis and curriculum in an effort to create a better learning situation for retarded children. Because in-depth diagnosis should be continuous, he has speculated that diagnostic centers might be established where children could go for several weeks or a month for thorough diagnosis; the children would return to the centers at intervals to evaluate progress and to revamp programs.

As far as curricular approaches are concerned, Dunn believes that considerable attention should be given to the development of a taxonomy of educational objectives for the mildly retarded. The areas to be included might be: environmental modification; motor development; sensory and perceptual training; cognitive and language development, including academic instruction; speech and communication training; connotative development; social interaction training; and vocational training. Many creative and imaginative activities and programs might be established in each of these areas; however, research is needed to determine just which activities would be most effective.

Since Dunn's article, the efficacy of special-education classes has been questioned anew. Hammons (1972) believes this article was symptomatic of a growing disenchantment with special-education practices. He indicates that not all authorities have agreed with Dunn. It would appear that no one method has been rated as superior in educating exceptional children. Also, no significant studies have shown the alternative models proposed to be efficacious. Hammons has suggested that changes in special education need to be explored in order to improve education for all exceptional children. In the interim, while an appropriate course of action is sought, the current level of education must be maintained and improved. Nelson and Schmidt (1971) also have indicated that logical and empirical testing is needed if special education is to move forward. They believe that we are not able to deal with the problem of efficacy because of our adherence to the past, failure to go beyond an *a priori* problem-solving approach, and failure to examine the constructs used.

Lilly (1971) has proposed a "zero reject" model for special education. Under this model, the possibility of a child's failing is denied; instead, the responsibility for failure rests on the teacher. The teacher would have complete responsibility for all children. Her skills would be such that she would rectify all classroom problems without referral. In contrast, Adamson and Van Etten (1972) have proposed an alternative called the "fail-save" operational model. In this system, if the regular system "fails" to meet all of a child's needs, the system is adapted in order to "save" him.

Kolstoe (1972) has outlined the major criticisms of programs for the mildly retarded and answered these criticisms. The basic criticisms of programs include:

1. Retardation evidenced during the school years disappears in the adult years.
2. Labeling harms children.
3. Special-class placement harms self-concept.
4. Segregated programs are not beneficial.
5. Teachers contribute to the self-fulfilling prophecy concerning low achievement.
6. Regular classrooms are capable of handling individual differences.

In discussing these criticisms, Kolstoe presented evidence to indicate that these criticisms are not completely justifiable. In many cases, special classes are not criticized as much as is the adminis-

tration of them. He recommended that the use of IQ to define
mental retardation be clarified, that re-evaluation be conducted on
a regular basis, and that provision be made to provide for continuing education into adult life.

Litigation and the Retarded

In recent years, a number of litigation cases have arisen which may
very well lead to changes in special education. These litigation cases
have questioned the labeling of children as retarded, educational
placement, testing procedures and interpretations, the parental role
in placement, and the psychological damage caused a child who is
placed improperly. Thus, the following cases may have great im-
pact for the future of special education as it now exists: *Hobson v.
Hanson* (1967), *Spangler v. Board of Education* (1970), *Diana v.
State Board of Education* (1970), *Covarrubias v. San Diego Unified
School District* (1971), *Arreola v. Board of Education* (1968), and
Stewart v. Phillips (1970).

In a ruling on *Hobson v. Hanson* (1967), Judge Skelly Wright
held illegal the method of testing and educational placement used
in Washington, D.C. public schools. Prior to this decision, the
Washington public schools had given the students a series of
standardized group tests. On the basis of their scores, they were
placed in honors, general, or special curriculum. In declaring the
"tracking" system that resulted illegal, the court noted that
standardized aptitude tests were not relevant because they were
standardized on middle-class white students and based upon a
knowledge of standard English. Thus, the tests were culturally
biased and lower-class and black students were being placed in
special classes in disproportionate numbers on the basis of socioeconomic or racial status rather than ability (*Hobson v. Hanson*,
pp. 514, 481).

In *Spangler v. Board of Education* (1970), the US District
Court for the Southern District of California also found that discrimination existed as a result of grouping students. First of all,
there was a conscious "racial imbalance" in terms of students and
faculty within the Pasadena School District. Second, there was
segregation existing within the integrated school as a result of
"interclass grouping" which took place on the basis of intelligence
tests and teacher recommendations. There was a higher percentage
of blacks in the slow classes in every subject matter. The testing

and "interclass grouping" were declared racially discriminatory, as they were based upon verbal achievement rather than on ability (*Spangler v. Board of Education*, p. 159).

In 1970, the District Court for the Northern District of California considered the case of nine Mexican-American public school children who contended they had been placed in special-education classes on the basis of inaccurate testing. They claimed the WISC and Stanford-Binet considered English verbal aptitude, were standardized on a white, native-American population, and thus discriminated against Mexican-Americans. In this case *Diana v. State Board of Education* (1970), the court agreed that:

1. Testing for all children would include their primary language as well as English.
2. Only sections of the test considered to be culturally unbiased would be given.
3. Mexican-American and Chinese-American students already in special-education classes would be retested and a summary of the retesting and re-evaluation would be submitted to each school district along with a plan to return these children to regular classes.
4. Revised IQ scores would be normalized to judge Mexican-Americans on the basis of their peers alone.
5. Where a disparity existed between Mexican-Americans in regular classes and those in special classes, an explanation for the disparity must be submitted (Ross, DeYoung, and Cohen, 1971).

Covarrubias v. San Diego Unified School District (1971) was similar to *Diana* in that it attacked the validity of testing methods for special education on behalf of twelve black and five Mexican-American students; however, it differed in two respects. First, the *Covarrubias* case sought money damages under the Civil Rights Act of 1871. Second, as a result of it, current teaching methods now must consider the culture of the ghetto environment in determining learning ability (Ross et al., 1971).

In *Arreola v. Board of Education* (1968), it was determined that parents should be involved in placement decisions. Eleven Mexican-Americans filed a complaint in Orange County, California to stop all special-education classes until a hearing was provided for placement, IQ tests recognized cultural differences, and a meaning-ful curriculum with periodic retesting was adopted (Ross et al., 1971).

Finally, the *Stewart v. Phillips* (1970) case, field in the Massachusetts Federal District Court, had three classes of plaintiffs: those students placed in classes for the retarded who were not retarded; those students who were retarded but had been denied special-class placement; and parents of retarded students who had been denied an opportunity to participate in placement decisions. The plaintiffs sought 20,000 dollars each for compensatory and punitive damages and asked that special-education classes be disbanded until a commission could be established to administer the program (Ross et al., 1971).

Of the cases mentioned, only one, *Hobson v. Hanson*, has gone to a Court of Appeals for a decision. Most cases are seeking settlement out of court.

Cruickshank (1972) has expressed the belief that too often in the past, special-education programs have been too mediocre and sterile and that the school system knows this. He has noted that cornerstones to a vital program include qualitive diagnosis, clinical teaching, environmental modification, and educational psychology related to psychopathology in perception. It would appear that increased accountability in education for the retarded will become a major concept in the future of special education as the nation comes to see education for all handicapped children not as charity or a desirable extra in the school program but as a fundamental right. This fact is evident in the "mandatory" legislation now being passed at state levels (Martin, 1972). Many states are seeking to provide appropriate education for the special child. In fact, a Federal District Court decision in Pennsylvania now holds the state responsible for such education (Martin, 1972). Texas now has a state plan to discard labels and provide for the education of all children within the framework of the regular school program (Hafner, 1972). Such actions appear to be a major trend for the future in special education.

FUTURE NEEDS

The following ten areas have been brought to the attention of the President of the United States by the Committee on Mental Retardation (1967) as being crucial areas of need.

1. Mental retardation services must be available to more of the nation's people.
2. More effective and extensive manpower recruitment and training programs for work with the mentally retarded are needed.
3. Fuller use of existing resources is necessary.
4. More public-private partnerships in program development services and research are needed.
5. A national mental retardation information and resource center should be developed.
6. Basic research, training in application of research, and rapid translation of research results into service programs need continuing encouragement.
7. Immediate, major attention should be given to early identification and treatment of the mentally retarded.
8. Social and institutional planning for the coming decades must take into account the special needs of the mentally retarded.
9. The legal status of the mentally retarded individual must be clarified and his rights guaranteed.
10. Everyone interested in helping the mentally retarded should give thought to imaginative ideas and approaches that will make new advances possible.[19]

In order to keep abreast of the current and future needs in the area of retardation, one should be aware that there are organizations with which to affiliate. These organizations include the National Association for Retarded Children (NARC), Council for Exceptional Children (CEC) and AAMD. In addition, the Bureau for the Education of the Handicapped (BEH) provides informative data.

SUMMARY

The field of mental retardation is one that is still plagued with controversy. In order that one can better understand the retarded, this chapter has presented the definitions, incidents, classifications, and causes of retardation. Theories of intelligence were examined, along with the scientific theories of the Gestaltists, Piaget, Hebb,

---

[19]President's Committee on Mental Retardation, pp. 19-30.

Skinner and Ellis, and Luria. In addition, the development of modern concepts of education was presented. Criticisms of present programs were discussed, as was the future of retardation and its needs. The first chapter has focused on the complete range of retardation. The remainder of the book will deal specifically with the educable and mildly retarded.

REFERENCES

Adamson, Gary, and Van Etten, Glen. "Zero Reject Model Revisited: A Workable Alternative," *Exceptional Children* 38 (May 1972): 735-38.

Arreola v. Board of Education, 160-577 (1968).

Baumeister, Alfred A. *Mental Retardation.* Chicago: Aldine Publishing Co., 1967.

Benoit, E.P. "Toward a New Definition of Mental Retardation." *American Journal of Mental Deficiency*, 63 (1959): 559-64.

Binet, A., and Simon, T. *The Development of Intelligence in Children.* Baltimore: The Williams & Wilkins Co., 1916.

Bugelski, B.R. *The Psychology of Learning Applied to Teaching.* New York: The Bobbs-Merrill Co., 1964.

Covarrubias v. San Diego Unified School District, 70-394, *Texas Reports* (February, 1971).

Cruickshank, William M. "Some Issues Facing the Field of Learning Disability." *Journal of Learning Disabilities* 5, 7 (August-September, 1972): 380-88.

Davis, Kingsley. "Extreme Social Isolation of a Child." *American Journal of Sociology* 45 (January 1940): 554-65.

Descoeudres, Alice. *The Education of Mentally Defective Children.* Translated by Ernest F. Row. Lexington, Massachusetts: D. C. Heath and Co., 1928.

Diana v. State Board of Education C-70 37 RFP. District Court for Northern California (February, 1970).

Doll, Edgar A. "The Essentials of an Inclusive Concept of Mental Deficiency." *American Journal of Mental Deficiency* 46 (1941): 215.

Douglas, Marcella E. "Some Concrete Contributions to Occupational Education in the Academic Classroom." *American Journal of Mental Deficiency* 48 (1944): 288-91.

Dugdale, R.L. *The Jukes: A Study of Crime, Pauperism, Disease, and Heredity.* New York: G.P. Putnam's Sons, 1877.

Duncan, John. *The Education of the Ordinary Child.* New York: The Ronald Press Co., 1943.

Dunn, Lloyd M. "Special Education for the Mildly Retarded—Is Much of It Justifiable?" *Exceptional Children* 35 (September 1968): 5-22.

Ellis, N.R. "The Stimulus Trace and Behavioral Inadequacy." In *Handbook of Mental Deficiency*, edited by N.R. Ellis, pp. 134-58. New York: Mc-Graw-Hill Book Co., 1963.

Furth, H.G. *Piaget for Teachers*. Englewood Cliffs, New Jersey: Prentice-Hall, Inc., 1970.

Galton, F. *Hereditary Genius*. London: The Macmillan Co., 1869.

Garrison, Karl C., and Magoon, R.A. *Educational Psychology: An Integration of Psychology and Educational Practices*. Columbus, Ohio: Charles E. Merrill Publishing Co., 1972.

Goddard, H.H. *The Kallikak Family*. New York: The Macmillan Co., 1912.

Goldstein, H., and Seigle, D. *The Illinois Plan for Special Education of Exceptional Children: A Curriculum Guide for Teachers of the Educable Mentally Handicapped*, Circular Series B-3, Number 12. Springfield: Illinois State Department of Public Instruction, 1958.

Guilford, J.P. "Intelligence: 1965 Model." *American Psychologist* (1966): 20-26.

_____. *The Nature of Human Intelligence*. New York: McGraw-Hill Book Co., 1967.

_____. "Three Faces of Intellect." *American Psychology* 14 (1959): 469-79.

Hafner, Donroy. "A Shift in Emphasis in Programing for Handicapped Children." *Exceptional Children* 39 (September 1972): 59-60.

Hammons, Gary W. "Educating the Mildly Retarded: A Review." *Exceptional Children* 38 (March 1972): 565-70.

Hebb, D.O. *The Organization of Behavior*. New York: John Wiley & Sons, 1949.

Heber, R. "A Manual on Terminology and Classification in Mental Retardation." *American Journal of Mental Deficiency* 64 (1959): 40.

_____. "A Manual on Terminology and Classification in Mental Retardation, Second Edition." A monograph of *American Journal of Mental Deficiency* (1961): 3-4.

Hobson v. Hansen, 269 F. Supp. 401 (1967).

Hungerford, R.H.; DeProspo, C.J.; and Rosenzweig, L.E. *The Nonacademic Pupil*. New York: New York City Teachers of Special Education, 1948.

Ingram, Christine P. *Education for the Slow-Learning Child*, 3rd ed. New York: The Ronald Press, 1960.

Inhelder, Barbel. *Le diagnostic du raisonnement chez les debiles mentaux*. Neuchatel, Switzerland; Delechaux et Niestle, 1944.

Inskeep, Annie D. *Teaching Dull and Retarded Children*. New York: The Macmillan Co., 1926.

Itard, J.M.G. *The Wild Boy of Aveyron*, translated by G. Humphrey and Mariel Humphrey. New York: Appleton-Century-Crofts, 1932.

Jensen, A.R. "How Much Can We Boost IQ and Scholastic Achievement?" *Harvard Educational Review* 39 (Winter, 1969): 1-123.

Johnson, G.O. "Psychological Characteristics of the Mentally Retarded." In *Psychology of Exceptional Children and Youth*, edited by W.M. Cruickshank, pp. 448-83. Englewood Cliffs, New Jersey: Prentice-Hall, Inc., 1963.

Kanner, Leo. *Child Psychiatry*, 3rd ed. Springfield, Illinois: Charles C. Thomas Co., 1957.

_____. "Feeblemindedness: Absolute, Relative, and Apparent." *Nervous Child* 7 (1948): 365-97.

Kanner, Leo, and Johnson, G.O. *Educating the Retarded Child.* Boston: Houghton Mifflin Co., 1951.

Kirk, Samuel A. *Early Education of the Mentally Retarded.* Urbana: University of Illinois Press, 1968.

_____. *Educating Exceptional Children.* Boston: Houghton Mifflin Co., 1962.

_____. "Research in Education." In *Mental Retardation: A Review of the Research,* edited by H.A. Stevens and R. Heber. Chicago: University of Chicago Press, 1964.

Kirk, S.A., and Johnson, O. *Educating the Retarded Child.* Boston: Houghton Mifflin Co., 1951.

Kolstoe, Oliver P. "Programs for the Mildly Retarded: A Reply to the Critics." *Exceptional Children* 39 (September 1972): 51-56.

_____. "Sensory Stimulation versus Specific Response." *Exceptional Children* 23 (1956): 2-4.

Lewin, K.A. *A Dynamic Theory of Personality.* New York: McGraw-Hill Book Co., 1935.

_____. *Field Theory in Social Science: Selected Theoretical Papers,* edited by D. Cartwright. New York: Harper & Row, Publishers, 1951.

Lilly, M.S. "A Training-Based Model for Special Education." *Exceptional Children* 37 (1971): 745-49.

Luria, A.R. "Psychological Studies of Mental Deficiency in the Soviet Union." In *Handbook of Mental Deficiency,* edited by N.R. Ellis, pp. 353-87. New York: McGraw-Hill Book Co., 1963.

_____. *The Role of Speech in the Regulation of Normal and Abnormal Behavior.* Washington, D.C.: United States Department of Health, Education, and Welfare, 1960.

Martens, Elise H., editor. *Curriculum Adjustments for the Mentally Retarded.* Washington, D.C.: United States Department of Health, Education, and Welfare Bulletin Number 2, 1950.

Martin, Edwin W. "Individualism and Behaviorism as Future Trends in Educating Handicapped Children." *Exceptional Children* 38 (March 1972): 517-25.

Masland, R.L.; Sarason, S.B.; and Gladwin, T. *Mental Subnormality.* New York: Basic Books, 1958.

Montessori, Maria. *Montessori Method,* translated by Anne E. George. New York: Stokes, 1912.

Nelson, Calvin C., and Schmidt, Leo J. "The Question of the Efficacy of Special Classes." *Exceptional Children* 37 (January 1971): 381-84.

Piaget, Jean. *The Construction of Reality in the Child.* New York: Basic Books, 1954.

_____. *Logic and Psychology.* New York: Basic Books, 1957.

_____. *The Origins of Intelligence in Children,* 2d ed. New York: International Universities Press, 1952.

_____. *The Psychology of Intelligence.* New York: Harcourt, Brace, Jovanovich, 1950.

President's Committee on Mental Retardation. *A First Report on the Nation's Progress and Remaining Great Needs in the Campaign to Combat Mental Retardation.* Washington, D.C.: Government Printing Office, 1967.

Robinson, H.B., and Robinson, N.M. *The Mentally Retarded Child: A Psychological Approach.* New York: McGraw-Hill Book Co., 1965.

Ross, J.L. Sterling; DeYoung, Henry G.; and Cohen, Julius S. "Confrontation: Special Education and the Law." *Exceptional Children* 38 (September 1971): 5-12.

Rothstein, Jerome H., editor. *Mental Retardation: Readings and Resources.* New York: Holt, Rinehart, & Winston, 1961.

Sarason, S.B. *Psychological Problems in Mental Deficiency,* 3rd ed. New York: Harper & Row, Publishers, 1959.

Sequin, E. *Idiocy and Its Treatment by the Physiological Method.* Albany, New York: Brandow, 1866.

Skeels, Harold M., and Dye, H.B. "A Study of the Effects of Differential Stimulation on Mentally Retarded Children." *Proceedings and Addresses of the Sixty-third Annual Session of the American Association on Mental Deficiency* 44 (1939): 114-36.

Skinner, B.F. "Are Theories of Learning Necessary?" *Psychological Review* 57 (1950): 193-216.

_____. *The Behavior of Organisms.* New York: Appleton-Century-Crofts, 1938.

Spangler v. Board of Education, 311 F. Supp. 501 (1970).

Spearman, Charles E. "General Intelligence Objectively Determined and Measured." *American Journal of Psychology* (1904): 201-93.

Stewart v. Phillips, 70-1199 F. (October 1970).

Strauss, Alfred A., and Lehtinen, Laura E. *Psychopathology and Education of the Brain-Injured Child.* New York: Grune & Stratton, 1947.

Terman, L.M. *The Measurement of Intelligence.* Boston: Houghton Mifflin Co., 1916.

Terman, L.M., and Merrill, Maud A. *Measuring Intelligence.* Boston: Houghton Mifflin Co., 1937.

Thorndike, E.L. "In the Symposium. Intelligence and Its Measurement." *Journal of Educational Psychology* 12 (1921): 124-27.

Thurstone, L.L., and Thurstone, Thelma G. "Factorial Studies of Intelligence." *Psychometric Monographs* (1941): 401-02; 409-10.

Tredgold, A.F. *A Textbook of Mental Deficiency,* 6th ed. Baltimore: William Wood and Co., 1937.

Wechsler, D. *Wechsler Adult Intelligence Scale: Manual.* New York: Psychological Corporation, 1955.

TWO

Components
of Reading

For an individual to relate the reading process to the needs of the retarded, it is necessary that he understand the developmental reading process and its components. Recent studies have found that no special reading approach can overcome all individual differences and that combinations of approaches are more effective than the utilization of one single method or approach (Stauffer, 1967; Bond and Dykstra, 1967). Therefore, the teacher must possess a knowledge of the reading skills that are incorporated in most reading approaches and must be able to utilize this knowledge in the best way.

Many volumes have been written about the reading process and reading skills; however, not all reading authorities are in agreement concerning all aspects of reading. Because sifting through the research and the controversy in order to develop effective programs may be a most difficult task for the special-education teacher, a familiarity with terminology used in discussing the reading characteristics of children may aid the teacher in establishing programs. The presentation of such terminology is the subject of this chapter.

DEFINITIONS OF READING

There are differing opinions regarding the definition of reading. In fact, there are almost as many definitions of reading as there are reading authorities. In addition, although in recent years there has been a marked change in the definitions, common to most of them is the belief that reading, thought, and language are closely related. For example, Gates (1949), an early reading expert, defined reading in the following manner:

> Reading is not a simple mechanical skill; nor is it a narrow scholastic tool. Properly cultivated, it is essentially a thoughtful process. However, to say that reading is a "thought-getting" process is to give too restricted a description. It should be developed as a complex organization of patterns of higher mental processes. It can and should embrace all types of thinking, evaluating, judging, imagining, reasoning, and problem-solving. Indeed, it is believed that reading is one of the media for cultivating many techniques of thinking and imagining. The reading program should, therefore, make careful provision for contributing as fully as possible to the cultivation of a whole array of techniques involved in understanding, thinking, reflecting, imagining, judging, evaluating, analyzing, and reasoning.[1]

A more recent reading authority, Dechant (1964), lists the following characteristics of reading:

1. Reading is a sensory process.

   Reading requires the use of the senses, especially vision. The reader must react visually to the graphic symbols. The symbols themselves must be legible, the eyes must see clearly and singly, and the light must be adequate.

2. Reading is a perceptual process.

   Reading occurs when meaning is brought to graphic stimuli. It is a progressive apprehension of the meanings and ideas represented by a sequence of words. It includes seeing the word, recognition of the word, awareness of the word's meaning, and relating the word to its context. This is perception in its fullest sense.

---

[1] Arthur I. Gates, "Character and Purposes of the Yearbook," *Reading in the Elementary School*, edited by Nelson B. Henry, Forty-eighth Yearbook of the National Society for the Study of Education (Chicago: University of Chicago Press, 1949), p. 3.

3. Reading is a response.

Reading is a system of responses made to some graphic stimuli. These include the vocal and/or subvocal muscular responses made at the sight of the word, the eye movements during reading, physical adaptations to the reading act such as postural changes, the critical and evaluative responses to what is being read, the emotional involvement of the reader, and meaningful reactions to the words.

4. Reading is a learned response.

Reading is a response that must be learned by the child and is under the control of the mechanisms of motivation and reinforcement.

5. Reading is a developmental task.

Developmental tasks have one basic characteristic: the child's readiness for them depends on the child's general development. Reading is a difficult task, and there is a most teachable moment for beginning reading and for each of the specific skills in reading. The child's level of achievement in reading depends on his over-all growth and development.

6. Reading can be an interest.

Reading may become an interest or a goal in its own right. It then may motivate other activity.

7. Reading is a learning process.

Reading may become one of the chief media for learning. The child can use reading to acquire knowledge and to change his own attitudes, ideals, and aspirations. Genuine reading involves integration and promotes the development of the reader. It opens up to him a world of ideas, takes him to distant lands, and lets him walk side by side with the great sages of time.

8. Reading is communication.

Reading is an active process. Communication from writer to reader occurs only if the reader can take meaning to the printed page. Without the reader, communication via the printed page is impossible.[2]

Dechant and many other reading authorities have stated that reading is a perceptual process. Goodman (1972), on the other

---

[2]E. V. Dechant, *Improving the Teaching of Reading* (Englewood Cliffs, New Jersey: Prentice-Hall, Inc., 1964), pp. 1-2. Copyright © 1964. Reprinted by permission of the publisher.

hand, has taken issue with the traditional definitions that emphasize the perception of words and letters. On this topic, Goodman
has stated:

> More simply stated, reading is a psycholinguistic guessing
> game. It involves partial use of available minimal language
> cues selected from perceptual input on the basis of the read-
> er's expectation. As this partial information is processed, tenta-
> tive decisions are made to be confirmed, rejected, or refined as
> reading progresses.[3]

Goodman also has stated prerequisites for the efficient reader:

> He must actively bring to bear his knowledge of language,
> his past experience, his conceptual attainments on the process-
> ing of language information encoded in the form of graphic
> symbols in order to decode the written language. Reading must
> therefore be regarded as an interaction between the reader and
> written language, through which the reader attempts to recon-
> struct a message from the writer.[4]

According to Goodman (1968), the reading process is a matter
of recoding, decoding, and encoding. In recoding, the child merely
"re-codes" the graphic symbols into aural symbols. This does not
mean that the child understands or "de-codes" the graphic mes-
sage. In fact, many teachers have observed children who can recode
without comprehending what they are reading. In beginning reading, the child must learn that "reading is supposed to make sense,
that is, that it can be decoded."[5]

Encoding involves obtaining the meaning while reading orally.
If the child is truly decoding the material that he reads silently,
he must decode or obtain meaning and then "encode meaning as
oral output"[6] when asked to read orally. Goodman has designated
"cues" or "cue systems" that must be used by the reader in obtaining meaning from written language. These systems will be discussed in Chapter Four.

---

[3]Kenneth S. Goodman, "Reading: A Psycholinguistic Guessing Game," in
Individualized Reading Instruction: A Reader, edited by Kenneth S. Goodman (New York: Holt, Rinehart & Winston, 1972), p. 15.

[4]Kenneth Goodman, ed., *The Psycholinguistic Nature of the Reading
Process* (Detroit: Wayne State University Press, 1968), p. 15.

[5]*Ibid.*, p. 21.

[6]*Ibid.*, p. 20.

There has been some research to substantiate Goodman's theory that reading is a "psycholinguistic guessing game." According to Ryan and Semmell (1969), a reader processes information according to his use of language. They have stated: "Thus, not all the information needed by the reader is on the printed page — nor are all the printed details needed by him."[7]

SKILLS FOR READING PROGRAMS

Although such authorities as Goodman feel that many "cues" necessary for reading are beyond the printed page, a perusal of many reading texts demonstrates the opposite viewpoint. Most reading texts include a myriad of discrete "reading skills" that are considered necessary for reading achievement. The market is overflowing with workbooks, filmstrips, tapes, and records that teach isolated reading skills. In order that the special education teacher might understand the nature of these skills, the remaining sections of this chapter are devoted to a discussion of skills that are usually included in most reading programs.

Word Attack Skills

Word attack skills include those techniques which are assumed to enable a child to "recode" an unknown word so that he can pronounce it and understand it as it is used in a contextual situation. Although many programs in word attack have been developed, these programs, in most cases, have become isolated word attack drills that do not foster independence in reading.

According to Wilson (1972), word attack can be grouped into three categories: phonic clues, structural analysis, and contextual clues. Other factors that have been included under word attack are: sight vocabulary, picture clues, configuration, and dictionary skills (Zintz, 1970). Most of these skills are ones that Goodman (1968) would term "cue systems within words" that are used by the reader for the purpose of recoding. Goodman cautions that an extensive use of these skills may result in an overemphasis on recoding.

Phonics Instruction: According to Heilman (1972), the purpose of phonics instruction "is to help the child develop the ability to

---

[7]Ellen Ryan and Melvin I. Semmel, "Reading as a Constructive Language Process," *Reading Research Quarterly* 5 (1969): 59-82.

work out the pronunciation (or approximate pronunciation) of printed word symbols which at the moment he does not know as sight words."[8] In early phonics instruction, the child learns to attach speech sounds to letters and letter combinations. The words that are used in phonics instruction should be in the child's speaking vocabulary (Heilman, 1972). Phonics instruction, therefore, aids him in identifying the printed word symbols that represent words he possesses in his oral language.

At one time, phonics instruction was used as a *method* of teaching reading. Many early readers, such as the *Beacon Readers* (1912), introduced many phonetic elements which the child was required to learn before beginning to read (Smith, 1965). Often, the sounds of the letters were taught in isolation. Smith (1965) has termed this approach alphabetic-phonetic.

Two basic approaches to teaching phonics — the analytic and synthetic—also have been delineated (Bagford, 1972). The analytic approaches are those which teach a limited number of sight words, usually seventy-five to 100, and then use these words in order to teach the letter sounds. For example, the teacher places the sight words *man, mouse,* and *monkey* on the board. Then, he asks the children to pronounce these words, stressing the first sound of the letter *m*. This technique is used in order to aid the children in learning the sounds of the letters. The synthetic approaches to teaching phonics are those that teach the sounds for certain letters first and then teach the child to blend these sounds into words. Most basal readers utilize the analytic approach, although the synthetic approaches have become rather popular recently (Bagford, 1972).

There is some evidence to suggest that the synthetic approach provides an earlier start in beginning reading than do the analytic methods (Sparks and Fay, 1957; Bliesmer and Yarborough, 1965). Additional longitudinal studies should be conducted in order to determine whether or not these early gains by children who have been taught by the synthetic method can be maintained throughout the grades.

A distinction should be made between the terms *phonics* and *phonetics*. Heilman (1964) has defined phonics as "a facet of reading instruction teaching speech sounds of letters and groups of letters in words" and phonetics as:

---

[8]Arthur W. Heilman, *Principles and Practices of Teaching Reading*, 3rd ed. (Columbus, Ohio: Charles E. Merrill Publishing Co., 1972), p. 245.

... that segment of linguistic science which deals with speech sounds, how these sounds are made vocally, sound changes which develop in languages, and the relation of speech sounds to the total language process. All phonics instruction is derived from phonetics, but phonics (as it relates to reading) utilizes only a relatively small portion of the body of knowledge identified as phonetics.[9]

Even though a knowledge of phonetic principles by the teacher may be beneficial to the teaching process (Bagford, 1972), many teachers do not possess an adequate background in phonetics and must rely upon information presented in basal reader manuals and workbooks (Austin and Morrison, 1963). Consequently, these teachers are aware of the content for phonics instruction but not of the phonetic generalizations underlying this instruction (Emans, 1972). Instruction in phonetic principles ought to be part of pre-service training for teachers who may be utilizing phonics approaches. Although a study of the broader topic of linguistics and applied linguistics may aid the teacher, a detailed discussion of these principles is beyond the scope of this text. If the reader is interested in pursuing the subject, he is referred to such books as *Linguistics in the Elementary Classroom* by Paul S. Anderson (1971) and *Applied English Linguistics* by Harold B. Allen (1958).

A list of phonics skills found in most phonics programs has been compiled by Heilman. It includes:

Steps in Teaching Phonics

1. Auditory-Visual Discrimination

2. Teaching Consonant Sounds
   a. Initial Consonant Sounds
   b. Consonant Digraphs (*sh, wh, th, ch*)
   c. Consonant Blends (*br, cl, str*, etc.)
   d. Substituting Initial Consonant Sounds
   e. Sounding Consonants at End of Words
   f. Consonant Digraphs (*nk, ng, ck, qu*)
   g. Consonant Irregularities
   h. Silent Consonants
   i. Sight-Word List — Nonphonetic Spellings
   j. Contractions

[9]Arthur W. Heilman, *Phonics in Proper Perspective*, 2d ed. (Columbus, Ohio: Charles E. Merrill Publishing Co., 1968), p. 2.

3. Teaching Vowel Sounds

    a. Short Vowel Sounds
    b. Long Vowel Sounds
    c. Teaching Long and Short Vowel Sounds Together
    d. Exceptions to Vowel Rules Taught
    e. Diphthongs (*oi, oy*)[10]
    f. Sounds of $\overline{oo}$ and oo

4. Syllabication

    a. Rules
    b. Prefixes and Suffixes
    c. Compound Words
    d. Doubling Final Consonants
    e. Accent[11]

For a very thorough study of phonics instruction, see Heilman's *Phonics in Proper Perspective* (1964). Chapter Seven will discuss the effectiveness of phonics instruction with the retarded.

Structural Analysis: Another skill included in most word attack programs is structural analysis; this skill involves the utilization of word parts, such as prefixes, suffixes, inflections, and compounds, in order to derive the meaning or pronunciation of words. In structural analysis, recognition is obtained through the structure of the word rather than the sound elements. Structural analysis includes such elements as inflectional variants; syllabication; compound words; and root words, prefixes, and suffixes.

The study of inflectional variants includes a study of word endings, such as possessives, plural nouns, verb changes, comparisons, and changing word endings (Zintz, 1970).

"The main concept in syllabication is that long words are made up of shorter elements, each containing a single vowel sound."[12] There are several rules of syllabication that hold consistently true, such as the double consonant rule ("pic-nic") and the twin consonant rule ("rab-bit"). A knowledge of several rules of syllabication may be beneficial for some children; however, too much stress on these rules may result in a series of exercises and drills that are completely meaningless to the child, especially if he is not able to apply them.

---

[10]This entry has been added by the authors of this text.

[11]Heilman, *Phonics in Proper Perspective*, 2d ed., pp. 23-24.

[12]Florence Roswell and Gladys Natchez, *Reading Disability: Diagnosis and Treatment* (New York: Basic Books, 1971), p. 98.

Identifying independent parts of compound words, such as "airplane," may aid the child in "unlocking" some unknown words.

A knowledge of the common prefixes and suffixes and their meanings may be helpful in word recognition. This skill is usually included in basic reading programs at the intermediate levels. Only the most common prefixes and suffixes should be taught, and this should be done only in meaningful situations rather than in isolated drill. Prefixes, such as *com, dis, ex, pre, re,* and *sub,* are frequently used in reading and the writing of elementary children (Stauffer, 1942), as are suffixes such as *tion, ment, ful,* and *less* (Kottmeyer, 1959). The child must learn to combine prefixes and suffixes with base words in order to change meanings of the root words.

Sight Vocabulary: The sight vocabulary of the child is dependent upon the ability of the child to recognize words instantly without the aid of word analysis or context clues. Many basal readers include a basic stock of words that children "should know automatically." Several lists of such words that are used most frequently in the beginning stages of reading have been compiled. In addition, Stone (1950), Dolch (1936), and Fry (1957) have developed lists of service words that pupils should know in order to be successful in reading. The Dolch list and word perception will be discussed in Chapter Five.

Picture Clues: Picture clues can be helpful in deriving meaning from the printed material. Such tools as diagrams and charts are very valuable in aiding comprehension for children should be taught to interpret pictures and illustrations. Picture dictionaries are also excellent tools for beginning or problem readers because they enable the reader to arrive at the meaning of a word by looking it up and then studying the corresponding picture. It should be noted though that an overemphasis on pictures may hinder the development of word attack skills, sight vocabulary, and independent reading.

Context Clues: "Studying the setting of the unknown word for clues to help in identifying the word is what is meant by context clues."[13] The reader uses the skill of guessing at the meaning of an unknown word by looking at the position of the word in a sentence or at the words surrounding the unknown word. The skill of using context clues can not be developed simply by telling the child to "read around" a word (Roswell and Nachez, 1971). The child must be taught to look for certain clues, such as definitions of the word

<hr/>

[13]Larry A. Harris and Carl B. Smith, *Reading Instruction through Diagnostic Teaching* (New York: Holt, Rinehart, & Winston, 1971), p. 223.

within the sentence, synonyms, or comparisons and contrasts, that may help him in securing the meaning. The use of the cloze procedure as a means of developing the child's use of context will be discussed in Chapter Six.

Configuration: Identifying words by their particular shapes is called configuration. The skill involves using certain cues such as stems above and below the line to aid the child in remembering the word. To accomplish this task, many teachers draw boxes around words in order to emphasize the shape. According to Durkin (1970) though, configuration uses irrelevant cues and actually may be of no help to the child in remembering words. She cites the following example as an illustration of her point.[14]

Durkin also has urged that the teacher encourage the child to attend to the actual details of letters in the words rather than use extraneous cues. A teacher must be cautious not to overemphasize word perception.

Dictionary Skills: If none of the methods of word attack are successful for the child in finding the meaning of a word, he may turn to the dictionary for help. Dictionary skills are especially important in the upper grades. From the dictionary the child is able to obtain the meaning of the word, the pronunciation, usage, and the derivations of the word. But in order for the child to use the dictionary successfully, he must be able to alphabetize, read the pronunciation keys, and have a fairly accurate knowledge of how the word is spelled. The recent development of picture dictionaries has made the use of the dictionary available at all levels of reading ability.

In summary, word analysis skills should be considered as part of the total process of moving toward independent reading. Many materials and devices have been developed in order to teach word attack, but many times these exercises become isolated drill and are, therefore, meaningless to the child. Care must be taken to see that this situation does not arise.

Reading Comprehension

Reading comprehension is one of the least understood skills in the reading process, and while many authorities have developed theo-

---

[14]Dolores Durkin, *Teaching Them to Read* (Boston: Allyn & Bacon, Inc., 1970), p. 208.

ries, models, and components of reading comprehension, none of them are accepted universally (Cleland, 1969). Although reading authorities are still not in agreement on a definition of reading comprehension, there are many materials and lessons available for the development of this skill. Specific skills (e.g., finding the main idea, inferring, and outlining) are placed under the headings of comprehension in basal series or reading texts. Most reading tests claim to measure reading comprehension as well.

One theory concerning reading comprehension states that comprehension is part of the cognitive process. Guilford has expressed the view that:

> Reading, when fully developed, is one of our most complex intellectual activities, involving many of the intellectual abilities, which we may regard as intellectual functions.[15]

Goodman (1972) has related reading to language and feels that comprehension should be the prime focus of reading instruction:

> Teaching and learning in reading must always be centered in comprehension. The importance of any particular letters and words in a sequence can be determined only in relationship to the message the whole sequence is conveying.[16]

If reading comprehension is part of the cognitive and language processes, it is, in turn, dependent upon these skills as well. Nearly every reading authority would agree that the child is not reading if he is not comprehending, yet if a child has a problem comprehending what he reads, it is more than a reading problem; it may be a "thinking problem" (Moffett, 1968). According to Goodman (1972), a child develops strategies for comprehension whereby he relates his past experiences to the materials and utilizes his present grammatical structures to predict upcoming messages as he processes written language.

Models and Taxonomies of Comprehension: Most models of comprehension develop hierarchies or levels of comprehension which may begin at locating facts and progress to such skills as evaluating

---

[15]J. B. Guilford, "Frontiers in Thinking That Teachers Should Know About," in *Elementary Reading Instruction*, ed. Althea Berry, Thomas C. Zarrett, and William Powell (Boston: Allyn & Bacon, Inc., 1969), p. 229.

[16]Goodman, "Reading: A Psycholinguistic Guessing Game," p. 508.

the author's opinion by the use of specific criteria. As authorities have applied these hierarchies to the questions that are asked in order to check or improve children's comprehension, they have found that most of the questions are of a factual nature (Hatcher, 1971). For example, the reading sessions in which children are asked questions at the end of the story usually are designed to "check" or "develop" comprehension skills. If the majority of these questions are factual, children may benefit very little from these sessions.

Numerous reading authorities have designed programs for the purpose of developing reading comprehension. Some, such as Spache (1963) and Barrett (Clymer, 1968), have placed these skills in the form of taxonomies or models. Spache (1963) has utilized Guilford's model as a guide for developing a comprehension model.

Comprehension Skills: Harris (1970) has cited the following as comprehension skills:

1. Ability to find answers to specific questions
2. Reading for main ideas
3. Reading to follow a sequence of events
4. Reading to note and recall details
5. Grasping the author's plan
6. Following printed directions[17]

Still another aspect of reading comprehension is critical reading. According to Painter, "Critical reading is critical thinking."[18] Skills usually included under critical reading are:

1. Judging fact from opinion
2. Differentiating between truth and fantasy
3. Determining opinions or biases of the author
4. Evaluating propaganda
5. Understanding and using figurative language[19]

An excellent source on critical reading or thinking is *Teaching for Thinking: Theory and Application* by Raths, et al.

---

[17]Albert J. Harris, *How to Increase Reading Ability* (New York: David McKay Co., 1970), pp. 423-31.

[18]Helen W. Painter, "Critical Reading in the Primary Grades," in *Reading Instruction: Dimensions and Issues,* ed. William K. Darr (Boston: Houghton Mifflin Co., 1967), p. 160.

[19]*Ibid.*, p. 160.

SUMMARY

A discussion of the definitions of reading and the terminology found in most reading programs was included in this chapter. Although reading authorities are not in total agreement as to the nature of the reading process, most concur that thought, language, and reading are closely related. The perceptual processes involved in reading also have been of interest to most who have developed reading programs. Exercises in word attack skills have centered around the perception of words and their perceptual and linguistic components, such as inflectional variants, root words, prefixes, suffixes, and compound words. Too often, lessons in word attack and word perception (e.g., the development of sight vocabulary) have resulted in isolated drill that is unrelated to the total reading process. A discussion of comprehension skills also was included in this chapter. Comprehension is considered to be the goal in most reading programs, and, as with the reading process itself, is closely related to thought and language. The terms "reading" and "comprehension" can not be separated from one another.

REFERENCES

Allen, Harold B., editor. *Readings in Applied English Linguistics*. New York: Appleton-Century-Crofts, 1958.

Anderson, Paul S. *Linguistics in the Elementary School Classroom*. New York: The Macmillan Co., 1971.

Austin, Mary, and Morrison, Coleman. *The First R*. New York: The Macmillan Co., 1963.

Bagford, Jack. "The Role in Teaching in Reading." In *Elementary Reading Today: Selected Articles*, edited by Wilma H. Miller, pp. 185-92. New York: Holt, Rinehart, & Winston, 1972.

Bliesmer, Emery P., and Yarborough, Betty H. "A Comparison of Ten Different Beginning Reading Programs in First Grades." *Phi Delta Kappan* 46 (1965): 500-04.

Bond, Guy L., and Dykstra, Robert. "Interpreting the First Grade Reading Studies." In *The First Grade Reading Studies: Findings of Individual Investigations*, edited by Guy L. Bond and Robert Dykstra. Newark, Delaware: International Reading Association, 1967.

Cleland, Donald. "Do We Apply What We Know about Comprehension? Pro-Challenger." In *Current Issues in Reading*. Newark, Delaware: International Reading Association, 13 (1969): 97-102.

Clymer, Theodore. "The Barrett Taxonomy—Cognitive and Affective Dimensions of Reading Comprehension." In *Innovations and Change in Reading Instruction: Sixty-Seventh Yearbook of the National Society for the Study of Education, Part II*, edited by Helen M. Robinson, pp. 19-23. Chicago: University of Chicago Press, 1968.

Dechant, E. V. *Improving the Teaching of Reading*. Englewood Cliffs, New Jersey: Prentice-Hall, Inc., 1964.

Dolch, E. W. "A Basic Sight Vocabulary." *Elementary School Journal* 36 (1936): 456-60.

Durkin, Dolores. *Teaching Them to Read*. Boston: Allyn & Bacon, Inc., 1970.

Emans, Robert. "History of Phonics." In *Elementary Reading Today: Selected Articles*, edited by Wilma H. Miller, pp. 175-84. New York: Holt, Rinehart, & Winston, 1972.

Fry, Edward. "Developing a Word List for Remedial Reading." *Elementary English* (November 1957): 456-58.

Gates, Arthur I. "Character and Purposes of the Yearbook." *Reading in the Elementary School*, edited by Nelson B. Henry. Forty-eighth Yearbook of the National Society for the Study of Education. Chicago: University of Chicago Press, 1949.

Goodman, Kenneth S., editor. *The Psycholinguistic Nature of the Reading Process*. Detroit: Wayne State University, 1968.

_____. "Reading: A Psycholinguistic Guessing Game." In *Individualized Instruction: A Reader*, edited by Kenneth S. Goodman. New York: Holt, Rinehart, & Winston, 1972.

_____. "Reading—The Key is in Children's Language." *The Reading Teacher* 25 (1972): 505-08.

Guilford, J. B. "Frontiers in Thinking That Teachers Should Know About." *Elementary Reading Instruction*, edited by Althea Berry; Thomas C. Zarrett; and William Powell, pp. 227-35. Boston: Allyn & Bacon, Inc., 1969.

Harris, Albert J. *How to Increase Reading Ability*. New York: David McKay Co., 1970.

Harris, Larry A., and Smith, Carl B. *Reading Instruction through Diagnostic Teaching*. New York: Holt, Rinehart, & Winston, 1971.

Hatcher, Thomas C. "The Development of Comprehension Skills in Selected Basal Readers." *Dissertation Abstracts* 3557-A, 1971.

Heilman, Arthur W. *Principles and Practices of Teaching Reading*, 3rd ed. Columbus, Ohio: Charles E. Merrill Publishing Co., 1972.

Kottmeyer, William. *Teacher's Guide for Remedial Reading*. Manchester, Missouri: Webster Publishing Co., 1959.

Moffett, James. *A Student-Centered Language Arts Curriculum Grades 11-13: A Handbook for Teachers*. Boston: Houghton Mifflin Co., 1968.

Painter, Helen W. "Critical Reading in the Primary Grades. In *Reading Instruction: Dimensions and Issues*, edited by William K. Darr. Boston: Houghton Mifflin Co., 1967.

Raths, Louis E., et al. *Teaching for Thinking: Theory and Application*. Columbus, Ohio: Charles E. Merrill Publishing Co., 1967.

Roswell, Florence, and Natchez, Gladys. *Reading Disability: Diagnosis and Treatment*. New York: Basic Books, 1971.

Ryan, Ellen, and Semmel, Melvin I. "Reading as a Constructive Language Process." *Reading Research Quarterly* 5 (1969): 59-82.

Smith, Nila B. *American Reading Instruction*. Newark, Delaware: International Reading Association, 1965.

Spache, George. *Toward Better Reading*. Champaign, Illinois: Garrard Publishing Co., 1963.

Sparks, Paul, and Fay, Leo C. "An Evaluation of Two Methods of Teaching Reading." *Elementary School Journal* 42 (1957): 386-90.

————. "A Study of Prefixes in the Thorndike List to Establish a List of Prefixes That Should Be Taught in the Elementary School." *Journal of Educational Research* 35 (1942): 453-58.

Stauffer, Russell G., editor. *The First Grade Reading Studies: Findings of Individual Investigations*. Newark, Delaware: International Reading Association, 1967.

Stone, Clarence. *Progress in Primary Reading*. McGraw-Hill Book Co., 1950.

Wilson, Robert M. *Diagnostic and Remedial Reading for Classroom and Clinic*, 2nd ed. Columbus, Ohio: Charles E. Merrill Publishing Co., 1972.

Zintz, Miles V. *The Reading Process: The Teacher and the Learner*. Dubuque, Iowa: William C. Brown Company, Publishers, 1970.

THREE

Reading
Deficits and
the Retarded

Describing the characteristics that may hinder the reading progress of mildly and borderline retarded children is not an easy task. Part of the problem stems from the fact that there is no substantial evidence concerning the predictors of reading success or characteristics that definitely hinder reading achievement. There is no evidence to support any one characteristic that could be the basis of all reading problems in the educable retarded (Spicker and Bartel, 1968). In addition, mentally retarded readers *should not* be regarded as a homogeneous group; individual differences are found in this group as well as in any group of normal readers.

This chapter attempts to enumerate some areas that have been indicated by researchers as being related to reading progress and the characteristics of educable and borderline retardates in these areas. Thus, several factors often cited as being related to reading skills are discussed including: experiential background, physical and intellectual factors; language; auditory, visual, and perceptual-motor perception; emotional and social adjustment; reading interests; skills and needs of the retarded; and learning disabilities in relation to the retarded.

EXPERIENTIAL BACKGROUND

Experiences, especially those related to the home, have been cited as being important in the development of reading skills and interests (Bond and Tinker, 1967), and the cultural level of the home is one of the best indicators of the child's background and experiences (Harris, 1970). A survey of the background of experiences of the educable retarded reveals that the homes are usually "culturally deprived" or "culturally different" since most mild retardation occurs within this societal context (Dunn, 1963; Wakefield, 1964). Although this is not to say that the culturally deprived lack experiences, it is true that the experiences of very few of them match the middle-class orientation of the public schools (Bloom, Davis, and Hess, 1965). In describing many of the differences in background of the deprived child, one must avoid drawing stereotypes which paint deprived children as being savages who must be civilized, who do not want to learn, and whose parents are absolutely not concerned about their children's academic achievement (Cuban, 1970; Heilman, 1972). Some legitimate general findings about the background of deprived children indicate the following areas of concern: substandard, crowded housing; inadequate food and clothing; alienation from the middle-class society; low educational level of parents; and few educational objects and materials in the home (Deutsch, 1963; Heilman, 1970).

Results of several studies made of the families of the mildly retarded show:

1. A greater prevalence of instability because of divorce and desertion.
2. More contact with social agencies and the courts.
3. Diverse and unsteady occupational histories of the parents.
4. Low achievement expectations of children by the parents, especially the mothers (Farber, 1968; Kennedy, 1948; Meyerowitz and Farber, 1966).

Although none of the studies show poor home conditions and low socioeconomic status to be a direct cause of reading failure, it seems certain that these factors can influence interest and motivation in reading (Wynn, 1967). Children whose parents are educated, take them on trips, read to them, and possess a wealth of books and magazines will be more likely to respond to the reading material presented in the schools than will their disadvantaged counterparts (Wilson and Hall, 1972; Karlin, 1972).

PHYSICAL FACTORS

Although controversy exists regarding the relationship of physical deficiencies to reading, several disabilities have been listed as possible causes of reading disability. They include: general health, visual and hearing disorders, speech defects, and motor disturbances (Bond and Tinker, 1967; Zintz, 1970; Roswell and Natchez, 1971). Another factor, neurological dysfunction, will be discussed under the subject of learning disabilities.

General Health

Chronic fatigue, malnutrition, endocrine disturbances, and other health-related factors that render the child listless and inattentive and lower his vitality can affect his reading progress, especially if these factors cause him to be chronically absent from school (Bond and Tinker, 1967; Eisenberg, 1967). Although it would be unwise to assume that mild mental retardation and poor health go hand-in-hand and that all mildly retarded children have health problems, research has found that culturally deprived children are typically in poor health. Many are anemic and some have kidney problems and other disorders related to malnutrition (Bereiter and Engelmann, 1966; Dunn, 1963). Health factors alone have not been designated as causes of reading disability, but they may be a contributing factor in the reading success of the mildly retarded child.

Visual and Auditory Defects

Far too many investigations to describe here have been conducted in order to determine the relationship between visual defects and reading.

> Ruling out the more serious visual defects which prevent the child from seeing printed word symbols, it is difficult, on the basis of published research, to come to a conclusion regarding the precise relationship between visual and reading deficiency.[1]

Although some investigators have found a great incidence of visual problems among school children, correlations between reading ability and scores on visual tests tend to be negligible (Bond

---

[1]Arthur W. Heilman, *Principles and Practices of Teaching Reading*, 3rd ed. (Columbus, Ohio: Charles E. Merrill Publishing Co., 1972), p. 133.

and Tinker, 1967). However, several other studies have found a higher incidence of hyperopia (farsightedness) among reading disability cases (Eames, 1934; Farris, 1934). More recently, binocular coordination has been named as a cause of reading disability (Spache, 1967). Eames (1964) has obtained evidence that correction of anisometropia in those with reading disabilities allows them to achieve greater success in reading. Anisometropia is a distortion of the images in the two eyes into different sizes of shapes which contributes to such complications as poor visual fusion and aniseikonia.

Even though there is no general agreement as to the exact relationship between reading and vision, there is a general consensus that visual dysfunction can cause a degree of discomfort and, perhaps, avoidance of reading as a result (Roswell and Natchez, 1971). Harris (1970), Bond and Tinker (1967), and Kottmeyer (1959) offer additional information on the relationship between poor vision and reading.

Visual problems do, of course, occur among the mildly retarded. More visual difficulties have been found among the mildly retarded than among normal groups; however, a substantial number of the retarded do not have such defects (Kirk, 1962). Thus, it can be safely said that the visual development and acuity of the retarded are very much like the mentally normal child (Kirk, 1940).

Hearing

Auditory acuity is the ability of the sense organ to receive impressions in order to hear. Just as there is controversy over the relationship of visual acuity and reading, there is also disagreement concerning the causal effects of auditory acuity on reading skills. Many studies have found no difference in good and poor readers in auditory acuity for pure tones. Robinson (1953) found acuity loss to be an infrequent cause of reading disability; however, Bond and Tinker (1967) have indicated that although no greater incidence of hearing deficiency is found in large groups of disabled readers, the individual clinical cases of poor readers who have hearing defects may not influence group comparisons in studies. Several investigators have found impaired hearing causally related to low reading ability; this seems to be especially true when losses are within high frequencies ranges (Betts, 1957; Kennedy, 1942; Henry, 1948; and Johnson, 1957).

On the subject of auditory acuity and poor reading, Bond and Tinker have concluded:

> There is ample evidence to indicate that certain children are handicapped by hearing impairment. This seems particularly true of cases with severe hearing loss, with high tone deafness, or when pupils with hearing loss are taught by auditory methods. Certainly every child who is a reading disability case should have a hearing test. While impairment of hearing seldom appears to be the sole cause of reading disability, it may be an important contributing factor in a pattern of causes.[2]

While the incidence of serious hearing loss in the normal population has been estimated as being 5 percent, a higher incidence of hearing loss (from 5 percent to 50 percent) has been reported among mentally retarded populations. Little information is available concerning the incidence of hearing loss among the borderline and educable retarded because most of the research has been conducted with the trainable, severely retarded, or institutionalized subjects (Siegenthaler, Sallade, and Lordibuono, 1972).

Reports of the incidence also fluctuate with the criterion of hearing loss, intelligence, age range of group studied, and the type of testing procedure, used (e.g., pure tone audiometer or speech hearing tests) (Kodman, Powers, Weller and Phillip, 1958; Berry and Eisenson, 1956). Although conclusions do indicate a higher loss of hearing in the retarded, more research is needed in this area in order to determine a better estimate of hearing loss among educable and borderline retarded children.

Speech Defects

Harris has noted two types of speech defects that are found most often among cases of reading disability; these are indistinctness with blurred consonant sounds and a "general thick quality, and a rapid, jerky, stumbling kind of speech which is sometimes called cluttering."[3] Occurrence of severe speech defects in school age children can be placed at 5 percent. An additional 5 percent of the

---

[2]Guy L. Bond and Miles A. Tinker, *Reading Difficulties: Their Diagnosis and Correction*, 2d ed (New York: Appleton-Century-Crofts, 1967), p. 112.

[3]Albert J. Harris, *How to Increase Reading Ability*, 5th ed (New York: David McKay Co., 1970), p. 259.

school age population have minor speech defects (Berry and Eisenson, 1956).

The classifications for speech disorders have been listed by Berry and Eisenson:

1. Defects of articulation (These include distortions, substitutions, or omissions of speech sounds)
2. Defects of voice production (These include significant deviations in quality, loudness, pitch, variety, or duration of vocalization)
3. Defects of rhythm (stuttering and cluttering)
4. Delayed speech development
5. Cleft-palate speech
6. Cerebral-palsy speech, including congenital aphasia
7. Impairment of language function (aphasia)
8. Speech defects associated with defective hearing[4]

The general consensus of most research is that the incidence of speech defects among the mentally retarded is higher than in the general population (Matthews, 1951, 1957; Jordan, 1972; and Keane, 1972). Many of the studies are not uniform concerning the nature of the speech problems or the criteria for standards of identification (Keane, 1972). A summary of the research indicates that a higher percentage of speech problems (57 to 72 percent) exists among institutionalized retardates and fewer among retardates in special classes (8 to 26 percent). Articulation problems constitute the largest percentage of speech difficulties among both mentally retarded and normal children (Spraldin, 1963).

After a review of the literature in regard to speech and intelligence, Keane has concluded that although there is no high positive correlation between intelligence and oral communication, it appears that the lower the IQ, the less evidence there is of speech. In addition, there is no one pattern of speech problem in the mentally retarded (Keane, 1972).

Motor Disturbances

As a group, disabled readers exhibit poor motor coordination (Bond and Tinker, 1967; Harris, 1970; Shedd, 1968; Rabinovitch, 1954). Rabinovitch has described these children's movements as having a nonspecific motor awkwardness which is exhibited in gait

---

[4]Mildred F. Berry and Jon Eisenson, *Speech Disorders: Principles and Practices of Therapy* (New York: Appleton-Century-Crofts, 1956), p. 3.

and performance of motor acts, such as dressing and closing doors. They do not possess obvious motor disorders but fall below average as a group, particularly in tests of locomotor coordination (Johnson and Myklebust, 1965). The present writers, through conferences with the parents of children with reading disabilities, have noted that many parents report that their children are uncoordinated and have difficulty in learning to ride bicycles, skip, and play sports such as baseball.

Although many reading disabled children do possess poor motor coordination, there is no evidence that this is a direct cause of reading disability, although poor reading and poor motor coordination may result from the same source (Harris, 1970). Berry has concluded from observations of children with language disorders and from reviewing the research that "motor awkwardness may be a notable sign of a central nervous deficit that also may have affected the child's language."[5]

Although educably and borderline mentally retarded children as a group are more like normal children in motor coordination, they are somewhat inferior in motor skills (Dunn, 1963). The retarded may be more noticeably disabled in finer motor skills, such as cutting and other manual activities, than in gross motor skills (Sloan, 1959). Finer motor skills will be discussed further later in this chapter.

INTELLECTUAL FACTORS

Intelligence (see Chapter One for a detailed discussion) scores have been designated as an important factor in determining reading readiness (Harris, 1970). Results of these tests are usually interpreted in terms of Mental Age (MA) and Intelligence Quotient (IQ). A particular MA, (e.g., 7.0) means that the child's score is equal to the score of a child who has an average intelligence score and is seven (7.0) years old. Although intelligence scores have been found to be important predictors of reading in the early years, a low IQ has not been shown to be a direct cause of reading disability (Vernon, 1957; Black, 1971). Nonetheless, a low IQ may lead to reading disability, if instruction is not adjusted to the child's lower intelligence in the early grades (Bond and Tinker, 1967). Intelligence factors also have been indicated as having a limiting effect on the child's potential level of reading success (Kirk, 1940).

[5]Mildred F. Berry, *Language Disorders of Children* (New York: Appleton-Century-Crofts, 1969), p. 191.

Mental age has long been related to reading readiness and success in reading. For example Morphett and Washburne (1931) concluded that a child must have a minimum mental age of six years six months (6.6) in order to learn to read. Special educators often have used this criterion as one measure of when a retarded child is able to learn to read and also of his level of success in reading (Cegelka and Cegelka, 1970; Kirk, 1940), although since the Morphett and Washburne study, other researchers have found that a mental age of 6.6 is not necessary for beginning reading (Gates, 1937; Edmiston and Peyton, 1950).

Not only have the earlier conclusions concerning the relationship between mental age and reading been challenged but the use of mental age as a predicting variable also has been questioned. A single predictor, such as mental age, should not be used to account for all individual differences (Heal, 1970); it is erroneous to assume that a twelve-year-old educable retarded child with a MA of 8.0 will perform in reading exactly like another twelve-year-old retarded child of the same mental age. Nor should a teacher of reading to the educable and borderline retarded base her reading instruction solely on the mental age of the child. An older retarded child with a lower mental age (e.g., 6.0) will not perform exactly like a normal six year old in reading tasks.

Specific Characteristics Related to Intelligence

Recently, approaches to mental retardation other than the general intelligence model have been developed because the "low intelligence concept of mental retardation does not really constitute a potent and productive explanatory or predictive system."[6] In other words, characterizing an educable mentally retarded child by his intelligence quotient alone does not provide sufficient evidence for the development of a curricular program. Since general intelligence scores are determined by performance on many specific tasks, investigators have researched the retarded child's performance on these tasks compared to that of the normal child. Research also has been conducted concerning the causal effects of these skills on reading disability. Among the abilities that have been considered are short and long-term memory and reasoning skills.

---

[6]Alfred A. Baumeister, "Learning Abilities of the Mentally Retarded," in *Mental Retardation*, ed. Alfred A. Baumeister (Chicago: Aldine Publishing Co., 1967), p. 199.

The approach of comparing specific skills assumes that the intelligence of mentally retarded children can be described according to learning deficiencies. The many studies that have been conducted comparing the learning abilities of mentally retarded children to those of normal children may be based on the premise that retarded children learn differently from normal children. This position has been challenged though (Iano, 1971) by those who hold a developmental theory of learning. Rather than assuming that intellectual development is based primarily on learning, researchers who accept the developmental view posit that "learning ability is primarily accounted for by level of intellectual development."[7] Piaget's work has influenced this theory of intellectual development for Piaget (1964) has determined that the usual sense of learning is too narrow. On the other hand, he views developmental learning as a gradual acquisition of general knowledge or structure due to the intricate relationship of biological maturation, general experience, and active participation of the individual. Iano, in summarizing this theory, has stated:

> For convenience and ease of communication, the acquisition of new and higher levels of intelligence can be termed development and the term learning can be restricted to its usual or narrower use. The mentally retarded then are viewed as being slow in development rather than in learning and as achieving a relatively low developmental level of maturity. However, the mentally retarded, as well as others, are viewed as capable of learning after mental maturity is attained.[8]

This theory essentially negates study after study on the learning differences and styles of the retarded. Because this developmental view has not been completely established, specific learning abilities or disabilities of the retarded and their relationship to reading also will be discussed in this chapter.

Memory

Memory refers to the operations of retention and reproduction of information (Guilford, 1967). It is discussed under a variety of terms, such as auditory memory, digit span memory, retrieval,

---

[7]Richard P. Iano, "Learning Deficiency versus Developmental Conceptions of Mental Retardation," *Exceptional Children* 38 (1971): 303.

[8]*Ibid.*, p. 304

visual memory, and sequential or serial memory. Difficult to test because of the inability to separate it from perception and other learning processes (Lerner, 1971), memory also poses other difficulties for researchers who wish to explore it. Biochemical explanations have been given for memory (Bogoch, 1968), but these explanations are not very practical for the special education teacher. Until more is understood about the neurological approaches, a behavioral approach is perhaps the most meaningful way in which the teacher can deal with memory.

Often referred to by the terms short-term and long-term, memory often is associated with the visual and auditory processes. For example, the ability to read with comprehension depends upon long-term memory, while immediate memory is necessary for rote learning (Myers and Hammill, 1969). Visual memory (storage of visual stimuli) and visual sequencing (remembering the order of a visual pattern) often have been related with problems in the ability to revisualize letters, words, or forms (Myers and Hammill, 1969; Guthrie and Goldberg, 1972).

Several researchers have linked memory deficits with academic failure, symbolic language disorders, and reading dysfunctions (Johnson and Myklebust, 1965; Gillespie, 1970; Shedd, 1968; Berry, 1956; Vergason, 1968; Van Riper, 1964; Robinson, 1953; and Kirk, 1971).

Many studies have discovered memory problems to be present in the educable retarded (Ellis, 1968; Stinnett and Prehm, 1970; Kirk and Kirk, 1971; Bateman and Wetherell, 1965; Burt, 1958; Prehm and Mayfield, 1970; Bliesmer, 1954; Wiseman, 1965; and McCarthy, 1965). However, it should be noted that these memory problems tend to occur more often when normal and retardates of the same age are compared. Johnson and Blake (1960) have found that when older retardates are matched with younger normal children of the same mental age, there are no significant differences in retention of material. Yet educable retarded children who are placed in the regular classroom are competing with normal children of the same age. If the retarded child is expected to remember material designated for the normal child, the level and meaningfulness of the material may hinder the child's memory (Dunn, 1964).

There is also evidence (Ellis, 1963) that mentally retarded children do retain material over an extended period of time after learning a fact or concept (Ellis, 1963; Vergason, 1962). It may be that the retarded have a more serious problem with short-term memory than with long-term memory. Ellis (1963) has hypothesized a "stimulus trace" theory to explain this possibility. This is a physiological explanation based upon the activity of the central nervous system. Ellis's theory holds that the retarded individual can not maintain the trace, or electrical charge, from stimuli resulting from receptive organs (e.g., visual stimuli). According to Ellis, this trace decays faster after a retarded child completes a learning trial than it does for a normal child. Thus, the theory relates to short-term rather than to long-term memory.

Attention, or the ability to attend, has been linked often with memory problems (Harris, 1970). Before a child can remember information, he must be able to concentrate, to attend to a particular stimulus, and to ignore distracting stimuli. Weaknesses in the ability to concentrate have been found among young disabled readers (Malmquist, 1958). In addition, according to Harris (1970), failure in many tasks on a test may be due to inattention rather than the lack of abilities for the tasks. Studies with the retarded have found that the retarded child may not attend to relevant stimuli and may be unable to ignore those stimuli that do not relate to the task. In many instances, while he is able to persevere in performing the task, he is attending to the wrong stimuli (Baumeister, 1967).

Reasoning Skills

Reasoning, cognitive, or "thinking" skills also have been linked with reading comprehension (Thorndike, 1917; Lerner, 1971). Many reading comprehension problems occur when the child is not able to reason beyond the literal level (Harris and Smith, 1971). Stauffer (1969) has referred to reading as a thinking process and indicated that reading comprehension involves the use of problem-solving, suspending judgments, and employing concepts. Piaget (1959), Guilford (1959), and Bloom (1956) also have made interpretations of reasoning skills. Guilford's model (see Chapter One) defines several operations related to reasoning — cognition, convergent thinking, divergent thinking, and evaluation (Guilford, 1967). Bloom's Taxonomy of Educational Objectives (1956) provides another framework for thinking skills. These levels are: knowledge or memory of details; comprehension or translation (putting information into one's own words); application utilizing learned materials; analysis (studying a subject with depth and recognizing or identifying its component parts); synthesis (solving a problem that requires original or creative thinking); and evaluation (judging material according to some criteria).

Some research studies have found retarded children to be deficient in reasoning and comprehension skills (Burt, 1958; Gallagher and Lucito, 1961). Although the evidence is not conclusive on these differences, several authors have cited such factors as deficiencies in abstractions, logical development, and manipulation of symbols as being areas of retardation among the disadvantaged children who comprise a large percentage of educable mentally retarded children (Bereiter and Engelmann, 1966; Cuban, 1970; Eisenberg, 1967; Tuckman, 1969). Other studies have found that retarded children have problems in applying spontaneous mediation (assigning distinctive labels to cues) or responding to implicit associations between materials; this problem appears to be especially common as the items increase in abstraction (Wallis, 1962; Rieber, 1964; Wallace and Underwood, 1964). For example, in learning a list of material, the normal subject tends to group (cluster) similar items together or to develop (mediate) some relationship between items in order to remember the material. "Quite likely, mental retardates not only have a smaller reservoir of mediators than normals, but also less experience in the use of them."[9] However, some evidence indicates that when retardates are taught to mediate cues with distinctive labels, their associative learning improves (Barnett, Ellis and Pryer, 1959; Cantor and Hattel, 1957; and Smith and Means, 1961).

The ability to cluster items has been related to reading comprehension by Braum (1963) and by Bilsky and Evans (1970). Here, the educable and borderline retardate's inability to deal with abstract relationships may hinder his ability to draw inferences and to make evaluations of the material that he reads.

In summary, the present authors stress that most of the learning characteristics of the educably retarded are not conclusive. Dunn (1964) has indicated that the educable retarded child is able to learn, retain, and reason just as well as the normal child of the same mental age.

LANGUAGE FACTORS

Although the evidence of a causal relationship between language and reading achievement is not clear (Weintraub, 1971), many

---

[9]Baumeister, p. 204.

authors have cited the importance of language skills to reading (Dechant, 1964; Durkin, 1970; Harris, 1970; Harris and Smith, 1972; Heilman, 1972; Loban, 1963; Strickland, 1969; and Zintz, 1970). The discussion of language is a multi-faceted one, and the "process of human communication is extremely complex."[10] No definite answers exist concerning the development and teaching of language skills. To further complicate matters, language and communication are not synonymous. "Communication is a broader term, encompassing nonverbal language such as gesture as well as oral language."[11]

Such factors as acquisition of language skills, the relationship of thinking skills to language, and linguistic investigations (lexical, phonological, morphological, and syntactic) are included in this section.

Acquisition of Language Skills

Language has been defined as "a body of sounds and meanings held in common by the members of a linguistic group."[12] A child learns this sound system very early in life as he acquires his language pattern through experiences, imitation of adults, and development of neurological processes. There are several theories regarding how a child acquires his language. According to the behavioristic theory developed by Skinner, the child learns by imitation and reinforcement. Other theorists, such as the nativists, believe that language development is biologically determined, neurologically based, and is paralleled by growth in motor and thinking skills. This theory stresses a "critical" period for language development which begins before the age of four. A third theory, influenced by Piaget, posits that the child takes an active role in learning language. His cognitive activity is an information process that develops through certain stages and is not able to work in a higher stage until he has mastered the problems in perception of the tasks in any given stage (Wanat, 1971). By the age of five, a child has mastered most of the complex components of the language, such as intonation (stress, pitch, and juncture) and specific word classes, phrases, and complexity in sentence structure. However, the child

---

[10]William A. Jenkins, "Language and Communication," in *Coordinating Reading Instruction*, ed. Helen M. Robinson (Glenview, Illinois: Scott, Foresman and Co., 1971), pp. 36-45.

[11]*Ibid.*, p. 36.

[12]Reprinted by permission of the publisher from Ruth Strickland, *The Language Arts in the Elementary School* (Lexington, Massachusetts: D. C. Heath & Co., 1969), p. 3.

is still learning dimensions of language until the ages of seven or eight years. During this period, he continues to make errors in such points of grammar as making subjects and verbs agree (Berry, 1969).

The acquisition of language has been related to many factors, including intelligence, home background, auditory acuity, and neurological development. At least some of these factors in language development are not favorable for the educable retarded child. Most educable retardates come from homes of low socioeconomic backgrounds and are at least one year behind normal children in the development of language skills (Bereiter and Englemann, 1966). Miller and Yoder (1972) have concluded that the retarded child develops the language in the same manner as the normal child but at a slower rate.

Language and Thought

Language and thought are closely related (Hilgard, 1962). On this subject, Strickland has remarked:

> The point at which real thinking begins in the life of a child is uncertain. He sees his mother put on her coat and pick up her purse to go to the market and runs for his sweater and cap to go with her. He sees Daddy leaving for work and runs to the window to wave good-bye. A dog will bring his leash when he wants to go out if the leash and going out are clearly associated in his mind, and a kitten will learn early to run to the kitchen when she hears the refrigerator door open. These are responses of association which may involve rudimentary thinking. Some authorities hold that a little child is incapable of much that can be called thinking until he learns to talk or at least until he senses the meaning of words. The three year old who accompanies his play with a running account of what he is doing is thinking aloud. In the process of acquiring speech, he must at many points use it orally if he is to use it at all.[13]

Does a child think before he acquires language? Researchers and psychologists, such as Piaget (1952), Vygotsky (1962), and Myklebust and Johnson (1965), have reviewed the child's preverbal ability (inner language or speech) to organize and structure experiences in order to answer this question. The inability to acquire such concepts as time, size, and direction, may be a deficiency of inner

---

[13]*Ibid.*, p. 23.

language. Myklebust and Johnson have hypothesized that such a deficit could affect reading comprehension.

Concepts are very much a part of the child's inner language. Concepts are symbols which stand for a class of objects or events with common properties (Hilgard, 1962); they may vary from the very concrete (chair) to the very abstract (honesty). The first words the child learns deal entirely with concrete things. Gradually, he develops more abstract concepts and generalizations concerning time, space, etc. This language is also a clue to his ability to see relationships and to utilize cause-and-effect thinking (Strickland, 1969). Such phrases in his oral vocabulary as "if this . . . then that" show this type of thinking. Concept development is important to word meaning and, therefore, is related to reading comprehension (Harris and Smith, 1971; Heilman, 1972; and Stauffer, 1969). A child may possess a wealth of concepts, but if they do not relate to the material which he is reading, he will experience difficulty in comprehension. This is a particular problem with reading material that emphasizes middle-class backgrounds and, therefore, does not relate to the experience of many educably mentally retarded children.

Concept formation in the mildly retarded has been studied by many educators (Furth, 1963; Griffith and Spitz, 1958; Griffith, Spitz, and Lepman, 1963; Jensen and Ronever, 1963; Milgram, 1966; Stephens, 1966). Their general conclusion is that concept formation is a special problem for the mentally retarded. Educable mentally retarded children deal more successfully with concrete concepts; many times their conceptual development lags behind their technical skills, such as word recognition (Goldstein and Seigle, 1961).

Oral Language

Studies to determine the nature of the oral language of the educable retarded have been conducted, but they do not give much idea of the nature of the language problems these children face (Dever, 1971). Miller and Yoder have stated: "There is very limited information on the development and use of the linguistic codes by the retarded child."[14]

A discussion of the supposed oral language problems of the retarded can be centered around the areas of lexicon (vocabu-

---

[14]Jon F. Miller and David E. Yoder, "On Developing the Content for a Language Teaching Program," *Mental Retardation* 10 (1972): 9-11.

lary), morphology (the smallest meaningful groups of sounds of the language, such as prefixes), and syntax (the ordering of the morphemes in the language) (Dever, 1971).

Lexical Problems

Knowledge of vocabulary has been indicated as being important to success in reading, especially to successful comprehension (Strickland, 1969; Harris and Smith, 1971). If the child has had no experiences with the words in the basal readers or has never heard the words spoken, he may have problems in comprehending the materials.

Significant vocabulary deficiencies have been found among the educable retarded (Dunn, 1964). Research has determined that the greater the extent of retardation, the greater the loss of speaking vocabulary (Keane, 1972). In fact, the very placement of children in special-education classes is dependent largely on vocabulary, since most individual intelligence tests are highly verbal in nature (Dever, 1971).

Although the vocabulary of the retarded may be deficient, there is very limited information concerning the exact nature of the retardation, especially among the educable and borderline retarded (Miller and Yoder, 1972).

Morphological Problems

Morphological difficulties in determining tense, person, number, and case may occur as the result of subcultures or background influences on the speech development of the educable retarded (Schiefelbusch, 1967; Valletutti, 1971). Findings of research studies indicate that retarded children respond in essentially the same ways on morphology as do culturally deprived when measured by the Grammatic Closure subtest of the *Illinois Test of Psycholinguistic Abilities (ITPA)* (Weaver and Weaver, 1967). Even when matched for mental age with normal children, educable retarded children have been found to be deficient in their ability in tense, number, and other morphophonemic features (Dever, 1971).

Morphemic analysis is considered part of the word recognition skills in reading (Harris, 1970). If a child does not use plurals when he speaks, he may have problems isolating them when he reads. Word attack skills, such as recognizing prefixes and suffixes, allow the child to become an independent reader. If the retarded child is limited in his ability to utilize these morphemic principles, he may have problems with word attack skills.

Syntactic Problems

Syntax is the order of the words in sentences and is usually studied in reference to variations in the normal acquisition of grammatical structure (Schiefelbusch, 1967). Most studies have concluded that mildly retarded children do have problems with syntax (Bateman and Wetherell, 1965; Goda, 1964; Semmel, Barritt, Bennett, and Perfetti, 1968; Siever, 1959). Syntax and reading have been related. In including syntactic skills under word attack, Harris and Smith have noted:

> Syntactic skills included context clues, punctuation cues, and identification of the position and function of the word in the structure of the sentence. The reader has certain internalized responses to the kinds of words that are underlined in the following sentence.

> (1)   (2)
> Justus was *warned* against swimming in the *lagoon*."

> Assuming he did not recognize instantly those underlined words, their positions and their functions indicate a past participle verb for 1 and a word for water in 2. The auxiliary verb *was* and the prepositional phrase *in the* create those expectations in the native speaker of the language. It is believed that most syntactic skills result primarily from the internalized language habit of the reader and not from the teaching scheme.[15]

Kirk and Kirk (1971) have stated that grammar is very important to academic skills because of its relationship to auditory reception (the ability to understand auditory symbols such as verbal discourse) and verbal expression.

In summary, it can be said that language development has been related often to progress in reading, although the exact relationship is not clear. In addition, educable retarded children appear to have language deficits in such areas as vocabulary. Because most of the mildly retarded and borderline retarded are from the lower socioeconomic classes, a question has been raised as to

---

[15]L. Harris and C. Smith, *Reading Instruction through Diagnostic Teaching* (New York: Holt, Rinehart, & Winston, 1972), p. 209.

whether this language disability is related to cognitive deficits or to cultural differences (Valletutti, 1971). More research is needed in this area as well as in the actual nature of language deficiencies of the educable retarded. Furthermore, the validity of many of the language measures used in determining language development of the retarded has been questioned (Dever, 1971). Schiefelbush, Copeland, and Smith (1967) provide a more thorough analysis of language and mental retardation.

PERCEPTION

Although perception is dependent upon the acuity of sense organs, it also depends upon the structures of the nervous system for the interpretations of the stimuli received from these organs (Hilgard, 1962) and upon the maturation and background experiences of the organism (Harris and Smith, 1971). As the child grows older, he is able to make more meaningful perceptions which develop as a result of his experiences with his environment. Three areas which have been related to reading are visual perception, auditory perception, and perceptual motor skills.

Visual Perception

"Visual perception is the cognition and interpretation of a visual sensation and the mental association of the present visual stimuli with memories of past experiences."[16] Visual perception has been indicated as being a very important skill for reading success (deHirsch, 1966; Harris and Smith, 1971; Heilman, 1972; Lerner, 1971), but the skill most often related to reading, especially in the beginning stages, is visual discrimination (the ability to note differences and likenesses among geometric forms, letters and words) (Barrett, 1965; Goins, 1958).

Visual Discrimination: Visual discrimination of letters and words also has a higher value of predicting reading success than visual discrimination of geometric designs and pictures (Barrett, 1965).

Another aspect of visual perception is spatial relation, which is the perception of the position of objects in space in relation to themselves and each other (Chalfant and Scheffelin, 1969). Spatial relations has been linked to such problems in reading as trans-

---

[16]Janet W. Lerner, *Children with Learning Disabilities: Theories, Diagnoses, and Teaching Strategies* (Boston: Houghton Mifflin Co., 1971), p. 34.

position of letters in words (Maslow, et al., 1964). Goodstein, Whitney, and Cawley (1970) have found spatial relations to be related positively to reading achievement. Other areas of visual perception have been defined as figure-ground (the ability to distinguish an object from the background surrounding it) and form constancy (ability to perceive similarities in form that persists when figures are altered in non-essential manners) by Frostig (1964). These areas have been related to reading disabilities by Maslow, et al. (1964) and by Goodstein, Whitney and Cawley (1970). The exact relationship between reading and these areas is not clear, and no claims should be made as to their accuracy as predictors of reading achievement (Cohen, 1969). Since the content validity of the subtests of some measures that determine visual perception such as the *Marianne Frostig Developmental Test of Visual Perception (DTVP)* has been questioned (Boyd and Randle, 1970), it is wise to see Chapter Four for a critique of the visual perception tests.

Studies have shown that culturally deprived children tend to have low scores in visual perception (Cohen, 1969; Deutsch, 1963; Goodstein, Whitney, and Cawley, 1970; Passamanick and Knabloch, 1958). Studies also have shown that visual perception and IQ scores are correlated (Lyons, 1954; Lloyd, 1966; Olson, 1966; Senger and Brunk, 1967). The high correlation could be due to the fact that many IQ tests include measures of visual perception (Cohen, 1969). Other reports have been given to indicate that educably retarded children, as a group, have visual perception deficits (Baumeister, 1967).

Other facets of visual perception such as eye-hand coordination and visual motor integration will be discussed under the topic of perceptual-motor development.

Auditory Perception

"Auditory perception is the ability to organize the sensory data received through the ear."[17] Auditory discrimination, blending, closure, and memory are the areas of auditory perception included in the following discussion.

Auditory Discrimination: Auditory discrimination is the ability to hear similarities and differences between and among two or more sounds. In a summary of the research on auditory discrimination

---

[17]*Ibid.*, p. 296.

and reading achievement, Dykstra (1966) concluded that many authorities, such as Monroe, Bond, and Robinson, have found auditory discrimination skills to be important in reading achievement. On the other hand, in his own study, Dykstra (1966) found that auditory measures, including auditory memory as well as discrimination, accounted for 38 percent of the variability in word recognition scores and did not have a high correlation with reading scores. However, Smith and Harris (1972) have concluded that, because of the unreliability of subtests on standardized tests, these results should be interpreted with some reservation.

Although a causal relationship may not exist between reading deficiency and auditory discrimination, many studies have shown poor readers to be low in auditory discrimination (Bond, 1935; Robinson, 1946; Schonell, 1958; Goetzinger, Dirks, and Vaer, 1960; and Christine and Christine, 1964). Durrell (1953) has found that retarded readers most often have problems with discriminating sounds in words.

Auditory Blending: "Auditory blending is the ability to reproduce a word by synthesizing its component sounds."[18] Kirk and Kirk (1971) also have related sound blending, as measured by the *ITPA*, to reading. Even if the child knows all the sounds, he has not mastered this skill if he can not synthesize sounds into words, therefore, he cannot read (Kirk and Kirk, 1971). Sound blending is a problem often encountered with problem readers (Golden and Steiner, 1969; Kass, 1965; Macione, 1969).

Auditory Closure: Auditory closure measures the child's ability to grasp a word when only part of that word is presented (Kirk and Kirk, 1971). This facet of auditory perception, which is measured on the *ITPA*, has been found to be deficient among poor readers (Kass, 1966).

Auditory Memory Span: Auditory memory span or auditory sequencing is the "amount of information an individual can retain in proper sequence, particularly for the purpose of immediate action or recall."[19] Some investigators have found that poor readers have problems with auditory sequencing ability as measured by tests

---

[18]Victoria Risko, "Differential Auditory Discrimination Skills as Related to Reading Achievement" (Ed.D. diss., West Virginia University, 1971), p. 9.

[19]Doris J. Johnson and Helmer Myklebust, *Learning Disabilities: Educational Principles and Practices* (New York: Grune & Stratton, 1967), p. 111.

employing digits (Gillespie, 1970; Golden and Steiner, 1969; Myklebust and Johnson, 1967; Poling, 1953; Wilhelm, 1968). Robinson (1953) found auditory memory span to be associated frequently with reading problems. However, the Kass (1966) and Macione (1967) studies on problem readers and the *ITPA* did not discover any significant differences between normal and disabled readers on the auditory-vocal sequencing.

Auditory Perception Problems and the Retarded: According to most studies, auditory perception deficits exist in the educable and borderline retarded (Bateman and Wetherell, 1965; Wiseman, 1965). A higher prevalence of auditory discrimination problems also has been indicated in children from lower socioeconomic backgrounds than in children from middle-class homes (Clark and Richards, 1966; Deutsch, 1965). The research in this area is scarce and more information is needed in order to determine the exact nature of the auditory perceptual deficiencies of the retarded.

Perceptual Motor Development

Perceptual motor development "refers to the interaction of the various channels of perception with motor activity." According to Kephart (1960), the separation of perception and perceptual-motor is impossible. He has stated: "In like manner, we cannot think of perceptual activity and motor activities as two different items; we must think of the hyphenated term *perceptual-motor*."[20] Perceptions result from the activities of the organism itself rather than from an input of stimuli which enters the organism for the purpose of motivating perceptual activity. The organisms must be active through firing nerve cells in order to generate nerve impulses that will translate and integrate outside energy.

Kephart views perceptual-motor processes as including a continuous feedback of information into the organism. Thus, the system receives information, integrates it with past and present information, correlates it with motor activity, and then feeds responses from this motor activity back into the system, thus creating a closed system which Kephart likens to an electric eye traffic light which senses the flow of traffic and acts accordingly. This system is illustrated in Figure 5.

---

[20]Newell C. Kephart, *The Slow Learner in the Classroom*, 2d ed (Columbus, Ohio: Charles E. Merrill Publishing Co., 1971), p. 115.

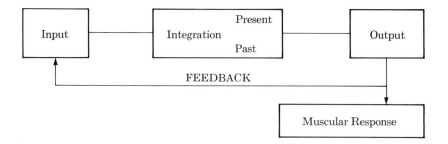

Figure 5:   Diagram of Feedback Mechanism in Perception[21]

Several factors, such as eye-hand coordination, visual motor integration, and laterality, have been included in perceptual-motor programs.

Since the first edition of Kephart's *Slow Learner in the Classroom* was published in 1960, much research has been conducted concerning the relationship between reading and perceptual-motor activity. Kephart's work itself was greatly influenced by Strauss who concluded that many brain-injured and retarded individuals also possess perceptual deficits (McCarthy and McCarthy, 1969).

Perceptual-motor deficits are found frequently in students with reading disabilities (Vernon, 1957). However, a causal relationship between reading skills and perceptual motor skills may not exist. In addition, training in perceptual-motor skills does not appear to improve children's reading scores significantly (Balow, 1971).

One important aspect of perceptual-motor development is eye-hand coordination, which is an integration of visual-tactual systems (Myers and Hammill, 1969). This skill is considered to be a fine-motor rather than a gross-motor task. Eye-hand coordination has been related to poor letter formation (Roswell and Natchez, 1971); However, eye-hand or eye-motor coordination, as measured by the Frostig *DTVP*, has been found to have very low positive correlation with reading tasks (Olson, 1966). Frostig (1964) has identified eye-hand coordination as well as the other measures on her test as being related to reading and spelling disorders, yet there is some controversy concerning these findings. Nonetheless, a higher incidence of eye-hand coordination problems does exist in disabled

[21]*Ibid.*, p. 108.

readers. Problems of eye-hand coordination also have been found among educable retarded children (Sloan, 1959; Wilson, 1971).

Laterality and Dominance: Kephart (1971) has included training in laterality in his perceptual-motor program. Lateral dominance is the "preferred use and superior functioning of one side of the body over the other."[22] Skillful use of the right hand for tasks such as writing would be indicative of right-hand dominance. A similar form of eye dominance exists as well which is considered crossed if the dominant hand and eye are on opposite sides of the body. Mixed handedness occurs if the individual does not prefer either hand consistently or performs equally well with either hand. Kephart (1971) has distinguished laterality from handedness and from the naming of left and right. He has posited that laterality is an internal awareness of the two sides of the body and their differences.

Brain dominance is another aspect of dominance that has occupied the attention of researchers. In 1937, Orton hypothesized that the centers for speech were located in the left hemisphere for a right-handed person and in the right hemisphere for a left-handed person. He also believed that reversals were caused by the mirror image's being made on the nondominant hemisphere. Since the 1930s, this theory has been discounted partially. Recent findings indicate that, in most cases of both right- and left-handed people, the left hemisphere is dominant for speech. Much research has been conducted concerning the relationship between laterality and reading achievement. Harris (1970), for example, has concluded that most of the research, which is very much in conflict, published in education journals can be criticized for not using "tests that are sensitive to mixed handedness and directional confusion."[23] Harris also has concluded that mixed handedness is related to poor reading while crossed dominance and mixed eyedness are not. Rice (1969), in a study of educable mentally retarded children compared to normal children, has found laterality confusion to be significantly related to intelligence as well as chronological age.

Directionality: Directionality, which is the awareness of the directions right and left outside the body, is dependent upon laterality. Once the child has developed laterality, he is able to project this awareness to his external environment (Kephart, 1971), for orien-

---

[22]Harris, p. 231.
[23]Harris, p. 242.

tation in space allows the child to move in a given direction upon command; for example, he can turn to the left when told to while square dancing. Directional confusion, as evidenced in such problems as reversals, has been related to problems in reading (Cohen, 1960; Harris, 1970; Roswell and Natchez, 1969). Although directional confusion and problems related to laterality appear in groups of poor readers, causal relationships between these factors and reading have not been completely established (Cohen, 1969).

Form-perception or Visual Motor Integration: Still another area of perceptual-motor programs is form perception, which is usually measured by the child's ability to copy geometric forms. Measurement of form perception is included in the *Purdue Perceptual Motor Survey* and the *Beery-Buktenica Test of Visual Motor Integration.* This ability has been found by some researchers to be related to reading achievement (Garrison and Magoon, 1972; Potter, 1949; Small, 1958).

Kephart's as well as other perceptual-motor programs, such as that of Getman (1968), include many other skills which may or may not be related to reading achievement; their relationship to reading skills has not been clearly established. Chapters Four and Five will provide additional analysis of perceptual tests and programs.

In summary, one can say that perceptual-motor skills have not been related causally to reading achievement, yet perceptual-motor deficiencies are found among poor readers. Finally, most of the literature indicates that mentally retarded children are inferior to normal children in perceptual motor development (Fisher, 1971; Erickson, 1965).

Emotional and Social Adjustment

A considerable controversy exists concerning emotional and social adjustment and reading failure. Which comes first — reading failure or emotional problems? Several studies have concluded that children who are emotionally stable when entering school can become emotionally upset after experiencing failure in reading tasks (Fernald, 1943; Newell, 1931; Preston, 1940). On the other hand, some researchers have concluded that emotional disturbances cause reading problems (Missildine, 1946; Raines and Tait, 1951), while still others hold that emotional disturbances and reading problems are interrelated (Gates, 1941; Robinson, 1953; Russell, 1947). By excluding severe emotional problems, such as childhood schizophrenia, the present writers have reached the opinion that while some children do come to school with social and emotional problems stemming from their homes, failure in school-related tasks contributes to emotional and social maladjustment in most cases. To be designated a failure at the age of six must be devastating to educable retarded children.

Emotional Disturbances: Studies have shown that the incidence of maladjustment among poor readers is greater than among good readers (Dechant, 1964). However, not all emotionally disturbed children are poor readers and not all poor readers are emotionally maladjusted. Repeated failure in reading skills may cause the child to withdraw his efforts and lack drive and interest in reading (Bond and Tinker, 1967). The saying "You can't fall out of bed if you sleep on the floor" is particularly applicable to the child who discontinues trying in order to avoid failure.

Studies with the educable retarded have found that, as a group, these children have a higher expectancy for failure than do normal children (Cromwell, 1961; Zigler, 1966; Zigler, 1967). Zigler (1968) contends that the retarded child, especially one from the lower socioeconomic classes, uses the classroom to satisfy his emotional needs more than does the normal child. Because of their anxiousness to please and their history of failure or negative responses from teachers, these children often approach learning situations that involve adults with great hesitance. Zigler (1966) also has indicated that retarded children are more outer-directed (dependent upon external cues such as praise or direction from the teacher) than normal children. This fact can be detrimental because it may reduce independence, spontaneity, and creativity (Carlson and Macmillan, 1970; Zigler, 1966). The writers of this text have observed these behaviors among educable retarded children in numerous circumstances, especially among older retardates. In reading tasks, the educable or borderline child often excuses his mistakes with such statements as "I did know that but I forgot." Role-playing, dramatization, reading orally, and other activities are hampered by the retarded child's fear of failure or ridicule.

Social Maladjustment: Several investigators have found that poor readers and educable and borderline mentally retarded children rank low in general social acceptance among their classmates (Buswell, 1953; Jordon and deCharms, 1959; Goodman, Gottlieb, and

Harrison, 1972; and Stevens, 1971). Retarded children also appear to be rejected more often for their behavioral problems than for their academic limitations (Johnson, 1950). Even when every effort is made to integrate the retarded children into most of the activities in the school (e.g., in a nongraded environment), they are still rejected more and accepted less often than nonretarded individuals (Goodman, Gottlieb, and Harrison, 1972; Lapp, 1959).

Thus, the retarded child may find himself a failure very early in his school career, and successive failure may lead to hostility, aggression, feelings of inferiority or withdrawal, and negative attitudes toward teachers, school, and academics. The outcome of such failures then becomes a detriment to further learning (Bond and Tinker, 1967; Guthery, 1971).

READING INTERESTS, SKILLS, AND NEEDS OF THE RETARDED

Understanding the reading interests, skills, and needs of the educable and borderline retarded should be important to a special educator who is involved in the reading program, and there is much work available for study on the reading interests of elementary and secondary students (Harris, 1970; Karlin, 1972). The educable retarded child reads less and sometimes has preferences which are immature for his age but more mature than those of younger children of his mental age (Lazar, 1937). However, at the secondary level there is little relationship between reading interests and intelligence (Norwell, 1950). Huber (1928) and Gates (1930) have found that the retarded child has essentially the same reading interests as those of the normal child.

The educable or borderline children should not be viewed as a group who all have the same interests. The range of individual likes and dislikes in reading are great regardless of intelligence or cultural background of the children doing the reading (Harris, 1970). However, one problem does exist in finding interesting reading material for the retarded. Books and basal readers geared to their age level are often too difficult for them to read, yet the material they are able to read is, in most cases, too juvenile for them. In a study with educable retarded children Koelsch (1969) found a low correlation between interest in basal readers that were on the children's reading level and in reading interests. Because of this problem, many high-interest, low-vocabulary series have been developed (see Appendix Four for listings).

Reading Skills

When matched by mental ages do educable retarded children perform differently from normal children in basic reading skills? Although the research is contradictory on this point, several studies have found differences in performance.

Dunn (1954) found that retarded boys who were matched to nonretarded boys with the same mental age were inferior in vowel understandings, contextual clues, sound omission, and both silent and oral reading. In 1930, Gates found that retarded subjects need more repetitions of words from basal readers (forty-five to fifty-five for retarded; thirty to thirty-five for normals) before learning them. In another study comparing bright normals and educable and borderline retardates with an IQ range of 72-84, Bleismer (1954) found the retarded children to be significantly inferior in total reading comprehension; specific comprehension skills, such as locating or recognizing factual details, recognizing main ideas, and drawing inferences and conclusions; and listening comprehension. Memory for factual details was slightly but not significantly higher for bright children. There were no differences between the groups in word meaning, word recognition, and reading rate.

Cawley, Goodstein, and Burrow (1972), as a result of their studies concerning the reading skills of the retarded, have concluded that mentally retarded children are inferior in reading skills that are related to linguistic development; this development encompasses the word attack skills discussed in Chapter Two. Shotick (1960) also has found differences between average and retarded boys in reading skills, specifically in the use of context clues and figurative language.

In relation to sex, retarded girls have been found to be superior in reading skills to boys (Bensberg, 1953; Jones, Gross and Van Way, 1960; Patterson and Philleo, 1943).

Several studies have considered the etiology of retardation as a factor in reading achievement. However, most often, no clear differences in reading skills were found between exogenous (brain-injured) or endogenous (unknown cause, familial) groups (Capobianco and Funk, 1959; Capobianco and Miller, 1958; Edwards, et al., 1971).

Finally, placement of the retarded has been studied in relation to reading success. Several investigators have found no greater gains in reading in special-class placement children than in cases of regular class placement (Ainsworth, 1959; Goldstein, Jordon, and

Moss, 1965). Some studies have found better gains in reading in regular class placement (Bennett, 1932; Cassidy and Stanton, 1959; Elenbogen, 1957), although Blatt (1958) did find better yearly gains in reading achievement for retarded children placed in special classes. Yet most of the studies contradict Blatt.

In a summary of the research by Kirk (1962), it is noted that educable retarded children do not usually read up to their mental age. However, in comparing superior students of the same mental age to retarded children, the studies indicate that the retarded children are closer to their capacity than the superior subjects (Kirk, 1964).

Some researchers have compared the differences between educable retarded subjects who are reading to capacity and those who are not. Differences, such as inability with automatic skills on the *Illinois Test of Psycholinguistic Abilities*, auditory memory, and lack of adequate word attack skills — especially phonics and contextual clues — have been found (Ragland, 1964; Shepherd, 1967).

Another study by Cawley, Goodstein, and Burrow (1972) involving differences between adequate and inadequate readers of average and slow learners using the *Gates-McKillop Reading Diagnostic Tests* found that poor readers made a significantly greater number of errors of omission, mispronunciation, repetition, and reversals than did good readers of comparable ability. Further discussion of oral reading errors can be found under the section on individual diagnostic reading tests in Chapter Four.

Still another factor related to mental age is determining at which point reading should be introduced to the educable retarded. As stated previously, the concept that a child must have a mental age of 6.6 has been questioned; however, some studies have found that when reading instruction is delayed until the retarded child's mental age is higher, (e.g., a mental age of 8.0), the retarded children learn reading more rapidly (Mechler, 1940). A follow-up of these subjects by Weiner (1954) found that their achievement was equal to a group of retardates who had not had a delay in instruction. Perhaps one advantage for delaying formal instruction is the alleviation of frustration and failure that occurs when reading is introduced earlier.

READING NEEDS OF THE RETARDED

The educable and borderline retarded need a certain number of reading skills for later job placement even though three-fourths of the retarded are placed in service, semiskilled, or unskilled occupations. Very few (10 percent) are found in white collar, clerical, and sales jobs, and fewer than 10 percent are placed in agriculture or skilled positions (Farber, 1968).

Although sophisticated reading skills may not be needed for many unskilled or semi-skilled jobs, the educable retarded will need to develop skill in filling out application forms for jobs, reading the newspaper, and reading instructions (Dunn, 1963). Other needed reading tasks include the ability to read street signs, telephone directories, public notices and warnings such as "high voltage," and labels on clothing and other products. With excellent instruction, the educable retarded and borderline retarded should develop the skill to do these tasks. By the age of sixteen, the child with an IQ of 70 should be able to read on approximately a fifth-grade level, (Bruekner and Bond, 1955) and the child with an IQ from 70 to 84 should achieve a grade level between 6.5 and 7.2.

Teaching the retarded the skill of reading is very necessary for job success. Although social adjustment is very important for success on the job, Guralnick (1956) and Kirk (1963) have found illiteracy to be a barrier to employment in many cases.

Specific Learning Disabilities

Traditionally, the term "specific learning disability" has been applied only to children with average or above average intelligence. Although many definitions for specific learning disabilities have been given, the most accepted one was formulated by the National Advisory Committee on Handicapped Children, or NACH, in 1968.

> Children with special learning disabilities exhibit a disorder in one or more of the basic psychological processes involved in understanding or in using spoken or written language. These may be manifested in disorders of listening, thinking, talking, reading, writing, spelling, or arithmetic. They include conditions which may have been referred to as perceptual handicaps, brain injury, minimal brain dysfunction, dyslexia, developmental aphasia, etc. They do not include learning problems which are due primarily to visual, hearing, or motor handicaps, to mental retardation, emotional disturbances, or to environmental disturbance.[24]

[24]National Advisory Committee on Handicapped Children, *Special Education for Handicapped Children: First Annual Report* (Washington, D.C.: United States Department of Health, Education, and Welfare, 1968), p. 4.

The incidence of specific learning disabilities in the school population ranges from 1 percent to 30 percent depending upon the criteria used. A conservative estimate of 1 to 3 percent was given by the NACH report to Congress in 1968. This estimated percentage is approximately the same as the estimate for the prevalence of mental retardation (2.3 percent) and speech disturbance (3.5 percent) although larger than populations of those who are deaf and hard of hearing (0.6 percent), visually handicapped (0.1 percent), crippled (0.8 percent), special health problems (0.8 percent), emotionally disturbed and socially maladjusted (2.0 percent), and gifted (2.0 percent) (Lerner, 1971).

According to Kirk and Kirk (1971), the term "specific" is very important when speaking of learning disabilities. If a specific learning deficit exists, it is not caused by a sensory deficiency or mental retardation. It also exists even though the child may have abilities in other areas. The term "discrepancy" is also very important. The child is said to have a specific learning disability if he has a significant discrepancy (two years or more) between his achievement and the level determined by tests and observations of the teacher and examiners to be expected of him (Minskoff, 1970).

Learning disabilities fall into three categories: academic disorders, nonsymbolic or perceptual motor disorders, and symbolic or language and communication disorders (Kirk and Kirk, 1971; Minskoff, 1970). Academic disorders usually are found in reading, writing, and spelling. Initially, most of the interest in specific learning disabilities grew out of the study of reading disabilities (Lerner, 1971). Many terms for reading disorders, such as strepsymbolia, psychic blindness, symbolic confusion, dyslexia, and alexia, have been found in the literature (Shedd, 1968).

Perceptual motor disturbances, which were discussed in a previous section of this chapter, have been found in children with specific learning disabilities. Much of the interest in perceptual disorders, specifically figure-ground, spatial relationships, etc., developed after the publication of the writings of Strauss and Lehtinen (1947). Strauss, who was influenced by principles of Gestalt psychology, considered these perceptual disorders to be caused by brain injury. Characteristics that Strauss listed for these "brain-injured" children are now known as the Strauss Syndrome (Johnson and Myklebust, 1967).

Also studied by Strauss were the symbolic or language disturbances that have been cited as areas of difficulties for children with specific learning disabilities (Kirk and Kirk, 1971). Such terms as auditory reception disabilities (inability to understand the spoken word although hearing is intact) have been used by Myklebust and Johnson (1967).

Although the NACH definition rules out mental retardation as one of the primary causes of specific learning disabilities, recent work by special educators has suggested that specific learning disabilities may exist among children who are placed in special classes for the educable and borderline retarded. According to Kirk and Kirk, the failure to discriminate between specific learning disabilities and other types of handicaps has caused confusion.

It should also be noted that there is often an overlap of handicapping conditions in the same child, with learning disabilities and other handicapping conditions both being present. Included in this set of children with learning disabilities are those who have also been classified as crippled, emotionally disturbed, and so forth. Some children are difficult to classify because (a) they are both a learning disability and another identifiable exceptionality (e.g., gifted but with a learning disability or emotionally disturbed plus a learning disability) or (b) they have a learning disability which sometimes misclassifies them as having a traditional form of exceptionality (e.g., a child who is misclassified as mentally retarded because of a low score on intelligence tests but who upon more intensive assessment is found to have normal abilities in some areas and very deficient abilities in other areas). These latter children will benefit most if their learning disability is treated directly while classroom adjustment is provided for their other types of handicaps. It is not sufficient merely to place them in special class for the other handicapped and assume that the learning disability will take care of itself.[25]

In a 1970 comparison of mildly retarded children with children designated as having learning disabilities, Sabatino and Hayden found that the EMR children lacked the symbolic conceptual power to mediate language concepts. However, both groups also possessed perceptual problems. Sabatino and Hayden (1970) suggest that educators also reexamine the label "educable mentally retarded."

---

[25]Samuel Kirk and Winifred Kirk, *Psycholinguistic Learning Disabilities: Diagnosis and Remediation* (Urbana: University of Illinois Press, 1971), p. 5. Reprinted by permission of the publisher.

They suggest two populations of EMR children — ones who lack central language abilities for mediation of symbolic word concepts and those who have difficulties in perceptual, expressive, and receptive language. The IQ's of the latter group tend to be slightly higher than those of the former. However, they do not achieve their potential academically because of these deficits.

Thus, in teaching EMR children reading, teachers may profit from the use of prescriptive techniques that are geared to specific learning disabilities for some of these children.

SUMMARY

An extensive amount of research has been conducted in order to determine causes of reading failure. Unfortunately, at the present time, no conclusive results have been formulated. Factors such as home background, low intelligence, sensory acuity, visual and auditory perception, language development, perceptual-motor disturbances, and social and emotional maladjustment are found more often in groups of disabled readers than normal readers. However, a causal relationship has not been clearly established between such problems and reading disabilities. The results of this research make it very difficult to assume that problems such as language deficiencies that exist among the educable and borderline retarded contribute to their failure in reading. Most of the factors related to reading failure that have been enumerated are more prevalent among educable retarded children, yet it would be erroneous to assume that all educable and borderline retarded children have the same reading deficiencies. Nonetheless, some research does indicate that these children have special reading problems.

REFERENCES

Ainsworth, S.H. *An Exploratory Study of Educational, Social, and Emotional Factors in the Education of Mentally Retarded Children in Georgia Public Schools.* Washington, D. C., U.S. Office of Education Project Number 171, 1959.

Balow, Bruce. "Perceptual-Motor Activities in the Treatment of Severe Reading Disability." *Reading Teacher* 24 (1971): 513-25.

Barrett, C.D.; Ellis N.K.; and Pryer, M.W. "Stimulus Pretraining and Delayed Reaction in Defectives." *American Journal of Mental Deficiency* 64 (1959): 104-11.

Barrett, Thomas C. "Visual Discrimination Tasks as Predictors of First-Grade Reading Achievement." *The Reading Teacher* 15 (1965): 276-82.

Bateman, D. and Wetherell, J. "Psycholinguistic Aspects of Mental Retardation."*Mental Retardation* 3 (1965): 8-13.

Baumeister, Alfred A. "Learning Abilities of the Mentally Retarded." In *Mental Retardation*, edited by Alfred A. Baumeister, pp. 181-204. Chicago: Aldine Publishing Company, 1967.

Bennett, A. "A Comparative Study of Subnormal Children in Elementary Grades." New York: New York Teachers College, 1932. Cited in *Handbook of Mental Deficiency*, edited by N.R. Ellis, p. 669. New York: McGraw-Hill, 1963.

Bensberg, C.J. "The Relationship of Academic Achievement of Mental Defectives to MA, Sex, Institutionalization, and Etiology." *American Journal of Mental Deficiency* 58 (1953): 327-30.

Berieter, Carl, and Engelmann, Siegfried. *Teaching Disadvantaged Children in the Preschool.* Englewood Cliffs, New Jersey: Prentice-Hall, Inc., 1966.

Berry, Mildred F. *Language Disorders of Children.* New York: Appleton-Century-Crofts, 1969.

Berry, Mildred F., and Eisenson, Jon. *Speech Disorders: Principles and Practices of Therapy.* New York: Appleton-Century-Crofts, 1956.

Betts, E.A. *Foundations of Reading Instruction.* New York: American Book Co., 1957.

Bilsky, Linda, and Evans, Ross. "Use of Associative Clustering Techniques in the Study of Reading Disabilities: Effects of List Organization." *American Journal of Mental Deficiency* 74 (1970): 771-76.

Black, William F. "An Investigation of Intelligence as a Causal Factor in Reading Problems." *Journal of Learning Disabilities* 3 (1971): 139-42.

Bliesmer, Emery P. "Reading Abilities of Bright and Dull Children of Comparable Mental Ages." In *Readings on Reading*, edited by Alfred R. Binter, John Dlabal, Jr., and Leonard K. Kise, pp. 189-98. Scranton, Pennsylvania: International Textbook Co., 1969.

Bloom, B. *Taxonomy of Educational Objectives Hand Book I: Cognitive Domain.* New York: David McKay Co., 1956.

Bloom, B.S.; Davis, H.; and Hess, R. *Compensatory Education for Cultural Deprivation.* New York: Holt, Rinehart, & Winston, 1965.

Bogoch, S. *The Biochemistry of Memory.* New York: Oxford University Press, 1968.

Bond, Guy. "The Auditory and Speech Characteristics of Poor Readers." *Contributions to Education*, Number 657. New York: Columbia University Teachers College, 1935.

Bond, Guy L., and Tinker, Miles A. *Reading Difficulties: Their Diagnosis and Correction*, 2d ed. New York: Appleton-Century-Crofts, 1967.

Boyd, Larry, and Randle, Kenneth. "Factor Analysis of the Frostig Developmental Test of Visual Perception." *Journal of Learning Disabilities* 3 (1970): 253-55.

Braum, J.S. "Relation between Concept Formation Ability and Reading Achievement at Three Developmental Levels." *Child Development* 34 (1963): 675-82.

Bruekner, L.J., and Bond, Guy L. *Diagnosis and Treatment of Learning Difficulties*. New York: Appleton-Century-Crofts, 1955.

Burt, C., *The Backward Child*. London: University of London Press, 1958.

Buswell, Margaret M. "The Relationship between the Social Structure of the Classroom and the Academic Success of the Pupils." *Journal of Experimental Education* 22 (1953): 37-52.

Cantor, G.N., and Hottell, J.V. "Psychomotor Learning in Defectives as Function of Verbal Pretraining." *Psychological Records* 7 (1957): 79-85.

Capobianco, R. J., and Funk, R. A. *A Comparative Study of Intelligence, Neurological, and Perceptual Processes as Related to Reading Achievement of Exogeneous and Retarded Children*. Syracuse: Syracuse University Research Institute, 1958.

Capobianco, R.J., and Miller, D.Y. *Quantitative and Qualitative Analysis of Exogeneous and Endogeneous Children in Some Reading Processes*. Syracuse: Syracuse University Research Institute, 1958.

Carlson, J.C., and MacMillan, D.L. "Comparison of Probability Judgments between EMR and Nonretarded Children." *American Journal of Mental Deficiency* 74 (1970): 697-700.

Cassidy, V.M., and Stanton, J.E. *An Investigation of Factors Involved in the Educational Placement of Mentally Retarded Children*. Washington, D. C.: U.S. Office of Education Project Number 43, 1959.

Cawley, J.F.; Goodstein, L.A.; and Burrow, W.H. *The Slow Learner and the Reading Problem*. Springfield, Illinois: Charles C. Thomas, Publisher, 1972.

Cegelka, Patricia A., and Cegelka, Walter J. "A Review of Research: Reading and the Educable Mentally Handicapped." *Exceptional Children* 37 (1970): 187-200.

Chalfant, James C., and Scheffelin, Margaret A. *Central Processing Dysfunction in Children: A Review of Research*. NINDS Monograph Number 9. Bethesda, Maryland: United States Department of Health, Education, and Welfare, 1969.

Christine, Dorothy, and Christine, C. "The Relationship of Auditory Discrimination to Articulation Defects and Reading Instruction." *Elementary School Journal* 65 (1964): 97-100.

Clark, Ann, and Richards, Charlotte. "Auditory Discrimination among Economically Disadvantaged and Nondisadvantaged Preschool Children." *Exceptional Children* 33 (1966): 259-62.

Cohen, Alice. "Relationship between Factors of Dominance and Reading Disability." In *Reading Disability and Perception*, edited by George Spache. *Proceedings of the Thirteenth Annual Convention of the International Reading Association*. Newark, Delaware, vol. 13, part 3 (1969): 38-45.

Cohen, S. Alan. "Studies in Visual Perception and Reading in Disadvantaged Children." *Journal of Learning Disabilities* 2 (1969): 499-503.

_____. *Teach Them All to Read: Theory, Methods, and Materials for Reaching the Disadvantaged*. New York: Random House, 1969.

Cromwell, R. "A Social Learning Approach to Mental Retardation." In *Handbook of Mental Deficiency*, edited by N.R. Ellis. New York: McGraw-Hill Book Co., 1963.

Cuban, Larry. *To Make a Difference: Teaching in the Inner City*. New York: The Free Press, 1970.

Dechant, Emerald. *Improving the Teaching of Reading*. Englewood Cliffs, New Jersey: Prentice-Hall, Inc., 1964.

DeHirsch, Katrina et al. *Predicting Reading Failure*. New York: Harper & Row, Publishers, 1966.

Deutsch, M. "The Disadvantaged Child and the Learning Process." In *Education in Depressed Areas*, edited by A.H. Passow, pp. 163-80. New York: Columbia University Teachers College, 1963.

_____. "The Role of Social Class in Language Development and Cognition. *American Journal of Orthopsychiatry* 35 (1965): 78-88.

Dever, Richard B. *The Use of Language by Mentally Retarded Children: A Review of the Literature*. Technical Report Number 1.24. Bloomington, Indiana: Indiana University Center for Research and Development of the Improvement of Teaching Handicapped Children, 1971.

Dunn, Lloyd M. "A Comparison of Reading Processes of Mentally Retarded Boys of the Same MA." In *Studies of Reading and Arithmetic in Mentally Retarded Boys*, edited by L.M. Dunn and R.J. Capobianco, pp. 7-99. *Monograph of the Society for Research in Child Development* 19 (1954): 7-99.

_____. "Educable Mentally Retarded Children." In *Exceptional Children in the Schools*, edited by L.M. Dunn, pp. 53-108. New York: Holt, Rinehart, & Winston, 1963.

Durkin, Dolores. *Teaching Them To Read*. Boston: Allyn & Bacon, Inc., 1970.

Durrell, Donald, and Murphy, Helen A. "The Auditory Discrimination Factor in Reading Readiness and Reading Disability." *Education* 73 (1953): 556-60.

Dykstra, R. "Auditory Discrimination Abilities and Beginning Reading Achievement." *Reading Research Quarterly* 1 (1966): 5-34.

Eames, T.H. "The Effect of Anisometropia on Reading Achievement." *American Journal of Optometry and Archives of American Academy of Optometry* 41 (1964): 700-02.

_____. "A Frequency Study of Physical Handicaps in Reading Disability and Unselected Groups." *Journal of Educational Research* 29 (1935): 1-5.

Edmiston, R.W., and Peyton, Bessie. "Improving First Grade Achievement by Readiness Instruction." *School and Society* 71 (1950): 230-32.

Edwards, R. Philip et al. "Academic Achievement and Minimal Brain Dysfunction in Mentally Retarded Children." *Exceptional Children* 38 (1971): 539-40.

Eisenberg, Leon. "Reading Retardation: Psychiatric and Sociologic Aspects." In *Disadvantaged Children*, vol. 1, edited by Jerome Hellmuth, pp. 410-31. Seattle: Special Child Publications, 1967.

_____. "Strengths of the Inner-City Child." In *Education of the Disadvantaged: A Book of Readings*, edited by A. Harry Passow, Meriam Goldberg, and Abraham J. Tannenbaum, pp. 78-87. New York: Holt, Rinehart, & Winston, 1967.

Elenbogen, M.L. "A Comparative Study of Some Aspects of Academic and Social Adjustment of Two Groups of Mentally Retarded Children in Special Classes and in Regular Grades." *Dissertation Abstracts* 17 (1957): 2497.

Ellis, N.R. "Memory Processes in Retardates and Normals: Theoretical and Empirical Considerations." Paper presented at the Gatenberg Conference on Research and Theory in Mental Retardation, March 1970.

Ellis, N.R.; McCarver, Ronald B.; and Ashurst, Hugh M. "Short-Term Memory in the Retarded: Ability Level and Stimulus Meaningfulness." *American Journal of Mental Deficiency* 72 (1970): 72-80.

Farber, Bernard. *Mental Retardation: Its Social and Cultural Consequences.* Boston: Houghton-Mifflin Co., 1968.

Farris, L.P. "Visual Defects or Factors Influencing Achievement in Reading." *California Journal of Secondary Education* 10 (1934): 50-51.

Fernald, Grace M. *Remedial Techniques in Basic School Subjects.* New York: McGraw-Hill Book Co., 1943.

Frostig, Marianne, and Horne, D. *The Frostig Program for Visual Perception.* Chicago: Follet Publishing Co., 1964.

Furth, H.G. "Conceptual Discovery and Control on a Pictorial Part-Whole Task as a Function of Age, Intelligence, and Language." *Journal of Educational Psychology* 54 (1963), 191-96.

Gallagher, J.J., and Lucito, L.J. "Intellectual Patterns of Gifted Compared with Average and Retarded." *Exceptional Children* 27 (1961): 479-82.

Garrison, Karl C. and Magoon, Robert A. *Educational Psychology: An Integration of Psychological and Educational Practices.* Columbus, Ohio: Charles E. Merrill Publishing Co., 1972.

Gates, A.I. *Interest and Ability in Reading.* New York: The Macmillan Co., 1930.

_____. "The Necessary Mental Age for Beginning Reading." *Elementary School Journal* 37 (1937): 497-508.

_____. "The Role of Personality Maladjustment in Reading Disability." *Journal of Genetic Psychology* 59 (1941): 77-83.

Getman, G.N.; Kane, E.R.; and McKee, G.W. *Developing Learning Readiness: A Visual-Motor Tactile Skills Program.* Manchester, Missouri: Webster Publishing, 1968.

Gillespie, Patricia H. "A Study of the Performance of Dyslexic and Normal Readers on the Slosson Intelligence Test for Children and Adults." Doctoral dissertation, West Virginia University, 1969.

Goda, S. "The Spoken Syntax of Normal Deaf and Retarded Adolescents." *Journal of Verbal Learning and Verbal Behavior* 3 (1964): 401-05.

Goetzinger, C.P.; Kirks, D.; and Baer, D.J. "Auditory Discrimination and Visual Perception in Good and Poor Readers." *Annals of Otology, Rhinilogy, and Laryngology* 69 (1960): 121. Also in *Readings on Reading,* edited by Alfred Binter, John J. Dlabal, and Leonard K. Kise, pp. 224-37. Scranton, Pennsylvania: International Book Co., 1969.

Goins, Jean. *Visual Perceptual Abilities and Early Reading Progress.* Supplementary Education Monograph Number 78. Chicago: University of Chicago Press, 1958.

Golden, Nancy E., and Steiner, Sharon R. "Auditory and Visual Functions in Good and Poor Readers." *Journal of Learning Disabilities* 2 (1969): 476-81.

Goldstein, H.; Jordon, L.; and Moss, J.W. "The Efficacy of Special Class Training in the Development of Mentally Retarded Children." Washington: Office of Education Project Number 162, 1965.

Goldstein, Herbert, and Seigle, Dorothy. "Characteristics of Educable Mentally Handicapped Children." In *Mental Retardation*, edited by Jerome H. Rothsten, p. 205-30. New York, Holt, Rinehart, & Winston, 1961.

Goodman, Hallace; Gottlieb, Jay; and Harrison, Robert H. "Social Acceptance of EMRs Integrated into a Nongraded Elementary School." *Journal of Mental Deficiency* 76 (1972): 412-17.

Goodstein, H.A.; Whitney, G.; and Cawley, J.F. "Prediction of Perceptual Reading Disability among Disadvantaged Children in the Second Grade." *Reading Teacher* 24 (1970): 23-28.

Griffith, B.C., and Spitz, H.H. "Some Relationships between Abstraction and Word Meaning in Retarded Adolescents." *American Journal of Mental Deficiency* 63 (1958), 247-51.

Griffith, B.C.; Spitz, H.H.; and Tipman, R.S. "Verbal Mediators and Concept Formation in Retarded and Normal Subjects." *Journal of Experimental Psychology* 58 (1959): 247-51.

Guilford, J.P. "Frontiers in Thinking That Teachers Should Know About." *Reading Teacher* 13 (1960): 176-82.

Guralnick, D. "Vocational Rehabilitational Services in New York City for the Mentally Retarded." *American Journal of Mental Deficiency* 61 (1956): 368.

Guthery, George H. "Differences in Attitudes of Educationally Handicapped Mentally Retarded and Normal Students." *Journal of Learning Disabilities* 4 (1971): 330-32.

Guthrie, John T., and Goldberg, Herman K. "Visual Sequential Memory in Reading Disability." *Journal of Learning Disabilities* 5 (1972): 41-46.

Harris, Albert J. *How to Increase Reading Ability*, 5th ed. New York: David McKay Co., 1970.

Harris, L., and Smith, C. *Reading Instruction through Diagnostic Teaching.* New York: Holt, Rinehart, & Winston, 1972.

Heal, Laird W. "Research Strategies and Research Goals in the Scientific Study of the Mentally Subnormal." *American Journal of Mental Deficiency* 75 (1970): 10-15.

Heilman, Arthur W. *Principles and Practices of Teaching Reading*, 3rd ed. Columbus, Ohio: Charles E. Merrill Publishing Co., 1972.

Henry, S. "Children's Audiograms in Relation to Reading Attainment." *Journal of Genetic Psychology* 70 (1947): 211-231; 71 (1948): 3-63.

Hilgard, Ernest R. *Introduction to Psychology.* New York: Harcourt, Brace, Jovanovich, 1962.

Huber, M.B. *The Influence of Intelligence upon Children's Reading Interest.* New York: Bureau of Publications, Teachers College, Columbia University, 1928.

Iano, Richard P. "Learning Deficiency versus Developmental Conceptions of Mental Retardation." *Exceptional Children* 38 (1971): 301-11.

Jenkins, William A. "Language and Communication." In *Coordinating Reading Instruction*, edited by Helen M. Robinson, pp. 36-45. Glenview, Illinois: Scott, Foresman and Co., 1971.

Jensen, A.R., and Rodehever, A.D. "The Effect of Verbal Mediation on the Learning and Retention of Paired Associates by Retarded Adults." *American Journal of Mental Deficiency* 68 (1963): 80-84.

Johnson, Doris J., and Myklebust, Helmer. "Dyslexia in Childhood." In *Learning Disorders*, vol. 1, edited by J. Hellmuth, pp. 259-92. Seattle, Washington: Special Child Publications, 1965.

————. *Learning Disabilities: Educational Principles and Practices.* New York: Grune & Stratton, 1967.

Johnson, G.O. "A Study of Social Position of Mentally Handicapped Children in the Regular Grades." *American Journal of Mental Deficiency* 55 (1950): 60-69.

Johnson, M.S. "Factors Related to Disability in Reading." *Journal of Experimental Education* 26 (1957): 1-26.

Jones, R.L.; Gross, F.P.; and Van Way, E.L. "A Longitudinal Study of Reading Achievement in a Group of Adolescent Institutionalized Mentally Retarded Children." *Training School Bulletin* 57 (1960): 41-47.

Jordan, T.E. *The Mentally Retarded*, 3rd ed. Columbus, Ohio: Charles E. Merrill Publishing Co., 1970.

Jordan, T.E., and deCharms, R. "The Achievement Motive in Normal and Mentally Retarded Children." *American Journal of Mental Deficiency* 64 (1959): 457-66.

Karlin, Robert. *Teaching Reading in High School*, 2d ed. Indianapolis, Indiana: The Bobbs-Merrill Co., 1972.

Kass, Corrine E., "Some Psychological Correlates of Severe Reading Disability (Dyslexia)." In *Selected Studies on the Illinois Test of Psycholinguistic Abilities*. Urbana: University of Illinois Press, 1963.

Keane, Vincent E. "The Incidence of Speech and Language Problems in the Mentally Retarded." *Mental Retardation* 10 (1972): 3-8.

Kennedy, H. "A Study of Children's Hearing as It Relates to Reading." *Journal of Experimental Education* 10 (1942): 238-51.

Kennedy, Ruby Jo Reeves. *The Social Adjustment of Morons in a Connecticut City*. Hartford, Connecticut: State Office Building, 1948.

Kephart, Newell C. *The Slow Learner in the Classroom*, 2d ed. Columbus, Ohio: Charles E. Merrill Publishing Co., 1971.

Kirk, Samuel. *Educating Exceptional Children*. Boston: Houghton-Mifflin Co., 1962.

_____. "Research in Education." In *Mental Retardation: A Review of Research*, edited by H.A. Stevens and R. Heber, pp. 57-99. Chicago: University of Chicago Press, 1963.

_____. *Teaching Reading to Slow-Learning Children*. Cambridge, Massachusetts: Riverside Press, 1940.

Kirk, Samuel, and Kirk, Winifred. *Psycholinguistic Learning Disabilities: Diagnosis and Remediation*. Urbana: University of Illinois Press, 1971.

Kodman, F., Jr.; Powers, T.; Weller, G.; and Phillip, P. "An Investigation of Hearing Loss in Mentally Retarded Children and Adults." *American Journal of Mental Deficiency* 63 (1958): 460-63.

Koelsch, G.J. "Readability and Interests of Five Basal Reading Series with Retarded Students." *Exceptional Children* 35 (1969): 487-88.

Kottmeyer, William. *Teacher's Guide for Remedial Reading*. St. Louis: Webster Publishing Co., 1959.

Lazar, May. "Reading Interests, Activities, and Opportunities of Bright, Average, and Dull Children." *Contributions to Education*, Number 207. New York: Teachers College Press, Columbia University, 1937.

Lerner, Janet, W. *Children with Learning Disabilities: Theories, Diagnosis, and Teaching Strategies*. Boston: Houghton Mifflin Co., 1971.

Lloyd, Bruce. "The Effects of Programmed Perceptual Training of Reading Achievement and Mental Maturity of Selected First Grade Pupils." *Journal of the Reading Specialist* 6 (1966): 49-55.

Loban, Walter. *The Language of Elementary School Children*. Champaign, Illinois: National Council of Teachers of English Research Report Number 1, 1963.

Lopp, E.A. "A Study of the Social Adjustment of Slow-Learning Children Who Were Assigned Part-Time to Regular Classes." *American Journal of Mental Deficiency* 62 (1957): 252-62.

Lyons, C.V., and Lyons, E.B. "The Power of Visual Training." *Journal of American Optometric Association* 26 (1954): 255-62.

McCarthy, J.M. *Patterns of Psycholinguistic Development of Mongoloid and Non-Mongoloid Severely Retarded Children*. Doctoral dissertation, University of Illinois, 1965.

McCarthy, James J., and McCarthy, Joan F. *Learning Disabilities.* Boston: Allyn & Bacon, Inc., 1967.

Macione, J.R. "Psychological Correlates of Reading Disabilities as Defined by the Illinois Test of Psycholinguistic Abilities." Doctoral dissertation, University of South Dakota, 1969. Reported in *Psycholinguistic Learning Disabilities,* edited by Samuel and Winifred Kirk, pp. 22-29. Urbana: University of Illinois Press, 1972.

Malmquist, Eve. *Factors Related to Reading Disabilities in the First Grade of the Eelementary School.* Stockholm, Sweden: Almquist and Wiksell, 1958.

Margaret, A., and Thompson, C.W. "Differential Test Responses of Normal, Superior, and Mentally Defective Subjects." *Journal of Abnormal Social Psychology* 45 (1950) : 163-67.

Maslow, P.; Frostig, M.; Lafever, D.W.; and Whittlesy, J.R. "The Marianne Frostig Developmental Test of Visual Perception, 1963 Standardization." *Perceptual and Motor Skills* 19 (1964) : 463-99.

Matthews, J. "Speech Problems of the Mentally Retarded." In *Handbook of Speech Pathology,* edited by L.E. Trouis. New York: Appleton-Century-Crofts, 1957.

Mechler, Ruth T. "Developmental Progress in Young Mentally Handicapped Children Who Received Prolonged Preacademic Training." *American Journal of Mental Deficiency* 45 (1940) : 267-73.

Meyerowitz, Joseph H., and Farber, Bernard. "Family Background of the EMR." In *Kinship and Family Organization,* edited by Bernard Farber, pp. 388-98. New York: John Wiley & Sons, 1966.

Milgram, N.A. "Verbal and Conceptual Classification of Trainable Mentally Retarded Children." *American Journal of Mental Deficiency* 70 (1966) : 763-65.

Miller, Jon F., and Yoder, David E. "On Developing the Content for a Language Teaching Program."*Mental Retardation* 10 (1972) : 9-11.

Minskoff, J. Gerald. "Understanding Learning Disabilities." *Reading Forum: A Collection of Reference Papers Concerned with Reading Disabilities,* edited by Louise Calkins. NINDS Monograph Number 1. Washington, D.C.: U.S. Department of Health, Education and Welfare, 1969.

Missildine, W.H. "The Emotional Background of Thirty Children with Reading Disabilities." *The Nervous Child* 5 (1946) : 263-72.

Morphett, Mabel V., and Washburne, C. "When Should Children Begin to Read?" *Elementary School Journal* 31 (1931) : 496-503.

Myers, Patricia L., and Hammill, Donald D. *Methods for Learning Disorders.* New York: John Wiley and Sons, 1969.

Newell, Nancy. "For Nonreaders in Distress." *Elementary School Journal* 32 (1931) : 183-95.

Norvell, George W. *The Reading Interests of Young People.* Lexington, Massachusetts: D. C. Heath, 1950.

Ohnmacht, F.S., and Olson, A. "Canonical Analysis of Reading Readiness Measures and the Frostig DVTP." Paper presented at AERA meeting, February, 1968, in Chicago.

Olson, A.V. "School Achievement, Reading Disability, and Special Visual Perception Skills in the Third Grade." *The Reading Teacher* 19 (1966) : 490-92.

Orton, Samuel T. *Reading, Writing, and Speech Problems in Children.* New York: W. W. Norton & Company, 1937.

Passamanick, B., and Knobloch, H. "The Contribution of Some Organic Factors to School Retardation in Negro Children." *Journal of Negro Education* 27 (1958): 4-9.

Patterson, R.M., and Philleo, C. "Academic Achievement of Deficient Groups at the Moron Level." *American Journal of Mental Deficiency* 47 (1943): 407-12.

Poling, Dorothy L. "Auditory Deficiencies of Poor Readers." *Supplementary Educational Monograph* 77 (1953): 107-12.

Potter, M.C. *Perception of Symbol Orientation and Early Reading Success. Contributions to Education*, Number 939. New York: Teachers College Press, Columbia University, 1949.

Prehm, Herbert J., and Mayfield, Sheryl. "Paired-Associate Learning and Retention in Nonretarded Children." *American Journal of Mental Deficiency* 74 (1970): 622-25.

Preston, Jary J. "Reading Failure and the Child's Security." *American Journal of Orthopsychiatry* 10 (1940): 239-52.

Rabinovitch, R. "Reading and Learning Disabilities." In *American Handbook of Psychiatry*, vol. 1, edited by S. Arieti. Toronto: University of Toronto Press, 1959.

Ragland, G.G. "The Performance of Educable Mentally Handicapped Students of Different Reading Abilities on the ITPA." *Dissertation Abstracts* 25 (1964): 3407-408.

Raines, Shirley, and Tait, A.T. "Emotional Factors in Reading Retardation." *California Journal of Educational Research* 11 (1951): 51-56.

Rarick, G. Lawrence; Widdap, James H.; and Geoffrey, D. Broadhead. "The Physical Fitness and Motor Performance of Educable Mentally Retarded Children." *Exceptional Children* 36 (1970): 509-20.

Rieber, M. "Verbal Mediation in Normal and Retarded Children." *American Journal of Mental Deficiency* 68 (1964): 634-41.

Risko, Victoria. "Differential Auditory Discrimination Skills as Related to Reading Achievement." Doctoral dissertation, West Virginia University, 1971.

Robinson, Helen M. "Personality and Reading." In *Modern Educational Problems*, edited by A.E. Trapler. New York: Educational Research Bureau, 1953.

_____. *Why Pupils Fail in Reading.* Chicago: University of Chicago Press, 1953.

Rossi, E.L. "Associative Clustering in Normal and Retarded Children." *American Journal of Mental Deficiency* 67 (1963): 692-99.

Roswell, Florence, and Natchez, Gladys. *Reading Disability: Diagnosis and Treatment*, 2d ed. New York: Basic Books, 1971.

Russell, D.H. "Reading Disabilities and Mental Health: A Review of Research." *Understanding the Child* 16 (1947): 24-32.

Sabatino, David A., and Hayden, David L. "Information Processing Behaviors Related to Learning Disability and Educable Mental Retardation." *Exceptional Children* 37 (1970): 21-30.

Schiefelbusch, Richard L.; Copeland, Ross H.; and Smith, James O. *Language and Mental Retardation: Empirical and Conceptual Considerations.* New York: Holt, Rinehart, & Winston, 1967.

Schonell, Fred J. *Backwardness in the Basic Subjects.* Edinburgh, Scotland: Oliver and Boyd Ltd., 1948.

Scott, Ralph. "Perceptual Readiness as a Predictor of Success in Reading." *The Reading Teacher* 22 (1968): 36-39.

Semmel, M.I. et al. "Grammatical Analysis of Word Association of EMR and Normal Children." *American Journal of Mental Deficiency* 72 (1968): 567-76.

Shedd, Charles. "Ptolemy Rides Again or Dyslexia Doesn't Exist?" *The Alabama Journal of Medical Sciences* 5 (1968): 481-503.

Shepherd, George. "Selected Factors in the Reading Ability of EMR Boys." *American Journal of Mental Deficiency* 71 (1967): 563-70.

Shotick, A. "A Comparative Investigation of the Performance of Mentally Retarded and Normal Boys on Selected Reading Comprehension and Performance Tasks." Doctoral dissertation, Syracuse University, 1960.

Siegenthaler, Bruce M.; Sallade, J.B.; and Lordibuona, J.S. "Speech-Hearing Measurements in an Intellectually Average to Below-Average Group of Children." *American Journal of Mental Deficiency* 76 (1972): 427-33.

Siever, Dorothy. "A Study to Compare the Performance of Brain Injured and Nonbrain Injured Children on the Differential Language Facilities Test." *American Journal of Mental Deficiency* 63 (1959): 839-47.

Singer, R.N., and Brunk, J.W. "Relation of Perceptual Motor Ability and Intellectual Ability in Elementary School Children." *Perceptual and Motor Skills* 24 (1967): 967-70.

Sloan, W. "Motor Proficiency and Intelligence." *American Journal of Mental Deficiency* 55 (1951): 394-406.

Small, V.H. "Ocular Pursuit Abilities and Reading." Doctoral dissertation. Purdue University, 1958.

Smith, M.P., and Meane, J.R. "Effects of Stimulus Pretraining on Discrimination Learning in the Mentally Retarded." *American Journal of Mental Deficiency* 55 (1951): 394-406.

Spicker, H.H., and Bartel, N.R. "The Mentally Retarded." In *Exceptional Children Research Review,* edited by G.O. Johnson and H.B. Blank, pp. 38-109. Arlington, Virginia: Council for Exceptional Children, 1968.

Spraldin, J.E. "Language and Communication of Mental Defectives." In *Handbook of Mental Deficiency,* edited by N.R. Ellis. New York: McGraw-Hill Book Co., 1963.

Stauffer, Russell G. *Teaching Reading as a Thinking Process.* New York: Harper & Row, 1969.

Stedman, D.J. "Associative Cluster of Semantic Categories in Normal and Retarded Subjects." *American Journal of Mental Deficiency* 67 (1963): 700-04.

Stephens, W.E. "Category Usage by Normal and Mentally Retarded Boys." *Child Development* 37 (1966): 355-62.

Stinnett, Ray D., and Prehm, Herbert J. "Retention in Retarded and Nonretarded Children as a Function of Learning Model." *American Journal of Mental Deficiency* 75 (1970): 39-46.

Strauss, Alfred A., and Lehtinen, Laura. *Psychopathology and Education of the Brain-Injured Child.* New York: Grune & Stratton, 1947.

Strickland, Ruth. *The Language Arts in the Elementary School.* Lexington, Massachusetts: D. C. Heath, 1969.

Thompson, C.W., and Thompson, M.A. "Differential Test Responses of Normal and Mental Defectives." *Journal of Abnormal Social Psychology* 42 (1947): 285-93.

Thorndike, E.L. "Leading as Reasoning: A Study of Mistakes in Paragraph Reading." *Journal of Educational Psychology* 8 (1917): 323-32.

Tuckman, Bruce W. "The Teacher and the Psychology of Culturally Deprived." In *Preparing to Teach the Disadvantaged*, edited by B. W. Tuckman and J.L. O'Brian, pp. 3-20. New York: Free Press, 1969.

Valletutti, Peter. "Language of the Mildly Mentally Retarded: Cognitive Deficit or Cultural Difference?" *Exceptional Children* 37 (1971): 455-59.

Van Riper, C. *Speech Correction*. Englewood Cliffs, New Jersey: Prentice-Hall, 1964.

Vergason, G.A. "Facilities of Memory in the Retardate." *Exceptional Children* 34 (1968): 589-96.

Vernon, M.D. *Backwardness in Reading*. Cambridge: Cambridge University Press, 1957.

Vygotsky, L.S. *Thought and Language*. Cambridge, Massachusetts: MIT Press, 1962.

Wakefield, R.A. "An Investigation of the Family Background of Educably Mentally Retarded Children in Special Classes." *Exceptional Children* 31 (1965), 143-46.

Wallace, W.P., and Underwood, B.J. "Implicit Responses and the Role of Intralist Similarity in Verbal Learning by Normal and Retarded Subjects." *Journal of Educational Psychology* 55 (1964): 362-70.

Wallis, R.R. "The Learning of Semiconcrete and Abstract Materials by Bright and Retarded Students." Doctoral dissertation, University of Oklahoma, 1963.

Wanat, Stanley F. "Language Acquisition: Basic Issues." *The Reading Teacher* 25 (1971): 142-47.

Weaver, S.J., and Weaver, A. "Psycholinguistic Abilities of Culturally Deprived Negro Children." *American Journal of Mental Deficiency* 72 (1967): 190-97.

Weiner, B.B. "A Report on the Final Academic Achievement of Thirty-Seven Mentally Handicapped Boys Who Had Been Enrolled in a Prolonged Preacademic Program." *American Journal of Mental Deficiency* 59 (1954): 200-19.

Wilhelm, Rowena. "Diagnostic Value of Test Score Differentials Found between Measures of Visual and Auditory Memory in Severely Disabled Readers." *Academic Therapy Quarterly* 2 (1968): 42-44.

Wilson, R.M., and Hall, M. *Reading and the Elementary School Child: Theory and Practice for Teachers*. New York: Van Nostrand Reinhold Co., 1972.

Wiseman, D.E. "The Effects of an Individual Remedial Program on Mentally Retarded Children With Psycholinguistic Disabilities." Doctoral dissertation, University of Illinois, 1965.

Wynn, S.J. "A Beginning Reading Program for the Deprived Child." *Reading Teacher* 21 (1967): 40-47.

Zigler, E. "Familial Mental Retardation: A Continuing Dilemma." *Science* 155 (1967): 292-98.

————. "Research on Personality Structure in the Retardate." In *International Review of Research in Mental Retardation*, vol. 1, edited by N.R. Ellis. New York: Academic Press, 1966.

Zintz, Miles. *The Reading Process: The Teacher and the Learner*. Dubuque, Iowa: William C. Brown Co., 1970.

FOUR

Overview of Diagnosis

Although the term *diagnosis* is not new to the field of special education, it is rapidly changing in nature. To date, much of the literature on diagnosis has been concerned with medical assessments that deal with the etiological factors of retardation. Although this type of assessment can be of value to the special educator, more information is needed in order to develop instructional programs. But if educational diagnosis extends only as far as placement or classification, it too can be of little benefit. For example, even if a child is administered the Stanford-Binet or the WISC, labeled as being educably retarded, "placed" in a class for the retarded, and instructed in a program planned for an entire group, he may not progress as he should.

Recently, the uses of such procedures have begun to change, and much literature has been written about interindividual and intraindividual differences (Smith, 1968). With the realization by educators that retarded children do possess individual learning styles, abilities, and disabilities, more diagnosis of these differences now is occurring. Because the majority of the programs for the educable retarded emphasize language arts, especially reading, much of the diagnosis has centered around reading skills and assumed correlates of reading, such as perceptual skills. But diagnosing the needs and skills of poor readers who are educably retarded is no simple matter. A multiplicity of factors related to reading diagnosis must be considered, and this chapter is the first of several that will discuss some of these factors. An overview discussion of the need for diagnosis, professionals involved in diagnosis, and present trends in reading diagnosis and their relation to the retarded is included in this chapter.

NEED FOR DIAGNOSIS

One of the first questions a special educator should ask in relation to diagnosis is: "What need is there to assess a child's strengths and weaknesses in reading?" If the special-education teacher plans to utilize the same program for all the children in his class, there is no need for specific diagnosis. However, if the educable mentally retarded are considered as a heterogeneous group rather than as a single group all possessing the same skills and backgrounds needed for reading achievement, specific diagnosis is necessary. The ultimate result of diagnosis should be a planned program for each child based upon *his* skills and interests, and knowledge which has been obtained from formal and informal measures. Although the matching of diagnostic results and specific reading programs or methods appears logical, the relationship between diagnosis and remediation has not been completely established, and these is a great deal of controversy concerning the nature of specific diagnosis (Tarnapol, 1970). Thus, since the nature of diagnosis depends upon one's philosophy of remediation, it is at this point that most of the controversy lies. This problem will be discussed in Chapters Seven through Ten.

The present authors support the need for individual diagnosis although we are aware of the disadvantages involved. One such drawback, validity and efficacy of individual diagnosis, has been discussed by Bateman (1970).

> The fundamental question of whether this approach works is a very slippery one. A child is diagnosed and then successfully remediated. Was the diagnosis necessary and sufficient prerequisite to the remediation? Might other remediation, not derived from the diagnosis, have been equally successful? A child is diagnosed but the remediation is not successful. Was the diagnosis inadequate or was an error made in deriving the

remediation? In any case, it is difficult to establish a valid relationship between diagnosis and remediation.[1]

The present authors feel that part of the problem exists because of a possible breakdown between the diagnostic and remediation processes. In many cases, diagnosis involves assessment by a clinician who then writes his report before consulting with the teacher. Thus, because of the lack of educational input, results of tests lack relevance to instructional programs (Bateman, 1970). Simply *reporting* that the child rotates figures on a perceptual test such as the *Bender-Gestalt* may leave the teacher with little knowledge of what to *do* with the information.

An additional problem exists because, too often, a problem is implemented and not reevaluated for a prescribed amount of time. In order for diagnosis to be used truly for prescriptive purposes, it must be continual. The terms *diagnostic* or *clinical teaching* have been given to such procedures (Smith, 1968; Lerner, 1971; Brison, 1967). In describing clinical teaching, Lerner has stated:

> In clinical teaching, diagnosis does not stop when the treatment procedure begins, and in fact, continuous diagnosis and treatment become the essence of clinical teaching. This means that the teacher modifies his teaching procedures and plans as new needs become apparent.[2]

Diagnostic or clinical teaching eliminates the potentially rigid and inflexible dichotomy between the diagnostic and remediational process. In fact, simply matching the results of a specific diagnosis with a specific treatment and assessing the program *after* the fact rather than continually may be the source of the problem described earlier by Bateman.

PROFESSIONALS INVOLVED IN READING DIAGNOSIS

Many disciplines, such as medicine, speech and hearing specialists, social services, psychology and special resources, may be involved

---

[1] Barbara Bateman, "The Role of Individual Diagnosis in Remedial Planning for Reading Disorders," in *Reading Forum* (Bethesda, Maryland: US Department of Health, Education, and Welfare, National Institute of Neurological Disease and Stroke Monograph Number 11, 1970), p. 130.

[2] Janet W. Lerner, *Children with Learning Disabilities: Theories, Diagnosis, and Teaching Strategies* (Boston: Houghton-Mifflin Co., 1971), p. 68.

initially in the reading diagnosis of the educable retarded. This team approach to diagnosis is beneficial in that each discipline is able to contribute its expertise toward total evaluation of the child. For example, a problem which appears educational may actually stem from a physical ailment such as anemia or from an emotional problem that may stem from the home. Although initial assessment may be conducted by resource personnel from other disciplines, the final responsibility for a child's prescriptive program rests with the special education teacher. If the teacher is to expect to make crucial instructional and curricular decisions, he should be very much a part of the diagnostic team.

Because the teacher spends the greatest amount of time with the child, his judgment, based upon observations and upon both formal and informal measures, should be respected. No prescription should be designed for a child by the rest of the team and given to the teacher for implementation without his input (Hammill, 1971). On this topic, Hammill has asserted:

> If assessment results that are meaningful for school use are to evolve from the total evaluation, the teachers and others charged with the diagnosis function must recognize that instruction and evaluation are not separate words, but that they are inseparately meshed. Successful teaching, namely, teaching where the child learns, is in itself, a reflection of a series of effective teacher assessments. This point of view is essential if the child is to be helped in a maximal fashion in the classroom.[3]

Therefore, the teacher should be trained in the administration and interpretation of diagnostic reading measures. If he lacks these skills, no amount of extensive diagnosis by the rest of the assessment team will be worthwhile.

TRENDS IN READING DIAGNOSIS

As was previously noted, diagnosis in reading skills is presently in a state of flux. Assessment ranges from a standard battery of standardized tests to informal measures and checklists that are based on observations of the teacher or the reading specialist. Some of the many different theories on diagnosis in the field of reading will

---

[3]Donald Hammill, "Evaluating Children for Instructional Purposes," *Academic Therapy* 6 (1971): 343.

be discussed in this section. These practices are assessment by standardized measures, criterion-based testing, modalities and processes, and learning styles.

Standardized Measures

More than a hundred group and individual standardized reading tests are available. Although many of these tests give specific information for educational plans, they do not always provide the detailed information which is needed to design a program for an individual child (Hammill, 1970). Most often, they measure general reading ability without identifying specific strengths and weaknesses in reading (Harris and Smith, 1972). Besides lacking specificity, standardized tests have several other drawbacks for use with the educable retarded. These tests are based upon a norm (i.e., comparison of an individual's score to the performance of many other individuals of the same age, grade, or level on the same measures). Because the norm of standardized reading tests is based on "average" children, there is some question as to the reliability, validity,[4] and effectiveness of such tests as diagnostic instruments with exceptional children (Hammill, 1970). Scores on standardized reading tests also are interpreted in terms of grade levels, a practice which is of little value to the special educator who is attempting to meet individual strengths and weaknesses of children. Grade level is a very arbitrary standard and interpretations tend to vary from test to test and reading series to reading series. Obtaining the knowledge that a child is reading on 2.0 grade level does not guarantee that the teacher will be able to match this finding exactly with second-grade materials in such areas as vocabulary and comprehension (Durost, 1971). In addition, it has been the authors' experience that educable retarded nonreaders will obtain a score as high as a third-grade reading level on standardized group reading tests. This finding is probably due to a guess factor (Fry, 1971).

In order to ameliorate the lack of specificity of standardized reading tests, especially group tests, some attempt has been made to do a task analysis of items. Diagnostic information can be obtained through analysis of the correct responses or errors on the tests (Ladd, 1971), although this is possible only if the teacher himself keeps the student's answer sheets. Most often, if the tests

---

[4]For a discussion of reliability and validity of tests see Oscar Buros, *Tests in Print* (Highland Park, New Jersey: The Gyphon Press, 1961).

are machine-scored, the teacher receives only the test scores. If the teacher does a task analysis of the answers on the test, he may have a better idea of the strengths and weaknesses of each pupil. Nonetheless, there are limitations to this procedure. There are usually too few items in any one category on the test to make a valid statement about the strengths or weaknesses in that area (Chalfant and Scheffelin, 1969). Even if a particular test is divided into subtests of particular skills, there is no assurance that the child's particular needs will be identified. "First of all, there is almost no evidence available that any of the subtests of standardized reading tests are valid measures of separate and distinct reading skill."[5]

Because of all the limitations to standardized reading tests— especially group tests, they are of limited value to the special educator. This is not to say that standardized reading tests should not be used. The teacher should realize that any measure has its limitations and there is nothing "mystical" about testing. He should use the tests to gather information that he feels is pertinent for instruction.

Criterion-Referenced Testing

Because of the limitations of standardized reading tests, especially their lack of specificity, educators are presently investigating the appropriateness of criterion-reference testing. Such tests are the outgrowth of a behavioristic task analysis approach to reading skills. In this approach, emphasis is placed on specific educational tasks (Bateman, 1966-67). Prescott has explained criterion- or content-referenced tests in the following way:

> In criterion-referenced or content-referenced-test interpretation, no attempt is made to compare the performance of an individual with that of others. Rather, one seeks to evaluate performance in terms of whether an individual has achieved or has failed to achieve specific instructional objectives. It seeks to answer the question, "What specific skills, knowledges, and understandings has a pupil acquired?" Can he, for example, spell the word "believe"? Can he suggest an appropriate title for

---

[5]Roger Farr, "Reading Tests and Teachers," in *Reading Diagnosis and Evaluation*, ed. Dorothy L. Debaer (Newark, Delaware: International Reading Association, 1970), p. 52.

a story? In its most elemental form, the response of each pupil to each test item is evaluated as correct or incorrect: the skill or ability or whatever, measured by a test item has either been mastered or it has not. The criterion is 100 percent mastery.[6]

Criterion-referenced tests do more than measure such global skills as "general reading ability."[7] Because they are so very specific, careful analysis of tasks to be learned is needed. Rather than just diagnosing a child as having problems in word analysis, the examiner must be able to analyze components of word analysis (e.g., knowledge of the prefix *un*) and report his findings in specifics rather than in generalities.

But just as norm-referenced testing has its problems so too does criterion-referenced testing. According to Prescott (1971), one important assumption of criterion-referenced assessment is that the skills to be measured can be placed in a hierarchy. In other words, it is assumed that one must master a certain skill before moving to another level or skill. This assumption creates a problem in reading because there is not yet proof of a clear-cut progression of learning how to read. There is a lack of general agreement or even evidence as to what steps are necessary to insure reading success (Prescott, 1971), although this limitation may be eliminated through future research in components of reading (Johnson and Kress, 1971). Although criterion-referenced testing is more absolute than standardized tests which measure a child's ability only in relation to that of another child, they still are not free from comparisons. The questions or tasks utilized still require a "base of reference."[8] The very decision to place a task at a certain chronological or mental age level implies that a certain response is expected from the child. The response is judged upon some criterion which has been considered "typical" for a certain age or capacity.

Other factors to be considered when using criterion-referenced tests are:

1. Children may get the right answers for the wrong reasons (e.g., by guessing or by knowing rather than really comprehending the skill).

---

[6]George A. Prescott, "Criterion-Referenced Test Interpretation in Reading," *The Reading Teacher* 24 (1971): 348.

[7]Marjorie S. Johnson and Roy A. Kress, "Task Analysis for Criterion-Referenced Tests," *The Reading Teacher* 24 (1971): 365.

[8]Prescott, p. 350.

2. The tests do not offer reasons for a child's inability to perform certain tasks.
3. No suggestion is given as what to do when the child doesn't learn the task initially. Usually, the assumption is made that if the child has not learned the task, he has not been taught properly or the skill has not been defined adequately (Bateman, 1966-67).

Criterion-referenced tests are beginning to come to the attention of educators. One such measure is part of the *Instructional Objectives Exchange* (IOX), a national depository for instructional objectives developed by Popham (1970). The special educator who is involved in testing reading skills could utilize the *Reading K-3* and *Reading 4-6* segments of IOX. The reading collection provides "measurement items, means of judging the adequacy of student-responses, and IOX rating for each objective."[9] Other criterion-referenced materials are listed in Appendix Three.

Criterion-referenced testing promises to be a valuable tool in reading diagnosis of the retarded for results from this type of testing gives the teacher specific information regarding the child's strengths and weaknesses in skill areas which can be transferred more readily into an educational program (Englemann, 1967). Although there are still limitations to these procedures, they represent a step in the right direction toward developing specific analyses of the reading process.

Assessment of Modalities

Another area of emphasis in diagnosis, especially in the field of learning disabilities, is modality testing. Wepman has stated of this area of diagnosis:

> A child's learning type — his maximal modality pathway of learning, his differential ability to learn by eye, or by ear, or even by touch, needs to be understood before a particular approach to reading can be determined for him.[10]

---

[9]Bill Blanton, "Eric/Crier," *The Reading Teacher* 25 (1971): 87.

[10]Joseph M. Wepman, "The Perceptual Basis for Learning," in *Educating Children with Learning Disabilities: Selected Readings*, ed. Edward C. Frierson and Walter B. Barbe (New York: Appleton-Century-Crofts, 1967), p. 355.

Many who have worked in the area of reading have advocated a modality approach (Cohn, 1964; deHirsch, Jansky, and Langford, 1966; Frostig, 1967; Johnson and Myklebust, 1967; and Wepman, 1967).

On the basis of tests designed to measure modalities, children are designated as visual, auditory, or tactile learners. Such tests as the Frostig *Developmental Test of Visual Motor Integration* (1963), *Illinois Test of Psycholinguistic Abilities* (Kirk, McCarty and Kirk, 1968), *Detroit Test of Learning Aptitude* (Baker and Leland, 1935), *Test of Auditory Discrimination* (Wepman, 1958), and *Southern California Kinesthetic and Tactile Perception Test* (Ayres, 1969) all have been used to test modalities. Many of these tests are discussed in more detail in a later section of this book.

Designating a child as a visual, auditory, or tactile-kinesthetic learner on the basis of tests is not as simplistic a process as it might sound because it is difficult to design a test that measures a single modality. Most of the tests, although they claim to measure one modality—such as visual perception, actually measure several modalities simultaneously (Lerner, 1971).

Another facet of learning through modalities is "intermodal transfer ability,"[11] or cross-modalities. In other words, the child is unable to transfer information via one modality (e.g., from a visual to another modality, such as auditory); therefore, he lacks integration skills. He may know the visual symbol of a letter and the sound of that letter but he is not able to integrate this knowledge. In the past, difficulties in reading have been attributed to problems in integration of modalities (Chalfant and Scheffelin, 1969; Johnson and Myklebust, 1967; Katz and Deutsch, 1963). The testing for cross-modal functioning is complex. Except for measures that have been devised for research purposes (Birch and Belmont, 1964) and for testing cerebral palsied children (Abercrombie, 1964), few tests have been developed in this area.

Even though matching modalities to materials or methods that are supposedly visual, auditory, or tactile is receiving favorable attention, several researchers have found this method to be no more successful than others (Bateman, 1968; Blanton, 1971). Perhaps lack of results on the use of such methods is due to the nature of the studies. If it is difficult to develop tests or materials that are unimodal, it is erroneous to assume that all the children who are

---

[11]*Ibid.*, p. 359.

included in these studies will be placed correctly according to modalities. For example, one child may score very high on a visual memory test, because he used his auditory skills (e.g., saying the letters over and over to himself in order to remember the words effectively rather than because he has adequate visual memory. After a child has been designated as a visual, auditory, or tactile-kinesthetic learner based upon results of testing, he is assigned a certain reading approach or material that is considered to be appropriate for a particular modality. But matching modalities to materials is difficult because reading materials or methods are not unimodal in nature. Finally, still other criticisms of modality testing have been raised. According to Wolpert (1971), it is fallacious to equate a child's perceptual skills with his learning processes. He has stated:

> This is a faulty practice for two reasons. First, perception is not synonymous with learning. Of course, perception is part of learning; however, a person's ability to perform better on a test of visual perception does not make him a "visual learner." Perhaps he might be more accurately termed a "visual perceiver." Second, the tests of perception used in determining modality strength are usually composed of nonreading tasks. To the extent that this type of perception plays a part in the reading process, this information may be of value. But what is this extent? Perception and reading are not synonymous any more than perception and learning are synonymous.[12]

Information Processing

Assessing a child's processing skills extends beyond merely identifying a child as a visual "perceiver" or "learner." Instead, assessment of processing skills requires the analysis of actions in some designated sequence. Process analysis is a determination of the sequence of steps or structure the individual learner uses to produce the responses he gives (Brown and Botel, 1972, p. 34). There have been attempts to isolate processes, especially those dealing with language learning (Chalfant and Scheffelin, 1969; Goodman, 1968; Osgood, 1957; Sabatino and Hayden, 1970; Wepman, 1960) and there are many interpretations of process assessment (Brown and Botel, 1972). Two of the earliest interpretations of processing skills are those of Osgood (1957) and Wepman (1960). Osgood designated

---

[12]Edward Wolpert, "Modality and Reading," *The Reading Teacher* 24 (1971): 641.

three language processes in his communication model, which has been used as part of the bases for the structure of the *Illinois Test of Psycholinguistic Abilities* (Kirk, McCarthy and Kirk, 1968). These processes are: *the receptive process* (decoding), which is the ability to recognize and/or understand what is received; *the expressive or encoding process*, which is the ability to express ideas verbally or nonverbally; and *the association or organization process*, which involves mediation of perceptions, concepts, or symbols. Wepman has described two processes—*transmission* and *integration*. The transmission process is composed of reaction and expression while the integration process translates the receptive materials or input into the appropriate output or expression.

Information processing can be related to reading. For example, a child who has difficulties with naming letters may be experiencing a problem with associating the name of the symbol. *The Illinois Test of Psycholinguistic Abilities* (ITPA) and combinations of perceptional and language tests have been used in order to determine the information processing skills of children (Sabatino and Hayden, 1970). Although process analysis is not synonymous with modality analysis, they are related. The modality the child uses to receive information material may influence the process of storing and recalling the material that is needed for a response (Shiffrin and Atkinson, 1969). Because there are so many different interpretations of process skills, implementation of these analyses for diagnotic purposes is rather difficult for the teacher at the present time (Brown and Botel, 1972); however, an understanding of processing is important for the design of diagnostic teaching lessons.

Although modality testing and information processing are controversial, they appear to have merit. Further research in the area of intersensory and intrasensory processing is needed in order to clarify such problems as those designated by Wolpert (1971) and Blanton (1971).

Diagnosis of Learning Styles

The diagnosis of learning styles often has been included in diagnostic teaching (Rosenberg, 1968; Wedell, 1970). In fact, the term *learning style* was defined by Rosenberg as "an individual's characteristic pattern of behavior when confronted with a problem."[13] He identified four characteristic learning styles: rigid-

---

[13]Marshall B. Rosenberg, *Diagnostic Teaching* (Seattle, Washington: Special Child Publications, 1968), p. 22.

inhibited style, undisciplined style, acceptance-anxious style, and creative style.

Some highlights of the styles designated by Rosenberg include the following:

1. *Rigid-inhibited style:* inability to adapt to change in routine; rigid adherence to rules.
2. *Undisciplined style:* destructive, negativistic attitude; making derogatory remarks to teacher and about subject matter.
3. *Acceptance-anxious style:* attempts to please others; fear of failure; sensitivity to criticism.
4. *Flexible style:* Initiative; persistent approach in finding answers.

Raths, et al. include other styles that they have termed "habitual disregard for thinking processes."[14] These are impulsiveness, overdependence upon the teacher, inability to concentrate, rigidity and inflexibility, dogmatic and assertive behavior, extreme lack of confidence, missing the meaning, and resistance to thinking.

The way a child attacks a problem situation is an important consideration in diagnosing his reading. If a child is "locked into" a rigid-inhibited style of learning, he may have problems transferring or directing his attention from one reading task to another. For further information on ways to identify learning styles, the reader can refer to Raths, et al. (1967) and Rosenberg (1968).

No one learning style should be considered as characteristic of retarded children. In fact, what appears to be a "learning style" may be the child's means of coping with failure. Because of a retarded child's early introduction to failure, he may be more fearful of failure and more concerned with pleasing adults than are normal children (Zigler, 1966). As was noted in Chapter Three, these characteristics reduce the child's feelings of independence and creativity (Carlson and MacMillan, 1970, Zigler, 1966).

SUMMARY

With the realization that children who are educable retarded are heterogeneous in relation to reading skills, the need for specific diagnosis has emerged. In the past, standardized measures have

---

[14]Louis Raths, et al., *Teaching for Thinking: Theory and Application* (Columbus, Ohio: Charles E. Merrill Publishing Co., 1967), p. 8.

been administered to retarded children in order to determine their needs, but, many limitations of the use of standardized measures with retarded children have been cited including lack of specificity and basis upon a norm which is very rarely standardized on groups of retarded children. New types of testing, such as criterion-referenced measures and modality testing, have been established. These new measures may provide for more specific diagnosis of individuals.

In addition to realizing and employing the development of new testing procedures, educators must begin to consider the special-education teacher as a central member of the diagnostic team. No matter how many professionals are involved in the reading diagnosis of the children, the teacher is ultimately responsible for their program. His input into the development of the diagnostic-prescriptive program should be respected.

REFERENCES

Abercrombie, M.L. *Perceptual Visuo-Motor Disorders in Cerebral Palsy.* London: Heinemann, 1964.

Ayres, Jean. "Patterns of Perceptual Motor Dysfunction in Children: A Factor Analytic Study." *Perceptual and Motor Skills Monograph Supplement* TV20 (1965): 335-68.

Baker, Harry, and Leland, B. *Detroit Test of Learning Aptitude.* Indianapolis, Indiana: The Bobbs-Merrill Co., 1935.

Bateman, Barbara. "The Efficacy of an Auditory and Visual Method of First-Grade Reading Instruction with Auditory and Visual Learners." In *Perception and Reading,* edited by Helen Smith. Newark, Delaware: International Reading Association, 1968.

_____. "The Role of Individual Diagnosis in Remedial Planning Disorders." *Reading Forum.* National Institute of Neurological Disease and Stroke Monograph Number 11, pp. 127-39. Bethesda, Maryland: United States Department of Health, Education, and Welfare, 1970.

_____. "Three Approaches to Diagnosis and Educational Planning for Children with Learning Disabilities." *Academic Therapy* 2 (1966-1967): 215-22.

Birch, H.G., and Belmont, Lillian. "Auditory-Visual Integration in Normal and Retarded Readers." *American Journal of Orthopsychiatry* 34 (1964): 851-61.

Blanton, Bill. "Eric-Crier." *The Reading Teacher* 25 (1971): 83-89.

Brison, David W. "Definition, Diagnosis, and Classification." In *Mental Retardation*, edited by Alfred Baumeister, pp. 1-19. Chicago: Aldine Publishing Co., 1967.

Brown, Virginia L., and Botel, Morton. *Dyslexia: Definition or Treatment?* Washington, D.C.: United States Department of Health, Education, and Welfare, Eric Clearinghouse on Retrieval of Information and Evaluation in Reading, 1972.

Buros, Oscar. *Tests in Print.* Highland Park, New Jersey: The Gryphon Press, 1961.

Carlson, J.C., and MacMillan, D.L. "Comparison of Probability Judgments between EMR and Nonretarded Children." *American Journal of Mental Deficiency* 74 (1970): 697-700.

Chalfant, James, and Scheffelin, Margaret. *Central Processing Dysfunctions in Children.* National Institute of Health Monograph Number 9. Bethesda, Maryland: United States Department of Health, Education, and Welfare Public Health Service, 1969.

Durost, W.N. "Accountability: The Task, the Tools, and the Pitfalls." *The Reading Teacher* 24 (1971): 291-324.

Engelmann, Siegfried. "Teaching Reading to Children with Low Mental Age." *Education and Training of the Mentally Retarded* 2 (1967): 193-201.

Farr, Roger. "Reading Tests and Teachers." In *Reading Diagnosis and Evaluation*, edited by Dorothy L. Debaer, pp. 49-54. Newark, Delaware: International Reading Association, 1970.

Frostig, Marianne. "Education for Children with Learning Disabilities." In *Educating Children with Learning Disabilities: Selected Readings*, edited by Edward Frierson and Walter Barbe, pp. 387-98. New York: Appleton-Century-Crofts, 1967.

Frostig, Marianne, et al. *The Marianne Frostig Developmental Test of Visual Perception: 1963 Standardization.* Palo Alto, California: Consulting Psychological Press, 1963.

Fry, Edward. "The Orangatang Score." *The Reading Teacher* 24 (1971): 360-61.

Goodman, Kenneth. *The Psycholinguistic Nature of the Reading Process.* Detroit: Wayne State University Press, 1968.

Hammill, Donald. "Evaluating Children for Instructional Purposes." *Academic Therapy* 6 (1971): 341; 353.

Harris, Larry, and Smith, Carl B. *Reading Instruction through Diagnostic Teaching.* New York: Holt, Rinehart, & Winston, 1972.

de Hirsch, Katrina; Jansky, Jeannette; and Langford, W.L. *Predicting Reading Failure: A Preliminary Study of Reading, Writing, and Spelling Disabilities in Preschool Children.* New York: Harper & Row, Publishers, 1966.

Johnson, Doris, and Myklebust, Helmer. *Learning Disabilities: Educational Principles and Practices.* New York: Grune & Stratton, 1967.

Johnson, Marjorie S., and Kress, Roy A. "Task Analysis for Criterion-Referenced Tests." *The Reading Teacher* 24 (1971): 355-59.

Katz, Phyllis, and Deutsch, Martin. *Visual and Auditory Efficiency and Its Relationship to Reading in Children.* Cooperative Research Project, Number 1099. Washington, D. C.: United States Department of Health, Education, and Welfare Office of Education, 1963.

Kirk, Samuel; McCarthy, James P.; and Kirk, Winifred. *The Illinois Test of Psycholinguistic Abilities*, rev. ed. Urbana: University of Illinois Press, 1968.

Ladd, Eleanor. "More than Scores from Tests." *The Reading Teacher* 24 (1971): 305-11.

Lerner, Janet W. *Children with Learning Disabilities: Theories, Diagnosis, and Teaching Strategies.* Boston: Houston Mifflin Co., 1971.

Osgood, C.E. *Contemporary Approaches to Cognition.* Cambridge: Harvard University Press, 1957.

Popham, W. James. *Reading K-3, K-6, K-12.* Los Angeles: Instructional Material Exchange, 1970.

Prescott, George A. "Criterion-Referenced Test Interpretation in Reading." *The Reading Teacher* 24 (1971): 347-54.

Raths, Louis, et al. *Teaching for Thinking: Theory and Application.* Columbus, Ohio: Charles E. Merrill Publishing Co., 1967.

Rosenberg, Marshall B. *Diagnostic Teaching.* Seattle, Washington: Special Child Publications, 1968.

Sabatino, David A., and Hayden, David. "Information Processing Behaviors Related to Learning Disabilities and Educable Mental Retardation." *Exceptional Children* 37 (1970): 21-29.

Shiffrin, R.M., and Atkinson, R.C. "Storage and Retrieval Processes in Long-Term Memory." *Psychological Review* 76 (1969): 179-93.

Smith, Robert. *Clinical Teaching: Methods of Instruction for the Retarded.* New York: McGraw-Hill Book Co., 1968.

Tarnapol, Lester. "Testing Children with Learning Disabilities." In *Learning Disabilities: Introduction to Educational and Medical Treatment*, 2d ed., edited by Lester Tarnapol, pp. 180-91. Springfield, Illinois: Charles C. Thomas Co., 1970.

Wedell, Klaus. "Diagnosing Learning Difficulties: A Sequential Strategy." *Journal of Learning Disabilities* 3 (1970): 311-17.

Wepman, Joseph. "Auditory Discrimination in Speech and Reading." *Elementary English Journal* 60 (1960): 325-33.

_____. *Auditory Discrimination Test.* Chicago: Language Research Associates, 1958.

_____. "The Perceptual Basis for Learning. In *Educating Children with Learning Disabilities: Selected Readings*, edited by Edward C. Frierson and Walter B. Barbe, pp. 353-62. New York: Appleton-Century-Crofts, 1967.

Wolpert, Edward. "Modality and Reading." *The Reading Teacher* 24 (1971): 640-43.

Ziegler, E. "Research on Personality Structure." In *International Review of Research in Mental Retardation*, vol. 1, edited by N. R. Ellis. New York: Academic Press, 1966.

FIVE

Formal Reading and Reading Related Tests

Formal reading measures usually include testing which can be either group or individual in nature, in the area of oral reading, word analysis, and comprehension. Because of the ineffectiveness of standardized group reading tests with the retarded, discussion of very few such tests is included in this chapter. Nonetheless, the teacher can utilize various sections of standardized individual diagnostic reading tests for prescriptive purposes. Although these tests yield grade levels, much diagnostic information may be obtained from them if the teacher is trained in doing so.

INDIVIDUAL DIAGNOSTIC READING TESTS

Because most individual reading tests are similar in nature, only a few examples are presented here, along with suggestions on how to obtain the most information from the particular test. Although these tests are not usually included in teacher training programs other than those in remedial reading, the special education teacher should be trained in administering and interpreting these tests. Chart 1 presents information on diagnostic individual reading tests. Standardized diagnostic individual reading tests can offer more information than group standardized reading tests, although they do have limitations. Four limitations are of particular importance—they give grade levels which are of very little diagnostic value to the special education teacher because of the lack of correlation of levels between tests and reading materials; they are time-consuming; they require considerable practice and study by the teacher before administering them; and they do not provide all the diagnostic information that is necessary in developing a program for the child, especially in the area of comprehension.

Components of the Tests

Most of the tests are comprised of word recognition lists, paragraphs for oral and silent reading, listening comprehension, phonetic analysis, and measurement of reading rate.

Word Recognition Lists: Most oral reading and word analysis tests include a section on word recognition. These lists are graded and are used to determine grade level, types of word analysis skills, and sight vocabulary (word recognition). Many of the lists are drawn randomly from basal readers or word lists such as *Thorndike and Lorge* (1944). The point at which a child is able to read all the words on the list successfully is considered his independent reading level, while the level at which he is unable to read the words is his frustration level. His instructional level lies between the independent and frustration levels (Froese, 1971).

Although all of these tests presume to determine grade-level placement in word recognition, many, especially used on the upper levels, do not correlate with each other (Froese, 1971). In addition, lists from which the words come usually are dated (Lobdell, 1965). This objection has been one of the chief criticisms of such isolated word lists as *Dolch Basic Word List* (Dolch, 1941), which is one of the most popular lists for use in determining word recognition (Johnson, 1971). The words used in compiling the *Dolch List* were taken from studies conducted in the 1920s. A more adequate and recent list can be found in Kucera and Francis's *Computational Analysis of Present-Day American English* (1967).

Word recognition lists, in addition to being used to determine level, have also been used for diagnostic purposes. An analysis of the errors a child makes and the words he pronounces readily can aid the teacher in establishing a reading skills program. Chart 2 on page 108 is an example of a child's responses on the Word

Chart 1: Individualized Standardized Reading Tests

Test	Publisher	Grades/Ages	Forms	Time	Measures	Price	Administrator	Validity	Reliability
Diagnostic Reading Scale	California Testing Service	Grades 1-8; Retarded Readers in Grades 9-12	One	No Time Limit	Word Recognition; Reading Comprehension; Phonics	$8.75 for Thirty-Five Record Booklets	Classroom Teacher	.64 to .92	.84 to .88
Durrell Analysis of Reading Difficulty	Harcourt, Brace, Jovanovich	Ages 6-11; Non-reader to Age 6	One	Ninety Minutes	Recall after Oral and Silent Reading; Listening Comprehension; Visual Recognition of Letters and Words; Ability to Sound Letters; Blends; Spelling	$3.70 for Examiner's Kit with Five Record Booklets; $3.75 for Thirty-Five Record Booklets	Classroom Teacher; Some Difficulty in Administration	No Data Available	No Data Available
Gates-McKillop Reading Diagnostic Tests	Teacher's College Press	Grades 1-8	Two	No Time Limit	Oral Reading; Word Perception; Phrase Perception; Blending Word Parts; Giving Letter Sounds; Naming Letters; Recognizing Visual Forms of Sounds; Auditory Blending; Spelling; Oral Vocabulary; Syllabication; Auditory Discrimination	$1.25 for Test; $.20 for Response Booklet; $.25 for Manual; $.10 for Tachisto-scope	Classroom Teacher; Some Difficulty in Administration	No Data Available	.68 to .97

Test	Publisher	Grades/Ages	Forms	Time	Measures	Price	Administrator	Validity	Reliability
Gilmore Oral Reading Test	Harcourt, Brace Jovanovich	Grades 1-8	Two	Fifteen to Twenty Minutes	Comprehension; Rate and Accuracy of Oral Reading	$1.70 per set of reading paragraphs; $2.10 for thirty-five record blanks	Classroom Teacher	.39 to .80	Accuracy, .4 to .84; Comprehension, .60 to .53; Rate, .70 to .54
Gray Oral Reading Test	The Bobbs-Merrill Co.	Grades 1-16	Four	No Time Limit	Rate and Accuracy of Oral Reading; Comprehension Questions	$3.20 for thirty-five tests; $1.60 for reading passage booklet	Classroom Teacher	High	.973 to .982

Chart 2:   Word List

~~1)~~ look	~~13)~~ ~~big~~ *get*	25) good	37) children
~~2)~~ come	~~14)~~ ~~milk~~ *make*	26) girl	38) live
~~3)~~ in *(NR)*	~~15)~~ dog	27) name	39) around
~~4)~~ the *(NR)*	~~16)~~ tree *(NR)*	28) away	40) barn
~~5)~~ you *(NR)*	~~17)~~ ~~are~~ *man*	29) this	41) other
~~6)~~ one	~~18)~~ run *(NR)*	30) bed	42) under
~~7)~~ she	~~19)~~ all *after*	31) call	43) cry
~~8)~~ ~~mother~~ *make*	~~20)~~ father *(NR)*	32) time	44) chicken
~~9)~~ me *4*	~~21)~~ door *(NR)*	33) sleep	45) breakfast
~~10)~~ yellow	22) like	34) fish	46) chair
~~11)~~ pig *(NR)*	23) ball	35) morning	47) rain
~~12)~~ it *(NR)*	24) eat	36) seen	48) asleep
			49) peep

NR = no response

Recognition List I of the *Spache Diagnostic Reading Scales* (California Test Bureau, 1963).

Although there are too few items in the word list in Chart 2 to make a final statement concerning this eight year old's responses, there are a few observations the teacher could make. The child tends to have three responses to words he does not know: he does not respond; he uses initial consonants as a cue; he guesses indiscriminately (e.g., *man* for *are*). The child's response to the word recognition list may give the teacher some clues regarding the nature of the problem; however, no placement in reading materials or final diagnosis should be based on the results of a word recognition list alone. Goodman (1965) has found that many of the words missed in isolation will be pronounced correctly by the child when read in content.

Analysis of Oral Reading Errors: From the word lists, the examiner obtains an idea of the child's reading level and of where to start in having the child read orally the graded selections of paragraphs found in an individualized reading test. The manuals suggest a standard system of marking the errors the child makes while reading orally. The following behaviors are classified as errors in most manuals:

1. Substitutions (e.g., *make* for *mat*).
2. Omissions of words, word endings, and punctuation.
3. Mispronunciations such as omissions of letter (e.g. *after*). Dialectal pronunciations are not counted as errors.
4. Hesitations. Most manuals suggest an amount of time for the child to hesitate in order to be regarded in error. Some tests don't consider hesitations to be errors.
5. Additions (e.g., He went to (the) town).
6. Repetitions of words, phrases, or sentences. (Some, but not all tests don't count the repetition of one word as an error.)
7. Aided pronunciation by the teacher. If the child hesitates for a period of time (e.g., five seconds), the teacher can pronounce the word for the child.

Kenneth Goodman (1965) has performed a systematic analysis of oral reading errors. He considers these "miscues" in oral reading very important to the teacher because they tell something about the child's language or reasoning skills. According to Goodman, these cues are based upon clues within words, such as letter-sound relationships or word configurations; the flow of the language in terms of operations as function order, inflection or inflectional agreement, intonation or reference to what comes prior or after the word in question; and cues external to language and the reader, such as his dialect and experimental and family background. Kenneth Goodman (1965) and Yetta Goodman (1970, 1972) both have gone considerably beyond the suggestions in the manuals in interpreting children's oral responses.

According to Yetta Goodman (1972), error analysis must be qualitative rather than quantative. If a child's errors are tallied merely to obtain a reading level on a passage and a placement in reading materials, the opportunity for diagnosis of the strategies the child uses when reading orally is lost. The teacher should evaluate such errors as regressions, omissions, substitutions, reversals, and insertions carefully. Although manuals suggest that the more errors a child makes, the less he is able to comprehend a particular passage, the teacher should realize that the child may, in reality, comprehend paragraphs on which he makes the most errors most readily. In some cases, if the child is not comprehending what he is reading, he may not attempt to make meaningful substitutions or insertions (Goodman, 1972). Miscues also may be indicative of the method the teacher has utilized in teaching word recognition skills (Barr, 1972), just as they may be representative of the child's entire thinking or language pattern (Ryan and Semmel, 1969).

An excellent source for analyzing a child's oral reading miscues is the *Reading Miscue Inventory* (Goodman and Burke, 1972). A copy of the coding sheet for the inventory is reproduced in this chapter.

Several studies of oral reading errors have been conducted with educable retarded readers (Dunn, 1954; Levitt, 1972; Levitt, 1970; Ramanauskas, 1970; Shepherd, 1967; Shotick, 1960). Some of the results of these studies *are* conflicting. For example, several studies have found that normals perform better than retarded children in use of contextual cues (Dunn, 1954; Shepherd, 1967; Shotick, 1960); however, Levitt (1970) has reported that normal first graders and retarded children reading on the first-grade level perform at essentially the same level on tests of content.

In another analysis of the oral reading errors of these children, Levitt (1972) found that the retardates did not attempt to obtain closure in meaning with the success that normals did and made errors that were not based upon problem-solving or adequate information-processing skills. Yet retarded children, according to Levitt, did use multiple cues [graphemic-phonemic (e.g., *play* for *put*) and graphemic-phonemic with context (e.g., *near the rear* for *near the road*)] more often than did the nonretarded children. The use of graphemic-phonemic cues, according to Goodman and Burke (1972), would not be desirable as a means of producing words with similar meanings. A child also may use graphemic-phonemic cues at the expense of grammatical relationships as well as meaning. Some

READING MISCUE INVENTORY CODING SHEET

© Carolyn L. Burke and Yetta M. Goodman 1972

Figure 6: Reading Miscue Inventory Coding Sheet[1]

[1]Carolyn Burke and Yetta Goodman, *Reading Miscue Inventory: Manual Procedure for Diagnosis and Evaluation* (London: The Macmillan Co., 1972). Copyright © 1972 by Carolyn L. Burke and Yetta M. Goodman. Reprinted by permission of the publisher.

Chart 3: Word Analysis Tests

Test	Publisher	Grades	Forms	Time	Measures	Price	Administrator	Variability	Reliability
Botel Reading Inventory	Follett Publishing Co.	Grades 1-12	Two	Ninety Minutes	Word Opposites; Word Recognition; Phonics	$3.00 for Examiner's Kit and Testing Forms; $1.38 for Thirty-Five Booklets	Class-room Teacher		
DOLCH Word List	General Press	Grades 1-3	One	No Time Limit	Word Recognition	Free	Class-room Teacher	No Data Available	No Data Available
SLOSSON Oral Reading Test	Slosson's Educational Publications, 140 Pine St., East Aurora, New York	Grades 1-12	One	Ten to Fifteen Minutes	Word Recognition	Part of Slossen's Intelligence Test; $3.10 per kit; $1.00 for extra answer sheets	Class-room Teacher		
WRAT Subtest (Reading and Spelling)	Guidance Association 1626 Gilpin Ave., Bloomington, Delaware	K-Adult	One	Twenty to Thirty Minutes	Word Recognition Spelling Mathematics	$2.75 for Specimen Set; $2.60 for Manual; $3.75 for Fifty Tests	Class-room Teacher		Reading and Spelling, .92 to .98; Arithmetic, .85 to .92

Test	Publisher	Grades	Forms	Time	Measures	Price	Administrator	Variability	Reliability
PIAT (Peabody Individual Achievement Test	American Guidance Service, Circle Pines, Minnesota 55014	Grades K-12+	One	Thirty-Forty Minutes	General Information; Reading Recognition Letter Names; Letter Sounds; Visual Discrimination of Letters and Words; Mathematics; Spelling; Reading Comprehension; Comprehension of Sentences	$20 for Fifty Tests	Class-room Teacher	No Validity Coefficient Available	Reading Recognition, .89; Reading Comprehension, −.64; Test is least reliable with Kindergarten
Doren Diagnostic (Group or Individual)	Educational Test Bureau, 720 Washington Ave., S.E. Minneapolis, Minnesota	Primary and Intermediate Grades	One	One to Three Hours; May Be Given In Sections	Letter Recognition; Beginning Sounds; Whole-Word Recognition; Words within Words; Speech Consonants; Ending Sounds; Blending; Rhyming; Vowels; Sight Words; Discriminate Guessing	$1.75 for Manual; $1.50 for Booklet; $4.85 for Twenty-Five Booklets	Class-room Teacher	1.-77 2.-88 3.-83 4.-92	.53 to .88; Median, .79

caution should be used in interpreting Levitt's findings. It is important to note that the retarded sample in Levitt's study were older children and had been exposed to reading instruction longer than the normal group of first graders. Levitt's findings were complicated by the limitation of having overlap between the two groups. Many of the children from the lower socieconomic populations and some of the children in the "normal" group of first graders were in the lower reading groups and might possibly be designated as retarded at a later date (Levitt, 1970).

In another study, Ramanauskas (1970), by using fewer categories of errors than Levitt, found that retardates made the same types of errors as the normals.

Still more research is needed though in the area of oral reading errors of the retarded in order to determine the progression of errors, such as a failure to give higher-order responses as the child learns to read; the relationship of reasoning and language skills to the cues or miscues; and the effect of repeated failure experienced in beginning reading on the strategies used by the retarded child in attempting to read orally.

Word Analysis Tests

Although some of the individual diagnostic reading tests include subtests on phonic skills, there are many other tests that are designed to measure certain aspects of word analysis, such as phonetic and structural analysis, as well as word recognition. Chart 3 includes some of these tests on page 112. These tests may be beneficial to the special educator because it appears likely from the results of several studies that retarded children are deficient in word analysis skills (Ragland, 1964; Ramanauskas, 1970; Shepherd, 1967). However, if the teacher is familiar with the word analysis skills materials, he can devise his own informal tests. An excellent source for informal testing of phonics skills is Guszak's *Diagnostic Instruction in the Elementary School* (1972).

Individual Tests of Reading Comprehension

Many of the individual diagnostic reading tests measure comprehension of oral and silent reading in addition to other skills. Most of these tests assess comprehension by asking a series of questions after the child has read a passage orally or silently. The manual for the test usually suggests what percentage of correct responses is considered to be indicative of adequate comprehension.

There are several disadvantages to the use of these tests to assess the child's reading comprehension. The majority of the questions test recall of factual information rather than the understanding of what is being read. Thus, they become a test of memory rather than of comprehension. Very few of the high-level skills of comprehension (e.g., inference skills) are measured in these tests. Most of the passages are too short to measure the child's ability to isolate main ideas, organize, or summarize material. Therefore, if the teacher wishes to obtain more diagnostic information, he might compose his own questions based upon a taxonomy of comprehension such as Barrett's (Clymer, 1968).

The *Reading Miscue Inventory* (Goodman and Burke, 1972) also gives suggestions and procedures for measuring comprehension of oral reading. With this test, rather than asking a series of questions about a short paragraph, the examiner asks the child to retell a story that has been read orally by the child. A scoring system of 100 points is employed and credit is given for character analysis, events, plot, theme, specifics, generalizations, and major concepts.

Most of the studies that have investigated the reading comprehension of the retarded have found that retarded children possess inadequate comprehension skills, especially such higher-level ones as inference (Bleismer, 1954; Cawley, Goodstein, and Burrow, 1972).

Formal Measures of Listening Comprehension

The Spache Diagnostic Reading Scales (1963) and *The Standard Reading Inventory* (1966) include provisions for testing of listening comprehensions. *The Durrell Listening-Reading Series* (Durrell, 1969) also measures listening comprehension at the primary and intermediate levels. The testing procedure on most tests requires the teacher to read the graded paragraphs to the child. Questions are then asked in order to determine listening comprehension. Manuals suggest percentages of correct items in order to obtain an adequate comprehension level.

Reading Related Tests

Many measures have been designed to predict reading readiness or failure. These tests attempt to measure areas, such as perception and language, which are considered to be related to reading achievement (see Chapter Three). Because of the frequency of the use of these tests in reading diagnosis of the retarded, this section concerning them is included. A description of the tests and their effectiveness as diagnostic instruments, especially with the retarded, is given and the following areas discussed: visual perception, auditory perception, perceptual-motor skills, and language.

Visual Perception: One of the most frequently used tests in the area of visual perception is the *Frostig Developmental Test of Visual Perception* (DTVP) (Frostig, et. al., 1963). According to Frostig (1963), visual perception skills are essential for the development of reading and writing skills. Five subtests of visual perception skills are measured on the DTVP. They are defined by Frostig et. al. (1966) in the following way:

Test I

Eye-Motor Coordination — a test of eye-hand coordination involving the drawing of continuous straight, curved, or angled lines between boundaries of various width, or from point to point without guide lines.

Test II

Figure-ground — a test involving shifts in perception of figures against increasing complex grounds. Intersecting and hidden geometric forms are used.

Test III

Constancy of Shape — a test involving the recognition of certain geometric figures presented in a variety of sizes, shadings, textures, and positions in space, and their discrimination from similar geometric figures. Circles, squares, rectangles, ellipses, and parallelograms are used.

Test IV

Position in Space — a test involving the discrimination of reversals and rotations of figures presented in series. Schematic drawings representing common objects are used.

Test V

Spatial relationships — a test involving the analysis of simple forms and patterns. These consist of lines of various lengths and angles which the child is required to copy, using dots as guide points.

Figures 7 through 11 illustrate each of these subtests.[2]

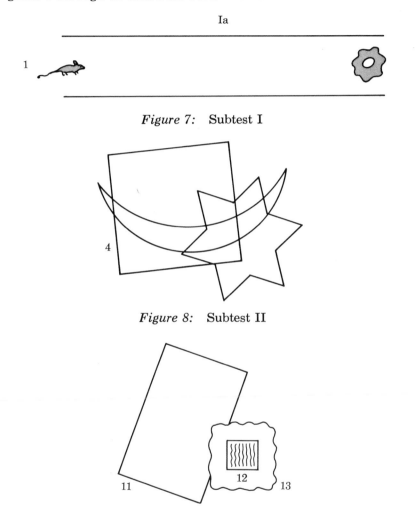

Ia

Figure 7: Subtest I

Figure 8: Subtest II

Figure 9: Subtest III

[2]Figures 7 through 11 are reprinted from *The Marianne Frostig Developmental Test of Visual Perception: 1963 Standardization Answer Booklet* (Palo Alto, California: Consulting Psychological Press, 1963), pp. IIa-Va, by permission of the publisher.

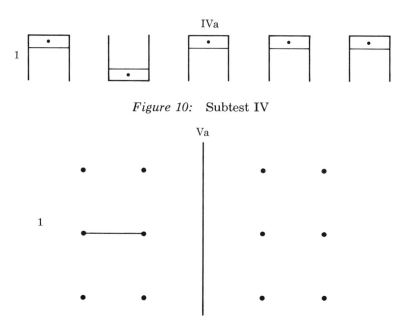

Figure 10:   Subtest IV

Figure 11:   Subtest V

According to the authors of the test, the *DVTP* may be used as a screening instrument in kindergarten or first grade or as a diagnostic instrument for older children who possess learning diffi-culties. The tests also may be given to groups or individually. It is suggested that the test not be given by the classroom teacher unless he has had some special training.

In this test, the raw scores are converted into a perceptual age (PA) equivalent which is based upon the chronological age (CA) of the average child who achieves such a score. The manual also gives suggestions for converting perceptual-age scores on sub-tests into scaled scores. For children under eight years of age, scaled scores may be obtained from the conversion table in the manual. If the children are between the ages of eight and ten, the teacher might employ this formula:

$$\frac{PA}{CA} \times 10 = \text{Scaled Scores}$$

A perceptual quotient, which is "a derivation scored determined from the sum of subtest scaled scores after correction for age variation"[3] also may be obtained. The manual suggests that the scaled scores and the perceptual quotients of mentally retarded children be computed using both the chronological and mental age (Frostig et al., 1966).

The standardization of the DVTP was made on 2116 school children in California who were, for the most part, white middle class. Very few Mexican-American or Oriental children were in the sample. No black children were included.

The reliability coefficients based upon test-retest reliability in two or three week intervals were .98, .80, and .69, with a range of .42 (Subtest II) to .80 (Subtest IV). Split-half reliabilities ranged from .35 (Subtest IV for children from eight to nine years old). The validity of the Frostig, obtained by correlating the DVPT and teacher ratings of classroom adjustment, motor coordination, and intellectual functioning, was .44, .50, and .50.

According to Frostig (1963), problems in the areas of these five subtests are related to failure in reading and writing skills. Specifically, problems in writing, word recognition, recognition of letters in different sizes or colors, reversals, and transpositions are related to eye-hand coordination, figure-ground perception, form constancy, position in space, and spatial relations respectively. Although the DTVP has been used as a screening device for predicting reading failure, the research is not in agreement concerning the relationship between the Frostig and reading skills. In addition, several studies have found that the DTVP has very low or insignificant correlations with reading achievement (Leibert and Sherk, 1970; Olson, 1966a; Olson, 1966b; Olson, 1968, Smith and Marx, 1972).

Research has been conducted to determine the correlations of items within the five subtests. If five discrete areas of visual perception are being measured, each item in a subtest should correlate highly with other items within the same subtest. Several such factor-analytic studies (the statistical technique used to determine the correlations within subtests) have been conducted (Allen, 1968; Ayres, 1965; Corah and Powell, 1963; Sprague, 1963; Smith and Marx, 1972). Although the studies vary somewhat in their results, the evidence suggests that the DTVP measures fewer than the five areas defined by Frostig. A general factor of perceptual organization, which may be more related to intelligence than to reading

---

[3]Marianne Frostig et al., *The Marianne Frostig Developmental Test of Visual Perception: 1963 Standardization* (Palo Alto, California: Consulting Psychological Press, 1963), p. 30.

achievement, has been identified by most of the studies (Smith and Marx, 1972). Some of the studies identify a second smaller factor composed of Subtests I and II. Smith and Marx (1972, p. 360) have stated that this second factor, if found to exist in future studies, may be one of motor steadiness.

Although the DTVP may be useful as a screening instrument for children who may have visual perception problems, the special educator must be cautious in using it as a diagnostic instrument because of its apparent limitations in measuring five separate areas (Allen, Haught, and Jones, 1965; Silverstein, 1965), its low reliabilities with some age levels, and its inability to discriminate above the age of ten — especially with the retarded (Silverstein, Ulfeldt, and Price, 1970). The test, as with most formal measures, was not standarized on exceptional children. The teacher must be very cautious in predicting reading achievement or reading failure on the basis of this one text.

Beery Developmental Test of Visual-Motor Integration: The Beery Developmental Test of Visual-Motor Integration (1967b) is another test that is used to assess difficulties in visual perception. Although the test was designed chiefly for use with preschool and early primary-grade children, it can be administered to groups or individuals from the ages of two to fifteen (Beery, 1967b). The test consists of a series of twenty-four geometric figures in booklet form. Because the administration and scoring procedures are very clear, a classroom teacher can give and score the test very easily. In fact, many illustrations of children's responses are given in the manual in order to aid the teacher in scoring. The consistency of scoring between raters has been determined to be high (Beery, 1967a; Ryckman and Rentfrow, 1971).

The test was standardized on a group of 1039 school children whose intelligent quotients ranged from normal upward. The children were from a middle-class suburban, rural, and lower middle-class urban populations (Beery, 1967b).

Coefficients for two-week test-retest reliability for the rural sample was .83 for boys and .87 for girls. A reliability coefficient for a group of educable retarded children was .90 (Beery, 1967a). A more recent study made with suburban youth found test-retest reliability to be .84 and split half reliability to be .74 (Ryckman and Rentfrow, 1971).

This particular test is age graded and correlates .89 between chronological age and number of correct forms. Approximately 25 percent of the variance can not be accounted for by chronological age. Beery (1967a) has speculated that mental age may be another factor measured by the test. Within small age ranges, MA appears to be highly correlated with geometric form reproduction.

One rationale for this test is that testing in the "levels of visual functioning (isolated part) and motor functioning (isolated part) separately does not always predict the level of visual-motor functioning."[4] According to Beery, the interaction of functions, which is presumed to be measured by the series of geometric forms included in the test, may be more significant than isolated functions. Geometric form reproduction may be correlated with a lack of functional organization resulting from developmental lag or neurological impairment.

Visual-motor integration has been correlated with reading achievement (Brown, 1971; Buktenica, 1966; Garrison and Magoon, 1972; Potter, 1949; Small, 1958). Although this correlation may be true, not enough is known presently about the relationship between reading and visual-motor integration in order for such a test as the *VMI* to be a truly diagnostic instrument for the teacher. Nonetheless, the *VMI* can be useful as a screening instrument for perceptual problems for the teacher of educable retarded children, for, as a group, retarded children perform below their mental age on geometric form reproduction (Beery, 1967a). This is not to say though that all retarded children need specific perceptual training or that this training will improve reading skills. Until more is known about the relationship between visual-motor integration and reading, it perhaps is true that such tests as the *VMI* are more diagnostic in nature for writing skills rather than reading.

Other tests of visual-motor integration are the *Perceptual Forms Test* (Sutphin, 1963); *Bender-Gestalt* Test (Koppitz, 1963); and parts of the *Purdue Perceptual Motor Survey* (Roach and Kephart, 1966).

Visual Discrimination Tests

Visual discrimination, especially of letters and words, has been related to success in reading by Barrett, 1965; Goins, 1958; Goldstein, and Moss and Jordan, 1965. To read, the child must possess the ability to discriminate among forms and then attach a verbal

---

[4]Keith Beery, *Visual Motor Integration: Monograph* (Chicago: Follett Publishing Co., 1967), p. 6.

label to the form; a basic problem in visual discrimination may be that the child does not attend to and discriminate among relevant forms. Mentally retarded children in particular have problems attending to significant details (Zeamon and House, 1963).

In assessing the visual discrimination skills of retardates, we feel that tests of discrimination of words and letters are more relevant to reading diagnosis than ones that include only geometric forms or pictures; however, if a child has extreme difficulty in discriminating letters and words, testing should include grosser measures as well as measures for visual acuity. Many reading readiness tests measure visual discrimination of letters and words; several such tests are the *Lee-Clark Reading Readiness Tests* (California Test Bureau, 1962); *Clymer-Barrett Prereading Battery* (Clymer and Barrett, 1967) and the *Murphy-Durrell Diagnostic Reading Readiness Tests* (Murphy and Durrell, 1964). If the teacher is familiar with these and other tests and with typical errors of letter and word discrimination, such as *b-d, was-saw,* that children make he can devise his own informal tests. For studies on visual discrimination of words and letters, the reader is referred to Barrett, 1965; Dunn, Rankin et al., 1968; Gibson et al., 1962; Guralick, 1972; Popp, 1964.

Visual Memory Tests

Visual memory, especially memory of words, is still another perceptual skill that has been related to reading achievement (Livo, 1970; Sutton, 1963). It is also a skill that is difficult to measure, for what appears to be a visual memory deficiency actually may be due to lack of concentration, inability to attend to relevent stimuli, and lack of associability. Most of the tests of visual memory do not differentiate among the various perceptual abilities (Frostig, 1968). Instead, memory and perceptual functions, such as visual motor integration, are combined in the same tests (Anastasi, 1968). For example, a child may do poorly on a visual memory test because of poor visual discrimination between similar looking forms rather that because of poor visual memory. Since most of the visual memory tests include the motor response, they actually are measuring visual motor memory instead of "pure" visual-spatial memory (Bannatyne, 1971).

One test that has attempted to assure visual-spatial memory is the *Bannatyne Visual-Spatial Memory Test (BVSMT)* (Bannatyne, 1971). Bannatyne has described the test in the following way:

The *Bannatyne Visual-Spatial Memory Test* was devised to assess a person's visual-spatial memory for designs in a "pure way without involving motor activity. Each of the fifteen separate stimulus designs is presented in turn for four seconds. Next a blank page is turned, an operation taking one second. This reveals a page of sight designs, from which the subject is required to select one design as the exact equivalent of the original stimulus design. The eight designs, which are randomized on the page, include the original design, a simplified version of it, a mirror image, a 90 degree rotation, a fragmentation, an out of proportion version of it, a complicated design and a symmetrical version. The subject is told beforehand that one design is the same as the original design and that he must select that particular one. . . .[5]

Several of the tests that measure visual-"motor" memory are: the *Memory Designs* (Graham-Kendall, 1960); the *Bender-Visual-Motor Gestalt Test (BVMGT)* (Bender, 1938; Koppitz, 1964); the *Benton Revised Visual Retention Test (BVRTS)* (Benton, 1963); and the *Slingerland Screening Test for Learning Disabilities* (Slingerland, 1967). Tests such as the *BVMGT* usually are administered by psychologists rather than by classroom teachers. These tests have been used quite extensively to determine brain damage or retardation. In general, mentally retarded children tend to have poorer scores on these tests than normal children (Koppitz, 1970). The *BVMGT* also tends to be related to overall school achievement and arithmetic more than to reading (Brenner et al., 1967).

Visual memory for letters and words can be measured by tests such as the *Visual Memory Subtest of the Durrell Analysis of Reading Difficulty* (Durrell, 1955); the *Slingerland Screening Test for Learning Disabilities* (1967), and the *Detroit Tests of Learning Aptitude-Visual Attention Span for Letters* (Baker and Leland, 1935).

Visual sequencing, or "the ability to organize visual stimuli in correct spatial order,"[6] is another facet of visual memory which often has been included in testing, although there are very few formal tests in this area. The "Visual Sequencing" subtest of the

---

[5]Alexander Bannatyne, *Language Reading and Learning Disabilities* (Springfield, Illinois: Charles C. Thomas, Publisher, 1971), p. 363.

[6]Robert Smith, *Teacher Diagnosis of Educational Difficulties* (Columbus, Ohio: Charles E. Merrill Publishing Co., 1969), p. 86.

Illinois Test of Psycholinguistic Abilities (Kirk, McCarthy, and Kirk, 1968) and the *Knox Cube Test* (Arthur, 1947) are two such formal measures, even though these tests may not measure the same type of skills (Paletz and Hirshoren, 1972) or skills that are necessary for remembering letters or words in a certain sequence.

Because of the lack of tests from which the teacher can adequately obtain diagnostic information for working with reading skills, he may need to develop informal tests. In doing so, the teacher should measure for both global memory forms and sequencing as well as tapping different levels of memory. For example, the teacher should explore the fact that it is harder for a child to recall or retrieve a geometric figure or letter with no cues than to select the correct one from among several alternatives (Wiseman, 1965). In addition, both short-term memory and long-term memory should be measured even though all the formal tests measure short-term memory. Although long-term memory problems may be indicative only of the existence of a perceptual problem or the fact that the child did not learn the material initially, this ability can be checked through diagnostic teaching lessons or observations. As was noted previously, a child may appear to have a visual memory problem when the cause of difficulty actually may be distractibility, lack of motivation, inability to associate, (e.g., transferring symbols to letter names, visual discrimination, or visual-motor integration difficulties). Careful and continual diagnosis by the teacher or clinician may determine the actual difficulty.

AUDITORY PERCEPTION

Tests of auditory perception are given quite often in order to predict reading failure or to develop skill programs in reading. The areas of auditory perception most often measured are: auditory discrimination, auditory blending, and auditory memory. Other areas, such as rhyming, also will be discussed in this section.

Auditory Discrimination Tests

The Wepman Auditory Discrimination Test (Forms I and II):   One of the most often used tools for measuring speech sound discrimination, this test (Wepman, 1958), which is designed to identify auditory deficits in children between the ages of five and eight, contains forty consonant sounds (e.g., *cad, cab*). The test is given individually and presented orally without the aid of visual cues. (The child is not allowed to watch the examiner's lips.) Several trial items are presented in order to determine whether the child understands the nature of the test. The child then is asked to respond "same" if the same word is presented twice and "different" if two different words are presented. The test is relatively short, requiring only minutes to administer. The score is determined by the number of errors the child makes; the manual indicates how many errors children at certain age levels need to make in order to demonstrate a difficulty in auditory discrimination. The test has been found to be sufficiently reliable (according to *Buros Sixth Mental Measurements Yearbook,* 1965) and its relationship to reading has been suggested by Wepman (1960). This relationship may not necessarily support the validity of the tests though because of the many variables related to reading achievement (Dicarlo, 1965).

The use of this test as a single measure to determine a child's difficulty in auditory discrimination has been questioned. Much of the criticism concerns the assertion that the use of minimal pairs is too gross of a measure of auditory discrimination (Blank, 1968; Byrne, 1962; Durrell, 1965; Myklebust and Johnson, 1967; Van Riper and Irwin, 1958). Although the test may determine whether the child is able to distinguish similarities between words, it may not identify children who have difficulty in perceiving sounds within words. A child who performs poorly in gross auditory discrimination is probably poor in analysis and synthesis of sounds; on the other hand, if the child does well in gross discrimination tasks, this is not necessarily an indication that he will not have problems with discrimination of individual speech sounds (Myklebust and Johnson, 1967).

Another criticism of the type of auditory discrimination test, which applies especially to culturally "different" children, is that the tests may be measuring the child's "unfamiliarity with standard English speech rather than deficits in auditory discrimination ability"[7] (Elenbogen and Thompson, 1972). Because many educable retarded children come from disadvantaged homes, this factor should be considered if a teacher chooses to administer tests of this nature. Another point to be considered is that many immature or retarded subjects have difficulty in grasping the task that is required

---

[7]Ruth Gottesman, "Auditory Discrimination Ability in Negro-Dialect-Speaking Children." *Journal of Learning Disabilities* 5 (1972): 94.

of them (responding "same" or "different") and therefore are not able to be tested. This is unfortunate because these are the very young or retarded children from whom a teacher desires to obtain information on auditory ability.

For other criticism of the *Wepman Auditory Discrimination Test* relative to the nature of the test, such as objections to its nominative table for determining number of errors at different levels and problems resulting from the types of responses required ("same" or "different"), see Vellutino, DeSetto, and Steger (1972) or Chalfant and Scheffelin (1969).

Other tests of auditory discrimination similar to the *Wepman* are the *PERC Auditory Discrimination Test* (1965), the *Sound Discrimination Test* (Templin, 1957), the *Picture Speech Discrimination Test* (Mecham and Rex, 1962), and the *Boston University Speech Sound Discrimination Picture Test* (1955). All of these tests are sufficient as screening measures, but are not extremely diagnostic in nature. If a teacher does a task analysis of the errors made by the child (e.g., the teacher determines that misses are minimal pairs of short vowel sounds), he may be able to apply this information directly to the teaching of reading skills. However, there is usually a lack of sufficient items of similar nature on the test to permit a sufficient item analysis. Therefore, these tests should not be used as a single indicator of the child's ability in the area of auditory discrimination.

Additional Measures of Auditory Perception

As was stated previously, there have been several criticisms of auditory discrimination tests. One test that has attempted to eliminate some of the problems related to other tests is the *Goldman-Fristoe-Woodcock Test of Auditory Discrimination* (1970). This is a pictorial test designed to provide measures of speech-sound discrimination ability in a setting that is relatively confounded by other factors.

> While the test is designed for use with children as young as four years of age, it can also be used with adults. It provides a measure of auditory discrimination under ideal listening conditions plus a comparative measure of auditory discrimination in the presence of controlled background noise.[8]

---

[8]Ronald Goldman, M. Fristoe, and Richard Woodcock, "A New Dimension in the Assessment of Sound Discrimination," *Journal of Learning Disabilities* 4 (1971): 365.

The effects of vocabulary or language development and the inconsistency of speaker's voice on the results of the test are controlled in this test. The vocabulary was chosen from words that are familiar to young children after an assessment of the word-picture associations has been completed with each child. Any additional training that is required after the assessment is then conducted prior to the actual testing. The subtests are presented on a standardized prerecorded tape.

The test consists of three parts: The Training Procedure, which familiarizes the subject with the word picture associations used in the subtests; the Quiet Subtest; and the Noise Subtest. The words selected for "this test are one syllable in length and are the consonant-vowel-consonant or consonant-vowel form when spoken."[9] This test is relatively new and additional research regarding its effectiveness as a screening or diagnostic instrument is needed. The manual contains information on the test's reliability and validity as well as normative data on its use with mentally retarded children. Although the test eliminates some discrimination problems that are related to the tests discussed previously, it still tests only minimal word pairs instead of individual speech sounds.

One test that goes beyond the measure of discrimination of minimal pairs is the *Lindamood Auditory Conceptualization (LAC)* (Lindamood and Lindamood, 1971). This is an individually administered test which measures the discrimination of such speech sounds as /p/ and /b/ and the "ability to perceive the number and order of sounds within a spoken pattern, as in perceiving the difference between *at, pat, tap,* and *apt.*"[10] The authors of the test stress the relationship of these skills to reading in the following statement:

> If a student cannot perceive contrasts in speech sound unit, or if he cannot conceptualize the order of sounds in syllables and words, he cannot easily associate the sound units with written symbols. This student learns to read and spell more through rote memory than through an understanding of the structural link between sound and symbol — between spoken patterns and the written patterns we use to represent them. Such rote learning can restrict progress in reading and spelling because it does not lend itself to extension and generalization to new and unfamiliar patterns.[11]

---

[9]*Ibid.*, p. 367.

[10]Charles H. Lindamood and Patricia C. Lindamood, *Auditory Conceptualization (LAC) Test* (Boston: Teaching Resources Corp., 1971), p. 7.

[11]*Ibid.*, p. 7.

The test, which can be used from a preschool to adult level, utilizes colored blocks which the subject manipulates in order to indicate his conceptualization of the speech sounds presented by the examiner. By the use of the blocks, the subject can show visually the order of the speech sounds presented. The color of the blocks the subject uses is not fixed. Instead, he may use any color he chooses to represent a speech sound as long as he consistently uses the same color for that sound. There are no rigid time requirements for the tests but the manual suggests that it can be completed within ten minutes, although retarded children may require more time.

Two forms are available, and the test consists of two subtests— Category I and Category II. Category I concerns isolated sounds in sequence and is divided into two parts. In Part A, for example, the subject must identify how many sounds he hears and their sequential order (e.g., /s/, /s/, /sh/). Category II concerns sounds within syllable patterns. Here, the subject must indicate changes in syllable patterns (e.g., /ab/ to /zab/ to /zaf/). This test essentially measures the skill to blend sounds.

According to the manual, prerequisites for the test are that the subject have the ability to judge sameness and difference, number concepts to four, and left-right progression. The manual is very explicit in describing the administration and scoring of the test and also contains information on the standardization, reliability, and validity of the test. The test was standardized on a full-range of socioeconomic and ethnic groups in kindergarten through sixth grade. The reliability obtained by means of test-retest with alternate forms of the *LAC* was high (.96). In order to determine validity, the test was correlated with the reading and spelling scores of the *Wide Range Achievement Test*. The correlations ranged from .67 to .81 at different grade levels, with an average of .73. Category I appears to be a better predictor of reading achievement at the lower levels, while Category II appears to be a better predictor at Grade 4.

This test is more diagnostic than most that are available, but, as with the *Goldman-Fristoe-Woodcock Test of Auditory Discrimination*, research is still needed, especially with the retarded, in order to determine the effectiveness of the *LAC* as a diagnostic instrument. The present authors' experiences with this test with retarded children indicates that these children have problems in grasping what is asked of them, especially with Category II.

Tests of Auditory Blending: Auditory blending is a complex auditory perceptual skill that often has been related to reading achievement (Bond, 1938; Carter and McGinnis, 1970; Chall, Roswell, and

Blumenthal, 1963; Dolch and Bloomster, 1937; Gates, 1947; Harris, 1970; and Myklebust and Johnson, 1962). Auditory blending can be related to auditory discrimination in that a child should be able to discriminate between separate sounds before he can blend them into words (Monroe and Backus, 1937). Although many educators in the field of reading have recognized auditory blending as an important skill, very few have developed instruments to measure it.

Tests that have been developed include: the *Roswell-Chall Auditory Blending Test* (1963) the "Sound Blending subtest" of the *Illinois Test of Psycholinguistic Abilities* (McCarthy, Kirk, and Kirk, 1968), the "Auditory Blending Subtest" of the *Gates-McKillop Reading Diagnostic Test* (1962) and the "Stanford Diagnostic Reading Test-Auditory Blending Subtest" and Category II of the *LAC*.

The *Roswell-Chall Auditory Blending Test* purports to measure the child's ability to blend sounds into whole words. It was developed for use in Grades 1 through 4 as well as with older children who are having problems in reading. It is an individual test which is administered orally. There are three parts to the test which consist of ten words each (e.g., /a/- /t/, /t/-/oa/-/t/). Parts I and II are subdivided into two parts with the former including consonant sounds and a vowel, and vowel digraph or diphthong, while the latter includes consonant combinations such as *st* and the remainder of the word. The third part of the test consists of three elements, with a consonant-vowel combination *(oa)* or a consonant combination. In administering the test, the examiner presents the sounds slowly to the child who must tell what the word is.

The test is more of an informal inventory than a standardized measure because it lacks many characteristics of adequate test construction (Aaron, 1965; Rackel, 1965). For example, the norming group consisted of sixty-two black children from New York City who were considered to be from the lower class, while another sample was composed of severely disabled readers. According to the *Buros Sixth Mental Measurements Yearbook*, the technical information for reliability and validity of the test is inadequate.

The "Sound Blending Subtest" of the *ITPA* is similar to the *Roswell-Chall Auditory Blending Test* in terms of presentation. In this test, the parts of the words are spoken individually at half-second intervals, and the child tells what word he hears. A wider range of age and difficulty (ages two to ten years) is included. At the lower end, pictures are employed, while at the upper end, nonsense syllables are included. The test-retest reliability coefficients at three different age levels are .69 (four years) .42 (six years) and .54

(eight years). Still, effectiveness of the "Sound Blending Subtest" as a diagnostic instrument with retarded children has been questioned. According to Hatch and French (1971), this subtest lacks stability, especially with retarded children, and caution should be used in utilizing it in developing remedial programs.

The "Auditory Blending Subtest" of the *Gates-McKillop* consists of fifteen words which are presented in parts with pauses of approximately one quarter of a second. The child responds verbally to the items.

The *Stanford Diagnostic Reading Test* (Karlsen, Madden, and Gardner, 1966) also contains a section on auditory blending. Unfortunately, the test requires the child to circle the letter that represents the sound. Thus, this subtest measures more than the auditory skill of blending.

Tests of Auditory Memory and Auditory Memory Span

"Auditory memory is the ability to store and recall what one has heard."[12] Auditory sequencing or auditory memory span "refers to the amount of information an individual can retain in proper sequence particularly for the purposes of immediate action or recall."[13] Most tests attempt to measure auditory memory span as it is defined in the previous sentences. The oral directions and the oral commissions of the *Detroit Test of Learning Aptitudes* (Baker and Leland, 1935) as well as the rhyming section of the *Screening Test of Auditory Perception (STAP)* (Kimmell and Stahl, 1969) purport to measure auditory memory, although any test of auditory perception requires the child to retain and recall information.

Just as other factors, such as attention, distractibility, and meaningfulness of material, may influence visual memory, so they also may influence auditory memory (Johnson and Myklebust, 1967; Berry, 1969). The teacher must consider this fact when he attempts to measure the auditory memory span of the child. Most of the auditory memory span tests utilize digits or nonsense syllables that are given orally at one-half second or one second intervals. The child then is asked to repeat the syllables. Some tests require that the child repeat some digits backwards as well as forwards.

---

[12]Janet W. Lerner, *Children with Learning Disabilities: Theories, Diagnosis, and Teaching Strategies* (Boston: Houghton-Mifflin Co., 1971), p. 134.

[13]Doris Johnson and Helmer Myklebust, *Learning Disabilities: Educational Principles and Practices* (New York: Grune & Stratton Co., 1967), p. 111.

Tests of digit recall include the *ITPA, Auditory Sequential Memory; Stanford-Binet* (Terman and Merrill, 1960), and *WISC Digit Span* (Wechsler, 1949).

Memory for digits, nonsense syllables, or unrelated words is considered by some to be a good measure of how well the child remembers language (Beery, 1969; Semmel and Bennett, 1970). Berry (1969) also suggests that such tests can measure auditory memory span and sensory-motor memory as well. In addition, tactile-kinesthetic perception is related to the perception of sound sequences. For a thorough discussion on this topic, see Beery (1969).

If a teacher chooses to use memory tests that are comprised of isolated word lists and syllables, such as the *Detroit Test of Learning Aptitudes*, rhythmic pattern, such as the *STAP*, or digits, such as the tests mentioned previously, he should also include measures of sentences and passages. Beery (1969) and Myklebust and Johnson (1967) suggest formal and informal techniques of this type.

In summary, assessments of auditory perception attempt to measure such abilities as speech-sound discrimination, blending, and memory, although other skills of auditory perception have been included in various tests. For example, *The Test of Nonverbal Auditory Discrimination (TENVAD)* (Buktenica, 1971) includes measures of pitch, loudness, and timbre, and *STAP* assesses rhyming and the memory of rhythmic patterns as well as discrimination of long and short vowels, consonants, and consonant blends. Assessment of auditory closure, which is defined by Kirk and Paraskevopoulos as the "child's ability to fill in missing parts which are deleted in auditory presentation and to produce a complete word"[14] is a subtest of the *ITPA*.

The present authors feel that assessment of auditory perception is important and that the teacher, if he realizes the limitation of formal tests, can use the tests available plus informal measures in order to determine the child's auditory abilities.

PERCEPTUAL-MOTOR TESTS

Although tests of visual and auditory perception are, in fact, measures of perceptual-motor abilities, a separate section is included in this chapter for perceptual-motor tests. The test included in the

---

[14]S. Kirk and J. Paraskevopoulos, *The Development and Psychometric Characteristics of the Revised Selevois. Test of Psycholinguistic Abilities* (Urbana: University of Illinois Press, 1969), p. 21.

following discussion may consist of subtests of auditory and visual perception, but they also may emphasize gross motor coordination. Presently, there is a great deal of controversy concerning the relationship between perceptual motor abilities and reading achievement (see Chapter Three). The present authors would caution teachers concerning any use of a perceptual-motor test as a predictor of reading achievement. Perceptual motor ability and reading may be related but not on a cause-and-effect basis. The knowledge obtained from perceptual motor tests may give valuable information to the teacher, but this information may not be readily transferable to reading instruction.

Several frequently used perceptual-motor tests include: the *Purdue Perceptual Motor Survey* (Roach & Kephart, 1966); the *Lincoln-Oseretsky Motor Development Scale* (Sloan, 1955); and the informal test developed by Cratty (1969). The *Purdue Perceptual-Motor Survey* contains the following subtests:

1. Walking board tasks, such as walking forward, backward, and sideways.
2. Jumping on both feet, the right foot, and the left foot.
3. Skipping.
4. Hopping
5. Identification of body parts.
6. Imitation of movements.
7. Covering an obstacle course, which measures how the child relates spatially to his environment.
8. Completion of the *Kraus-Weber Test.*
9. Playing "angels in the snow," which is "useful in detecting problems with right-to-left sidedness."[15]
10. Chalkboard exercises for perceptual-motor matching, which require the child to draw a circle and double circles and to copy various motifs.
11. Ocular pursuits, which are designed to measure the ability of a child "to establish and maintain visual contact with a target."[16]
12. Copying visual achievement forms, which measures visual-motor integration.

The manual for this test contains specific instructions for the age levels suitable for each subtest as well as for the administration and scoring of the subtests. Many suggestions for observation of re-

---

[15]E.G. Roach and N.C. Kephart, *The Purdue Perceptual-Motor Survey* (Columbus, Ohio: Charles E. Merrill Publishing Co., 1966), p. 44.
[16]*Ibid.*, p. 58.

sponses during the test are also given. Information concerning the reliability and validity of the test are included in the manual.

The Lincoln-Oseretsky Motor Development Scale (Sloan, 1955) and the Cratty test (1969) are similar in nature. Examples of items from the Lincoln-Oseretsky include walking backwards for a distance of six feet, touching the nose, jumping and turning about, and standing on one foot.

Informal observations of children also give the teacher some information concerning their motor performance. For a thorough discussion on perceptual-motor development in children see Kephart's *The Slow Learner in the Classroom* (1971).

Tests of Language: Considerable research has been conducted concerning the language development of the retarded and its relationship to reading achievement. Unfortunately, there are no tests available to measure language adequately (Bordie, 1970); Dever, 1971; Rosenberg, 1970). Most of the tests do not exemplify the present research and theories of language development (Rosenberg, 1970).

Although the tests available are insufficient for making adequate diagnostic statements about children's language, several tests do purport to measure language skills and are used frequently with the retarded. Two of these are the *Illinois Test of Psycholinguistic Abilities (ITPA)* (Kirk, McCarthy, and Kirk, 1968) and the *Peabody Picture Vocabulary Test (PPVT)* (Dunn, 1965). These tests supposedly measure linguistic abilities and speech disabilities, such as articulation disorders.

The Revised Edition of the *ITPA* (Kirk, McCarthy, and Kirk, 1968), which was designed as a diagnostic instrument for children between the ages of thirty months and nine years, tests specific abilities in order to develop remediational programs. The basis for the test is the model of communication developed by Osgood (1957). Three dimensions are hypothesized in Osgood's model: processes of reception (decoding), organization (association), and expression (encoding); levels of organization — projection, integration, and representation; and such channels of communication as the auditory and visual. For a more thorough discussion of the model, see Osgood (1957) and Kirk and Paraskevopoulos (1969).

The *ITPA* consists of ten subtests and two supplementary tests. The definitions of the subtests are included in the following passages from Kirk and Paraskevopoulos.

    1. *Auditory reception subtest.* Auditory reception (decoding) involves the ability to gain meaning from auditorily

received stimuli. This skill is measured by giving sentences orally in question form, e.g., "Do birds fly?" The child is to answer *yes* or *no.* (Representational level — Receptive Process)

2. *Visual reception subtest.* The term visual reception denotes the ability to gain meaning from visually received stimuli. This test consists of forty photographic items, each consisting of stimulus picture on one page and four alternative pictures on a second page. He is shown the picture which is removed; then he is shown the four optional pictures. He is asked to point to the correct picture that is conceptually most like the first picture. (Representational level—Receptive Process)

3. *Auditory association subtest.* Auditory association is the ability to relate auditorily received stimuli in a meaningful way. (On my hands I have fingers; on my feet I have _____.) The response of the child is vocal. (Representational Level — Association Process)

4. *Visual association subtest.* Visual association describes the ability to relate visually received stimuli in a meaningful way. The lower level of the test is comprised of twenty items in each of which the subject is required to select from among four pictures the one which most meaningfully relates to a stimulus picture. The upper level of the test is comprised of twenty-two visual analogies which are comparable to the analogies on the auditory association subtest. (Representational Level — Association Process)

5. *Verbal expression* is the ability to convey ideas in words. It is measured by the child's responses to an open-ended question, "Tell me all about _____!" as he is handed in sequence a ball, a block, an envelope, and a button. (Representational Level — Expressive Process)

6. *Manual expression subtest.* Manual expression is the ability to express ideas by gestures. It is representative of a larger function involving the use of body and facial expression to transmit ideas. The child is shown a picture of a common object and is asked, "Show me what we do with a _____." (Representational Level — Expressive Process)

7. *Grammatic closure subtest.* Grammatic closure, defined operationally, refers to the child's ability to make use of the redundancies of oral language in acquiring habits for handling syntax and grammatic inflections. The test is

essentially nonmeaningful closure, testing the child's use of grammatic form. (Automatic Level)

8. *Visual closure subtest.* Visual closure refers to the ability to perceive visual material presented in incomplete form by making use of his previous experiences with visual stimuli. For present purposes, visual closure is defined as the ability to recognize the whole from part. The test consists of four scenes, presented separately each containing either fourteen or fifteen objects in varying degrees of concealment. The child's task is to point to particular objects which are particularly hidden. It is primarily a test of perceptual speed in a visual closure task, since there is a specified time limit. (Automatic Level)

9. *Auditory sequential memory subtest.* Auditory sequential memory involves the ability to reproduce from memory, immediately after presentation, sequences of stimuli which have been auditorily received. The Auditory Sequential Memory Subtest of the *ITPA* consists of twenty-eight digit sequences ranging in length from two to eight digits. Digits are presented at the rate of two per second. Two trials per sequences are allowed, with more credit given (two points) for success on the first trial than on the second (one point). The digits are given at shorter intervals in order to lower the age to which the test is appropriate. The shorter the interval, the easier the task. (Automatic Level)

10. *Visual memory subtest.* Visual sequential memory involves the ability to reproduce from memory sequences of visually received stimuli. The Visual Memory Subtest is comprised of twenty-five sequences of discrete, nonmeaningful, abstract figures varying in length from two through eight figures. The child is shown each sequence of figures for five seconds and then asked to put chips of corresponding figures in the same order. As with auditory memory, two trials are allowed per sequence when necessary. (Automatic Level)

11. *Auditory closure subtest.* Auditory closure refers to the ability to recognize and reproduce a word by filling in the missing parts which were omitted or distorted during presentation. The auditory closure subtest requires the expression of a complete word when a sound or syllable has been deleted. It consists of thirty items of mutilated words such as "bo/le," "tele/one," presented to the child with the direction "What am I talking about?" (Automatic Level)

12. *Sound blending subtest.* Sound blending refers to the ability to synthesize two or more discrete and isolate sounds

into a whole. The test was discussed under the Auditory Perception section. (Automatic Level) [17]

There have been several major criticisms of the use of the *ITPA* as a diagnostic instrument. For example, the subtests of the *ITPA* were based on the theory of Osgood's Model of Language, and although Osgood has changed his model recently, the *ITPA* does not reflect this change (Osgood, 1968; Rosenberg, 1970). Also, these subtests do not appear to test the theory that was earlier presented by Osgood adequately (Weener, Barrett, and Semmell, 1967). In addition, other problems exist in attempting to use the subtests for diagnostic purposes. Although the overall language score is reliable, the reliability of the subtests is too low for diagnostic statement from individual profiles to be made (Weener, Barrett, and Semmell, 1967).

As with the *DTVP* (Frostig, 1963), the *ITPA* should assess "single abilities which are mutually exclusive."[18] No factor analytic study has supported the assumption that the test assesses single skills, although it may render a general language factor, especially at the lower age levels (Ryckman and Wiegerink, 1969). Because of this difficulty, caution should be used in establishing remedial programs based upon individual subtests. Yet even if the teacher chooses to use the total language score, the results may not be specific enough to begin a program in language for the child (Van Hattum, 1969).

Another test that is used as a measure of language is the *Peabody Picture Vocabulary Test (PPVT)* (Dunn, 1965), the *Ammons Full-Range Vocabulary Test* (Ammons and Ammons, 1958) and the *Van Alstyne* (Van Alstyne, 1959), both of which are similar to it. The *PPVT* is an individually administered test which requires no verbal response from the child. The age range is from age two to adults, although the test is more suitable for children four years and older (Beery, 1969). The test consists of plates containing four stimulus pictures. The examiner pronounces the words and the child

---

[17]S. Kirk and J. Paraskevopoulos, *The Development and Psychometric Characteristics of the Revised Selevois Test of Psycholinguistic Abilities* (Urbana: University of Illinois Press, 1969), pp. 29-48. Reprinted by permission of the publisher.

[18]David E. Ryckman and Ronald Wiegerink, "The Factors of the *Illinois Test of Psycholinguistic Abilities:* A Comparison of Eighteen Factor Analyses," *Exceptional Children* 35 (1969): 107.

is to point to the picture that represents the word. Designed to measure the child's verbal intelligence, it can provide an intelligence score from the child's raw score. However, it is more of a measure of the child's comprehension of word meanings. This test can not be given as a single diagnostic measure of language because it provides only gross information about the child's receptive vocabulary (Van Hattum, 1969). For information about standardization, reliability, and validity of the *PPVT*, see Dunn (1965), Wolfensberger (1962), and Hammill and Irwin (1965).

Although no tests existing at the present time adequately measure the language of retarded children (Dever, 1971; Rosenberg, 1970), the assessment of language skills can give the teacher valuable information for the development of reading programs. There also is some evidence to support the fact that a child utilizes his knowledge of language and its operation in respect to his reading (Goodman, 1968) and that reading can be considered a language process (Ryan and Semmell, 1969). For further information on language testing, see Dever (1971) and Beery (1969).

SUMMARY

Formal reading and reading-related tests may best be utilized by the teacher if he has some specific objectives for administering them. Although there are many standardized group diagnostic reading tests, the special-education teacher will obtain little information that will be beneficial in developing programs from them. Individual diagnostic reading tests will yield valuable information as measurements of word recognition, sentence reading, and comprehension, if the teacher is trained in interpreting the results. Newer tests, such as the *Reading Miscue Inventory*, allow the teacher to diagnose the reading "strategies" or "cues" employed by children as they read.

Tests that purport to measure correlates of reading, such as visual auditory perception and language, also were discussed in this chapter. These measures are usually administered in order to determine readiness for reading or to develop remedial reading programs for children who have reading problems. Since there is some controversy as to the relationship between these correlates and reading achievement, a teacher should understand the nature of these tests and the types of information that may be obtained from them before he administers them.

REFERENCES

Aaron, Ira. "Roswell-Chall Auditory Blending Test." *The Sixth Mental Measurement Yearbook*, edited by Oscar K. Buros, p. 1114. New Jersey: Gryphon Press, 1965.

Allen, R.F., "Factor Analysis of the Developmental Test of Visual Perception: Performance of Educable Mental Retardates." *Perceptual Motor Skills* 26 (1968): 257-58.

Allen, R.M.; Haught, T.D.; and Jones, R.W. "Visual Perceptual Abilities and Intelligence in Mental Retardation." *Journal of Clinical Psychology* 21 (1965): 299-300.

Ammons, R.B., and Ammons, Helen S. *The Full-Range Picture Vocabulary Test*. New Orleans: R.B. Ammons, 1958.

Anastasi, Anna. *Psychological Testing*, 3rd ed. London: Collier-Macmillan Limited, 1968.

Arthur, Grace. *A Point Scale of Performance Tests, Revised Form II (Knox Cube Test)*. New York: The Psychological Corporation, 1947.

Ayres, A. Jean. "Patterns of Perceptual Motor Dysfunction in Children: A Factor Analytic Study." *Perceptual and Motor Skills Monograph Supplement TV20* (1965): 335-68.

Baker, Harry, and Leland, B. *Detroit Test of Learning Aptitude*. Indianapolis, Indiana: The Bobbs-Merrill Co., 1935.

Bannatyne, Alexander. *Language Reading and Learning Disabilities*. Springfield, Illinois: Charles C. Thomas Co., 1971.

Barr, Rebecca C. "The Influence of Instructional Conditions on Word Recognition Errors." *Reading Research Quarterly* 7 (1972): 509-29.

Barrett, Thomas. "Visual Discrimination Tasks as Predictors of First-Grade Reading Achievement." *The Reading Teacher* 15 (1965): 276-82.

Beery, Keith E. *Developmental Test of Visual Motor Integration: Administration and Scoring Manual*. Chicago: Follett Publishing Co., 1967a.

_____. *Visual Motor Integration: Monograph*. Chicago: Follett Publishing Co., 1967b.

Beery, Mildred. *Language Disorders of Children: The Bases and Diagnosis*. New York: Appleton-Century-Crofts, 1969.

Bender, L. "A Visual Motor Gestalt Test and Its Clinical Use." *American Orthopsychiatric Association, Research Monograph Number 3*, 1938.

Benton, A.L. *Revised Visual Retention Test: Manual*. New York: Psychological Corporation, 1963.

Blank, Marion. "Cognitive Processes in Auditory Discrimination in Normal and Retarded Readers." *Child Development* 39 (May 1968): 650-65.

Bliesmer, Emery P. "Reading Abilities of Bright and Dull Children of Comparable Mental Ages." *Journal of Educational Psychology* 45 (1954): 321-31.

Bond, Guy. The Auditory and Speech Characteristics of Poor Readers. *Teachers College Contribution to Education* No. 637 (1938).

Bordie, J.G. "Language Tests and Linguistically Different Learners: The Sad State of the Art." *Elementary English* 47 (1970): 814-29.

The Boston University of Speech Sound Discrimination Test. Boston: Boston University, 1955.

Brenner, May Woolf, et al. "Visual-Motor Disability in School Children." *British Medical Journal* 47 (1967): 259-62.

Brown, Doug. "Multi-Variate Factor Analysis of Upper and Lower Elementary School Children: Learning Patterns within and between Social Class and Race." Unpublished Study, Indiana University, 1971.

Buktenica, N.A. "Auditory Discrimination: A New Assessment Procedure." *Exceptional Children* 38 (1971): 237-40.

_____. *Relative Contribution of Auditory and Visual Perception to First-Grade Language Learning*. Doctoral dissertation, University of Chicago, 1966.

Buros, Oscar K. editor. *Sixth Mental Measurements Yearbook*. Highland Park, New Jersey: Gryphon Press, 1965.

Byrne, M. *The Wepman Auditory Discrimination Test as a Clinical Pool*. Paper presented to American Speech and Hearing Association, 1962, in New York.

Carter, Homer L.J. and McGinnis, Dorothy. *Diagnosis and Treatment of the Disabled Reader*. New York: Macmillan Company, 1970.

Cawley, J.F.; Goodstein, H.A.; and Burrow, W.H. *The Slow Learner and The Reading Problem*. Springfield, Illinois: Charles C. Thomas Co., 1972.

Chalfant, James, and Scheffelin, Margaret. *Central Processing Dysfunctions in Children*. National Institute of Health Monograph Number 9. Bethesda, Maryland: United States Department of Health, Education, and Welfare, Public Health Service, 1969.

Chall, Jeanne; Roswell, Florence; and Blumenthal, Susan. "Auditory Blending Ability: A Factor in Success in Beginning Reading." *The Reading Teacher* 17 (1963): 113-18.

Clymer, Theodore, and Barrett, Thomas. "The Barrett-Taxonomy-Cognitive and Affective Dimensions of Reading Comprehension." In *Innovation and Change in Reading Instruction: Sixty-Seventh Yearbook of the National Society for the Study of Education. Part H*, edited by Helen M. Robinson, pp. 19-23. Chicago: University of Chicago Press, 1968.

_____. *Clymer-Barrett Prereading Battery*. Boston: Personal Press, 1967.

Corah, N.L., and Powell, B.J. "A Factor Analytic Study of the Frostig DTVP." *Perceptual and Motor Skills* 16 (1963): 59-63.

Cratty, B. *Motor Activity and the Education of Retardates*. Philadelphia: Lea and Febriger, 1969.

Dever, Richard B. *The Use of Language by Mentally Retarded Children: A Review of the Literature*. Technical Report 1.24. of the Center for Research and Development on the Improvement of Teaching Handicapped Children. Bloomington: Indiana University, 1971.

Dicarlo, Louis M., *"The Auditory Discrimination Test." The Sixth Mental Measurements Yearbook*, edited by C. K. Buros. Highland Park, New Jersey: Gryphon Press, 1965.

Dolch, E.W., and Bloomster, M. *Dolch Basic Word List*. Champaign, Illinois: Garrard Press, 1941.

_____. "Phonic Readiness." *Elementary School Journal* 38 (1937): 201-05.

Drake, Charles. *PERC Auditory Discrimination Test*. Wellesley, Massachusetts: Perceptual and Education Research Center, 1965.

Dunn, L.M. "A Comparison of the Reading Processes of Mentally Retarded Boys of the Same Mental Age." In *Studies of Reading and Arithmetic in Mentally Retarded Boys*, edited by L.M. Dunn and K.J. Capobiance, pp. 7-99. Monograph of the Society for Research and Child Development, pp. 7-99, 1954.

_____. *Peabody Picture Vocabulary Test*. Minneapolis, Minnesota: American Guidance Service, 1965.

Dunn, L.M.; Rankin, P.A.; Leton, D.A.; and Shelton, V.F. "Congruency Factors Related to Visual Confusion of English Letters." *Perceptual and Motor Skills* 26 (1968): 659-66.

Durrell, Donald. *Durrell Analysis of Reading Difficulty*. New York: Harcourt, Brace, Jovanovich, 1955.

_____. The Durrell Listening-Reading Series. New York: Harcourt, Brace, Jovanovich, 1969.

_____. Improving Reading Instruction. New York: Harcourt, Brace, Jovanovich, 1965.

Elenbogen, Elaine, and Thompson, Glen. "A Comparison of Social Class Effects in Two Tests of Auditory Discrimination." *Journal of Learning Disabilities* 5 (1972): 209-12.

Froese, Victor. "Word Recognition Tests: Are They Useful beyond Grade Three?" *Reading Teacher* 24 (1971): 432-38.

Frostig, M. "Education for Children With Learning Disabilities." In *Progress in Learning Disabilities*, edited by H.R. Myklebust. New York: Grune & Stratton, 1968.

Frostig, M.; LeFevre, W.; and Whittlesey, J.R.B. *Administration and Scoring Manual, Marianne Frostig Developmental Test of Visual Perception, 1966 Revised*. Palo Alto, California: Consulting Psychological Press, 1966.

Frostig, M. et al. *The Marianne Frostig Development Test of Visual Perception: 1963 Standardization*. Palo Alto, California: Consulting Psychological Press, 1963.

Garrison, Karl C., and Magoon, Robert A. *Educational Psychology: An Integration of Psychological and Educational Practices*. Columbus, Ohio: Charles E. Merrill Publishing Co., 1972.

Gates, A., and McKillop, A. *Improvement of Reading*. (3rd Edition) New York: Macmillan, 1947.

_____. *Reading Diagnostic Test*. New York: Teachers College Press, 1962.

Gibson, E.J., et al. "A Developmental Study of the Perception of Letter-like Forms." *Journal of Comparative and Physiological Psychology* 55 (1962): 897-906.

Goins, Jean. *Visual Perceptual Abilities and Early Reading Progress*. Chicago: University of Chicago Press Supplementary Education Monograph Number 78, 1958.

Goldman, Ronald; Fristoe, M.; and Woodcock, Richard. "A New Dimension in the Assessment of Sound Discrimination." *Journal of Learning Disabilities* 4 (1971): 364-68.

_____. *Test of Auditory Discrimination*. Circle Rines, Minnesota: American Guidance Service, 1970.

Goldstein, H.; Moss, J.W.; and Jordon, L.J. *The Efficacy of Special-Class Learning in the Development of Mentally Retarded Children*. Cognitive Research Project Number 619. Washington, D.C.: United States Department of Health, Education, and Welfare Office of Education, 1965.

Goodman, Kenneth. "A Linguistic Study of Cues and Miscues in Reading." *Elementary English Review* 42 (1965): 639-43.

Goodman, Yetta. "Reading Diagnosis — Qualitative and Quantitative." *The Reading Teacher* 25 (1972): 32-37.

_____. "Using Children's Reading Miscues for New Teaching Strategies." *Reading Teacher* 23 (1970): 455-59.

Goodman, Yetta, and Burke, Carolyn L. *Reading Miscue Inventory: Manual Procedure for Diagnosis and Evaluation.* London: Collier-MacMillan, Limited, 1972.

Gottesman, Ruth. "Auditory Discrimination Ability in Negro-Dialect-Speaking Children." *Journal of Learning Disabilities* 5 (1972): 94-101.

Graham, F., and Kendall, B. *Memory for Design's Test.* Missoula, Montana: Psychological Tests Specialists, 1960.

Guralick, Michael J. "Alphabet Discrimination and Distinction Test. Research in Edition." *Journal of Learning Disabilities* 5 (1972): 428-34.

Guszak, Frank J. *Diagnostic Reading Instruction in the Elementary School.* New York: Harper & Row, Publisher, 1972.

Hammill, Donald, and Irwin, O.C. "PPVT as a Measure of Intelligence for Mentally Retarded." *Teaching School-Bulletin* 62 (1965): 126-31.

Harris, Albert. *How to Increase Reading Ability,* 5th ed. New York: David McKay Co., 1970.

Hatch, Erich, and French, Joseph T. "The Revised ITPA. Its Reliability and Validity for Use with EMR's." *Journal of School Psychology* 9 (1971): 16-23.

Johnson, Dale D. "The Dolch List Reexamined." *The Reading Teacher* 24 (1971): 449-57.

Johnson, Doris, and Myklebust, Helmer. *Learning Disabilities: Educational Principles and Practices.* New York: Grune & Stratton, 1967.

Karlsen, B.; Madden, R.; and Gardner, E.F. *Stanford Diagnostic Reading Test.* New York: Harcourt, Brace, Jovanovich, 1966.

Kephart, N. *The Slow Learner in the Classroom,* 2d ed. Columbus, Ohio: Charles E. Merrill Publishing Co., 1971.

Kimmell, Geraldine M., and Stahl, J. *The STAP (Screening Test of Auditory Perception).* San Rafael, California: Academic Therapy Publications, 1969.

Kirk, S.; McCarthy, J.P.; and Kirk, W. *The Illinois Test of Psycholinguistic Ability,* rev. ed. Urbana: University of Illinois Press, 1968.

Kirk, S., and Paraskevopoulos, J. *The Development and Psychometric Characteristics of the Revised Selevois. Test of Psycholinguistic Abilities.* Urbana: University of Illinois Press, 1969.

Koppitz, E. *The Bender Gestalt Test for Young Children.* New York: Grune & Stratton, 1964.

_____. "Brain Damage, Reading Disability, and the Bender Gestalt Test." *Journal of Learning Disabilities* (1970) 429-33.

Kucera, H., and Francis, W.N. *Computational Analysis of Present-Day American English.* Providence, Rhode Island: Brown University Press, 1967.

Ladd, Eleanor. "More than Scores from Tests." *Reading Teacher* 24 (1971): 305-11.

Lee, J.M., and Clark, W.W. *Reading Readiness Tests.* Monterey, California: California Test Bureau, 1962.

Leiburt, Robert E., and Sherk, John K. "Three Frostig Visual Perception Subtests and Specific Reading Tasks for Kindergarten, First, and Second Grade Children." *The Reading Teacher* 24 (1970): 130-37.

Lerner, Janet W. *Children With Learning Disabilities: Theories, Diagnosis, and Teaching Strategies.* Boston: Houghton-Mifflin Co., 1971.

Levitt, Edith. "The Effect of Context on the Reading of Retarded and Normal Children at the First-Grade Levels." *Journal of Special Education* 4 (1970): 425-29.

————. "Higher-Order and Lower-Order Reading Responses of Mentally Retarded and Nonretarded Children at the First-Grade Level." *American Journal of Mental Deficiency* 77 (1972): 13-20.

Lindamood, Charles H., and Lindamood, Patricia C. *Auditory Conceptualization (LAC) Test.* Boston: Teaching Resources, 1971.

Livo, Norman J. "Reading Readiness Factors and Beginning Reading Success." *The Reading Teacher* 24 (1970): 124-29; 163.

Lobdell, L.C. "Let's Update the Word List." *Elementary English* 42 (1965): 156-58.

McCracken, R. *Standard Reading Inventory.* Klanath Falls, Oregon: Klanath Printing Co., 1966.

Mecham, M.J., and Rex, J.L. *Picture Speech Discrimination Test.* Provo, Utah: Brigham Young University Press, 1962.

Monroe, Marion, and Backus, Bertie. *Remedial Reading.* Boston: Houghton-Mifflin Co. 1937.

Murphy, Helen, and Durrell, Donald. *Murphy-Durrell Diagnostic Reading Readiness Tests.* New York: Harcourt, Brace, Jovanovich, 1964.

Olson, A.V. "Factor Analytic Studies of the Frostig DTVP." *Journal of Special Education* 2 (1968): 429-33.

————. "The Relation of Achievement Test Scores and Specific Reading Abilities to the Frostig DT of VP." *Perceptual and Motor Skills* 22 (1966A): 179-84.

————. "School Achievement, Reading Ability, and Specific Visual Perception Skills in the Third Grade." *The Reading Teacher* 19 (1966B): 490-92.

Osgood, C.E. "A Behavioristic Analysis of Perception and Language as Cognitive Phenomena." In *Contemporary Approaches to Cognition,* pp. 75-118. Cambridge, Massachusetts: Harvard University Press, 1957.

————. "Toward a Wedding of Insufficiencies." In *Verbal Behavior and General Behavior Theory,* edited by T.R. Dixon and D.L. Horton. Englewood Cliffs, New Jersey: Prentice-Hall, Inc., 1968.

Paletz, Merrill D., and Hirsheren, A. "A Comparison of Two Tests of Visual Sequential Memory Ability." *Journal of Learning Disabilities* 5 (1972): 102-03.

Popp, H. "Visual Discrimination of Alphabet Letters." *The Reading Teacher* 18 (1964): 221-26.

Potter, M.C. "Perception of Symbol Orientation and Early Reading Success." In *Contribution to Education.* Number 939. New York: Columbia University, Teacher's College, 1949.

Rackel, H. Van. "Roswell-Chall Auditory Blending Test." In *The Sixth Mental Measurements Yearbooks,* edited by Oscar K. Buros, p. 114. Highland Park, New Jersey: Gryphon Press, 1965.

Ragland, G.C. "The Performance of Educable Mentally Handicapped Students of Different Reading Abilities on the ITVA." *Dissertation Abstracts* 25 (1964): 3403-408.

Ramanauskas, S. "Oral Reading Errors and Cloze Comprehension of Mentally Retarded Children." Storrs: University of Connecticut, 1970.

Roach, E.G., and Pephart, N.C. *The Purdue Perceptual Motor Survey.* Columbus, Ohio: Charles E. Merrill Publishing Co., 1966.

Rosenberg, S. "Problems of Language Development in the Retarded." *Social-Cultural Aspects of Mental Retardation*, edited by H.C. Haywood, pp. 203-16. New York: Appleton-Century-Crofts, 1970.

Roswell, Florence, and Chall, Jeanne. *The Roswell-Chall Auditory Blending Test.* New York: Essay Press, 1963.

Ryan, Ellen, and Semmel, M. "Reading as a Constructive Language Process." *Reading Research Quarterly* 5 (1969): 59-83.

Ryckman, David B., and Rentfrow, Robert. "The Beery Development Test of Visual Motor Integration: An Investigation of Reliability." *Journal of Learning Disabilities* 4 (1971): 333-34.

Ryckman, David B., and Wiegerink, Ronald. "The Factors of the Illinois Test of Psycholinguistic Abilities: A Comparison of Eighteen Factor Analysis." Exceptional Children 35 (1969): 107-14.

Semmel, M. I., and Bennett, S. M. "Effects of Linguistic Structure and Delay on Memory Span on a Modified Cloze Task." *American Journal of Mental Deficiency* 74 (1970): 681-88.

Shepherd, G. "Selected Factors in the Reading Ability of Educably Mentally Retarded Boys." *American Journal of Mental Deficiency* 71 (1967): 563-70.

Shotick, A. "A Comparative Investigation of the Performance of Mentally Retarded and Normal Boys on Selected Reading Comprehension and Performance Tasks." Doctoral dissertation, Syracuse University, 1960.

Silverstein, A.B. "Variance Components in the DTVP." *Perceptual and Motor Skills* 20 (1965): 973-76.

Silverstein, A.B.; Alfeldt, V.; and Price, E. "Clinical Assessment of Visual Perception Ability in the Mentally Retarded." *American Journal of Mental Deficiency* 74 (1970): 524-26.

Slingerland, Beth. *Screening Tests for Identifying Children with Specific Language Disability.* Cambridge, Massachusetts: Educators Publishing Service, 1967.

Sloan, W. *The Lincoln-Oseretskey Motor Development Scale.* Los Angeles: Western Psychological Services, 1955.

Small, V. H. "Ocular Pursuit Abilities and Reading." Doctoral dissertation, Purdue University, 1958.

Smith, Philip A., and Marx, Ronald W. "Some Cautions on the Use of the Frostig Test: A Factor Analytic Study." *Journal of Learning Disabilities*, 5 (1972): 357-62.

Smith, Robert. *Teacher Diagnosis of Educational Difficulties.* Columbus, Ohio: Charles E. Merrill Publishing Co., 1969.

Spache, George. *Diagnostic Reading Scales.* Monterey: California Test Bureau, 1963.

Sprague, R. "Learning Difficulties of First-Grade Children Diagnosed by *DTVP*." Doctoral dissertation, Wayne State University, 1963.

Sutphin, F.C. *Perceptual Testing-Training Handbook for First-Grade Teachers.* Winter Haven, Florida: Lions Research Foundation, 1967.

Sutton, P.P. *The Relationship of Visual Ability to Reading.* Masters' thesis, University of Illinois, 1963.

Templin, M. *Certain Language Skills in Children.* Minneapolis: University of Minnesota Press, 1957.

Terman, L.M., and Merrill, M.A. *Stanford-Binet Intelligence Scale: Manual for the Third Revision. Form T-B.* Boston: Houghton-Mifflin, 1964.

Thorndike, E.K., and Lorge, I. *The Teacher's Word Book of 30,000 Words.* New York: Columbia University Teacher's College Press, 1944.

Van Alystyne, D. *Van Alystyne Picture Vocabulary Test: 1959 Revision.* New York: World Book, 1969.

Van Hattum, R.J. *New Dimensions for the Speech and Hearing Program in the School: Language and the Retarded Child.* Paper presented at California State Department of Education, November, 1969, at San Diego.

Van Riper, C., and Irwin, J. *Voices and Articulation.* Englewood Cliffs, New Jersey: Prentice-Hall, Inc., 1958.

Vellutino, Frank; De Selto, Louis; and Steger, Joseph. "Categorical Judgment and the *Wepman Test of Auditory Discrimination.*" *Journal of Speech and Hearing Disorders* 37 (1972) : 252-57.

Wechsler, David. *Wechsler Intelligence Scale for Children.* New York: Psychological Corporation, 1949.

Weener, P.; Barritt, L. S.; and Semmel M. I. "A Critical Evaluation of the *Illinois Test of Psychological Abilities.*" *Exceptional Children* 33 (1967) : 373-80.

Wepman, Joseph. "Auditory Discrimination in Speech and Reading." *Elementary English Journal* 60 (1960) : 325-33.

_____. *Auditory Discrimination Test.* Chicago: Language Research Associates, 1958.

Wiseman, D. "A Classroom Procedure for Identifying and Remediating Language Problems." *Mental Retardation* 3 (1965) : 20-23.

Wolfensberger, W. "Correlation between *PPVT* and Achievement Scores among the Retarded." *American Journal of Mental Deficiency* 66 (1962) : 450-51.

Zeamon, D., and House, B. "The Role of Attention in Retardate Discrimination Learning." In *Handbook of Mental Deficiency: Psychological Theory and Research,* edited by N.R. Ellis, pp. 159-223. New York: McGraw-Hill 1963.

SIX

Informal Procedures
and Steps of Assessment

Informal diagnosis is not optional but is very necessary for the teacher because standardized measures will give the teacher all the information that is needed for instruction only very rarely. The present authors have experienced the frustration that results from using formal diagnostic measures or specific assessment measures, such as criterion-referenced tests, only to find that we needed more information after the scores or results were analyzed. When such a problem arises, informal measures or procedures must be utilized in order to develop specific objectives for instruction.

The term *informal* may lead the teacher to feel that this type of assessment does not require skill. This is not the case. A teacher must have great skill in order to develop informal measures. He should be trained thoroughly in employing observation skills, informal reading and reading-related tests, diagnostic or trial teaching lessons, and sequential steps to diagnoses.

OBSERVATIONAL SKILLS

A very important aspect of informal diagnosis is observation of the child's performance.

> Observing involves the intentional and methodical viewing of some object of activity. Observing is more than mere seeing; it entails planned, careful, and focused active attention by the observer.[1]

The point that observation must be planned and focused can not be stressed too strongly. Many teachers observe behavior but do not attempt to develop any systematic analysis of what they observe; consequently, many activities that could give valuable diagnostic information are lost. Observation should be conducted during testing sessions or diagnostic teaching lessons, during the child's free time, during group activities, and during activities involving reading and academic skills.

Much information can be obtained from careful observation of a child during the testing session, but in order to remember the behavior of the child during the session, the teacher should attempt to take notes. An informal checklist of behaviors can be devised by the teacher or clinician in order to gather information without being obvious or interrupting the child's responses.

The way a child responds during the assessment may give the teacher an idea of his learning styles, attitudes, and manners of coping with failure. For example, if a child is constantly giving any answer that occurs to him or asking, "How did I do?" or "Did I fail that one?" he may be expressing a strong fear of failure. (A more thorough analysis of responses of children is included in the section on diagnostic teaching lessons).

What a child does with his free time also is extremely important for purposes of assessment. Such information can be gained only if the teacher allows children time to choose their own unsupervised activities. In this situation, the child's interests and ability to structure his time or environment can be determined from observation. Thus, a teacher should reserve time for observing children in free situations instead of always using such time for planning of activities with other children.

How a child performs in a group situation also may reveal information about his physical, perceptual, linguistic, or personal development. A teacher might find a clue in a child who is very quiet in the classroom but an incessant talker with his friends on the playground. Similarly, if the child is never asked to participate in physical activities, he may be experiencing a gross motor difficulty.

---

[1] Ronald T. Hyman, *Ways of Teaching* (Philadelphia: J.B. Lippincott Co., 1970), p. 256.

Observation of Reading Performance

Observing the child's behavior in relation to reading and academics is an especially important aspect of informal observation. Analyzing activities that are cognitive (e.g., activities on a comprehension level) are easier to analyze than affective responses toward academics, especially reading. Darling (1969) has suggested the use of a taxonomy of affective behavior [i.e., the *Krathwohl Taxonomy* (1964)] as a basis for such observation. The five levels of this taxonomy are: receiving, responding, valuing, organizing, and characterizing. "The continuum extends from a simple awareness on one extreme to complete internalization on the other."[2] How involved a child is in the reading process can be analyzed by the use of the taxonomy and from this analysis, a chart of behaviors can be developed in order to facilitate careful observation. The following chart is an example for the first three levels of the taxonomy. For more information see Darling (1969) and Krathwohl (1964).

Chart 4:   Levels of the Krathwohl Taxonomy[3]

I. Receiving

A. Awareness

1. Does the child appear to attend to the reading task?
2. Does he daydream frequently during the reading lessons?
3. While doing free reading, does he spend much of his time attending to the environment?

B. Willingness to Receive

1. Does he appear interested in the reading activity by responding in some way (e.g., sitting quietly, smiling, etc.)?
2. Does he attend to a task to completion while working in a group?
3. Does he attend to a task to completion while working in a tutorial situation?

[2]David Darling, "Evaluating the Affective Domain of Reading," in *Elementary Reading Instruction*, ed. Althea Beery, Thomas Barrett, and William Powell (Boston: Allyn & Bacon, 1969), p. 304.

[3]*Ibid.*, pp. 135-40. Paraphrased by permission of David Darling and the International Reading Association.

II. Responding

    A. Acquiescence in Responding

        1. Does the child respond orally when asked a question in a group?
        2. Does the child respond orally when asked a question in a tutorial situation?

    B. Willingness to Respond

        1. Does the child volunteer a response in a group?
        2. Does the child volunteer a response in a tutorial situation?
        3. Is the child uncooperative in answering questions or carrying out activities?

III. Valuing

    A. Acceptance of a Value

        1. Does the child obtain satisfaction from reading in any form (e.g., stories, his own writing, books, etc.)?

    B. Preference of a Value

        1. Does the child exhibit a special reading interest?

    C. Commitment of a Value

        1. Does the child choose to read in his free time?
        2. Is the child involved very frequently in a reading activity as a means of obtaining information or recreation?

Observation Systems

Even though observations by the teacher are very important, many times he may need to know to what extent his own interaction with the child is influencing his behaviors in reading. Thus, several formal observation systems have been developed (Fink, 1971; Flanders, 1965; and Werry and Quay, 1969) for this purpose. An impartial observer is required for some of the observation in these measures because if an observer, such as the school psychologist or counselor, is employed, the teacher may discover that his behavior (e.g., facial expression, verbal reprimands, etc.) may be influencing the child's responses during reading sessions.

INFORMAL READING MEASURES

Many informal reading measures have been developed for use by teachers, and there is general agreement among most reading authorities concerning the usefulness of such informal reading tests. However, there is little information concerning the effectiveness of informal reading measures in relation to standardized ones. In addition, criteria for scoring such informal measures as the *Informal Reading Inventory* is conflicting (Kinder, 1969). Finally, developing informal measures that assess reading skills requires that the teacher possess a knowledge of what authorities consider the reading process to be as well as the ability to interpret results of the measures adequately (Kinder, 1969).

Informal Reading Inventory

One of the most popular informal reading tests is the *Informal Reading Inventory (IRI)*. This inventory is a general check done by the teacher to determine the pupil's reading power (Kennedy, 1966). It consists of a series of paragraphs, usually taken from one basal series and arranged in increasing order of difficulty. Basically, the *IRI* helps the teacher determine on what level of reading performance the child is working. As outlined by Betts (1946), these levels include: the independent level, the instructional level, the frustration level, and the probable capacity level.

At the independent level, the child is able to read the material easily in a rhythmical, well-phrased conversational tone, which is free from tension. Comprehension of reading is 90 percent or better. The instructional reading level uses challenging material of which the child is able to comprehend at least 75 percent. There is no more than one word-recognition error per twenty words after silent study at this level. The child is able to read rhythmically in a conversational tone with good phrasing. The frustration level is indicated when the child shows extreme difficulty in reading by exhibiting such symptoms as tension, finger pointing, and withdrawal. His oral reading may show lack of rhythm, meaningless substitutions, trouble with word recognition, or a high pitched voice. Comprehension at this level is usually less than 50 percent. Finally, the probable capacity level or listening level is found by reading to the child and checking his comprehension. This level is indicated by the child's ability to relate experiences to what he hears and to use the vocabulary and language structure of the selection read. The listening comprehension at this level should be approximately 75 percent.

When constructing an *IRI* to be used with educable mentally retarded children, a teacher should observe a certain note of caution. Although the authors are not completely basal-oriented regarding construction for EMR children, we do believe that if a basal series is to be used for some children, an *IRI* on that basal series should be given before the child is placed in it because of the variations in basal series regarding the introduction of vocabulary and concepts.

To build an *IRI*, the teacher should choose a well-graded series of readers which the child has not used previously. The teacher then selects two selections from the first part of each book, starting with the preprimer; one of these selections is to be used for oral reading and the other for silent reading (Kennedy, 1966). Selections from the preprimer through the second reader should contain from sixty to 120 words; for Grades 3 to 6, 100 to 200 words might make up an appropriate selection (Zintz, 1970). The teacher next prepares three to five comprehension questions based on various levels of Barrett's Taxonomy (See Chapter 2). He should avoid questions which can be answered with a "yes" or "no." In addition, he prepares a word list to check sight vocabulary by using every third or fourth word from the word list in the back of the reader and plans a way of checking which is similar to those suggested in manuals of standardized individual reading tests. A code or check sheet will be most useful in this respect (Kennedy, 1966).

Information gained from an *IRI* can be helpful in assigning instructional material for each child (Harris and Smith, 1972). In addition, it can enable the teacher to meet the child at his own level of functioning. The teacher is able to use materials that are at hand and get needed answers quickly. Because the basal series is used, this inventory is probably more valuable in terms of textbook reading than other types of tests (Betts, 1946).

It is important to remember that the *IRI* is only as good as the teacher who administers it (Zintz, 1970). Spache (1964) also has criticized it because reading series are not accurately graded and the reading passages usually are not sufficiently long to allow for an adequate check of comprehension, although this criticism is true with standardized oral reading tests too. The authors believe that prepared comprehension questions do not always reflect the various aspects of comprehension — factual, inferential, judgmental, etc. In addition, if an EMR child cannot read at all, the *IRI* cannot be beneficial. The teacher should realize that the *IRI* does not measure all specific aspects of reading and that it should not be used as the only reading measure.

Cloze Tests

Another informal measure of reading level and comprehension is the cloze technique (Taylor, 1953). This procedure involves selecting a passage of approximately 260-275 words in length on varying levels of difficulty. Words, usually every fifth one, are deleted from the passages. The child then is asked to write in the missing words, and the number of correct responses are changed to percentages. Rankin and Culhane (1969) consider the child to be on the independent reading level if 61 percent or more of the deleted words are correct, on the instructional level if 41 percent or more are correct, and on the frustrational level if 40 percent or fewer are correct.

According to Guszak (1972), this type of measure is rather difficult for students below a fourth-grade reading level to use. This criticism may be true for retarded children readers, especially younger ones, although the technique has been utilized in studies of language and comprehension of the retarded (Ramanauskas, 1970; Semmell, Barrett, and Bennett, 1970). Retarded children appear to have more difficulty with cloze tasks than would be predicted by their mental age. This may be due to a problem related to weak grammatical decoding strategies of retarded children (Semmell, Barrett, and Bennett, 1970).

The cloze procedure appears to correlate with test scores from reading comprehension tests (Bloomer, 1966; Hafner, 1965). Because of the problems of testing reading comprehension, such as testing memory rather than reading comprehension, the cloze procedure also may be used to check comprehension. The procedure has possibilities that are diagnostic in nature if an attempt is made to analyze why a child makes certain errors. For example, errors may be analyzed according to the child's basic linguistic components, cognitive types, and reasoning skills (Hafner, 1965). If a teacher chooses to utilize the cloze technique, he must be aware of the fact that he is tapping more than reading skills when he asks the child to write in the correct answer.

INFORMAL READING AND READING-RELATED TESTS

Informal Checklists

The development of checklists of reading skills by the teacher in order to diagnose and record specific skills that children may be lacking is a useful informal technique. For a checklist, if specific in nature, will allow a teacher to make careful analysis of certain skills. These checklists are constructed more easily in the areas of phonics and structural analysis than in comprehension. Although such taxonomies as Barrett (Clymer, 1968) can be utilized for comprehension.

One basic problem with checklists is that many assume hierarchies of reading skills which are based upon logic rather than research. For example, there is no guarantee that developing auditory discrimination of the short vowel sounds will lead to overall reading achievement for the child.

The teacher should remember that too much reliance on checklists may cause him to stress too heavily the teaching of skills without the application of them. However, used properly these lists can be very diagnostic. An example of a compact list of reading skills is the *Reading Skills Checklist* developed by Guszak (1972).

Other Informal Tests

Another nonstandardized instrument similar in nature to a checklist is *A Psychoeducational Inventory of Basic Learning Abilities* (Valett, 1968). This inventory encompasses more than reading skills. Forty-three learning tasks in the area of gross motor development, sensory-motor integration, perceptual-motor skills, and social skills are included. A five-point rating scale is utilized in determining the skills of the child. Although this inventory can give the teacher a preliminary analysis of the child's problem, still more assessment is needed. In fact, many of the categories do not include enough tasks to make an adequate judgment of the problem areas.

DIAGNOSTIC TEACHING LESSONS

Regardless how extensive the diagnostic tests, formal or informal, may be, there is still much that is the teacher's responsibility to ascertain. Because of need for further assessment, the teacher must be able to develop lessons that teach and test simultaneously.

> Diagnostic teaching is an extension and a continuation of the diagnostic process in which the teacher through careful observation and reporting aids in arriving at a behavioral description of the child's specific difficulties.[4]

Myers and Hammill (1971) have stated two reasons for the use of diagnostic teaching — intrasubject variability and lack of complete test information. Because children's responses vary from day

---

[4]Patricia Myers and Donald Hammill, *Methods of Learning Disorders* (New York: John Wiley & Sons, 1971), p. 71.

to day, testing results obtained during only a short period may not be sufficient to determine a consistent pattern of performance. Tests sample behaviors rather than testing all possible aspects; consequently, there are usually not enough items in a test from which to draw conclusions.

Although the development of diagnostic teaching lessons or trial lessons (Roswell and Natchez, 1965) is no simple matter, one systematic attempt to formalize diagnostic teaching lessons is the *Mills Learning Methods Test* (Mills, 1970). This test includes a series of lessons which teach word recognition according to various methods — visual, auditory, kinesthetic, and combination approach. In it, the assessment of how many words a child learns and retains after a fifteen-minute teaching session is made. The test requires a series of five days of sessions for completion. Based upon the results of the test the child is considered to learn through visual, auditory, kinesthetic, or combination approaches. The manual gives suggestions for teaching recognition of those words used in the test, utilizing various methods. Although the procedure is a good example of steps that can be taken in diagnostic teaching lessons, the test has certain limitations, one of which is that the visual and auditory methods are not purely visual or auditory but a combination of visual *and* auditory; however, as has been stated previously, it is very difficult to obtain a unimodal presentation. In addition, the appropriateness of certain procedures in teaching the words through various other methods has been questioned. For example, drawing boxes around the words in the visual approach has been cited as only adding extraneous material that may not be beneficial in learning a word (Durkin, 1970).

In order to develop diagnostic teaching lessons, a teacher must be able to decide what types of information are needed and then find ways of obtaining this information. This task requires the ability to ask specific questions and the ability to analyze educational tasks. Task analysis thus is a behavioral approach to diagnosis (Bateman, 1966; Bateman, 1966-67; Johnson, 1967). About the behavioral task-analysis approach, Bateman states:

> In this behavioristic task-analysis approach there is a relative emphasis on assumed processes within the child and more emphasis on what specific educational tasks he needs to be taught. A related emphasis is placed on analyzing the tasks into their component sequential steps.[5]

---

[5]Barbara Bateman, "Three Approaches to Diagnosis for Children with Learning Disabilities," *Academic Therapy* 2 (1966-1967): 219.

Criterion-referenced questions enable the teacher to analyze specific skills in reading, and they should be the first step in developing a diagnostic teaching lesson. Objectives included in the *Instructional Objectives Exchange* (Popham, 1970) can aid the teacher in developing behavioral objectives. The following sentence is an example of such an objective. "Given a word orally and a list of four other words, the student will identify the word on the list having the same initial three-letter consonant blend as the one given orally."[6] Teachers should be skilled in writing clear, concise objectives. Excellent sources that explain the process of preparing behavioral objectives are Mager (1962) and Vargas (1972).

The behavioral task-analysis approach works best with specific reading skills, such as structural analysis; however, consideration of reading task as unitary skills is presumptuous. Many abilities are being measured while requesting the child to "give the sound of the consonant letter." An assessment which assumes to tap "single functions" may be far from diagnostic (Keogh, 1971, 546). The recording of whether a child has mastered or failed a task gives no information concerning how the child arrived at his answer (Keogh, 1971). Therefore, the learning strategies and the modalities of the child should be considered as well as specific skills. Although modality teaching is still controversial, the present authors feel that children possess different manners or styles of learning. Thus, a diagnostic teaching lesson should include an analysis of the types of responses of children and the modes of presentations of skills.

Johnson has explained her system of task analysis in the following way:

> By analysis of the nature of a task, considering the expected mode of response and the processes necessary to complete it, and then noting a child's performance, a teacher can learn a great deal about the learning disability and areas to remediate.[7]

Johnson (1967) added that through this procedure the teacher will focus on processes as well as subject matter. An analysis of tasks according to Johnson (1967) includes:

1. Is the task intrasensory or intersensory? For example, if the child is asked to circle the letter *t* after the teacher pronounces the sound/t/, he is using motor integration as well as auditory perception.

---

[6]James W. Popham, *Reading K-3, K-6, K-12* (Los Angeles: Institutional Material Exchange, 1970), p. 2.

[7]Doris J. Johnson, "Educational Principles for Children with Learning Disabilities," *Rehabilitation Literature* 28 (1967): 317-22.

2. An analysis of the sensory modalities, auditory, visual, or tactile should be made.
3. An analysis of the presentation, verbal or nonverbal, (e.g., visual) is concluded.
4. The level of the task should be analyzed. Johnson employs the levels perception, memory, symbolization, or conceptualization. Other hierarchies could be considered, such as those developed by Osgood (1957), Bloom (1956) or Gagne (1964).

Gagné (1964) has arranged these forms of behavior in a hierarchy from the simple to the complex. Gagne has stated:

> ... The major reason for doing this is to indicate that the *learning conditions* for the more complex forms may be described most clearly if the *preconditions* are first identified. In fact, these preconditions constitute one of the most important things that can be said about the learning of these kinds of behaviors. The hierarchy of behaviors has this appearance:

The learning of

Problem-Solving and *Strategy-Using*

require the prelearning of:

Principles

which require the prelearning of:

Concepts

which require the prelearning of:

Associations

which require the prelearning of:

Chains

which require the prelearning of:

Identifications

which require the prelearning of:

Responses[8]

---

[8]Robert Gagné, "The Implications of Instructional Objectives for Learning," in *Defining Educational Objectives*, ed. M. Lindvall (Pittsburgh, Pennsylvania: University of Pittsburgh Press, 1964), p. 45.

5. The expected mode of responses of the child is another important task analysis.

In developing a diagnostic teaching lesson, the teacher must analyze previous information gathered from formal and informal tests or observations. For example, the teacher may have observed that a child has some difficulty with discimination of short vowel sounds. He then designs a series of lessons that will teach this discrimination as well as analyze the tasks outlined by Johnson (1967).

The steps of a diagnostic teaching lesson are illustrated in Chart 5.

Chart 5: A Diagnostic Teaching Lesson[9]

I. Objectives Written in Behavioral Terms

II. Analysis of Task Presentation

    A. Manner of presentation — auditory, visual, tactile-kinesthetic, or combinations

    B. Content analysis (The specific nature of the content should be noted. See Adamson and Van Etten, 1970 for a discussion of content analysis.

    C. Environment — one-to-one or group presentation

III. Analysis of Pupil Performance

    A. Modality

        1. Intrasensory — visual or auditory (very rare to obtain unimodal response)

        2. Intersensory — auditory-motor integration or visual-motor integration

    B. Process-receptive — integrative (associative) and expressive

    C. Level of Response (Johnson, Gagné, Bloom, etc.)

    D. Affective Response

IV. Results of Lessons and Remarks (This would include how the child performed on the tasks as well as his behavior during the task)

---

[9]Many parts of the preceding chart were influenced by Doris J. Johnson, "Educational Principles for Children with Learning Disabilities," *Rehabilitation Literature* 28 (1967): 318-19, by permission of the journal.

Based upon results of a trial lesson, a teacher may find it necessary to teach several such lessons in order to determine a consistent pattern. The present authors feel that diagnosis is not sufficient without the inclusion of diagnostic teaching lessons. The development of these lessons requires that a clinician work in the classroom as well as in the "testing booth." More importantly, it mandates a very skilled teacher because he will bear most of the responsibility of developing, conducting, and evaluating these lessons. Chapter Ten contains examples of diagnostic teaching lessons.

Steps in Diagnosis

If the diagnostician or classroom teacher utilizes diagnostic teaching, there may be a first step, but there should not be a final step until the child leaves the program. Because diagnosis is continual and ongoing, the teacher should be modifying his program based upon new information constantly. Every lesson is part of the assessment. If a teacher is trained to "field" problems, he will be able to assess the student's needs as well as the materials and methods used in the program (Hammill, 1971). Unfortunately, due to lack of training, teachers too often blindly follow programs regardless of their effectiveness. If a diagnosis is to be effective, it *must not end* after the preliminary assessment is made.

Inquiry Based Diagnosis: Diagnosis of reading problems is a problem-solving or inquiry approach. Therefore, thorough understanding of what is involved in diagnosis through the inquiry method can aid the teacher in making better instructional decisions.

Goldmark (1968) has given a very adequate development of the components of inquiry which the authors will relate to reading skills in the following passages. An important part of the inquiry method is the process of asking questions. If a problem is felt to exist (e.g., in the area of reading), the teacher asks specific questions, such as, "Does the child know the consonant sounds?" He uses the tools, such as a phonics survey, available in solving his problem. Questions may be on various levels. For example, if the teacher asks the question, "What letter sounds does the child know?" he is asking a question at the *descriptive* or *substantive* level. This type of questioning is typical of criterion-referenced tests. However, if the teacher asks, "Why doesn't the child know the letter sound?" he is searching for a general principle or rule which can be applied. This is a question which often may be asked if a teacher is interested in modalities. These "why" questions are asked in search of a *criteria* that can be applied to a judgment. An even higher level of questioning asks "Why this law, rule, or principle?"[10] At this point, the teacher may ask if there is value in testing for modalities. The answer is that this level of questioning is very important because it allows the special-education teacher to continually search for the *assumptions* involved with techniques such as modality testing. Because of it, he may ask, "Is there research to substantiate the testing of modalities?"

The final step of questioning is what Goldmark calls "inquiry into inquiry."[11] At this step, the teacher questions his own steps in diagnosis. For example, he may ask, "Why have I chosen to use standardized tests rather than informal measures?" Thus, in order for diagnosis to be a continual, effective process, the teacher must investigate his own diagnostic procedures. In summary, Goldmark has presented a definition of inquiry:

> Inquiry is a reflexive, patterned search, which takes questions from the *substantive* level, to the *criteria* level, to the value and *assumption* level, where new assumptions can be posed and new alternatives constructed.[12]

Process of Inquiry: An important part of inquiry is the process or steps involved in questioning. Beyer (1971, p. 50) presents a model of the process of inquiry developed for social studies. This model can also be used effectively in reading diagnosis.

The narrative of this chart in Figure 12 may help the teacher in understanding the process of reading diagnosis as the authors of this book view it.

The Problem

Becoming Aware of the Problem: Several approaches have been used to determine the severity of a reading problem. Most often, a child is said to have difficulty in reading if there is a discrepancy between his reading potential and actual reading level. Although the capacity of the child is usually equated with his intelligence and/or mental age, one should be cautious in using one single factor, such as intelligence, as a predictor of reading potential (Cawley, Goldstein, and Burrow, 1972). In addition the relationship between

---

[10]Bernice Goldmark, *Social Studies: A Method of Inquiry* (Belmont, California: Wadsworth Publishing Co., 1968), p. 4.

[11]*Ibid.*, p. 5.

[12]*Ibid.*, p. 7.

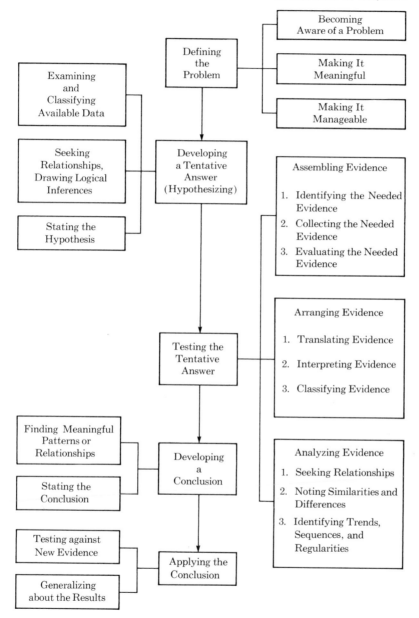

Figure 12: The Process of Inquiry[13]

[13]Berry Beyer, *Inquiry in the Social Studies Classroom: A Strategy for Teaching* (Columbus, Ohio: Charles E. Merrill Publishing Co., 1971), p. 50. Reprinted by permission of the publisher.

IQ and reading achievement is not clear, especially in populations of lower intelligence (Quay, 1963). For instance, several studies have actually found retarded children to be performing above their mental age in reading (Kirk, 1964).

Many formulae have been developed in order to determine the child's reading expectancy. Those developed by Harris (1970) and Bond and Tinker (1967) are used quite often. Although Harris considers intelligence to be an important factor in determining reading potential, he includes other factors, such as visual and auditory perception, which tend to develop with age. Because of this factor, his formula includes chronological age as well as mental age:

$$\text{Reading Expectancy Age} = \frac{2MA \ x \ CA}{3}$$

By doubling the MA, Harris gives priority to intelligence. A reading quotient is obtained by the following formula:

$$\text{Reading Expectancy Quotient} = \frac{RA^* \ x \ 100.}{R \ Exp \ A}$$

If a child's quotient falls within 90 and 110, he has no severe problem.

Bond and Tinker (1967) have included the number of years in school plus another year that accounts for the grade score given to the child when he entered Grade 1. According to them, reading expectancy is determined by the following formula:

$$(\text{Years in School x IQ} = 1.0).$$

This formula is rather unrealistic for use in determining expectancies of children who are not within the normal range of intelligence (Guszak, 1972).

Another approach utilized for estimating the child's reading potential is to measure his listening comprehension (Durost, 1962; Durrell, 1955; Harris, 1970; Ladd, 1971; and Spache, 1963). With this method, the assumption is made that if a child can understand the material that is read to him, he has the potential to read it himself (Guszak, 1972; Ladd, 1970). Such formal tests of listening com-

---

*Reading age is obtained by adding 5.2 years to the present reading level of the child. This is to account for a 5.2 year difference between the grade level and age of the child (age of entry to school is 6.2).

prehension include: the *Durrell Listening-Reading Series* (1969); the *Spache Diagnostic Reading Scales* (1963); the *McCracken Standard Reading Inventory* (1966). The *Metropolitan Reading Achievement Tests* (Durost, 1962) suggest testing for understanding by reading aloud to the child all the items and possible answers as he reads silently. An equivalent form, which the child reads without assistance, then is given. If the child receives a substantially higher score on the first test, his potential may be higher than his present reading level. Thus, informal reading inventories may be used as informal measures of listening comprehension.

The main criticism of reading formulae or procedures being used to estimate a child's reading potential is that the amount of retardation depends upon the formula or procedure that is used to determine it (Reed, 1970; Simmons and Shapiro, 1968). Thus, a child's potential may vary according to the formula used. Because of this problem and the fact that IQ is not a good single predictor of reading potential, Reed (1970) has suggested that potential is related more to the materials and/or approaches used with the child than to the child's actual ability. Many factors should be considered in determining the severity of a reading problem (Cawley, Goodstein, and Burrow, 1972), some of which include: the response of the child to the reading materials and tasks being presented; the attitude and background of the child; and the background, skills, and experiences of the teacher.

Determining the problem in this manner requires skillful observation on the part of the teacher and experience in using different reading methods and approaches. The problem should not be defined merely in terms of whether the child is reading to potential, but, rather, on other cognitive and affective characteristics of the child. Some of these characteristics will be discussed in a later section.

Making the Problem Meaningful and Manageable: In diagnosing reading difficulties of the retarded, a teacher must be able to understand the nature of the problem. If a teacher is to be expected to establish an instructional program for the child, he must define the problem in educational terms. Although this requirement does not completely eliminate medical diagnosis, much of clinical findings, such as those based upon etiology (e.g., mongolism), may not make the problem any more meaningful for the teacher. Educational diagnosis in the areas of reading skills or related correlates gives more vital information to the teacher that is needed for instruction.

DEVELOPING A TENTATIVE ANSWER (HYPOTHESIZING)

After a teacher determines that problems exist, he will want to know the exact nature of those problems and what he can do about them. This being the case, it will be necessary for him to formulate hypotheses. Beyer has defined an hypothesis as:

> . . . an educated guess — a statement of a possible answer, solution, or alternative that is derived from the learner's past experience and his quick analysis of the present, available data. Hypothesis is an inductive process — that is, it involves working with separate, often, disparate, bits of information and coming up with (inferring) a general statement which apparently explains the proper relationship between all that information and any additional, but as yet unavailable, relevant data. A hypothesis reaches beyond the evidence from which it is derived.[14]

Considerable skill is required in order for a teacher to make appropriate hypotheses regarding the nature of a child's reading difficulties. Because hypothesizing is basically an inductive process, the teacher must be able to adequately collect all available data.

Examining and Classifying the Data

In the first step of inquiry, defining the problem, the teacher made use of observational skills. However, this observation was accomplished at random or simply as a collection of bits and pieces of information. In developing a tentative answer, these observations must be classified and related to learning problems. In addition, the teacher will want to examine additional *unavailable* data and classify it. Such data will consist of information regarding: past educational experiences of the child; home or environmental background; and physical, social, and psychological development. A few teachers of educable mentally retarded children are fortunate enough to be part of interdisciplinary teams where such information already is completed, but if such data is not accessible, the process of establishing sound hypotheses becomes more tedious. One solu-

---

[14]*Ibid.*, p. 38.

tion may be for the teacher to become aware of referral agencies on the state and local level. Regardless of the limited amount of information a teacher might obtain, he still develops a hypothesis about the child's problems, realizing the limitations of his tentative answers.

Seeking Relationships, Drawing Logical Inferences

After examining and classifying data, the teacher attempts to seek relationships among the evidence and matches the separate fragments of data to each other in order to reach a possible explanation of the problem. For example, if a medical record reports a chronic illness of the child, if the school attendance record shows repeated absences — especially in the earlier grades, and if certain basic reading skills are lacking, the teacher may infer that illness is a major contributor to the reading problem. Thus, a number of relationships may be made, with the teacher designating one problem as primary. On the other hand, the teacher may isolate numerous problems, such as emotional maladjustment, perceptual problems, or inadequate instruction, and all of these problems may be a basis for stating hypotheses.

Stating the Hypothesis

Once inferences are drawn, they become possible explanations or hypotheses which can serve as guides for further investigation (Beyer, 1971). In order for a hypothesis to be an effective tool, it should be recorded in explicit terms. To hypothesize that a child's reading problem is caused by physical defects lacks conciseness; however, to state that auditory perception is contributing to the child's inability to learn phonics generalizations makes the hypothesis more manageable educationally for the teacher. Nonetheless, although such a statement is more concise, it is still only an "educated guess" and should be considered tentative, for it has been based on fragments of information and provides only a guide for further inquiry. Too often, professionals involved in diagnosis have been guilty of considering the hypothesis as the final step. For example, designing educational programs for children on the basis of two hours of psychological testing is erroneous. Such programs often fail because they do not take into consideration that the initial diagnosis was fragmentary and incomplete. Thus, the hypothesis is transferred to fact very hastily or without allowing room for its being tested.

TESTING THE TENTATIVE ANSWER

Since tentative hypotheses have been formed on the basis of available evidence, it now becomes necessary to take these hypotheses and assemble, arrange, and analyze additional information which can be gained from the testing process (Beyer, 1971). This means going from the general hypothesis back to the particulars through the process of deduction. Such a process is the key to diagnosis of clinical teaching.

Assembling, Arranging, and Analyzing Evidence

The teacher is first concerned with what additional information must be collected in order to test the hypotheses. Depending upon the nature of the hypotheses, the information then can be assembled and analyzed. For example, if the teacher hypothesizes that auditory blending problems are causing difficulty with phonics generalizations, he could assemble additional information on this hypothesis by administering one or more standardized auditory blending tests, conducting diagnostic teaching lessons, making further observations on materials used, and using checklists. These techniques should constantly be evaluated as they are used, and the data should be arranged in some meaningful way. To accomplish this, the teacher could make a profile on the child, look for various patterns within it, and then analyze the new information in it. For example, the child may have no problems in blending consonant sounds but problems in blending vowel sounds. Thus, with this information, the teacher can form relationships and discover similarities and differences. This type of testing for tentative answers cannot be compiled in one day. It is a continual search for answers to find trends; therefore, it is an ongoing process.

DEVELOPING A CONCLUSION

The ultimate goal of inquiry is to develop a conclusion. In order for such a conclusion to be educationally significant, the teacher must determine what meaningful relationship it has to the child's reading achievement. Because there is considerable controversy between the relationship of some correlates and reading achievement, the teacher must utilize evidence that he sees as being related most directly to the problem. Stating a conclusion that is related to reading achievement must be based upon his own philosophy of the reading process. For example, where one teacher may choose to state that the child has a visual perception difficulty that is limiting his reading process, another teacher may develop conclusions which are only descriptive in nature (e.g., limited sight vocabulary). Chapters Eight and Nine contain discussions on different philosophies of instruction.

APPLYING A CONCLUSION

"No conclusion may be considered final or definitive until it has been checked against all the relevant data."[15] Because of all the variables involved in reading instruction, no conclusions can be considered to be definitely final. Although the teacher must select materials or approaches that may fit his conclusions, it is necessary that he constantly evaluate the child's reactions. If no progress occurs, the teacher must return to step of developing a tentative answer in the inquiry process.

SUMMARY

Informal diagnosis of reading achievement requires that the teacher be skilled in techniques of observation and analysis of reading tasks, for every reading lesson is part of the total diagnostic or clinical teaching process. Inquiry or problem-solving procedures prevent the teacher or diagnostician from planning programs that are based upon insufficient knowledge or data. If a teacher follows inquiry process, he will be evaluating constantly the effectiveness of any program he implements.

REFERENCES

Adamson, Gary, and Van Etten, Carleen. "Prescribing via Analysis and Retrieval of Instructional Materials in the Educational Modulation Center." *Exceptional Children* 36 (1970): 531-37.

Bateman, Barbara. "Learning Disorders." *Review of Educational Research* 33 (1966): 93.

---

[15]*Ibid.*, p. 47.

_____. "Three Approaches to Diagnosis for Children with Learning Disabilities." *Academic Therapy* 2 (1966-1967): 215-22.

Betts, E.A. *Foundations of Reading Instruction.* New York: American Book Co., 1946.

Beyer, Barry. *Inquiry in the Social Studies Classroom: A Strategy for Teaching.* Columbus, Ohio: Charles E. Merrill Publishing Co., 1971.

Bloom, Benjamin S., editor. *Taxonomy of Educational Objectives Handbook I: Cognitive Domain.* New York: David McKay Co., 1956.

Bloomer, R.H. *Nonovert Reinforced Cloze Procedure.* Project Number 2245. Washington, D.C.: United States Department of Health, Education, and Welfare Office of Education, 1966.

Bond, Guy, and Tinker, Miles A. *Reading Difficulties: Their Diagnosis and Correction,* 2d ed. New York: Appleton-Century-Crofts, 1967.

Cawley, J.F.; Goodstein, H.A.; and Burrow, W.H. *The Slow Learner and the Reading Problem.* Springfield, Illinois: Charles C. Thomas Co., 1972.

Clymer, Theodore. "The Barett-Taxonomy-Cognitive and Affective Dimensions of Reading Comprehension." In *Innovation and Change in Reading Instruction: Sixty-seventh Yearbook og the National Society for the Study of Education, Part H,* edited by Helen M. Robinson, pp. 19-23. Chicago: University of Chicago Press, 1968.

Darling, David. "Evaluating the Affective Domain of Reading." In *Elementary Reading Instruction,* edited by Althea Beery, Thomas Barrett, and William Powell, pp. 303-10. Boston: Allyn & Bacon Co., 1969.

Durkin, Delores. *Teaching Them All to Read.* Boston: Allyn & Bacon Co., 1970.

Durost, W. N. *Metropolitan Manual for Interpreting.* New York: Harcourt, Brace, Jovanovich, 1962.

Durrell, Donald. *Durrell Analysis of Reading Difficulty.* New York: Harcourt, Brace, Jovanovich, 1955.

_____. *The Durrell Listening-Reading Series.* New York: Harcourt, Brace, Jovanovich, 1969.

Fink, Albert H. *Fink Interaction Analysis System.* Paper presented at the meeting of the American Educational Research Association, February 1971, in New York City.

Flanders, N.A. *Teacher Influence, Pupil Attitudes, and Achievement.* Washington, D.C.: US Government Printing Office, 1965.

Gagné, Robert. "The Implications of Instructional Objectives for Learning." In *Defining Educational Objectives,* edited by M. Lindvall. Pittsburgh: University of Pittsburgh Press, 1964.

Goldmark, Bernice. *Social Studies: A Method of Inquiry.* Belmont, California: Wadsworth Publishing Co., 1968.

Guszak, Frank J. *Diagnostic Reading Instruction in the Elementary School.* New York: Harper & Row, Publisher, 1972.

Hafner, L. "Importance of Cloze." In *The Philosophical and Social Bases for Reading 14th Yearbook,* edited by E.T. Thurstone and L.E. Hafner. Milwaukee, Wisconsin: National Reading Conference, 1965.

Hammill, Donald. "Evaluating Children for Instructional Purposes." *Academic Therapy* 6 (1971): 341-53.

Harris, Albert. *How to Increase Reading Ability,* 5th ed. New York: David McKay Co., 1970.

Harris, Larry, and Smith, Carl B. *Reading Instruction through Diagnostic Teaching.* New York: Holt, Rinehart, & Winston, 1972.

Hyman, Ronald T. *Ways of Teaching.* Philadelphia: J.B. Lippincott Co., 1970.

Johnson, Doris J. "Educational Principles for Children with Learning Disabilities." *Rehabilitation Literature* 28 (1967): 317-22.

Keogh, Barbara. "A Compensatory Model for Psycho-educational Evaluation of Children with Learning Disorders." *Journal of Learning Disabilities* 4 (1971): 544-48.

Kennedy, Eddie C. *Essentials in Teaching Reading.* Parsons, West Virginia: McClain Printing Co., 1966.

Kinder, Joseph. "How Useful Are Informal Reading Tests?" *In Elementary Reading Instruction: Selected Materials,* edited by Althea Beery, Thomas Barrett, and William Powell. Boston: Allyn & Bacon Co., 1969.

Kirk, Samuel. "Research in Education." In *Mental Retardation: A Review of Research,* edited by H.A. Stevens and P. Heber, pp. 57-99. Chicago: University of Chicago Press, 1964.

Krathwohl, David R.; Bloom, Benjamin; and Bertram, B. *Taxonomy of Educational Objectives: Handbook II. Affective Domain.* New York: David McKay Co., 1964.

Ladd, E. "More than a Score of Tests." *The Reading Teacher* 24 (1971): 305-11.

Mager, R. *Preparing Instructional Objectives.* Palo Alto, California: Fearon Publishers, 1962.

McCracken, Robert A. *Standard Reading Inventory.* Klamath Falls, Oregon: Klamath Printing Co., 1966.

Mills, Robert E. *Learning Methods Test.* Fort Lauderdale, Florida: Mills Center, 1956.

Myers, Patricia, and Hammill, Donald. *Methods of Learning Disorders.* New York: John Wiley & Sons, 1969.

Osgood, C.E. *Motivational Dynamics of Language Behavior: Nebraska Symposium on Motivation.* Lincoln: University of Nebraska Press, 1957.

Popham, James W. *Reading K-3, K-6, K-12.* Los Angeles: Instructional Material Exchange, 1970.

Quay, Herbert. "Academic Skills," In *Handbook for Mental Deficiency,* edited by Norman Ellis. New York: McGraw-Hill Book Co., 1963.

Ramanauskas, S. *Oral Reading Errors and Cloze Comprehension of Mentally Retarded Children.* Storrs: University of Connecticut, 1970. Reported in Cawley, John; Goodstein, Henry; and Burrow, Will H. *The Slow Learner and the Reading Problem.* Springfield, Illinois: Charles C. Thomas Co., 1972.

Rankin, E.F., and Culhane, J.W. "Comparable Cloze and Multiple-Choice Comprehension Test Scores. *Journal of Reading* 13 (1969): 193-98.

Reed, James C. "The Deficits of Retarded Readers—Fact or Artifact?" *The Reading Teacher* 23 (1970): 347-52.

Roswell, Florence, and Natchez, Gladys. *Reading Disability: Diagnosis and Treatment.* New York: Basic Books, Inc., 1964.

Semmel, M.I.; Barrett, L.; and Bennett, S. "Performance of EMR and Nonretarded Children on a Modified Cloze Task." *American Journal of Mental Deficiency* 74 (1970): 681-88.

Simmons, G.A. and Shapiro, P.J. "Reading Expectancy Formulas: A Warning Note." *Journal of Reading* 11 (1968): 626-29.

Spache, George. *Diagnostic Reading Scales.* Monterey: California Test Bureau, 1963.

_____. *Reading in the Elementary School.* Boston: Allyn & Bacon, 1964.

Taylor, W.L. "Cloze Procedure: A New Tool for Measuring Reliability." *Journalism Quarterly* 30 (1953): 415-33.

Valett, Robert. *A Psychoeducational Inventory of Basic Learning Abilities.* Belmont, California: Fearon Publishers, 1968.

Vargus, Julie. *Writing Worthwhile Behavioral Objectives.* New York: Harper & Row, Publishers, 1972.

Werry, John S., and Quay, Herbert C. "Observing the Classroom Behavior of Elementary School Children." *Exceptional Children* 35 (1969): 461-70.

Zintz, Miles. *The Reading Process: The Teacher and the Learner.* Dubuque, Iowa: William C. Brown Co., 1970.

SEVEN

Developmental Reading Approaches and Skills

Matching instructional materials and approaches to the needs of children is a vital educational process, in which the classroom teacher plays an important role. As he should with diagnostic procedures, the teacher should be very skilled in the selection and evaluation of instructional techniques and commercially prepared materials. However, the processes of evaluating instructional materials and methods may not be as systematic as it could be. For example, in some instances, teachers select materials on the basis of suggestions from other teachers or from the advertisements of commercial vendors (Drew and Martinson, 1971). This informal means of disseminating information and assessing the efficacy of materials and methods is an insufficient one in many cases for meeting the specific learning abilities of children.

One of the questions about materials most frequently asked by special education teachers is: "What reading series would be the best for my classroom?" There is no answer to this question at the present time, and perhaps, never will be. There is no agreement among authorities as to what approach works best with a particular child or groups of children; "there seems to be no definitive support for asserting the superiority of one method over another."[1]

In reviewing the results of their first grade reading studies, Bond and Dykstra (1967) have suggested that teachers utilize a diagnostic approach to teaching reading and combinations of approaches rather than one method taught in isolation. But if a teacher is to use a diagnostic approach, the selection of appropriate strategies for an individual child depends upon a thorough assessment of the child *and* the materials available. This point cannot be stressed too strongly, for how a teacher views the effectiveness of a method or materials may actually influence the achievement of children with whom he uses these materials (Bogatz, 1971). For example, utilization of a material based solely upon the expectancies of what it *should* do for a certain group or "type" of child is a very superficial manner of selection. On this point Johnson and Kress (1971) have stated:

> Perhaps the basic guideline is this: preconceived notions about children and school programs cannot guide the learning process. Only actual observation of each child and honest searching for the best use of the assets as a stepping stone for further learning can be an adequate guide for his program.[2]

CRITERIA FOR SELECTION OF INSTRUCTIONAL MATERIALS AND APPROACHES

Educators have been attempting to answer the question of what criteria a teacher should use in the selection of materials to meet individual needs in the area of reading for some time. The most popular manner for investigating the effectiveness of materials has been the comparison of one method with another one, usually using groups of children for the experiment. This approach does not necessarily provide information that will be beneficial for a teacher who chooses to teach diagnostically though, for in such comparison, it is very difficult to define how one approach is truly different from another. Most methods contain similar elements, such as the teaching of the alphabet, comprehension, structural analysis, or word

---

[1]M.C. Sitko; D.C. Semmel; G. Wilcone; and M.I. Semmell, "The Relationship of Word and Sentence Association of EMR Children to Reading Performance" (Bloomington: University of Indiana Center for Innovation in Teaching the Handicapped, School of Education, 1972), p. 2.

[2]M.S. Johnson and Roy A. Kress, "Matching Children and Programs," *The Reading Teacher* 255 (1971): 442.

recognition. In addition, comparison studies do not reveal the strong or weak points of a program (Engelmann, 1967). Therefore, the results of the studies often yield little information that will aid the teacher in developing materials for the individual child.

Systematic Analysis

Because so many new materials and methods are being introduced in the field, it is becoming more important that the teacher have the *skills* necessary to evaluate materials and approaches rather than merely the knowledge of what all these materials are. To insure that teachers have such skills, some systematic attempts to evaluate instruction and materials have been developed (Armstrong, 1969; Bogatz, 1971; Drew and Martinson, 1971; Lazar, 1970). Also, one step toward evaluation of materials and the dissemination of information has come through the development of the federally-funded Special Education Instructional Materials Centers (SEIMC) in various locations across the country. One purpose of these centers is the development of systematic assessment of instructional materials. One such model for the ongoing assessment of instructional methods and materials is presented in Figure 13 on p. 172.

This model is very similar to the inquiry model presented in Chapter Six in that the teacher constantly is establishing and testing hypotheses about the needs of the child and the types of materials and methods that would meet these needs. If a teacher has specific objectives in mind when utilizing a particular technique or material, effectiveness can be determined by whether or not these objectives are met. In addition, the teacher will be better able to develop his own materials and procedures and avoid the trap of selecting materials without any specific objectives for using the material or procedures.

The decision to select a particular material should be made as systematically as the selection of instructional objectives and the actual assessment itself. An analysis of the manner of presentation (e.g., auditory, visual, tactile-kinesthetic) and the content of the material are two important factors to consider. Drew and Martinson, (1971, p. 119) have suggested other criteria: reading level, concept introduction level, interest level, amount of review, stimulus complexity, construction durability, illustration quality, initial and ongoing cost, supplementary activities, storage requirements, and relevance to urban and rural children.

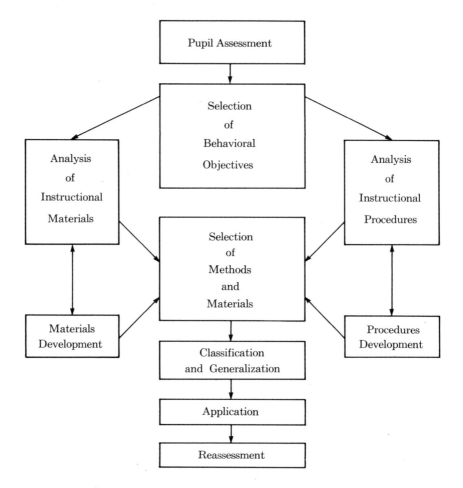

Figure 13:   Model for Ongoing Assessment of Instructional
Materials[3]

Lazar (1970) has also developed a very systematic procedure
for the analysis of reading tasks. As does Armstrong (1969), he
begins his procedure with the assessment of children's needs.
Highlights of his procedure are:

---

[3]Jenny R. Armstrong, "Teaching An Ongoing Process of Assessing, Selecting, and Developing, Generalizing, Applying, and Reassessing." *Education and Training for the Mentally Retarded* 4 (1960): 168. Reprinted by
permission of the Council for Exceptional Children and the author.

1. The development of individual and group profiles
2. Construction of instructional objectives
3. Establishment of criterion for success
4. Short-range and long-term objectives and assessments
5. Evaluation of methods to be used in terms of individual, small-group, or total-group involvement
6. Evaluation based on self-evaluation, joint evaluation, and evaluation by others — perhaps resource personnel

In Lazar's procedure, if the program selected proves to be successful, it is continued; if it is not, the process starts again with reassessment of the needs and skills of the children.

In summary, if the teacher has an adequate knowledge of the needs of his children and criteria for evaluating the effectiveness of materials and methods, he should be more competent in individualizing instruction.

SPECIFIC READING APPROACHES

A presentation of reading methods, approaches, and materials utilized in developmental reading are included in this chapter as is some of the research related to these programs. Most of the investigation has been in the form of comparison studies and, as was stated in the introduction, the results of such comparison studies will not necessarily aid the teacher in prescribing materials and approaches for the individual child. Any teacher or supervisor who is developing a reading program for retarded children must realize there is *no one best approach or one panacea* for the development of reading skills. Before the selection of any program is made, an assessment of the skills and learning styles of the children should be considered.

Most developmental reading approaches have been used with retarded children. However, there are some approaches, techniques, and methods that have been designed specifically for special reading problems. These will be discussed in Chapter Eight. Those under discussion in this chapter are *simply applicable* to retarded children.

Basal Reader Approach

The basal reader approach, a highly organized method of teaching reading, is used by over 95 percent of the primary teachers and over

90 percent of the intermediate-grade teachers in the school systems in the United States (Austin and Morrison, 1963). With this approach, the use of a graded series of basic reading textbooks and teacher's manuals serve as the core of the program. The series starts in the first grade with reading readiness materials, such as charts, word cards, ditto sheets, games, audiovisual materials, and usually continues through Grade 8. Such books as preprimers, first readers, and the "big book," which is a large reproduction of the first few stories in the first preprimers, are included in the program for the first year.

Some important characteristics of this type of program are: a controlled vocabulary, especially in the early grades, and an organized, sequential, and logical system of teaching the reading skills (Dechant, 1964).

According to Wilson and Hall (1972), basal readers have several advantages:

1. They provide a carefully graded set of materials with a systematic progression of difficulty in vocabulary and reading skills.
2. The vocabulary is carefully controlled in beginning readers to promote success in the initial stages, although this control is not necessarily considered an advantage by all authorities.
3. The skills of both decoding and comprehension are stressed.
4. They are colorful and attractive and contain numerous illustrations.
5. Teachers can simultaneously use materials of various levels of difficulty for the pupils who are working at different levels in the same class.
6. The detailed teacher's guides contain clear explanations of the total reading procedure and step-by-step outlines for each lesson.
7. The accompanying manuals provide numerous suggestions for enriching the total reading program used in a class.
8. Basal readers save teacher time and effort with the readily available books, workbooks, and other supplementary materials.[4]

On the other hand several authors (Heilman, 1972; Kerfoot, 1965; Niemeyer, 1965; Wilson and Hall, 1972) have cited weaknesses of the approach:

---

[4]From Robert M. Wilson and MaryAnne Hall, *Reading and the Elementary School Child* (New York: Van Nostrand Reinhold Co., 1972), p. 58. Copyright © 1972 by Litton Publishing, Inc. Reprinted by permission of the publisher.

1. Lack of variety in sentence structure.
2. On the whole, much of the content materials lack literary merit.
3. Content and materials are drawn almost exclusively from the middle class strata, although some attempt has been made to change this.
4. The language patterns are relatively simple and therefore removed from the child's oral language which is more complex in nature.
5. The teacher's manuals present a very structured program and don't allow for flexibility or adaptability.
6. Children may be grouped by the teacher but in many cases, unless multiple level texts are used, children are grouped inappropriately.
7. No provision for individual differences is usually made beyond the usual three group structure.

Research regarding the use of basal readers with retarded children is sparse and limited in scope; however, research dealing with the basal reader in general can provide insight into this approach. Many investigations reported in the First Grade Studies sponsored by the US Office of Education compared the basal-reader approach to other approaches. These yielded the following conclusions as outlined by Bond and Dykstra (1967a):

> With respect to the i.t.a. versus basal, basal plus phonics versus basal, linguistic versus basal and phonic/linguistic versus basal treatment comparisons, the following conclusions can be drawn:
> 1. Programs which were superior in the various basal versus nonbasal comparisons tended to be superior across all levels of intelligence. There was no indication that approaches operated differentially for pupils with high or low intelligence.
> 2. Programs which were superior in the various basal versus nonbasal comparisons tended to be superior across all levels of auditory discrimination ability. There was no indication that approaches operated differentially for pupils with high and low auditory discrimination.
> 3. Programs which were superior in the various basal versus nonbasal comparisons tended to be superior across all levels of preinstructional letter knowledge. There was no indication that approaches operated differen-

tially for pupils with high or low ability to recognize letters.

4. There is no basis for using test information of the nature employed in this analysis to place pupils differentially in a basal program or any other instructional program utilized in this investigation. A teacher who is successful with a given instructional program will probably be successful with that approach for pupils of varying degrees of readiness and capability.

Conclusions from the basal versus language experience comparison are less clear-cut. There is some indication that low readiness pupils are more successful in a basal program, while high readiness pupils profit more from a language experience program. However, this trend must be studied further in light of the fact that the finding in this investigation on which the conclusion is based may have resulted from sampling problems.[5]

In another investigation, Criscuolo (1967) used the Houghton Mifflin series for enrichment and achievement programs with lower socioeconomic students. On the basis of the *Metropolitan Achievement Test*, he found the enrichment program in this case to be superior. He has indicated that basal readers can "produce highly satisfactory reading achievement if used long enough to allow for complete mastery and extension of reading skills."[6]

Koelsch (1969) investigated the readability and interests of five third-grade level basal reading series, which included those published by The American Book Company, Harper and Row, J.B. Lippincott, Macmillan, and Scott, Foresman, with educable mentally retarded students. (The mean chronological age among these students was 13.11; the mean mental age was 3.6.) He found no significant differences in readability among the series and that little relationship existed between interest categories and interest patterns of the students. In addition he found interest content among basal readers to be significantly different from that of their peers.

---

[5]Guy Bond and Robert Dykstra, "The Cooperative Research Program in First-Grade Reading Instruction," *Reading Research Quarterly* 2 (1967a): 125-26. Reprinted by permission of Guy Bond and the International Reading Association.

[6]Nicholas P. Criscuolo, "Enrichment and Acceleration in Reading," *Elementary School Journal* 68 (1967): 145.

Finally, he concluded that uninteresting materials must be adapted to the special student in order to maintain interest in reading.

Blake, Aaron, and Westbrook (1967) investigated the basal reading skills of children who were and were not mentally handicapped in fifty basal reading skills in the areas of sight, phonetic analysis, dictionary usage, word functions, and comprehension skills; they used the Scott Foresman *New Basic Readers Series* for the study. Aaron (1971) believes that the following implications can be drawn from that investigation:

1. Mentally retarded children can learn the skills of reading. At the primary level, the mentally retarded group compared favorably with the normal group on thirty-nine of forty-eight skills. At the intermediate level, the retarded group compared favorably with the normal group on only twenty-two of fifty skills.
2. Pupils, especially the superior pupils, should be taught the skills at earlier ages.
3. Teachers should expect pupils to achieve at higher levels.
4. Teachers should differentiate methods and materials in a way appropriate for the pupils' particular learning and motivational characteristics.
5. Secondary programs for mentally retarded students should give more attention to developmental reading.
6. Programs such as the one used in this investigation appear to be better suited to normal than to retarded and superior students.[7]

In summary, we see advantages in the use of basal readers, especially by beginning teachers. However, many of the stories, workbook exercises, and supplementary materials are of little value for the retarded reader. In fact, the misuse of basal readers with retarded readers can deaden the child's interest in reading and actually impede his progress.

It is becoming rather difficult at the present time to make generalizations concerning basal readers because of the variations of materials included in each approach. Many are adding multisensory aids, behavioral objectives, and criterion-referenced tests as well as

---

[7]Era E. Aaron, "Learning of Basal Reading Skills by Mentally and Nonmentally Handicapped Children," in *Meeting Individual Needs in Reading,* ed. Helen K. Smith (Newark, Delaware: International Reading Association, 1971), pp. 89-90.

other features (e.g. soft-cover books and materials for culturally disadvantaged children) to their programs. It is important to remember that, as with any approach, no series should be used exclusively with an entire group of children and that if teachers use the basal reader in the traditional manner, interest or motivation may be impaired.

Phonics Approaches

Although approaches using basal readers include instruction in phonics, phonics approaches themselves concentrate more heavily on the teaching of phonetic principles and do not necessarily encompass all areas of reading instruction; most of the supplementary approaches that emphasize phonics instruction are also synthetic in nature (see Chapter Two).

Even though there has been considerable controversy concerning the effectiveness of phonics instruction, there is some evidence to indicate that beginning reading programs with a strong code emphasis — either phonetic or linguistic — are more successful than traditional basal reader programs or programs, such as individualized reading, that do not emphasize phonics (Bliesmer and Yarborough, 1965; Chall, 1967).

Some research has indicated that phonics instruction is successful with educable retarded children (French, 1950; Hegge, 1934; Kirk, 1940; Santin, 1971; Warner, 1967). However, there is also some disagreement concerning the use of intensive phonics with these children. Some authorities feel that retarded children are unable to learn phonics generalization (Gates, 1947; Tansley and Gulliford, 1960), even though earlier studies reported that those children who had a mental age of seven were able to benefit from phonics instruction (Smith, 1957). Therefore, the research is not conclusive as to the effectiveness of concentrated phonics instruction with retarded children (Cawley, Goodstein, and Burrow, 1972). After reviewing nine studies concerning the effectiveness of phonics instruction with slow-learning children, Chall stated:

> The evidence is sparce. However, if the limited findings from these nine studies are accurate and can be replicated, they may be explained as follows: Systematic phonics is probably more effective for slow-learning pupils because it can be made easier than intrinsic phonics.[8]

---

[8]Jeanne Chall, *Learning to Read: The Great Debate* (New York: McGraw-Hill Book Co., 1967), p. 127.

Chall has concluded that intrinsic phonics, an inductive approach which requires children to draw generalizations, may give these children more difficulty than a direct phonics approach.

The present authors feel that the controversy over the effectiveness of a particular approach (e.g., phonics) with a group of children is unwarranted. The decision to utilize phonics instruction should be based upon the strengths and weaknesses of an individual child rather than upon some evidence that phonics instruction is successful with a particular group of children. The characteristics of the individual child should be considered. For example, if the child has severe auditory discrimination problems, the teacher should consider the possibility that the child may not profit initially from phonics instruction.

No one phonics method or program is entirely like another, and many of the programs that incorporate phonics instruction utilize varying methods of presentation (e.g., programmed or multisensory approaches). Several of the different phonics programs are described in the following pages.

The Phonovisual Method: This approach (Schoolfield and Timberlake, 1944 and 1960) is a supplementary phonics program which utilizes materials that consist primarily of one wall chart with twenty-six consonants represented by meaningful pictures, such as pictures of *pig* for /p/ and *sun* for /s/, and another wall chart of the vowels with similar representations (e.g., the picture of a cat for the short vowel sound /a/). Other materials include small individual charts similar to the wall charts, practice sheets and books, magnetic boards (which are also reproductions of the wall charts), filmstrips, duplicating masters, game materials, readiness and transition books, and teacher's handbooks. A *Phonovisual Textbook for Teachers* (Smith, 1971) is a supplementary text giving background to the program and suggestions for utilizing the materials at various levels of instruction. A *Phonovisual Diagnostic Test* is also included.

The approach is a systematic synthetic phonics program that is to be taught to the total group in separate lessons every day; the lessons last from fifteen to thirty minutes. These skills learned are then applied during the language arts periods. The manual gives suggestions for incorporating the phonovisual method with basal readers and library books.

There has been some criticism that synthetic methods that taught during isolated periods they develop skills that are separated from the reading process (Hildreth, 1957), and it is true that many of these phonics drills can become boring to children

(Chall, 1967). The phonovisual method attempts to eradicate this problem by using interesting presentations and games.

Phonetic Keys to Reading: Another supplementary phonics approach is *Phonetic Keys to Reading* (Harris, Creekmore, and Greenman, 1967). This program consists of teacher's guide and workbooks for Grades 1 through 3. An urban edition (1971) of *Phonetic Keys to Reading* is also available. The "keys" to reading are forty separate phonetic generalizations which are introduced in the beginning stages of the program, with the vowels being introduced before the consonants. The program also attempts to include the aspect of reading comprehension by asking comprehension questions after the stories, although Chall (1967) has criticized the comprehension checks for asking too many needless questions and thereby tending to cause the reading lessons to be boring. The program also has a heavy concentration on learning rules. Several authorities feel though that many retarded children have problems in learning such phonic generalizations. Discussion of additional phonics approaches that have been used in remedial programs are included in Chapter Eight.

Currently there are many phonics programs and supplementary phonics aids on the market. Also, several basal reader programs are placing more emphasis on phonics instruction. Appendix Two lists additional phonics materials that were not discussed in this chapter.

Individualized Reading

With the increasing interest of teachers in individual differences of children, adoption of instruction to suit the individual needs and skills of children has developed (Heilman, 1972). However, it is important to note that individualized reading is not synonymous with individualized instruction. It is a specific approach to teaching reading which encompasses the philosophy of meeting the needs of children; it is not like many other approaches on the market used in individualized instruction.

According to Wilson and Hall (1972), the major features of the individualized reading approach are:

1. Pupils select their reading material from a wide variety of books available in their classroom and/or school library.
2. Each pupil reads different material and moves at his own pace through the material he has selected.

3. Direct instruction occurs in a pupil-teacher conference rather than in a reading group.
4. The reading materials are trade (library) books rather than basal readers.[9]

Several disadvantages of the individualized reading program have been given. Heilman (1972) contends that the approach requires a great number of reading materials which many systems may not be able to afford. He adds that this is not a problem unique to the individualized reading program but may be said of many programs. Wilson and Hall (1972) cite such disadvantages as inadequate skill development, if the teacher is not highly structured; the extensive record keeping which may be time-consuming; and the difficulty in scheduling conferences with children. Another limitation designated by Kerfoot (1965) is the difficulty in judging the reading level of the books.

Research on the individualized reading program with the retarded learner is limited, and in studies completed so far with intellectually average or above average students, findings do not agree. For example, Sartain (1960) found that the individualized approach with second-grade students did not produce better gains in reading than did a strong basal reader program. In the same way, MacDonald (1966) found no significant difference between individualized (experimental) and group instruction (control) in terms of student achievement or school-related anxiety; however, in this case, the experimental group preferred reading to a significantly greater degree than did the control group. Huser (1965) also found a more favorable attitude toward reading among children taught by the individualized approach, although there were no significant gains in their achievement. In addition, the *First Grade Studies*, which were discussed earlier, failed to show the superiority of the individualized approach.

In working with retarded readers, Parker (1965) found the individualized approach to be superior over the basal readers with all his subjects except for the lowest reading group.

Meiselman (1963) found no significant difference between the individualized approach and basal readers with fourth, fifth, and sixth grade urban blacks. However, the subjects did develop more positive attitudes toward reading when the individualized approach was used.

---

[9]Wilson and Hall, p. 4.

In summary, it would appear that the individualized approach is in no way superior to any other approach. However, when properly instructed, students can make reading achievement gains and develop more positive attitudes toward reading using this approach.

Numerous individualized reading programs, usually in kit form, are now available. Appendix Two contains a list of these programs.

The Language Experience Approach

According to Harris (1964), the experience method, which consists of the teacher's writing down stories dictated by children, is the forerunner of the language experience approach. The language experience method began in San Diego with Doris Lee as Supervisor of Reading. A textbook, first written in the 1930s and revised in 1963, was written to explain the approach (Lee and Allen, 1963).

The basic philosophy of this method is built upon the oral experiences of the individual child and is used from Grades 1 through junior high school. The approach builds on and continues to provide individual experiences for each child, while, at the same time, increasing the common group experiences. It also provides for maximum development of each child through increasing his self-confidence and self-direction.

This method of learning to read makes possible the continuing use of each child's own experiential background in listening and speaking. It is built on the theory that communication skills are related and are essential to success in academic achievement, and, consequently, does not consider reading as a separate subject. Instead, its proponents contend that reading permeates all communications and experiences of the child.

Some of the major principles behind this method are:

1. What a child thinks about he can talk about.
2. What he can talk about can be expressed in painting, writing, or some other form.
3. Anything he writes can be read.
4. He can read what he writes and what other people write.
5. As he represents his speech sounds with symbols, he uses the same symbols (letter) over and over.
6. Each letter in the alphabet stands for one or more sounds that he makes when he talks.
7. Every word begins with a sound he can write down.
8. Most words have an ending sound.
9. Many words have something in between.

10. Some words are used over and over in our language and some words are used very often.
11. What he has to say and write is as important to him as what other people write for him to read.[10]

Several of the advantages of the language experience approach include the emphasis placed on meaning; the high degree of interest (Wilson and Hall, 1972), and the close relationship between oral and written language.

Heilman (1972), though, has cited several disadvantages of overreliance on such a program:

1. It is difficult to control vocabulary. Too many words may be introduced at one time.
2. Basic sight words may not be repeated often enough to insure mastery.
3. When used exclusively as a method, it puts too much burden on the teacher, demands much time, and a high level of training.
4. It is difficult to adapt this type of instruction to the needs and abilities of all children.
5. It encourages memorization rather than mastery of sight words.[11]

The Ashton-Warner Approach: A unique language experience method is referred to as the Ashton-Warner approach. This approach uses the concept of organic reading. In organic reading, "key vocabulary" is chosen by the child himself; this self-selection gives it its meaning and emotion. Ashton-Warner (1963) has stated: "First words must mean something to the child. First words must have intense meaning for a child, they must be part of his being."[12]

Thus, children relate their experiences and feelings in story form from functional vocabulary lists and words which correspond to their basal reading level. Through the children's involvement, interest is insured rather than assumed.

Although many teachers find it difficult to use this method because of the time and resourcefulness it requires and because of its lack of systematization (Sitko, et al., 1972), it has been recom-

---

[10]Doris M. Lee and R. V. Allen, *Learning to Read through Experiences,* 2d ed. (New York: Appleton-Century-Crofts, 1963), pp. 5-8. Reprinted by permission of the publisher.

[11]A.W. Heilman, *Principles and Practices of Teaching Reading,* 3d ed. (Columbus, Ohio: Charles E. Merrill Publishing Co., 1972), p. 210.

[12]Sylvia Ashton-Warner, *Teacher* (New York: Bantam Books, 1963), p. 30.

mended for the culturally disadvantaged and retarded children (Sitko, et al., 1972; Packer, 1970).

Research regarding the use of the language experience approach with retarded children is scanty. One research review by Hall (1972) does provide an excellent picture of the language experience approach with the culturally disadvantaged though. Of the studies cited, many may have applicability to the retarded. In a study in San Diego County, California (1961), sixty-seven teachers participated in a study of the teaching of reading by the individualized, basal, and language experience approach during the 1959-1960 school year. By standardized testing, those conducting the test concluded that through the language experience approach, children could make as much or more progress in learning reading skills as through the other approaches. However, the language experience approach was not considered to be superior.

Brazziel and Terrell (1962) found the use of experience materials (especially experience charts) to result in significantly higher scores on the *Metropolitan Readiness Test* for the experimental group of twenty-six culturally disadvantaged children than for the three control groups when those charts were used with other readiness activities and materials. Hall (1965) developed and evaluated a program with first-semester, first-grade, disadvantaged black children in the Washington, D.C. schools. To accomplish this study, he used five experimental groups ($N = 151$) and five control groups ($N = 121$). The experimental groups were favored significantly in terms of reading readiness as well as in terms of word recognition and sentence reading on a standard reading test; they were not at an advantage on a word recognition test developed by the investigator. In addition, teachers rated the language experience approach as being more effective than the basal reader.

Lamb (1971) also investigated the language experience approach in beginning reading with culturally disadvantaged children in Indianapolis, Indiana. He found no significant difference between the experimental and control groups, which used a modified basal reader approach, in terms of achievement and attitude as measured by the *California Reading Test* and *The Primary Pupil Reading Attitude Inventory*. However, in another study, Giles (1966) found that language experience techniques for teaching oral language to first graders caused greater achievement. This was true for male more so than female students.

The *First Grade Studies* sponsored by the US Office of Education contained twenty-seven separate studies, six of which concerned the language experience approach. One of these studies by Harris (1966, 1967, 1969) dealt specifically with the disadvantaged. Harris studied economically disadvantaged urban children over a three-year period using a skills-centered approach rather than a language experience approach. At the end of the three-year period, there was no significant differences between methods in any of the tests given.

With those beyond the elementary level, Becker (1970) conducted an experience program with a vocational emphasis on four nonreaders at the Woman's Job Training Program in Charleston, West Virginia. At the end of eleven months, two of the women were reading on the third-grade level, one on the fourth, and one on the fifth.

Wilson and Parkey (1970) conducted a study with educationally retarded seventh graders using the language experience approach in social studies, mathematics, and science. While they found little difference in reading achievement between the experimental and control group as measured by the *Botel Word Opposites Test,* the experimental group did view themselves more favorably as learners.

In a study with retarded children, Woodcock (1967) compared the language experience approach with several other methods, including i.t.a. (in both its basal reader and language experience presentations), basal readers (i.t.a. and rebus presentations), and basal readers using traditional orthography. No significant differences were found in achievement.

Thus, research in the language experience approach seems to indicate that it can be beneficial to the reading program, but cannot be considered to be the only successful approach. The present writers have used this approach with older retarded children and found it very successful, especially in developing interest. If the teacher is interested in a commercially constructed program, *The Language Experience in Reading (LEIR)* (Encyclopedia Britannica Educational Corporation, 1970) is recommended.

The Linguistic Approach

What is commonly termed the linguistic approach to teaching reading was first advocated by Bloomfield in 1933, although his steps for teaching reading were not described until an article in the *Elementary English Review* in 1942. His entire approach to teaching reading (alphabetic linguistics) was published in *Let's Read* (Bloomfield and Barnhart, 1961).

Bloomfield asserted that one should teach beginning reading by concentrating exclusively on carefully selected monosyllabic words which show a particular spelling pattern. He divided the monosyllabic words into regular and irregular words and insisted that a child learn only regular words until he had overlearned them. He developed three basic steps to beginning reading — name the alphabet, master left-to-right order, and begin on three letter words (such as *man*, *pan*, and *ran*). The child is taught to name every letter in each word in a spelling approach.

All lessons include words from previous lessons. There are thirty-six lessons in the basic patterns and by lesson ninety-seven, the child has been exposed to only three irregulars: *a*, *an* and *the*. By the end of the third grade, the child has completed 245 lessons.

Rather than teaching the child to associate sounds and symbols, Bloomfield assumed that this process was learned automatically. He criticized phonics because he felt the methods of teaching phonics confused writing with speech and unnecessarily isolated speech sounds.

In the *Let's Read* program, there is little initial emphasis on meaning. Instead, the program stresses the mechanics of reading rather than comprehension first. Also, nonsense syllables are used in order to enable the child to apply his ability to read regular spelling patterns.

After Bloomfield's introduction of his linguistic approach to teaching reading, several men expanded and modified his techniques. One of the best known is Charles Fries, author of the *Merrill Linguistic Readers* (1966). Fries also advocates the regular spelling pattern approach, but he emphasizes whole words rather than individual letters. He has suggested the spelling pattern approach which includes a minimal list of words and structures put into a teachable sequence of contrasts and structures (Fries, 1963). Children are taught to develop the ability to see the significant contrasting features of separate letters. For example, some of these spelling patterns would be *tap-pat*, *tip-pit*. Initially, words are presented in capital letters only. As with Bloomfield's program, comprehension is not emphasized in the beginning and pictures are not included in the series.

Still another linguist, Carl Lefevre, attempted in his book *Linguistics and the Teaching of Reading* to give a "comprehensive application of linguistic data to reading and writing processes with primary emphasis on the sentence."[13] Rather than concentrating only on the phonemes (sound units) and morphemes (smallest meaningful units — e.g., prefix *un*, word *dog*, or plural *s*), Lefevre applied other linguistic principles, such as syntax and intonation, to reading. According to Lefevre, syntax leads to comprehension of the "entire meaning bearing pattern,"[14] while intonation is the tune of rhythm of speech which is represented in writing by punctuation marks; intonation is an integral part of comprehension. The saying "It's not what you say but how you say it" is an example of the importance of intonation. In this context, oral reading can be used as a means of developing comprehension and motivating children to read silently (Lefevre, 1969).

Another version of the linguistic programs developed by Bloomfield and Fries is the phonic-linguistic approach (Hughes, 1969). In this case, intensive phonics instruction combined with controlled patterns, such as *c-v-c*, and controlled introductions of phonics principles are given the main emphasis. Two such programs are the *Open Court* series (1963) and Lippincott's *Basic Reading* (1966).

There have been several reading series that incorporate "linguistic principles" in their programs. Some of these include: *Merrill Linguistic Readers* (1966), *Miami Linguistic Readers* (D. C. Heath, 1970), *SRA Linguistic Readers* (1966), *Patterns, Sounds and Meaning* (Allyn and Bacon, 1971), *Linguistic Readers* (Benzinger, 1971), *Structural Reading* (1966), and *Linguistic Science Readers* (Harper and Row, 1963). However, according to Goodman (1969), there is no linguistic approach to the teaching of reading. Rather than designating one series as *the* linguistic approach, Goodman notes that all phases of reading are linguistic in nature. If one views reading as a part of the language process, linguistic principles must apply in all reading instruction regardless of the approach used. Therefore, the linguistic approach to reading advocated by Bloomfield becomes a very narrow interpretation of linguistics (Lefevre, 1969).

Science of Linguistics: The science of linguistics extends far beyond the realm of spelling patterns. "Linguistics is a scientific in-

---

[13]Carl A. Lefevre, "A Comprehensive Linguistic Approach to Reading," in *Readings on Reading*, edited by Alfred Binter, J. Daebel, and L. Kise (Scranton, Pennsylvania: International Textbook Co., 1969), p. 448.

[14]Ibid., p. 451.

quiry into language which results into a body of verifiable facts."[15] Eisenhardt points out that linguists specialize in such areas of our language as the sound system, the history of the language, meanings which depend upon the settings of the words (semantics), dialects, and syntax.

Another area of linguistics — psycholinguistics — has been considered to be very much an integral part of the reading process. On this subject, Goodman has stated: "As we come to see the reader as a user of language, we will understand that reading is a psycholinguistic process, an interaction between thought and language."[16]

From this standpoint, linguistics, rather than being applied to reading instruction, "reading instruction is applied to linguistics"[17] rather than linguistics being applied to reading instruction. According to Goodman, in order for reading programs to best utilize linguistic principles, natural language should be included; programs should be language centered; grammatical patterns of children should be considered; and language variances (e.g. dialect) should be a part of the program. *The Scott Foresman Reading Systems* (1970) has attempted to incorporate many of the psycholinguistic principles advocated by Goodman.

Research and the Linguistic Approach: In comparison studies of the effectiveness of linguistic series such as Bloomfield's (alphabetic linguistics), overall results do not show these series to be any more effective than other approaches, such as the traditional basal reader programs (Fidelia, 1959; Schreyer, 1967; Sheldon and Lashinger, 1967). The phonic-linguistic approaches fair somewhat better in comparison studies (Hughes, 1969). In summarizing the *First-Grade Reading Studies*, Bond and Dykstra (1967) have stated that a combination of modified linguistics approaches and basal readers seems to be more effective than either approach used in isolation.

Initial Teaching Alphabet (i.t.a.)

The Initial Teaching Alphabet (i.t.a.) is not a method of teaching reading but a change in the medium or the letter symbols (Downing, 1967c). It is a basal reader approach that employs "a simplified

---

[15]C. Eisenhardt, *Applying Linguistics in the Teaching of Reading and the Language Arts* (Columbus, Ohio: Charles E. Merrill Publishing Co., 1972), p. 6.

[16]K.S. Goodman, "Behind the Eye: What Happens in Reading," in Reading Process and Program, ed. K.S. Goodman and O.S. Niles (Champaign, Illinois: National Council of Teachers of English, 1970), p. 6.

[17]*Ibid.*, p. 271.

and regularized writing system."[18] This system was first introduced in the English schools in 1961 by Sir James Pitman and to American children in 1963 by Anita Metzer in New Jersey and Albert Mazurkiewicz in Pennsylvania (Block, 1972).

According to Downing, i.t.a. has three main characteristics:

1. It is an augmented alphabet that has forty-four characters. This number consists of twenty-four letters from the conventional Roman alphabet (*q* and *x* are omitted because they are redundant) and twenty new characters for those phonemes (sound units) of English which have no single letter of their own in t. o. (traditional orthography).
2. i.t.a. has regularized spelling. For instance, the words "one" and "done" are written "wun" and "dun" in i.t.a. to match the regularity of the spelling patterns in words like *bun, fun, run, sun.*
3. i.t.a. is a transitional writing-system. The i.t.a alphabet and its use in i.t.a. spellings are designed deliberately to facilitate the change from i.t.a. reading to t.o. reading.[19]

Other characteristics of the program include: use of lower case letters, writing, and creative expression at the same time to develop reading skills. Transition usually occurs at the end of the first grade.

Since the introduction of i.t.a., many studies have been conducted comparing its effectiveness to approaches that utilize traditional orthography. Block, director of the i.t.a. foundation at Hofstra University, has on file seventy-six comparison studies. From these studies, he concludes that "i.t.a. is clearly superior."[20] However, not all reading authorities are in agreement about the success of i.t.a. After summarizing many of the research studies utilizing i.t.a., Dawson (1969) concluded that the research is still inconclusive for several reasons — the studies have not been longitudinal in nature and controls used were not adequate because the Hawthorne effect was not adequately considered as a variable.

Gillooly (1969) concurs with Dawson's analysis of the research methodology of most of the studies. He has added that many of the studies did not take into account all the variances, such as differences in materials or approaches, used in the studies. For

---

[18]John Downing, "Progress Report on I.T.A." in *Readings on Reading,* ed. Alfred R. Binter, John J. Daebel, and Leonard K. Kise (Scranton, Pennsylvania: International Textbook Co., 1969b), p. 469.

[19]*Ibid.*, p. 469-70.

[20]J.R. Block, "Newsreport Interview," *Reading Newsreport* 6 (1972): 6.

example, he questions whether, if i.t.a. is found to be superior to one basal reader series in a particular study, is this result to be interpreted to mean i.t.a. will be superior to all basal reader series? (Gillooly, 1969).

The research concerning the effectiveness of i.t.a. with retarded children is also inconclusive. Some reports indicate that retarded children can learn to read utilizing the approach (Downing, 1967b; Downing, 1969; Mazurkiewicz, 1966; Orman, 1966; Stewart, 1969). In comparison studies though, not all of the results are that encouraging. In the Woodcock study (1967), i.t.a. was no more effective than the other approaches (e.g. programmed readers, basal readers, rebus) used in the study.

Downing (1967b) also has reported that slow-learning children showed insignificant improvement on test results after the third year and that many of these children need at least three years of i.t.a. before transition.

As was noted previously, i.t.a. is a medium and not an approach. Although a basal reader approach is used to teach i.t.a., a great deal of variability may occur in methodology. According to Downing (1969a), how i.t.a. is taught is very important. At the present time, the i.t.a. foundation is sponsoring research to determine what methods should be used in teaching reading utilizing the i.t.a. medium most effectively (Block, 1972). Downing (1969b) has recommended combining of the language experience approach with i.t.a. and placing an emphasis on creativity in writing rather than on learning formation of letters and words through isolated drills. Mazurkiewicz (1966) has suggested combining a multisensory method, such as Fernald's, with i.t.a. for use with slow learners. Other modifications could be the use of sand-box tracing of letters and words, flashcard drills, and blending exercises using small symbol cards (Mazurkiewicz, 1966).

Although retarded children can learn to read using i.t.a., it should not be considered as a total approach for all retarded children. No one approach or medium can serve as a panacea for all children. Our observation has been that retarded children require longer for transition and sometimes continue to spell a few words in i.t.a. after they have made the transition in reading.

SUMMARY

The most frequently used developmental reading approaches were discussed in this chapter. Among these, the basal reader approach is the popular form of teaching reading in our country. Discussion

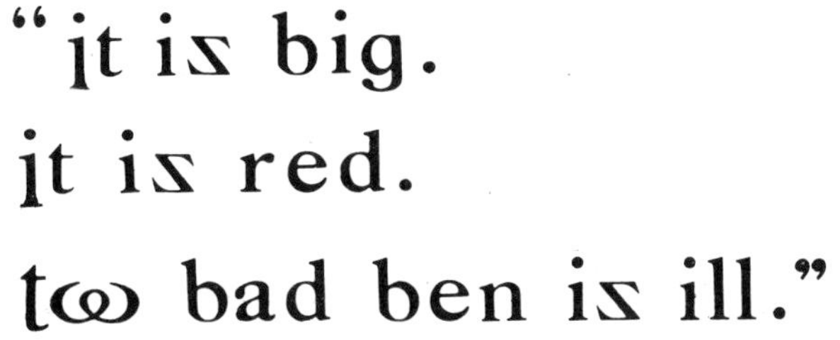

"ɪt iꙅ big.
ɪt iꙅ red.
tꙍ bad ben iꙅ ill."

Figure 14: Example of i/t/a[21]

was included of many of the techniques of teaching reading, such as phonics and linguistics, encompassed in basal programs. Programs such as i.t.a. are taught within the framework of the basal reader approach. Approaches that depart completely from the basal reader are language experience and individualized reading.

Research concerning the effectiveness of these programs with the retarded also was discussed in this chapter. Much of the research which has been conducted was in the form of comparison studies which, unfortunately, yield little information that will enable a teacher to design diagnostic-prescriptive programs for children. As was stated previously, no one method has been found to be more effective than another with groups of children.

Additional methods, such as programmed instruction and multisensory techniques, which usually are used with normal children, will be discussed in Chapter Eight because of their frequent use with the retarded or problem readers.

REFERENCES

Aaron, Ira E. "Learning of Basal Reading Skills by Mentally and Nonmentally Handicapped Children." In *Meeting Individual Needs in Reading,* edited by Helen K. Smith, pp. 89-90. Newark, Delaware: International Reading Association, 1971.

Allen, R.V., and Lee, Doris M. *Language Experiences in Reading.* Chicago: Encyclopedia Britannica Educational Corporation, 1970.

[21]Reprinted from *Dinasaur Ben* by Annie DeCaprio, in *Early to Read i/t/a Program* by A. Mazurkiewicz and H. Tanyzer (New York: i/t/a Publications, 1969), p. 21, by permission of the publisher.

Armstrong, Jenny R. "Teaching: An Ongoing Process of Assessing, Selecting, and Developing, Generalizing, Applying, and Reassessing." *Education and Training for the Mentally Retarded* 4 (1969): 168-76.

Ashton-Warner, Sylvia. *Teacher.* New York: Bantam Books, 1963.

Austin, Mary, and Morrison, Coleman. *The First R: The Harvard Report on Reading in Elementary Schools.* New York: The Macmillan Co., 1963.

Becker, John T. "Language Experience Approach in a Job Corps Reading Lab." *Journal of Reading* 13 (1970): 281-84; 319-21.

Blake, K.A.; Aaron, I.E.; and Westbrook, H.H. *Learning of Basal Reading Skills by Mentally Handicapped and Nonmentally Handicapped Pupils.* BEH Project Number 5,0391. Washington, D.C.: United States Department of Health, Education, and Welfare Office of Education, 1967.

Bliesmer, Emery P., and Yarborough, Betty H. "A Comparison of the Ten Different Beginning Reading Programs in First Grade." *Phi Delta Kappan* 56 (1965): 500-04.

Block, J.R. "Newsreport Interview." *Reading Newsreport* 6 (1972): 4-8; 47.

Bloomfield, Leonard. "Linguistics and Reading." *Elementary English Review* 19 (1942): 125-30; 183-86.

_____. "Why a Linguistic Society?" In *Language* edited by L. Bloomfield, New York: Holt, Rinehart, & Winston, 1933.

Bloomfield, Leonard, and Barnhart, C. *Let's Read: A Linguistic Approach.* Detroit: Wayne State University Press, 1961.

Bogatz, Boris E. An Investigation of Teacher Expectancies of Instructional Materials." *Exceptional Children* 38 (1971): 233-36.

Bond, Guy, and Dykstra, Robert. "The Cooperative Research Program in First-Grade Reading Instruction." *Reading Research Quarterly* 2 (1967a).

_____. "Interpreting the First-Grade Reading Studies." In *The First-Grade Reading Studies: Findings of Individual Investigations,* edited by Russel G. Stauffer, pp. 1-9. Newark, Delaware: International Reading Association, 1967b.

Brazziel, W.F., and Terrell, Mary. "For First Graders: A Good Start in School." *Elementary School Journal* 62 (1962): 352-55.

Cawley, J.F.; Goodstein, H.A.; and Burrow, W.H. *The Slow Learner and the Reading Problem.* Springfield, Illinois: Charles C. Thomas Co., 1972.

Chall, Jeanne, *Learning to Read: The Great Debate.* New York: McGraw-Hill Book Co., 1967.

Criscuolo, Nicholas P. "Enrichment and Acceleration in Reading." *Elementary School Journal* 68 (1967): 142-46.

Dawson, M.A. "How Effective is i.t.a. in Reading Instruction?" In *Current Issues in Reading,* edited by Nila B. Smith, pp. 224-37. Newark, Delaware: International Reading Association, 1969.

Dechant, E.V. *Improving the Teaching of Reading.* Englewood Cliffs, New Jersey: Prentice-Hall, Inc., 1964.

Downing, John A. "E.S.A. School Teachers Assess i.t.a." *Special Education* 56 (1967a), 12-16.

_____. "How Effective is i.t.a.?" In *Current Issues in Reading,* edited by Nila B. Smith, pp. 238-44. Newark, Delaware: International Reading Association, 1969a.

_____. "Progress Report on i.t.a." In *Readings on Reading,* edited by Alfred R. Binter, John J. Daebel, and Leonard K. Kise, pp. 469-76. Scranton, Pennsylvania: International Textbook Co., 1969b.

_____. "Self-Discovery, Self-Expression, and the Self-Image in the i.t.a. Classroom." In *Readings on Reading,* edited by Alfred R. Binter, John J. Daebal, and Leonard K. Kise, pp. 477-83. Scranton, Pennsylvania: International Textbook Co., 1969c.

_____. "What's Wrong with i.t.a.?" *Phi Delta Kappan* 48 (1967b): 262.

Drew, C.J., and Martinson, M.C. "Educational Methodology: An Examination Approach." *Exceptional Children* 38 (1971): 117-20.

Eisenhardt, C. *Applying Linguistics in the Teaching of Reading and the Language Arts.* Columbus, Ohio: Charles E. Merrill Publishing Co., 1972.

Engelmann, Siegfried. "Classroom Techniques: Teaching Reading to Children with Low Mental Ages." *Education and Training of the Mentally Retarded* 2 (1967): 193-201.

Fidelia, Sister Mary. "The Relative Effectiveness of Bloomfield's Linguistic Approach to Word Attack as Compared with Phonics We Use." Doctoral dissertation, University of Ottawa, 1959.

French, E.L. "Reading Disability and Mental Deficiency: A Preliminary Report." *Training School Bulletin* 47 (1950): 47-57.

Fries, C.C. *Linguistics and Reading.* New York: Holt, Rinehart, & Winston, 1963.

Fries, C.C.; Fries, Agnes C.; Wilson, Rosemary; and Rudolph, Mildred K. *Merrill Linguistic Readers.* Columbus, Ohio: Charles E. Merrill Publishing Co., 1966.

Gates, A.I. *The Improvement of Reading,* 3rd ed. New York: The Macmillan Co., 1947.

Giles, Douglas E. "The Effect of Two Approaches to Reading Instruction upon the Oral Language Development of First-Grade Pupils." Doctoral dissertation, North Texas State University, 1966.

Gillooly, W.B. "How Effective is i.t.a. in Reading Instruction?" In *Current Issues in Reading,* edited by Nila B. Smith, pp. 245-53. Newark, Delaware: International Reading Association, 1969.

Goodman, Kenneth S. "Behind the Eye: What Happens in Reading." In *Reading Process and Program,* edited by Kenneth S. Goodman and O.S. Niles, pp. 3-38. Champaign, Illinois: National Council of Teachers of English, 1970.

_____. "The Linguistic Approach: Pro-Challenger." In *Current Issues in Reading,* edited by Nila B. Smith, pp. 268-76. Newark, Delaware: International Reading Association, 1969.

Hall, MaryAnne. "The Development and Evaluation of a Language Experience Approach to Reading with First-Grade Culturally Disadvantaged Children." Doctoral dissertation, University of Maryland, 1965.

_____. *The Language Experience Approach for the Culturally Disadvantaged.* Newark, Delaware: International Reading Association, 1972.

Harris, Albert J. "Progressive Education and Reading Instruction." *The Reading Teacher* 18 (1964): 128-38.

Harris, Albert J., and Morrison, Coleman. "The Craft Project: A Final Report." *The Reading Teacher* 22 (January 1969): 335-40.

Harris, Albert J., and Serwer, Blanche L. "Comparing Reading Approaches in First-Grade Teaching with Disadvantaged Children." *The Reading Teacher* 19 (May 1966): 631-35.

Harris, Albert J.; Serwer, Blanche L.; and Gold, Lawrence. "Comparing Reading Approaches in First-Grade Teaching with Disadvantaged Children — Extended into Second Grade." *The Reading Teacher* 20 (May 1967): 698-703.

Harris, Theodore; Creekmore, Mildred; and Greenman, Margaret. *Phonetic Keys to Reading.* Oklahoma City, Oklahoma: Economy Co., 1964.

Hegge, T.G. "Special Reading Disability with Particular Reference to the Mentally Deficient." *American Journal of Mental Deficiency* 39 (1934): 224.

Heilman, Arthur W. *Principles and Practices of Teaching Reading,* 3rd ed. Columbus, Ohio: Charles E. Merrill Publishing Co., 1972.

Hilbreth, Gertrude. "New Methods for Old in Teaching Phonics." *Elementary School Journal* 57 (1957): 436-41.

Hughes, Ann. "The Linguistic Approach: Con-Challenger." In *Current Issues in Reading,* edited by Nila B. Smith, pp. 277-82. Newark, Delaware: International Reading Association, 1969.

Huser, Mary K. "The Efficacy of Individualized Reading in Achievement and Attitude." Ed.D. dissertation, University of Illinois, 1965.

Johnson, M.S., and Kress, Roy A. "Matching Children and Programs." *The Reading Teacher* 255 (1971): 402; 442.

Kerfoot, James F., editor. "First-Grade Reading Programs." In *Perspectives in Reading, Number 5.* Newark, Delaware: International Reading Association, 1965.

Kirk, Samuel. *Teaching Reading to Slow-Learning Children.* Boston: Houghton Mifflin Co., 1940.

Koelsch, G.J. "Readability and Interests of Five Basal Reading Series with Retarded Students." *Exceptional Children* 35 (February 1969): 487-88.

Lamb, Rose. "The Language Experience Approach to Teaching Beginning Reading to Culturally Disadvantaged Pupils." Final Report Project Number D-E-005, Grant Number OEG-5-70-0013 (010). Washington, D.C.: United States Department of Health, Education, and Welfare Bureau of Research, January 1971.

Lazar, Alfred L. "Reading Programs and Materials for the Educable Mentally Retarded—A Point of View." Paper presented at the International Reading Association Conference, May 1970, at Anaheim, California.

Lee, Doris M., and Allen, R.V. *Learning to Read through Experience,* 2d ed. New York: Appleton-Century-Crofts, 1963.

Lefevre, C.A. "A Comprehensive Linguistic Approach to Reading." In *Readings on Reading,* edited by Alfred R. Binter, John J. Daebal, and Leonard K. Kise, pp. 445-62. Scranton, Pennsylvania: International Textbook Co., 1969.

————. *Linguistics and the Teaching of Reading.* New York: McGraw-Hill Book Co., 1964.

MacDonald, J.B. "Individualized versus Group Instruction in First-Grade Reading." *The Reading Teacher* 19 (1966): 643-46; 652.

McCracken, G. *Lippincott Basic Reading Program.* Philadelphia: J.B. Lippincott Co., 1966.

Mazurkiewicz, A.J. "The Initial Teaching Alphabet." In *The Disabled Reader: Education of the Dyslexic Child,* edited by John Money and Gilbert Schiffman, pp. 161-74. Baltimore: The Johns Hopkins Press, 1966.

Meiselman, Max Sidney. "A Comparison of Two Reading Programs for Retarded Readers." Ed.D. dissertation, New York University, 1963.

Niemeyer, John H. "The Bank Street Readers: Support for Movement toward an Integrated Society." *The Reading Teacher* (1965): 542-45.

Orman, J. "Introduction to Reading through the Initial Teaching Alphabet." *Teaching and Training* 4 (1966): 189-213.

Packer, A.B. "Ashton-Warner's Key Vocabulary for the Disadvantaged." *The Reading Teacher* 23 (1970): 559-64.

Parker, Clea Edward. "Effect of an Individualized Reading Program on Achievement in Reading." Ed.D. dissertation, Louisiana State University, 1965.

Rasmussen, D. *SRA Linguistic Readers.* Chicago: Science Research Associates, 1964.

Santin, Sylvia E. *Report of an Experiment in the Teaching of Reading to Adolescent Trainable Retarded.* Ontario: Guelph University and Ontario Association for the Mentally Retarded, 1971.

Sartain, Harry W. "The Roseville Experiment with Individualized Reading." *The Reading Teacher* 13 (1960): 277-81.

Schneyer, J.W. "Reading Achievement of First-Grade Children Taught by a Linguistic Approach and a Sisel Reader Approach." *In The First-Grade Reading Studies: Findings of Individual Investigations,* edited by Russel G. Stauffer, pp. 119-24. Newark, Delaware: International Reading Association, 1967.

Schoolfeld, Lucille D., and Timberlake, Josephine. *Phonovisual Products.* Washington, D.C.: Box 5625, Friendship Station, 1960.

San Diego Department of Education. *Improving Reading Instruction: Descriptions of Three Approaches to the Teaching of Reading.* Monograph Number 2. San Diego: San Diego Department of Education, May 1961.

Sheldon, W. D., and Lashinger, D.R. "Effect of First-Grade Instruction Using Basal Readers, Modified Linguistics Materials, and Linguistic Readers." In *The First-Grade Reading Studies: Findings of Individual Investigations,* edited by Russell G. Stauffer, pp. 125-28. Newark, Delaware: International Reading Association, 1967.

Sitko, M.C.; Semmel, D.C., Wilcone, G.; and Semmell, M.I. "The Relationship of Word and Sentence Association of EMR Children to Reading Performance." Bloomington: University of Indiana Center for Innovation in Teaching the Handicapped, School of Education, 1972.

Smith, E.B. *Phonovisual Textbook for Teachers.* Rockville, Maryland: Phonovisual Products, Inc., 1971.

Smith, Nila B. "What Research Supports about Phonics Instruction." *Journal of Educational Research* 51 (1957): 1-9.

Stern, C. *The Structural Reading Series.* Syracuse, New York: The L.W. Singer Co., 1966.

Stewart, R. "i.t.a. after Two Years." in *Readings on Reading,* edited by Alfred Binter, John J. Daebal, and Leonard Kise, pp. 484-92. Scranton, Pennsylvania: International Textbook Company, 1969.

Tansley, A.E., and Gulliford, A. *The Education of the Slow-Learning Child.* London: Routiledge & Kegan Printers, 1960.

Warner, Delores. *Experimental Phonetic Reading Programs for Exceptional Pupils.* Los Angeles: California University, 1967.

Wilson, Robert M., and Hall, MaryAnne. *Reading and the Elementary School Child.* New York: Van Nostrand Reinhold Co., 1972.

Wilson, Robert M., and Parkey, Nancy. "A Modified Reading Program in a Middle School." *Journal of Reading* 13 (March 1970), 447-552.

Woodcock, R. *The Peabody-Chicago-Detroit Reading Project—A Report of Second Year Results.* Nashville, Tennessee: George Peabody College, 1967.

EIGHT

Remedial Reading Approaches

Although developmental reading approaches have been adapted to meet the needs of retarded children, specific approaches have also been developed for other children with reading problems. Some of the approaches that have been used with retarded children were developed originally for normal readers and are still used with normal readers (e.g., programmed reading). Because these methods have been used with retarded readers and, in many cases, modified, they are placed for discussion in this chapter.

MULTISENSORY READING APPROACHES

Various reading approaches have been categorized as multisensory, although, in actuality, very few reading programs are unisensory in nature. *Most* approaches combine auditory as well as visual presentation in their teaching methods. Even though a program may be considered to be visual, auditory presentation is usually included (through pronouncing the words or giving verbal directions, etc.). Therefore, the term "multisensory" is applied to an approach that makes an apparent concerted attempt to include more than one mode of presentation—visual, auditory, and/or kinesthetic (muscle sense). The multisensory method which was utilized by early educators, such as the Greeks (Fernald, 1943), in recent years has been used mostly in the area of remedial reading and special education. A "bombardment approach in which the child is encouraged to hear it, feel it, and see it"[1] has composed much of the training in special education.

The kinesthetic, or tactile (sandpaper letters, etc.), component of the multisensory approach has been stressed especially in training special educators. According to some authorities, the kinesthetic perception is considered to be as important as auditory perception in language learning (Berry, 1969). Because motor patterns are learned very early and communication is motoric before it is anything else, some authorities feel that kinesthesis may serve as a mediator between auditory stimuli and perception (Brain, 1961).

Although the research is not conclusive, there is some evidence to support the multisensory approach with retarded readers and retarded children (Cawley, 1967; Edwards, 1966; Kline and Lee, 1970; Linn and Ryan, 1968; Stuart, 1963). With retarded children as well as with normal ones, the auditory-visual modes of presentation, especially if concrete visuals are utilized, may be superior to an auditory approach (Day and Beach, 1950). Again, this point is also controversial (Hill and Hecker, 1966; Katz and Deutsch, 1964).

Many specialists are in favor of the utilization of a multisensory technique; however, some authorities caution against using the approach indiscriminately (Johnson and Myklebust, 1967). In describing the possible limitations of the approach, Johnson and Myklebust have stated:

> A number of children manifest disturbances only when more than one process is required at a time. It is in this context that the concept of overloading takes on value and is significant in education. The multisensory approach, if used promiscuously can be damaging.[2]

There is some neurological evidence to support the assumption that bombarding a child with all modes of presentation actually may confuse him (Berry, 1969). Some advocates of unisensory

[1]Milton C. Blue, "Influence of Mode of Presentation, Age, and Intelligence on Paired-Associates Learning," *American Journal of Mental Deficiency* 74 (1970): 527.

[2]Doris Johnson and Helmer Myklebust, *Learning Disabilities* (New York: Grune & Stratton, 1967), p. 31.

methods advise blocking one channel (e.g. vision through blind-folding) in order to aid the child in perceiving auditorily and/or kinesthetically. Thus, it is apparent that, as with any approach, multisensory or unisensory techniques should not be used as a total program for a class but according to needs of individual children.

There are several approaches having multisensory components that have been used in teaching reading to the retarded. These include: Fernald and its adaptations, Montessori, Gillingham-alphabetic method, multisensory linguistic techniques, and basal reader-multisensory combined approaches.

Fernald Method

This visual-auditory-tactual-kinesthetic (VATK) method of teaching reading emerged from the work of Grace Fernald and Helen B. Keller at the University of California at Los Angeles Clinic School in the 1920s. The technique was developed for teaching reading to children and adults who were of normal intelligence but had "extreme disabilities along specific lines."[3] The cases of extreme disability were labeled "word-blindness." Because Fernald felt that these individuals had not learned to read through a visual or auditory approach because of perceptual or sensory defects, she believed that tracing letters and words would aid their learning to read. Fernald described her basic method:

> The essentials of our technique consists of (1) the discovery of some means by which the child can learn to write words correctly, (2) the motivating of such writing, (3) the reading by the child of the printed copy of what he has written, (4) extensive reading of materials other than own compositions.[4]

In the initial stages of the method, the child is allowed to choose words that he wants to learn to read and write. As the child learns to write these words, he is encouraged to write stories. Words that he needs for his stories are written by the teacher. The child then learns these words by the VATK procedure. Finally, his stories are typed for him within twenty-four hours in order that he can

---

[3]Grace Fernald, *Remedial Techniques in Basic School Subjects* (New York: McGraw-Hill Book Co., 1943), p. 3. Reprinted by permission of the publisher.
[4]*Ibid.*, p. 33.

remember the original wording. The specific steps for the technique are summarized in the following passages from Fernald:

Stage One: The word is written for the child with crayon in large cursive or manuscript writing. The child traces the word, pronouncing it slowly as he traces. He writes the word and checks his copy with the original. He continues this procedure until he can correctly reproduce the word from memory. The word is added to a story which is typed for him by the teacher, and he then reads aloud his story in print. The words that have been learned by this procedure are then placed in alphabetical order in a file. Fernald stresses several points in this stage: (1) Finger contact in tracing is very important; (2) the child should not refer to the copy when writing the word; (3) if a child makes an error, he must start over entirely so that words will always be written in units; and (4) words should always be meaningful to the child.

Stage Two: According to Fernald, as the child progresses he is able to eliminate the tracing of the word. He looks at the word, pronounces it, and writes it from memory. He continues writing stories and keeping a word file.

Stage Three: In this stage, the word is no longer written for the child. He looks at a word on the printed page, says it, and then writes it. In this stage, the child begins to read books and read freely. The teacher consistently checks the retention of the words that are learned by the child.

Stage Four: After the child has learned a number of words, he is able to generalize and to "attack" new words based upon their similarity to known words. This is similar to the approach used by many basal reader programs in beginning reading, i.e., a child learns a stock of sight words and from these words phonics skills are taught. However, there is no deliberate attempt to teach phonics skills in the Fernald approach. "The child is never made to sound the words when he is reading nor is it sounded out for him by his teacher" (Fernald, 1943, p. 53). Instead the teacher tells the child unknown words. He writes the word in order to develop word recognition. In the final stage, the child is reading books of interest.[5]

During remedial training, teachers and parents do not read to the child. A rationale for this practice is that children with severe

---

[5]*Ibid.,* pp. 33-53.

reading problems are read to so often in order to have information imparted to them that they learn to expect this practice rather than attempting to develop necessary skills so that they can read themselves. After the child has learned to read, this practice of not reading to the child is eliminated. Even then, though, the child is read to only if he desires to listen.

There are more aspects to the approach utilized by Fernald. For example, she was interested in developing techniques for alleviating emotional stress which she felt to be a concomitant part of the reading disorder in many cases. Consequently, she developed methods so that success was stressed considerably, even though the weaknesses of the children were not emphasized.

VATK and Retarded Children: Fernald offered specific suggestions for using her method with retarded children. Essentially, she advocated the same methods as the ones she used with extreme disability cases. Some suggestions for modification include careful supervision of tracing and promoting or showing pictures to aid in story writing because of the lack of "ideational drive" among many retarded children (Fernald, 1943).

The *VATK* method has been found to be effective with some retarded children, although not with all (Kirk, 1933; McCarthy and Oliver, 1965). Cawley, Goodstein and Burrow have recommended the use of the VATK method with slow learners who have severe reading problems and "accompanying associative and sensory deficits."[6]

According to some authorities, the success of the method may not be a result so much of the tracing or writing of words as of the careful attention and concentration given to the word (Johnson, 1963; Morris, 1958; Ofman and Schaevitz, 1963; Tansley and Gulliford, 1960). Thus, children with visual discrimination, memory, or sequencing deficits may benefit more from the *VAK* or *VAKT* program than children with auditory problems (Myers and Hammill, 1969).

Adaptations of the VATK Approach: Variations of the *VATK* method employed by Fernald have been developed by reading specialists and special educators such as Monroe (1932), Johnson (1966), and Cawley, Goodstein, and Burrow (1972). Monroe's remedial instruction for children with severe reading problems encorporates a "sound tracing technique." Unlike Fernald, Monroe

---

[6]J. F. Cawley; H. A. Goodstein, and W. H. Burrow, *The Slow Learner and the Reading Problem* (Springfield, Illinois: Charles C. Thomas Co., 1972), p. 275.

placed considerable emphasis on drill and phonics instruction. Blending and articulation of sounds also are an integral part of his approach.

Based upon her experience with children with severe reading problems Johnson (1966) also modified Fernald's technique. She made no extreme changes in the technique but did supplement the stages slightly. Specific steps to be followed with her method depend upon the explicit needs of the child. For example, some children are introduced to the *VATK* procedure, while others may utilize *VAK* only if they do not trace the word. Tracing is done with the index and the middle fingers rather than with just one or two fingers as Fernald suggested. Finally, the child must write two correct copies of the word before he places it in his story.

An adaptation of the Fernald method for slow learners has been suggested by Cawley, Goodstein, and Burrow (1972) and accomplished by breaking down the *VATK* steps into three levels: *Level I — AV, VA*; *Level II — VAK*; and *Level III — VAKT*. The first level is used with children who can learn successfully through visual and auditory presentations. The *AV* implies a heavier stress on phonics where the *VA* indicates a stress on sight vocabulary development with an auditory component which does not necessarily place a heavy emphasis on phonics. Cawley, Goodstein, and Burrow caution against teachers or specialists perceiving reading as being either auditory or visual in nature. "Reading is not an either-or-activity and we feel it is essential that the treatment specialist retain this orientation for the slow learner."[7]

The second and third levels of this adaptation are utilized with children who have severe reading problems accompanied by associate and synthesis deficits. According to Cawley, Goodstein, and Burrow, the slow learner may trace the words as many as fifty times before he can reproduce it from memory. Progress is slow and the technique is one which is difficult to apply to a classroom setting because it requires individual attention by the teacher. We would tend to agree that this approach is a difficult one to implement in a classroom setting; it is not impossible to use though, if the teacher plans his lessons, activities, and grouping very carefully.

Montessori's Approach to Teaching Reading

Although Maria Montessori's methods extend far beyond reading skills, for the purpose of this discussion, only her approach to teaching reading will be included.

---

[7]*Ibid.*, p. 275.

Even though there are many Montessori schools in our country at the present time, these are for middle- or upper-middle class children, Montessori's methods emerged from her work as a physician at the Psychiatric Clinic of the University of Rome with "idiot" children who were institutionalized in insane asylums (Orem, 1969). She was very much interested in the educational aspects of mental retardation and had studied the works and methods developed by Itard and Sequin for working with the retarded. In order to develop a knowledge of the characteristics of retarded children in educational settings, Montessori spent two years (1898-1900) teaching retarded children and directing the activities of the other teachers in her institute (Orem, 1969). From her studies of the methods of other special educators, courses in experimental psychology, and actual experiences with retarded children, she developed her methods of teaching reading and writing and, because of the success of these methods with retarded children, decided to apply her techniques to the education of normal children as well.

The Montessori approach to teaching reading is multisensory in nature. It incorporated as many senses as possible in teaching the letters (e.g. tracing of sandpaper letters involves looking at the letter; hearing the sound of the letter pronounced by the teacher involves auditory skill; studying it carefully requires visual attention) (Montessori, 1912). The approach to teaching reading could be described as being synthetic in its beginning stages for the child learns to associate shapes of the letters with isolated letter sounds. Reading is taught initially as a mechanical process with no attention being given to comprehension.

Montessori's method (1964-65) combines writing in teaching reading and includes exercises for holding and using a pencil as a preparation for writing. As the child learns the alphabet through multisensory methods, he learns to write it also. From these letters, he is taught to compose words by using a movable wooden alphabet.

There has been little research reported specifically concerning the effectiveness of Montessori's methods of teaching reading with retarded children (Datta, 1969) even though Montessori's work began with retarded children, and she herself reported very good results in achievement in reading, writing, and mathematics (Datta, 1969). For a thorough discussion of Montessori's methods, see *Montessori and the Special Child* (Orem, 1969), *The Montessori Method* (Montessori, 1912), *A Montessori Handbook* (Orem, 1965), and *Dr. Montessori's Own Handbook* (Montessori, 1965).

The Gillingham-Stillman Alphabetic Approach

As were the techniques developed by Fernald, the Gillingham alphabetic method came about as the result of clinical work with children with extreme reading problems in the 1920s and 1930s. Samuel T. Orton, who was the director of the Language Research Project of the Neurological Institute and who is sometimes referred to as the "father of dyslexia" in America, was responsible for much of the research dealing with children who had learning difficulties (Orton, 1937). However, since Orton was interested in developing educational programs as well as conducting research on etiological and physiological factors of learning disorders, he requested Anna Gillingham, who was one of his research fellows as well as a former school psychologist and teacher to develop materials and programs for "dyslexic" children. Gillingham and Bessie Stillman, a remedial teacher, developed a remedial program which they termed the *alphabetic method* and which was described in their published manual, *Remedial Training of Children with Specific Disability in Reading, Spelling, and Penmanship* (Gillingham and Stillman, 1936). The manual is presently in its seventh edition (1965).

The Gillingham approach to teaching reading, spelling, and writing was based upon observations of characteristics that many children with reading problems possess, such as reversals, problems in written expression, and difficulties in associating sounds with symbols. The approach is multisensory because training involves association of visual, auditory, and kinesthetic presentations (Gillingham and Stillman, 1965; Orton, 1937).

Blending of discrete units of sound (a synthetic approach) is an important part of the training. In describing the basis of the method, Gillingham stated:

> The technique in this book is based upon the constant use of association of all the following, —how a letter or word looks, how it sounds, and how the speech organs or the hand in writing feel when producing it.[8]

Materials developed for the method include: phonetic drill cards, phonetic words (the Jewel case), syllable concepts, and little stories. Phonetic associations are taught by explicit procedures that

---

[8]A. Gillingham and B. Stillman, *Remedial Training for Children with Specific Disability in Reading, Spelling, and Penmanship*, 7th ed. (Cambridge: Education Publishing Service, 1965), p. 17.

attempt to record visual, auditory, and kinesthetic impression on the brain. Associations of the visual symbol with the name of the letter and of the visual symbol with the sound of the letter are taught by the use of the phonetic drill cards. In addition, associations of the name of the letter to the sound is developed. After these skills have been taught, the child learns to write the letter by tracing a copy made by the teacher, copying the letter itself, writing the letter from memory as well as writing it with eyes averted. Then, the child writes the letter after the teacher has given the sound. The individual letters combine into three letter-phonetic words which are found on the phonetic word; after the child learns to read and write three-letter words, these words are combined into stories which contain such sentences as "fat Sam had a bat."[9] These stories also are used for dictation purposes. A considerable amount of spelling also is part of the program.

The alphabetic method was not designed for retarded children, although Gillingham and Stillman have stated that some retarded children may profit from it (Gillingham and Stillman, 1936). Although it is important to remember that, as with any method, this program will not benefit all retarded children, this approach has been criticized especially because of its rigidity, lack of interesting reading material, and emphasis on phonics which may hinder a child with severe auditory perception difficulties (Frostig, 1966; Gates, 1947).

Remedial Reading Drills

Remedial Reading Drills (Hegge, Kirk, and Kirk, 1955) which is considered to be a complete program, was developed initially for use with retarded children. The contents of the program are contained in one book, although the approach was discussed by Kirk in 1940. This single-letter phonics program utilizes a multisensory or kinesthetic approach in learning the letter that represents the sounds. The sounds are blended into words as they are learned, and the changes in one syllable words that are blended are made generally in order to minimize confusion. Those who have used the program with retarded children have reported success (Hegge, 1934; Kirk, 1940).

---

[9]*Ibid.*, p. 60.

Multisensory Linguistic Programs

Several linguistic approaches to the teaching of reading include multisensory presentations: *The Intersensory Reading Method* (Pollack, 1969); *Multisensory Linguistic Approach* (Hillis, 1971); and the *Alphabetic-Phonetic-Structural-Linguistic Approach* (*APSL*) (Shedd, 1968).

The Intersensory Reading Approach was developed by Pollack for use with young dyslexic children. It combines a linguistic approach with visual, auditory, and kinesthetic modalities. "Under this method, reading, writing, and spelling are taught simultaneously."[10] At the prereading level, the program introduces a phonics readiness set and uses concrete objects to represent sounds. Blending of sounds and word building with the concrete object also are taught. After this stage is mastered, letter cards are introduced; workbooks in reading and writing are added at the first-grade level.

"The learning sequence is carefully programmed to reduce confusion and to build concepts in small steps. The vocabulary of 403 words is phonetically controlled and organized into linguistic spelling patterns."[11]

A variation of this approach, *The Hip Reader*, has been developed for use with inner-city nonreaders (Pollack, 1970).

The Multisensory Linguistic Approach (Hillis, 1971) combines the learning of forty-four phonemes with the auditory, kinesthetic, and visual senses. Hillis also developed physical signals to represent each phoneme. With this approach, much emphasis is placed upon the position of the mouth in producing the sound. In fact, the sounds are introduced according to the similarity of physical production (e.g. ten breath sounds, voiced consonant, nasal consonant, and glides [*l, r, y*], long and short vowel patterns). The child also is shown the positions in the mouth where the sounds originate.

One of the most important features in the approach is the use of the chalkboard. Hillis has stated:

> During the course of a morning, each child has his chance
> to perform at the chalkboard. This is the key to success in the

---

[10]S. Brown, ed., "A Hip Reader for Cool Cats," *Reading Newsreport* 4 (1970): 15.

[11]C. Pollock, *The Intersensory Reading Method* (New York: Book Lab, Inc., 1969), p. 2.

method. It is here that the children learn to listen to the sounds
that letters stand for, produce the symbols that make the word
look right on the lined chalkboard, and read the word back to
the group.[12]

After the child learns the ten breath sounds, he is introduced
to the vowels so that words can be written. Blending of sounds is
emphasized at this stage. Long vowel sounds are introduced in
linguistic patterns which are arranged "on jet black composition
board with white felt numbers and symbols."[13] For example, a circle
stands for a vowel while a square represents a consonant. One such
pattern would be: for no, we, go.

There is no empirical information in the literature as to the
effectiveness of this program, although such facets as board work
may be motivational for some retarded children.

*The Alphabetic-Phonetic-Structural-Linguistic Approach
(APSL)* was developed by Shedd (1968) while he was working with
dyslexic children and male adult illiterates. Shedd has described
the overall program:

> Seven years of research with dyslexic children employing
> different variables indicates that when highly structured mate-
> rial is employed in a one-to-one situation utilizing a multisen-
> sory approach, success may be obtained. The instructors do not
> need to be utilized. No special relationships need be established
> between the instructor and the student, no inticement need be
> employed, for student participation.[14]

Despite this statement, Shedd makes no claim that his method
is *the* method for working with all dyslexic children; however, he
has reported gains in achievement in reading as the result of this
individual tutoring program.

The approach is termed alphabetic-phonetic because the child
learns the name of the letter, how to reproduce the letter by memory, and the sound of the letter. The procedure in learning these
skills follows explicit steps. The letter is presented to the student
in reduced visibility; the student is asked the name of the letter; he
traces a model of the letter; he reproduces the letter on sandpaper
with his finger; and then he writes it on paper. A sound is given to

---

[12]Viola Hillis, "The Multisensory Linguistic Approach: The Key to Language Problems?," *Reading Newsreport* 6 (1971): 20.

[13]*Ibid.*, p. 24.

[14]C. L. Shedd, "Ptolemy Rides Again or Dyslexia Doesn't Exist," *The
Alabama Journal of Medical Science* 5 (1968): 500.

the letter, and the child is asked to write the letter and make the sound simultaneously. As individual letters are learned, they are immediately blended into words such as *at* for the blending of *a* and *t*. In the structural-linguistic aspect of the program, the consonants with "maximal discrimination" and short vowels are introduced initially (Shedd, 1968). The program progresses in complexity until a college-level vocabulary of 18,000 words has been introduced. Spelling is an important part of the program, and the children learn to spell as they read.

There are no pictures included in the materials and the passages are not interesting in content. However, motivation, in many cases, comes from the immediate success that is usually felt at the beginning of the program. The program requires a one-to-one situation which is very difficult to achieve in a classroom setting.

In summary, a combination of multisensory presentations and linguistics has some merits (e.g., it is highly structural, a fact which aids in spelling especially). Limitations include the restricted type of reading, the lack of motivations, or the lack of interesting material.

Multisensory Basal Reader Approaches

Recently, some basal reader programs have incorporated multisensory techniques in their developmental programs. Five of these programs are: *The Beginning to Read, Write, and Listen* (Rowland, 1971); *The Scott Foresman Reading Systems* (Scott Foresman, 1971); *Learning about Sounds and Letters* (Ginn, 1972); *The Open Court Reading Program* (Open Court, 1963); and *First Experiences* (McGraw-Hill, 1972).

The Beginning to Read, Write, and Listen is a multisensory program that was developed to introduce skills that fall between readiness and actual reading. The materials consist of workbooks and cassette tapes. This program adds the sense of smell to the multisensory approach by presenting a treated paper which releases a scent when scratched. In introducing the letter, many aids are provided; among these are those that give the scent of the objects (e.g. roses); textured letters, which help the child to remember the shape of the letter in easily remembered forms (e.g. the tail of the skunk forms an *s*); and the sounds of the letters on cassette tapes.

The Scott Foresman Systems offer many multisensory devices for primary reading. Word and alphabet blocks, alphabet records, and raised letters for tactile sensation are all part of its supplementary materials.

The Learning about Sounds and Letters Program, first part of the *Ginn 360 Series*, consists of a "sense kit" which includes materials that children can touch, see, feel, and hear. The kit contains three-dimensional plastic alphabets, a plastic easel, picture words, cards, records, duplicating masters, and a teacher's guide.

The First Experience is a multisensory approach for teaching letters and sounds. All modalities, including the tactile and kinesthetic, are utilized.

The Open Court Correlated Language Arts Program, consisting of the foundation program with supplementary workshop kit and basic readers, includes multisensory techniques as an integral part of the foundation program. Its kindergarten program (1970) is also multisensory in nature and includes trace-and-copy alphabet boards (seven large, wipe-clean cards) and exercises in tracing and copying letters. Such devices as alphabet puzzles which consist of ten different shapes from which all the letters can be made are part of the foundations program. Other tactile aids are the plastic alphabet, tracing sandpaper, alphabet paper — which contains faint letters for the child to trace, and the printer's box which contains movable letters. The sounds of the letters are taught by the use of a record and wall sound charts that contain concrete illustrations and mnemonic devices that enable the child to remember the sounds of the letters. For example, the sound of the letter *h* is illustrated by a man running. With this approach, the children write the letters as soon as they learn their names. For a detailed discussion of this approach, see the *Special Education Guide to the Open Court Program* (Robins, 1970).

Because many companies who publish reading materials are developing multisensory materials, the special-education teacher has many choices from which to select aids for multisensory teaching; however, if the teacher lacks money for purchasing these materials, most of these aids can be made by the teacher himself.

PROGRAMMED INSTRUCTION

Programmed instruction for the teaching of reading to the retarded has been utilized since the early 1960s (Malpass, 1967). Although many of the principles of programmed instruction are used in most classrooms, the method of teaching itself possesses specific characteristics. For example, in presenting a definition of programmed instruction method, Bigge (1964) has stated:

> Programmed instruction is a system of teaching and learn-
> ing within which pre-established subject matter is broken down
> into small, discrete steps and carefully organized into a logical
> sequence in which it can be learned readily by students. Each
> step builds deliberately upon the preceding one. The learner can
> progress through the sequence of steps at his own rate and he is
> reinforced immediately after each step; either he is given the
> correct response or he is permitted to proceed to the next step
> after he registers the correct response. Programmed instruction
> may be accomplished with or without the use of teaching ma-
> chines.[15]

In most programmed reading programs, units of materials are presented in frames which are designed to be self-explanatory and are one "logically related to the other."[16] The probability of error should be relatively low. Most programs attempt to arrive at not more than a 5 percent error rate; however, according to Malpass, this rate is difficult to achieve with retarded children. In this case, not more than a 15 percent error rate is advised (Malpass, 1967).

Two important aspects of programmed materials with retarded children are repetition and feedback for these aspects seem to provide for better acquisition and retention of materials (Malpass, 1967).

A number of studies have been conducted concerning the effectiveness of programmed instruction in teaching reading to the retarded (Greene, 1966). The results of the majority of these studies are that retarded children are able to learn to read by means of programmed instruction presented by the use of programmed texts, machines, or tutors. In studies dealing with methods of presentation, there has been no agreement regarding the best approach for presenting words or sight vocabulary (Greene, 1966).

Several investigators have compared the effectiveness of programmed reading instruction to other reading methods. In the majority of these studies, no significant differences between pro-

---

[15]Morris L. Bigge, *Learning Theories for Teachers* (New York: Harper & Row, Publishers, 1964), p. 134.

[16]Leslie F. Malpass, "Programmed Instruction for Retarded Children," in *Mental Retardation; Appraisal, Education, and Rehabilitation*, ed. Alfred A. Baumeister (Chicago: Aldine Publishing Co., 1967), p. 216.

grammed instruction and traditional methods were found (Greene, 1966; Hofmeister, 1971; Kaplan, 1971; Malpass, et al., 1963, 1964). In the Malpass, et al. studies, automated instruction was found to be superior to traditional methods but not to individual human tutoring.

Another technique of programmed instruction was developed by Ellson, et al. (1965) and is termed "programmed tutoring" because a tutor is used to reinforce the child's oral responses. Basal readers are used as the basis for instruction, but, in this program, classroom teaching of reading is supplemented by fifteen-minute sessions of individual tutoring. Nonprofessionals who are trained in teaching letter and word recognition, use of phonics rules, word analysis, and comprehension skills are employed in addition to teachers. The tutors also are trained to use specific sequential steps for teaching skills. A branching technique of instruction is utilized (i.e., if errors are made by the child, the tutor is to take specific carefully designed steps for correcting such errors). Programmed tutoring has been used with disadvantaged and slow children, and conclusions from the research conducted indicate that programmed tutoring is effective, especially when it is combined with classroom teaching (Ellson, et al., 1965).

Programmed instruction in reading may be an effective means of teaching reading skills in that it provides for the individualization of instruction and overlearning that may be necessary for the retention of some skills (Cegelka and Cegelka, 1970). Whether or not the teacher decides to use programmed teaching machines or textbooks, he first must make a careful analysis of the content and mode of presentation. Careful programming requires a knowledge of the sequential steps in learning a particular skill and the amount of information that should be presented in any one step. Such knowledge is difficult to obtain in the area of reading. In order to construct programmed reading materials, one must know what words are the easiest to learn and what steps are important in learning the skill, yet most of this information has not been confirmed. Some research is presently being conducted which may yield some knowledge concerning the discrete skills employed in learning to read (Coleman, 1970). If this information becomes available, it can be utilized in the construction of programmed reading materials.

As with any method, programmed instruction should not be used exclusively in teaching reading to the retarded. Indeed, if every child in the classroom receives the same programmed materials, it may become individualized only in terms of pacing. The mode of presentation is the same for every child; therefore, programmed instruction provides for the needs of the child only if his needs are matched to the information obtained from diagnostic procedures.

According to Hofmeister (1969), programmed instruction in reading may be very effective if modified to meet the needs of the students. He believes that criteria for judgment of use of the materials should be: the objectives of the program, the placement and vocabulary level of the materials, the length of the program, the reusability and cost factors, and the supporting materials (e.g. films, tapes, and records) available.

Programmed Textbooks

Sullivan Programmed Readers: The *Sullivan Programmed Readers* (Buchannon and Sullivan Associates, 1963) is a programmed workbook and textbook approach to teaching reading for Grades 1 through 6. In this program, discrete units of reading skills are presented in frames in a linear manner. In such linear programs, the steps follow a single pattern, with one bit of material following another regardless of the response of the child, although some programs do employ branching which establishes alternative steps depending upon the response of the participant.

The *Sullivan* program is a programmed linguistic approach which starts with the teaching of the alphabet in addition to the letter sounds. As each single letter sound is introduced, it is combined with a previously learned letter sound such as /a/-/t/. The short vowel and consonant sounds are taught first, along with some sight words, such as *the*.

Before the child begins the program, he must know the names of the letters of the alphabet, how to print all the letters, the concept that letters make words, and various phonics skills. These skills are taught by the teacher with the aid of ditto materials and board work.

The effectiveness of this particular program with both normal and retarded children has been studied (Hammill and Mattleman, 1969; Hofmeister, 1969; McNeil, 1964; Ruddell, 1965; Jones, 1966; and Woodcock, 1967). The overall results of these studies suggest that children are able to learn to read by using this program but that there is no significant increase in their reading achievement over that of children using traditional methods.

Although the program has all the advantages that other programmed materials possess (e.g. self-pacing, immediate feedback), some of its disadvantages are: the material is not highly motivating or interesting to all children; children frequently obtain the correct answers without understanding the reason for them; and the mode of presentation does not place much emphasis on the auditory channel.

Another programmed series, the *M. W. Sullivan Reading Program* (Behavioral Research Laboratories, 1966), includes twenty programmed texts, correlated readers that are of high interest/low vocabulary, and correlated tapes. These tapes provide a means for auditory presentation. The format is designed in such a manner that it can be appealing to an adult as well as a child.

Progressive Choice Method: Like the Sullivan series, the progressive choice method combines elements of programmed construction and the linguistic approach to reading. An attempt has been made by Woolman (1955), who originally developed the program, to combine several principles of learning theory into an approach to teaching reading. Discrimination learning, built-in success, active response of the participant, immediate feedback, and multisensory presentation are some of the learning principles considered in this program (Woolman, 1965).

The program is unique in that it attempts to simplify the complexity of the reading materials presented in the earlier stages of reading. For example, the basic inconsistencies of the English language are eliminated in the beginning by very systematically introducing letters and sounds that correspond easily and can be discriminated easily as well as word patterns that are highly controlled. Each letter has only one sound, one shape (upper case), and one form (the singular). As each additional letter is introduced, it is combined with previously learned ones.

As the child learns the sound and name of the letter, visually, he also traces the entire letter; then, he traces a dotted form of the letter; and finally, he writes it on his own. In addition, comprehension is considered because the words presented supposedly are already part of the child's listening and speaking vocabulary; the reading vocabulary thus is introduced and reinforced in meaningful context.

A motivational factor, the use of incentives via peer recognition, is utilized in this program. As the child progresses through the program, he earns the privilege to assist other students and has titles such as "student instructor" awarded to him.

The progressive choice method has been designed specifically for retarded learners and children with perceptual programs. *Lift Off to Reading* (Woolman, 1966) is a three-cycle program which was developed for elementary children, while *Reading in High Gear* (Woolman, 1965) was designed for retarded and disadvantaged adolescents.

Research conducted on the success of the program indicates that it is an effective program for both normal and retarded learners (Bloomer, 1960; Davy, 1962), although it has been criticized by some for vocalizing the sounds of the consonants (e.g. *guh* for the letter sound of /g/). Some reading authorities feel that the consonant sounds should not be presented to children individually because, in reality, they possess no sounds of their own but are merely positions in the mouth that come before or after uttering a vowel sound (Edwards, 1966). In addition, Woolman has been criticized for utilizing nonsense syllables for some of the phoneme-grapheme relationships (Edwards, 1966). Some distinct advantages to the program are: the use of incentives for motivational purposes, systematic instruction, and incorporation of teaching and writing and spelling skills. Finally, the program attempts to minimize visual discrimination difficulties which have been reported to be a problem for disabled readers and retarded children (Barrett, 1965; Blackman and Burges, 1970).

Peabody Rebus Reading Program: The Rebus Reading Program (Woodcock and Clark, 1969) is a programmed reading approach which employs rebuses (pictures of symbols of printed words) in the beginning stages of reading. The program consists of five workbooks containing 400 frames each. The child is able to work independently through the program because each frame provides feedback. In this process, the child applies water to his answer, and if if he is correct, the space turns green; if he is wrong, the space turns red. Fillers and water wells are provided for the marking system.

Words are introduced gradually throughout the program; by the completion of Book Five, the child has been exposed to 120 words. The child also has learned sentence reading because the symbols are placed in sentence form early in the program.

A supplementary lessons kit, which aids in group instruction, is available for use with Books One and Two. This material consists of rebus word, picture, and sentence cards; answer strips; and review masks for covering students' responses in the workbooks.

As with most programs already discussed, *The Rebus Reading Program* is effective in teaching word recognition to retarded children; however, it does not appear to be superior to traditional approaches (Woodcock, 1967). It has the advantage of being motivational to some children, especially those who have experienced considerable failure in reading in the past. There is also some evidence to indicate that young children, normal as well as retarded, learn very effectively by a visual-pictorial method (Bruininks and Clark, 1972), although retarded children may have more difficulty than normals in processing information presented visually, especially when it is presented in a complex manner (Olson, 1971).

Edmark Reading Program: Another program that utilizes aspects of programmed instruction is the *Edmark Reading Program* developed by Bijou and associates (Edmark Associates, 1972). This approach, which is the result of research and development at the Rainier Schools, Buckleu, Washington, was designed specifically for teaching retarded children or nonreaders to read. The program teaches the comprehension and use of a 150-word vocabulary. There are 227 lessons of four kinds: word recognition lessons, which teach one or two words per lesson, with distractors of increasing difficulty used in each frame; direction books, which teach the child to follow printed directions; picture-phrase matching lessons; and storybook lessons, sixteen separate stories which are read orally by the student.

The program incorporates many operant learning principles, such as training in making discriminative responses, cueing, shaping, fading, and stimulus response chaining (Bijou, et al., 1966). Elements of programmed instruction included are: lessons that are broken down into small discrete sequential steps; reinforcement which is used by the teacher in the form of verbal praise (token reinforcement may be used but this is optional); and progression by the children at their own rate. A small teaching machine, the Grolier Min/Max, may also be used for the purpose of framing the lessons. Lessons may be taught individually or in small groups.

Although the program is not primarily self-instructional, the publishers claim that no special training is needed on the part of the teacher for it. The manual gives specific procedures and reponses which the teacher is to use in each lesson. For example, in the Word Recognition Lesson One (HORSE), the child is asked to point to the word *horse*, which is among such distractors as *it* and *un*. If the child is correct, the teacher verbally reinforces the child with "very good" and continues the lesson by asking the child to read the word orally. If the child points to the incorrect word, the teacher's response is "no"; he then points to the word *horse* while saying, "This is the word *horse*" (Edmark Associates, 1972, p. 12). After the teacher receives the correct response, the child is moved to the next frame.

Other features of the program include procedures for charting the progress of children, pretests and review tests, and a prereading unit for determining if the student has the necessary skills in order to benefit from the program.

The development of the program extended over a ten-year span and included research on the achievement of retarded children. Although token reinforcement has been used with these lessons, many children achieve equally well without the use of tokens (Edmark Associates, 1972). Bijou and associates have reported considerable success with this reading program in teaching the retarded (Lent, 1968).

Advantages of the program are that it is consistent, sequential, requires no special training for the teacher or tutor, is moderate in cost, and allows for monitoring of the child's progress. Limitations are that it almost requires a one-to-one relationship and does not have substantial supplementary reading materials for the better readers.

Fitzhugh Plus Program: The *Fitzhugh Plus Program* (Fitzhugh and Fitzhugh, 1966) combines a perceptual approach with programmed instruction. The child receives immediate feedback similar to the rebus program by means of a special pencil which marks in green if the child is correct. The program consists of workbooks that introduce spatial organizations, language, and numbers.

In the workbooks consisting of spatial organizations, bits of information are presented in frames which are divided into columns. The child is to match the figure in the left column with the correct one among other figures in the right column. These workbooks attempt to develop the child's ability to perceive objects in space and time.

The language and number skills are presented in a similar manner. Skills, such as identification of pictures, numbers, letters, and words, and some mathematical operations are presented in this workbook.

This approach is not a total program to teaching reading. Instead, it may be used as supplementary material in introducing or reinforcing such skills as letter recognition; the decided advantage of it is that it allows the child to work independently. There are two apparent disadvantages of the program: The exercises for developing the ability in spatial organization may not necessarily improve letter or word recognition (Guralnick, 1972); the format is dull, and, therefore, may not sustain a child's interest. Although this program may be very effective with some children, it is still true that there is no one method of visual-motor discrimination that seems to be the best for all children (Jenson and King, 1970).

PROGRAMMED INSTRUCTION AND TEACHING MACHINES

Some attempt has been made to teach programmed reading through the use of machines in the same fashion as with programmed textbooks. The results of comparison studies of the use of teaching machines as opposed to programmed tests indicate no significant differences in retention of the material, although there is some evidence that children complete more frames using programmed texts than they do with teaching machines (Goldstein and Gotkin, 1963). Also, according to Blackman and Capobianco (1965), retarded children can learn to read as effectively through traditional methods as through the use of machines. As do programmed textbooks, teaching machines have the advantages of individualizing instruction, enabling self-pacing, being motivational, and reducing distractions (Malpass, 1967). However, a teaching machine is only as effective "as the program that goes in it."[17] Disadvantages include the fact that many such machines are beyond the cost that most school systems can afford. In addition, skills such as critical reading or comprehension are not emphasized as much as word recognition skills in these programs (McCreary, 1970), although this is also true of programmed textbooks. Several teaching machines that have been used with the retarded are presented in the following section even though some of these do not utilize programmed material.

Edison Responsive Environment (ERE)

The *Edison Responsive Environment* was developed in a cooperative effort by O. K. Moore and associates and the engineering team of the Thomas A. Edison Research Laboratory, McGraw-Edison

---

[17] *Ibid.*, p. 220.

Company, West Orange, New Jersey (Moore, 1964). In developing the program, which employs a "talking typewriter," Moore made several assumptions regarding teaching reading and writing skills:

1. There is a one-to-one correspondence between spoken and written forms of English.
2. Written English is visual speech, while spoken English is audible writing.
3. Writing is "on a par with speaking and reading with listening."[18]

In teaching the child the reading, writing and listening skills, the teacher follows a specific program.

Phase I: Free Exploration. Prior to this stage, a child is introduced to a booth where the *ERE* is housed. A special environment, free of distractions and windows, was designed specifically for the *ERE*. The child's fingernails are painted with nontoxic water colors to match the colors on the key board. In this phase, the child is allowed to explore freely. If a child strikes a key, the tape system of the *ERE* pronounces the name of the character struck. The system is highly mechanized, consisting of a computer input and read-out device, three memory systems, an audio-recording system, and two visual exhibition systems. Frustration for the child is eliminated because the keys will not jam, and the machine is virtually errorless.

Phase II: Search and Match. After a certain time in exploratory activities, the length of which depends upon the child, letter and punctuation marks are presented. The child is to find the proper key and match it to the punctuation.

Phase III: Word Construction. In this phase, words are introduced and the skills of reading and writing are developed. Words and the pictorial representations are presented; however, pictures are used sparingly. Words from stories, such as *Aesop's Fables*, are employed. In the writing phase, children dictate stories into a microphone. These stories usually are generated in the "transfer" room which is similar to a classroom.

---

[18]O. K. Moore, "Autoletic Responsive Environments and Exceptional Children," in *The Special Child in Century 21,* ed. J. Hellmuth (Seattle, Washington: Special Child Publications, 1964), p. 95. Reprinted by permission of the publisher.

Phase IV: Reading and Writing. In this phase, children read and develop stories.

In Moore's program, a child is allowed to leave the *ERE* booth whenever he desires, but he may not stay for more than thirty minutes. A classroom setting, the transfer room, provides transfer of skills learned independently in the booth.

Although no research, except for reports of case studies, has been conducted to verify the success of the *ERE* with retarded children, the program does seem to have many advantages in teaching reading and writing to exceptional children; for example, it is self-pacing, motivational, and errorless (Cegelka and Cegelka, 1970). Unfortunately, if research does prove this program to be superior to other methods of teaching reading to the retarded, it still has the severe limitation of being extremely expensive. One typewriter costs forty thousand dollars, and this price does not include the cost of maintenance.

Computer Assisted Instruction (CAI)

Computer Assisted Instruction (CAI) also has been offered as a method of individualizing instruction (Atkinson and Fletcher, 1972; Mendelsohn, 1970; and Wills, 1971). Although at first the cost of the program was beyond what most school districts could afford, recent attempts have been made to lower the cost of *CAI*. One *CAI* developed at Stanford University in 1965 was designed to teach reading skills in kindergarten through third grade. In the earlier stages of its development, the program was designed to require very little dependence on teacher assistance; however, because of the cost of such a program, the newer *CAI* is designed to be a supplement to classroom instruction.

In describing this present program, Atkinson and Fletcher have stated:

> The aim of the reading project during the last three years has been to design and implement a low cost *CAI* curriculum that would act as a supplement to normal classroom instruction. A student terminal in the current program consists only of a "model 33" teletypewriter with an audio head set. There is no graphic or photographic capability at the student terminal, and the character set of the teletypewriter includes only upper case letters. On the other hand, audio for the *Stanford CAI System* is quite flexible. The audio messages are stored in digitized form

on magnetic discs; the system provides for rapid (thirty milliseconds) random access to any one of the 6000 recorded words and messages.[19]

More expensive versions of *CAI* include television sets or cathode ray tubes (CRT's) which can present any type of material that can be presented in books; the child can respond directly on the picture tube by pointing or using a "talking pencil"; the response then is recorded electronically. If a child points to the wrong item, the computer provides the next sequence on the screen that would aid the child in learning the necessary skill in order to make a correct response.

If a school utilizes *CAI*, a terminal that links the system to a control computer is placed in the school. These terminals may be located at some distance from the central computer. Program components may be divided into several parts or strands to develop such skills as reading readiness and vocabulary. Procedures for teaching a skill may include the student's receiving two cues — spoken and written words and responding with both a visual and auditory correction if the child makes an error.

CAI has been used effectively with normal, disadvantaged, and educationally handicapped children (Atkinson and Fletcher, 1972; Brown, 1970; Mendelsohn, 1970). Unfortunately, as with the *ERE*, the cost factor is a limitation. According to Atkinson and Fletcher (1972), the cost of their program is eighty dollars per student per year for a daily twelve-minute session. Companies such as Quick Responses Systems Inc. have developed less expensive systems.

The MAST Teaching System

The MAST Teaching System distributed by Keystone View Company is an automated teaching machine developed by MAST (1962). The machine consists of a projector, filmstrips, and means for providing responses to the child. In this procedure, the child copies a letter, word, etc. on recording paper. He then presses a button which reveals the correct answer. Because both images appear simultaneously, he is able to compare his response with the one provided by the machine. This machine has been found to be a

---

[19]Richard C. Atkinson and John D. Fletcher, "Teaching Children to Read with a Computer," *The Reading Teacher* 25 (1972): 319.

reliable teaching device and is relatively free from mechanical flaws (Malpass, 1967).

Tutorgram

An inexpensive teaching device is the *Tutorgram* distributed by the Enrichment Reading Corporation of America. This compact device is designed to give immediate feedback to a child. When instructional cards are placed on the machine, the child uses an "electric pointer" to select his answers which are adjacent to holes punched in the card. If he is correct, the light and buzzer on the instrument will respond. The software for the Tutorgram consists of fifty-four cards in series on the following subject areas: preschool awareness and identification, social studies, mathematics, language arts, and science. The reading cards include lessons on word recognition and phonics skill (through a visual approach). There are also blank cards so that the teacher can make his own lessons.

Hoffman Reading Achievement Program

The Hoffman Reading Program distributed by Hoffman Information Systems has been used with retarded children from the preschool to the intermediate and junior high level. The hardware for this system includes a compact machine combining a filmstrip projector and a record player. Filmstrips are accompanied by a paced record. The program introduces study units that are for developing reading skills in children from preschool through Grade 6. As with the other program discussed, the program is fairly expensive.

Language Master

Bell & Howell's *Language Master* is a compact machine which does not utilize programmed material but does provide feedback for the child by means of a flash card which has a word printed on the front and a strip of magnetic tape on the bottom. This card moves across a track in the machine as the recorded voice pronounces the word. Provision is made for the child to record a response. The cards available provide instruction in visual and auditory discrimination skills, phonetic skills, and sight vocabulary. There are thirty-six card programs available for kindergarten through twelfth grade as well as blank tapes to introduce reading skills material developed by the teacher. Although the program is moderately expensive, the price is not beyond the limit of many school systems. The present authors have used this program with retarded children and have found it to be highly motivating. Children who appear to be distractible and to have short attention spans can work constructively for long periods of time on this machine. In fact, a controlling influence on behavior of children seems to be a general characteristic of many teaching machines (Malpass, 1967).

Audio Flashcard Reader

The *EFI Audio Flashcard Reader* distributed by Electronic Futures is similar to the *Language Master*. In this case, the software for the program consists of reading readiness and phonetic-linguistic skills on a prekindergarten and kindergarten level. Much of the program is semiconcrete in that the visual presentation includes pictures and auditory environmental sounds.

TTC Magnetic Card Reader

Teaching Technology Corporation's machine is similar to the Language Master and the Audio Flashcard Reader.

Audio Tape Recorders

One of the most versatile technological aids available for classroom use is the tape recorder, reel, or cassette. This is especially true when the equipment is provided with headphone sets. A teacher may purchase available supplementary reading programs or devise his own to use with a tape recorder. We have found the tape recorder to be a highly motivating and effective device for working with retarded children. Addresses of several tape recorders and taped reading programs are listed in the Appendix.

Machines for Improving Perceptual Speed and Reading Rate

A multitude of machines for improving perceptual speed or reading rate have been developed. Although many teachers report that these machines are highly motivating to students, research results do not substantiate their effectiveness in improving and maintaining reading rate or efficiency of eye movements (Witham, 1969):

In describing these devices, Witham has stated:

> There are presently available over twenty forms of instrumentation and training films for the reading teacher. Approximately one-half of these are designed to improve perceptual skills through some form of tachistoscopic training. This type of visual exercise has a variety of goals: accurate form perception and increased visual discrimination; rapid visual perception (the ocular and mental intake of visual material); organized retention for a stronger visual memory, better directional attack and an awareness of components as parts of the whole; and finally such by-products as increasing attention, concentration, eye-hand coordination and so on.[20]

We have seen several of these types of machines in use in countless special classes. In most cases, teachers did not fully understand the objectives of the devices and did not use them correctly. Because the present research does not support the overall effectiveness of these devices and because they are expensive, we recommend that money for reading materials be invested elsewhere, especially if the teacher is on a limited budget.

See Witham (1969) for a more detailed discussion of these machines. There are many more teaching machines available that were not discussed in detail. The appendix at the end of the book gives addresses of the distributors of several of these devices.

UNIQUE READING APPROACHES

There are other approaches used in remediation which contain elements of various approaches but retain a definite uniqueness which does not allow them to be categorized except under multiple categories. These programs were designed for special reading cases and include: *Words in Color, Psycholinguistic Color System, Distar, Modern Reading,* and *The Neurological Impress Method.*

---

[20]Anthony P. Witham, "The Index to Reading Material (Devices and Films for Improving Readings)," in *Readings on Reading,* ed. Alfred J. Binter, John J. Daebel, and Leonard K. Kise, pp. 499-506 (Scranton, Pennsylvania: International Textbook Co., 1969).

Words in Color

"*Words in Color* is a system of writing the language in a phonetic manner by having a distinct color for each phoneme."[21] This approach, which was developed by Gattegno (1962), includes thirty-nine shades of color to match the thirty-nine phonemes which Gattegno has named in the English language. Large wall charts with black backgrounds are employed in order to teach the colors and their corresponding letters. When the teacher writes on the board, he uses colored chalk coded with the same colors as the charts. The remainder of the printed material, such as the books, is in black and white.

A transfer is made from color to regular print by using the assumption that the child has learned the sounds of the letters and will no longer need the color as an aid. Zintz (1970) feels that this program is very complicated and probably not very useful in the teaching of reading as a thinking process. Spache (1972) agrees with Zintz and has stated that no supporting statistics exist to indicate that *Words in Color* offers any particular advantage. In addition, he has indicated:

> . . . that, when given a stimulus containing several clues learners tend to select a single clue for retention, adding a clue such as color, a different typeface, or even different symbols. . . . tends to complicate the learning task. Moreover, these additional clues must be discarded in the transition to normal reading, and [are] therefore of no help in transfer.[22]

On the other hand, some research does favor the use of color. Jones (1965) found color too highly significant as a factor in visual perception in early reading, while Hinds (1966), in studying the use of *Words in Color* with illiterate adults, found the *Words in Color* group to have significantly better scores in both mean vocabulary and comprehensive scores compared to the group using a conventional method of teaching reading. Dodds (1966), in comparing *Words in Color* to traditional basal readers, found the *Words in*

---

[21]Miles V. Zintz, *The Reading Process: The Teacher and the Learner* (Dubuque, Iowa: William C. Brown Co., 1970), p. 411.

[22]G. D. Spache, *The Teaching of Reading* (Bloomington, Indiana: Phi Delta Kappa, Inc., 1972), p. 62.

Color group to have significantly different word recognition skills and spelling at the end of the first grade and to have mean comprehension scores which were also significantly higher during second grade. These findings were not true for the primary-age children.

Other studies have found no significant differences in the use of *Words in Color* compared to the use of other methods, such as basal reader (Hill, 1967; Kaufman, 1972). In a study with borderline retardates, Lockmiller and DiNello (1970) found no significant differences in reading achievement between *Words in Color* and a basal reader program.

Psycholinguistic Color System

Although the phonemes are color coded in this approach, only seventeen vowel phonemes are color coded as opposed to forty-seven colors used in *Words in Color*. Bannatyne designed the program in 1968 to be used with kindergarten and first-grade children (Bannatyne, 1971, p. 647). In stating the theory behind this program, Bannatyne has writen:

> The theory behind the system is that most dyslexic children suffer from an inability to remember constantly changing paterns of sound-symbol associations and therefore the simultaneous manual, auditory, and visual sequencing of phoneme and letters is the essential element in learning to read. The letters of the system are used for systematic word and sentence building, for syllabication practice, for the analysis and synthesis of successive sounds, and for various activities and word games.[23]

The materials for the teacher's guide series include programmed workbooks, colored pencils, games, flash cards, and wall charts containing the color coded phoneme/grapheme relationships.

Distar

The Distar program (Engelmann and Bruner, 1969) was designed specifically for teaching beginning reading to culturally deprived and slow-learning children. According to Engelmann (1967), this program should enable children who have mental ages of four or

---

[23]Alexander Bannatyne, "The Color Phonics System," in *The Disabled Reader: Education of the Dyslexic Child,* ed. John Money and Gilbert S. Chuffman (Baltimore: Johns Hopkins Press, 1966), p. 193.

above to learn to read. Thus, he refutes the traditional belief that a child must have a mental age of 6.6 years in order to learn to read. Some authorities in the field of special education have suggested that educable retarded children's reading instruction be delayed until they have mental ages of 6.6 or above, but with Engelmann and Bruner's program, this would not be necessary. Engelmann has stated:

> The major implication of our work seems to be that children with relatively low mental ages (initially less than four years) can learn to read if the instruction is adequately geared to give them instruction in all of the subskills demanded by the complex behavior we call reading. Furthermore, virtually all children with mental ages of four or over can learn to read. Their progress is relatively slow, but all can progress from one subskill to the next until they are reading. With the emphasis on subskills, the teacher is in a position to know what skills a child has not learned. She therefore knows which skills to work on. When a child masters a given skill, the teacher can proceed to the next one.[24]

The Distar program incorporates the teaching of skills that are considered to be necessary for learning to read. It is assumed that normal children naturally possess these skills while problem readers and retarded children must be taught them systematically in order to learn to read (Bruner, 1968).

Initially, the program emphasizes sequencing, left-right progression, and the association of sound with a symbol. The children are taught that these sounds occur in fixed orders in words and to spell by orally pronouncing the sounds (e.g., /c/-/at/). The program stresses the skills that are considered to be difficult for slower children to master (e.g., blending and rhyming). Children are taught that words that are said slowly (/c/-/a/-/t/) can be blended by saying them fast. In order to minimize confusion in learning the sounds and symbols, a basic set of nine phonemes that are not similar in sound or visual appearance are presented initially, with the symbols formed in a manner that reduces visual discrimination confusions; some symbols are joined together (e.g., th). After twenty sounds have been introduced, the children are able to read story books that contain from one to twenty-five words. Sounds

---

[24]Siegfried Engelmann, "Classroom Techniques: Teaching Reading to Children with Low Mental Age," *Education and Training of the Mentally Retarded* 2 (1967): 199.

that have not been introduced are represented in small print in words and diacritical marks are placed over the vowels.

Materials for the program consist of teacher presentation notebooks and take-home materials. In *Reading I*, teacher materials consist of the teacher's guide, the related skills book, *Sounds and Reading Sounds — Books A, B*, and *C*. Records on the sounds presented in the program as well as techniques for teacher presentation also are included.

Student materials include take-home blending sheets, take-home sound-symbol sheets, take-home stories, take-home writing sheets, and workbooks containing the worksheets (Engelmann and Bruner, 1969).

Reading II contains a continuation of *Sounds and Reading Sounds* with *Books D, E*, and *F*, a recycling book, and other supplementary materials, such as progress indicators. Take-home items are also included in *Reading II*, and the materials are intended to be used for a two-year program.

In presenting the materials, the teacher conducts lessons with small homogeneous groups of children (determined by pre-tests) who are seated around him for twenty to thirty minutes. The presentation booklets are placed in easel form so that the teacher can hold them in his lap. Suggestions for reinforcement, pacing, and correction of children are given in the manual. Children are able to monitor their progress by crossing out the sounds on the plastic-coated sound pages in the teacher's notebook (Engelmann and Bruner, 1969). The *Distar Library Series Preschool-Grade 2* (Engelmann and Bruner, 1971) has been developed to reinforce the skills in the *Distar Reading I* and *II*.

Engelmann (1967) has reported that the program has been successful with culturally deprived children, many of whom were on the "fringe of the mentally handicapped."[25] Another study, conducted by Williamson (1970) reported that children of all ability groups profited from the Distar program, while Guinet (1971) found that teachers who used the program had very favorable opinions of students' progress as well as its effectiveness in motivating children to learn to read.

More research is needed before a true appraisal of the effectiveness of Distar with retarded children can be made. A few of the assumptions behind the program are not ones on which total

---

[25]*Ibid.*, p. 195.

agreement would be held by all reading authorities. For example, Engelmann takes issue with the assumption that children learn differently and must be treated differently; he has stated that if the criterion of performance (ability to translate symbols into words) is the same for all children, the steps for reaching this criterion should be the same.

Because of Engelmann's belief, variations in the Distar program are obtained through the use of pacing. A very slow child may need more time, and a faster child may possibly require a considerable number of repetitions before either child can learn a given skill (Engelmann and Bruner, 1969). Criterion tests are included so that children can be tested after each segment. If they do not pass the test, presentations are repeated.

In addition, the assumption that the program "is designed so that every skill the child needs in order to read is taught"[26] may provoke comment by some authorities, although at the present time, the reasearch is not conclusive concerning the prerequisite skills for learning to read for all children.

Modern Reading

The Modern Reading Program (Clark, 1967) is not widely distributed. It consists of features from various reading methods or approaches. In describing her program, Clark has stated:

> It is a combined phonetic-linguistic-sight method of teaching reading. It is taught in a dramatic way almost without verbal instructions in order to emphasize physical and visual learning. Much use is made of repetition and imitation in brief game-like lessons. Slow pupils are especially benefited by racing games. The curricula is enriched with imagery and rhyme to stimulate general language appreciation. Special techniques are described to improve the child's ability to concentrate and finish a task.[27]

In the beginning stages of the program, individual sounds are taught. As the child progresses, he learns to read words such as *rock, rush,* and *room.* As with other programs, such as Distar at-

---

[26]Siegfried Engelmann and E. C. Bruner, *Distar Reading: An Instructional System* (Chicago: Science Research Associates, 1969), p. 19.

[27]Hulda R. Clark, *Teachers' Guide to Modern Reading.* Orange City, Florida: Humanitas Curriculum, 1967.

tempts are made to eliminate visual discrimination difficulties. Reinforcement is also utilized in the form of praise or prizes.

In the early stages of the program, the child and teacher read orally together, but, gradually the child is allowed to read alone. He is also encouraged to memorize the words in the books. The lessons are planned so that the teacher can introduce them to children in individual or small-group settings.

Material consists of small paperbound books, tag board strips consisting of letters and words, and two records. Specific supplementary reading materials also are suggested.

The Modern Reading Program was designed especially for problem readers and culturally disadvantaged children with its main focus on the motivation and concentration of the children as well as on teaching groups of words that are phonetically and linguistically controlled. Suggestions are given in the manual for working with hyperactive and slow-reacting children. The program is very inexpensive and may be of benefit to some children who are extremely hard to motivate or who need additional assistance in phonetic skills.

Neurological-Impress Method

This technique for teaching reading was first used by Heckelman in 1952 with children who had average or above intelligence but had not learned to read to their potential. Heckelman has described his program:

> The neurological-impress method is a system of unison reading whereby the student and the teacher read aloud, simultaneously at a rapid rate. The disabled reader is placed slightly to the front of the teacher with the student and the teacher holding the book jointly. As the student and teacher read the materials in unison, the voice of the teacher is directed into the ear of the student at close range.[28]

Other features of the program include no need for special preparation of the materials prior to the unison reading session; the teacher's use of his finger to follow oral reading; the fact that the

---

[28]R. G. Heckelman, "The Neurological Impress Method of Remedial Reading Instruction," *Academic Therapy* 4 (1969): 278.

teacher does not teach any phonics skills or word recognition; and the lack of specific comprehension questions from the teacher after the reading session, although the child may volunteer any information he desires about the material.

The rationale for the approach is that the feedback to the child may affect a neurological change. Heckleman has hypothesized that this method involves a combination of reflexive neurological systems. He has stated:

> It is further hypothesized that this method of reading is probably one of the most direct and fundamental systems of reading. It involves a combination of reflexive neurological systems. In a sense it could be said to bypass the associational reading processes. The child is exposed only to accurate, correct reading patterns. The correct systems are deeply impressed. Using these reflex systems as a basic vehicle for the correct reading process, the child can begin to read.[29]

In a study conducted by Heckelman, the results indicated that the program was successful with problem readers (Heckelman, 1962), but another study conducted by Hollingsworth (1970) utilizing the *EFI Wireless System* and taped stories for the unison reading rather than the teacher found the method to be ineffective. As a result, Hollingsworth hypothesized that the program may depend upon the personal involvement of the teacher with the child. One of the limitations of the program is that it is time-consuming (Heckelman's study utilized unison reading fifteen minutes a day, five days a week.) and requires a one-to-one relationship. In addition, teachers may find it difficult to decide what children especially would profit from such a method. It is apparent that more investigation is needed to determine why this program is effective with some children.

MATERIALS AND APPROACHES FOR INTERMEDIATE AND SECONDARY EDUCABLE RETARDED

Most of the approaches that have been reviewed in this chapter are used for teaching beginning reading, although many (e.g. basal readers) continue instruction through the intermediate or secondary grades. But because retarded children have special problems

---

[29]*Ibid.*, p. 282.

in the intermediate and secondary school years, special materials and techniques have been developed for their needs in reading instruction, including high interest/low vocabulary readers and materials, occupationally-oriented reading programs, and materials for skill development and reading in the content areas.

High Interest/Low Vocabulary Materials

Many of the available reading materials, especially basal readers, do not contain topics of interests for older retarded children who are reading on a particular level in the series (Koelsch, 1969). Because this same problem can exist with children of average intelligence and/or culturally disadvantaged children, many materials have been developed that are of high interest to older children who have simpler vocabularies. Retarded children have many varied interests, and the teacher should attempt to provide materials which possess a wide variety of subjects as well as reading levels.

Materials have been developed commercially in kit form that provide short, high interest stories on various reading levels and are accompanied by vocabulary and word attack exercises. One such series of kits by D. H. Parker is published by Science Research Associates (SRA).

Kits also have been developed which have short selections from literature on various reading levels by Science Research Associates and Noble and Noble. Several such kits or laboratories are listed among the high interest/low vocabulary materials in Appendix One. Other sources for high-interest/low vocabulary material, such as books and audio-visual devices, include: Kottmeyer (1959); Cushenberry (1969); Anderson, Hemenway, and Anderson, (1969); and Spache (1970).

Obtaining and Developing Reading Interests

As was stated previously, retarded children have a variety of reading interests. The teacher must attempt to ascertain these interests as well as being instrumental in developing reading interests. Many educable retarded children may read little because of the difficulty in finding books on their level. For many, it is a chore to complete, let alone enjoy, a book which they have selected at random. Harris (1970) has suggested several ways of obtaining the interests of children: observation; "hobby clubs," or periods for sharing of interests;

interviews with children; and questionnaires. Many questionnaires (often called interest inventories) have been developed, but it has been our experience that retarded children often have difficulty in reading and completing the inventories. Nonetheless, the teacher may want to develop a short inventory which he can complete after an interview with or observation of the child. An example of an interest inventory follows.

Reading Interest Inventory[30]

---

1. Name _____ Age _____ Grade _____

2. From what source do you secure most of your free reading books?

   Friends _____ School Library _____

   Community Library _____ Church Library _____

3. How many books have you borrowed during the past month? _____

   How many of the books did you read completely? _____

   Give the titles of some of the books. _____

   _____

4. Check the kinds of books which you like to read.

   Fiction _____ Mysteries _____ Sports _____

   Romance _____ Heroes _____ History _____

   Science _____

5. What kinds of hobbies do you have? _____

   _____

---

[30]From the book *Reading Improvement in the Elementary School* by D. Cushenberry, pp. 141-42. Copyright © 1969 by Parker Publishing Co., Inc. Published by Parker Publishing Co., Inc., West Nyack, New York. Reprinted by permission of Prentice-Hall, Inc.

6. List the names of three television programs you like best.

_____

7. Give a list of the states and countries which you have visited.

_____

8. Mention the names of three of your favorite newspapers.

_____

9. Which of the following sections of the newspaper do you usually read?

A. National and Local News _____   D. Editorials _____

B. Comics _____   E. Sports _____

C. Feature Stories _____   F. Other _____

10. If you had at least two hours a day to devote to free reading, what kinds of material would you probably select? Why?

_____

_____

_____

_____

Some questions in this inventory concerning reading habits apply only to older children who already are able to read. The teacher may want to use the following questionnaire for younger children.

Interest Inventory

Name _____ Age _____

1. What are your favorite animals? _____

Do you have a pet? _____ What is it? _____

2. What are your favorite TV shows? _____

_____

3. What do you like to do most in your spare time? _____

_____

4. What are your hobbies? _____

5. Do you like to listen to stories? _____

What kind? _____

6. Who is your best friend? _____

What do you do together? _____

7. What are your favorite sports? _____

Do you participate in a sport? _____

8. Do you like to read? _____ What are your favorite stories?

_____

_____

Developing Reading Interests: Many children have life interests (e.g., cars) but are unaware that reading materials concerning their interests are available. The teacher can alert these students to such materials through the use of interesting bulletin boards, interest corners, and sharing sessions. Oral presentations, such as reading stories, playing records or excerpts from books, or the showing of filmstrips and films, also can be used to develop and expand such interests. We have employed small-group projects and interest groups successfully as techniques for motivating older retarded children to read. However, before a teacher can be successful in developing the reading interests of children, he must be knowledgeable of the variety of materials available.

Readability of Materials: If the teacher is unable to obtain many commercially produced materials specifically developed for high interest/low vocabulary reading, he may need to survey the books in the classroom or school library for their readability levels. Readability formulas have been developed that can aid teachers in determining the level of a book. Because many of the earlier formulas have been criticized for their lack of predictiveness for all materials (Bormuth, 1969) and because the calculation involved in the use of these formulas is time-consuming, several attempts have been made at developing easier and quicker formulas (Fry, 1968). Williams (1972), for example, has developed an efficient system for determining the revised Dale-Chall readability formulas. The cloze procedure discussed in Chapter Four also has been used to determine the readability of materials (Rankin, 1965; Taylor, 1953). If a teacher is interested in using readability formulas, he should read the references already cited as well as Dale and Chall (1948); Koenke (1971); Powers, et al. (1958); and Spache (1953). The results of the Spache readability projects, which include thousands of titles and their approximate reading levels and are published in booklet form, offer other aids for teachers in determining readability level. Three of these projects are *Books for Slow Readers* (Spache, 1969); *Correlation to Basal Readers* (Spache, 1969); and the *Readability Level Catalog* (Spache, 1969).

Occupationally and Socially Oriented Reading Programs and Materials

As the educable retarded child advances in his reading skills and maturity, emphasis in curriculums usually is placed on specific job preparation, work skills, and social adjustment (Dunn, 1963). Low-vocabulary series that focus on job skills and are appropriate for such a curriculum have been published. For example, a list of some of the series compiled by Anderson, Hemenway, and Anderson (1969) can be found in Appendix One. Most of these series such as the *New Rochester Reading Series* (Goldberg and Brumher, 1963) are designed for low reading levels and have exercises in vocabulary and related reading skills. Although many of these series are available, the teacher should adapt those he uses to meet the needs of the particular student in his local environment (Anderson, Hemenway, and Anderson, 1969).

An experience approach also can be adapted to the teaching of reading skills needed for occupational and social activities (Hafner and Karlin, 1967). With this approach, learning to read road maps, street signs, specific directions, and notices can be done in the context of the common experiences of the group. Field trips to various places, such as an employment office, are good motivational experiences for students who must learn to fill out job application blanks, applications for social security cards, etc. Students will be more likely to want to learn the necessary reading skills related to their future occupational and social life if an experience approach is utilized.

Skills Development: Older retarded students often need additional assistance in the area of reading skills. The ability to follow directions, to use the dictionary, to read directions in such aids to daily living as cookbooks are reading skills which should be taught to older retarded students and often can be taught through an experience approach, although there are many series that emphasize skill development through the use of high interest materials. Some of these series are listed in Appendix One.

Reading in the Content Areas: Although there are many reading series available that are high-interest/low vocabulary, there are fewer low vocabulary series in such content areas as the social studies. This dearth of material presents a problem in that many basic concepts in these fields must be presented in some manner (e.g., films), other than writing. Recently, however, publishers have developed low vocabulary materials in the subject areas. Some of these materials include: *World Traveler* — a magazine about such topics as the trips to the moon, other countries, animals, and nature (National Geographic, 1970); *America: Land of Change* — a series for junior high and high school students with low reading levels (Shapiro, McCrea and Beck, 1970); *American Adventures*, (Cebulash, 1970); and *The Training Skills Series*, (Hunter and LaFollette, 1971). For other low vocabulary reading materials in the content areas, see Anderson, Hemenway, and Anderson's *Instructional Resources for Teachers of the Culturally Disadvantaged and Exceptional* (1969).

Approaches and Materials for Enhancing Reading Comprehension

Enhancing the reading comprehension of educable retarded children is a concern for many teachers. Although reading comprehension may be an area of difficulty for many retarded children (Bleismer,

1969), differences in levels of reading comprehension may be related more to reading achievement than to intelligence (Smith, 1967); thus, a child of lower intelligence is able to profit from instruction in reading comprehension. After reviewing the studies on intelligence and instruction in reading comprehension, Caskey concluded:

> Thus it appears that if the pupil has skills adequate for dealing with the material at his level, a higher level of comprehension is dependent not so much upon intellectual ability as it is upon the kind of instructional assistance that is given him.[31]

Several of the numerous materials and techniques available for the teaching of reading comprehension are discussed in this section.

Directed Reading Lesson: All basal readers attempt to teach comprehension skills either specifically or incidentally. This particular framework has become so standardized that it is often referred to as the *directed reading lesson.* The basic procedure begins with establishment of a purpose for reading the selection. In establishing such a purpose, the teacher often draws upon the experiential background of his students to allow him to use information about the story or subject to develop interest or motivation. The new vocabulary and new concepts then are introduced to facilitate the reading; silent reading follows. During this time period, the teacher is supposedly active observing student habits, such as lip reading, or holding the book close to the eyes. After silent reading, discussion of the story occurs. Such discussion should include not only factual information but also such skills as the ability to understand the main idea, form judgments, and detect propaganda. Oral reading, the next step, can occur along with discussion to help support or refute an argument. If oral reading is presented to the whole class in a form such as a report or play, it should be practiced in advance to prevent gross reading errors because students should hear only *good* oral reading if they are to be aided in their own improvement and if boredom is to be eliminated. Thus, the teacher must consider carefully his objectives for oral reading. The final step, follow-up or enrichment, includes such activities as practicing additional word attack skills, reading books on the same topics, or doing library work.

All too often, the directed reading lesson is used without awareness of its limitations. Usually, more time is spent on intro-

---

[31]Helen Caskey, "Guidelines for Teaching Comprehension," *The Reading Teacher* 23 (1970): 651.

ducing the purposes for reading than on the rest of the lesson. In addition, purposes for reading usually are established by the teacher, although it has been recommended (Stauffer, 1969) that children be encouraged to establish their own reasons for reading the selection. On this subject, Stauffer has remarked:

> Self-declared purposes are of special significance. As directive influences and motivators, they are authoritative and trustworthy, especially to the degree that they are promoted by the facts at hand and the reader's motives, attitudes and experiences. They avoid the pitfalls of assigned purposes and the artificiality of ready-made questions. They make the reader a student of what he is reading rather than a servant to recitation. They develop traits of open-mindedness, whole heartedness, and responsibility, of alertness, flexibility, and curiosity. Possession of the ability to declare purposes makes the difference between an able reader and an intellectual bungler.[32]

The practice of introducing vocabulary or concepts prior to reading also has been criticized by Stauffer (1969). The child should be trained to be an independent reader, and this process entails learning to use context clues, the glossary, or a dictionary if he does not know a word (Stauffer, 1969). According to Goodman (1967), a child does utilize his background experiences and language to anticipate the meaning of the text. He views reading as a "psycholinguistic guessing game" in which the child utilizes cues to arrive at the meaning. If this is true, presenting words before the reading lesson will not allow the child to develop adequate comprehension strategies. If the teacher does choose to present words prior to the lesson, they should never be introduced in isolation (Goodman 1969).

In discussion, questioning techniques are used often for the development of reading comprehension. One of the most frequently used forms of questioning, found in the manuals of many basal reader series, is for the teacher to ask numerous questions, a large majority of which are factual in nature, after the children have read the story or selection (Forsyth, et al. 1971; Hatcher, 1971). Because of these characteristics, the lessons tend to be boring and children often lose interest in the selection. One of the present authors recalls a child remarking to the teacher after one such

---

[32]Russell G. Stauffer, *Teaching Reading as a Thinking Process* (New York: Harper & Row, Publishers, 1969), pp. 20-21 © 1969 by Russell G. Stauffer. Reprinted by permission of the publisher.

session, "Why do you ask all those questions? I read the story once."

Many series suggest that the story be broken into sections and that questions be asked after each part. In addition, questions or statements to prompt children to read subsequent selections are utilized. Too often, though, children resent being interrupted, and if they are truly interested in the story, they need no prompting to read the entire selection. If adult readers were subjected to this procedure of developing comprehension, it is doubtful they would complete many novels.

Although many suggestions for the development of reading comprehension in basal series may be valuable, the teacher may have to supplement the manual with questions which go beyond the factual levels. The use of models (Spache, 1963) or taxonomies (Clymer, 1968) can aid in the selection of questions.

After reviewing the research on questioning techniques and comprehension, Schneyer remarked:

> These investigations agree that the nature of the questions employed by the teacher and the strategies she uses in leading pupils' thought from one level to another are central in influencing the depth of thinking developed among pupils. The use of clarifying questions and slow-paced teacher-pupil interaction which allows time for pupil thinking are vital teacher strategies.[33]

Particularly good sources for questioning skills are the *Teaching Skills* manuals and films (Allen, Ryan, Bush, and Cooper, 1969). Although most of these manuals are for secondary students, many suggestions are included. Other sources include: *Ways of Teaching* (Hyman, 1970) *Thinking in Elementary School Children* (Taba, Levine, and Freeman, 1964).

Skills in questioning should be applied to teaching comprehension to the retarded. Herman (1967) has found that teachers are less flexible and more teacher-centered in discussions with children of lower intelligence. Because the teacher may think that these children are not capable of higher-level thinking skills, he may ask only factual questions or not attempt to stimulate the use of skills such as divergent thinking (Cawley, Goodstein, and Burrow, 1972).

---

[33]J. Schneyer, "Wesley Research, Classroom Verbal Instruction, and Pupil Learning," *The Reading Teacher* 28 (1970): 369-71.

Still another approach which extends the directed reading lesson is Stauffer's (1969) directed reading-thinking activity *D-R-T-A*. The *D-R-T-A* approach follows:

I. Identifying Purposes for Reading

    A. Examining clues available

        1. Title and subtitles
        2. Pictures, maps, graphs, and charts
        3. Materials adjusted to the information as it is read and to the readability

    B. Declaring purposes:

        1. In terms of the reader's background of experience, intellect, language facility, interests, and needs
        2. In terms of experience, abilities, interests, and needs of the group
        3. In terms of the content of the material (e.g., time, place, people, number, science, aesthetic, and humor)

II. Guiding the Adjustment of Rate to Purposes and Material

    A. Skimming: To read swiftly and lightly

    B. Scanning: To read carefully from point to point

    C. Studying:: To read and reread to pass judgment

III. Observing the Reading

    A. Noting abilities to adjust rate to purpose and material
    B. Recognizing comprehension needs and providing help by clarifying:

        1. Purposes
        2. Concepts
        3. Need for silent or oral rereading

    C. Acknowledging requests for help with word-recognition needs by providing immediate help in the use of:

        1. Context clues: Meaning clues
        2. Phonetic clues: Sound cues

      3. Structural clues: Sight clues
      4. Glossary clues: Meaning, sound, and sight clues

IV. Developing Comprehension

    A. Checking on individual and group purposes
    B. Staying with or redefining purposes
    C. Recognizing the need for other source material
    D. Developing concepts

 V. Fundamental Skill-Training Activities: Discussion, Further Reading, Additional Study, Writing

    A. Increasing powers of observation or directed attention
    B. Increasing powers of reflection by:

      1. Abstraction: Recognizing old ideas, conceiving new ideas, and making inductions and analyses
      2. Judgment: Formulating propositions and asserting them
      3. Reasoning: Inferring, demonstrating, and systematizing knowledge inductively

    C. Mastering the skills of word recognition: Picture and language context analysis, phonetic and structural analysis, and dictionary usage

    D. Developing adeptness in the use of semantic analysis: Levels of abstraction, shifts of meaning, referential and emotive language, definite and indefinite terms, and concept development[34]

Necessary Comprehension Skills

Regardless of the approach utilized in teaching reading, the expected outcome is the acquisition of basic skills in reading comprehension. These include: word, sentence, and paragraph meaning; organizational skills; and critical reading skills. It is not necessary for these skills to be taught within the framework of a directed reading lesson; indeed, many approaches (e.g., individualized reading) do not involve the use of directed reading lessons. Yet the child is expected to comprehend what he reads.

---

[34]Stauffer, pp. 20-21.

Word Meanings: Before the child can relate to the printed word, he must have had some experience with the concept which the word represents. Because of this fact, the teaching of word meanings or vocabulary involves more than matching the word to the meaning or filling in a workbook page. According to Stauffer, "words are the coins of the concept realm."[35] Therefore, if vocabulary development is to be meaningful, one must acquire concepts in order to acquire word meaning.

Concept development of this type has been cited as a special problem for retarded children (See Chapter Three.) Educable retarded children may have more success with concrete concepts than abstract ones. Although concepts of size, space, and time are difficult necessary concepts to be developed for some retarded children, attributes of objects, such as texture, color, weight and size, also can pose difficulties. For example, a ball may be smooth, round, hard, and red, or rough, round, soft, and blue. As a child begins to perceive the world around him, he may begin to place objects into categories (e.g., a rose and lily are both flowers), for he must learn to see likenesses and differences among objects. The development of these concepts should be concrete and as meaningful as possible. For example, in learning attributes of an object, it is necessary for the child to use a multisensory approach in manipulating the object; in other words, the child must experience the object. However, it must be realized that the child brings certain experiences to the learning situation, even though it may be necessary for the teacher to augment these experiences.

Several language programs and early childhood materials incorporate concept development, including Bereiter and Engelmann (1966) and the *Peabody Language Development Kits* (Dunn, et al., 1965, 1967, 1968). There are also materials such as the *Attribute Games* (Teaching Resources, 1972), and programs such as *Science: A Process Approach* (Xerox, 1967), all of which deal with concept development and reasoning skills.

Sentence Meaning: The learning of word meanings cannot be accomplished by isolated word lists. Because of the multiple meanings of many common words, words in isolation essentially convey no meaning. For example, the word *iron* may have various meanings depending upon the experiences of the readers. Some may consider *iron* to be a metal, an instrument for pressing clothing, or a

---

[35]*Ibid.*, p. 139.

tablet to be taken internally. Thus, sentence reading should be used in the initial stages of reading in order for the child to develop adequate comprehension of word meanings. The cloze procedure (See Chapter Four) also may be an effective method of introducing word meaning in context.

Paragraph Meaning: "Understanding a paragraph depends, to a great extent, upon the appreciation of the interrelationships among its sentences."[36] Children should be able to locate a topic sentence and those sentences in a paragraph which support it. Many workbooks in comprehension provide exercises in identifying main ideas. Basal reader series and reading texts also suggest activities, including such ideas as writing headlines, selecting main ideas, identifying extraneous parts, and creative paragraph writing.

The teacher should remember that word concepts and sentence sense must be developed before paragraph meaning. In addition, the teacher should be willing to use supplemental exercises which extend the suggestions found in basal readers or workbooks. In fact, workbook exercises may stifle the child's creativity and reduce the development of paragraph meaning to a rote exercise.

Organizational Skills: The ability to organize verbal materials may be a problem for retarded children (Sitko, et al., 1972). Consequently, since organizational ability is important for reading comprehension (Evans, 1970), a retarded child may profit from instruction in organizational skills (Bilsky and Evans, 1970). If materials to be presented are introduced in a highly organized fashion, this instruction may aid the retarded child's comprehension (Sitko, 1970). The development of organizational skills may be accomplished through oral and/or written activities.

If the child is taught that materials are organized logically through such techniques as headings or subtitles, he may be able to retain more information (Stauffer, 1969). For example, reading in the content area may be facilitated if the child is able to utilize the organizational structure of the material in obtaining information. Under organizational abilities, Bond and Wagner (1963) place the skills of sequencing relationships, classifying, summarizing, relating materials from various sources, and following directions.

Critical Reading: Too often, special-education teachers ignore the area of critical reading or thinking skills. This is unfortunate be-

---

[36]Guy Bond and Eva Bond Wagner, *Teaching the Child to Read* (New York: The Macmillan Co., 1960); p. 205.

cause adult educable retarded individuals are often faced with the necessity of utilizing critical thinking and reading skills. For example, judging the worth of a product for itself rather than by the claims made by advertisers, investigating sources of information, and differentiating between fact and opinion are reasoning skills which aid in social living.

Teachers may introduce critical thinking skills in beginning reading. Through discussion of fairy tales and folk stories, children may be lead to realize the difference between fact and fantasy. Also, relating stories to their own experiences and evaluating the worth of statements or stories are skills that can be introduced in story reading or listening comprehension.

SUMMARY

This chapter contains the basic remedial reading approaches, categorized under multisensory programmed instruction, teaching machines, and other unique programs. Programs for intermediate and secondary instruction also were included. All of the approaches discussed were developed for children with special reading problems. As a general statement, we can say that because of the variety of programs available and their adaptability to the retarded, it is necessary that the teacher be aware that no one particular program is not a panacea for all reading instructions. Programs must be utilized on the basis of the individual's needs.

REFERENCES

Allen, Dwight, et al. *Teaching Skills.* Morristown, New Jersey: General Learning Corporation, 1969.

Anderson, R. M.; Hemenway, R. E.; and Anderson, Janet W. *Instructional Resources for Teachers of the Culturally Disadvantaged and Exceptional.* Springfield, Illinois: Charles C. Thomas Co., 1969.

Atkinson, Richard C., and Fletcher, John D., "Teaching Children to Read With a Computer." *The Reading Teacher* 25 (1972): 319-27.

Attribute Games. Boston: Teaching Resources, 1972.

Audio Flashcard Reader. North Haven, Connecticut: Electronic Futures, Inc., 1962.

Bannatyne, Alexander. "The Color Phonics System." In *The Disabled Reader: Education of the Dyslexic Child,* edited by John Money and Gilbert S. Chuffman. Baltimore: Johns Hopkins Press, 1966.

————. *Language, Reading, and Learning Disabilities.* Springfield, Illinois: Charles C. Thomas Co., 1971.

————. *Psycholinguistic Color System: A Reading, Writing, Spelling, and Language Program.* Urbana, Illinois: Learning Systems Press, 1968.

Berry, Mildred M. *Language Disorders of Children: The Basis and Diagnosis.* New York: Appleton-Century-Crofts, 1969.

Bereiter, Carl, and Engelmann, Seigfried. *Teaching Disadvantaged Children in the Preschool.* Englewood Cliffs, New Jersey: Prentice-Hall, Inc., 1966.

Bigge, Morris L. *Learning Theories for Teachers.* New York: Harper & Row, Publishers, 1964.

Bijou, S. W., et al. *The Edmark Reading Program.* Seattle, Washington: Edmark Associates, 1972.

————. "Programmed Instruction as an Approach to Teaching of Reading, Writing, and Arithmetic to Retarded Children." *The Psychological Record* 16 (1966): 505-22.

Bilsky, L., and Evans, R. A. "Use of Associative Clustering Technique in the Study of Reading Disability: Effects of List Organization." *American Journal of Mental Deficiency* 74 (1970): 701-76.

Blackman, L. S., and Burges, A. L. "Psychological Factors Related to Early Reading Behavior of Educable Mentally Retarded and Normal Children." Interim Report of the Research and Demonstration Center for the Education of Handicapped Children. New York: Columbia University Teacher's College, 1970.

Blackman, L. S., and Capobianco, R. J. "An Evaluation of Programmed Instruction with the Mentally Retarded utilizing Teaching Machines." *American Journal of Mental Deficiency* 70 (1965): 262-69.

Bleismer, Emery O. "Teaching Abilities of Bright and Dull Children of Comparable Mental Ages." In *Readings on Reading,* edited by Alfred R. Binter, John Deabel, and Leonard K. Kise, pp. 189-98. Scranton, Pennsylvania: International Textbook Co., 1969.

Bloomer, R. H. "An Investigation of an Experimental First Phonics Program." *Journal of Educational Psychology* 53 (1960): 188-93.

Blue, Milton C. "Influence of Mode of Presentation, Age, and Intelligence on Paired-Associates Learning." *American Journal of Mental Deficiency* 74 (1970): 527-32.

Bond, Guy, and Wagner, Eva Bond. *Teaching the Child to Read.* New York: The Macmillan Co., 1960.

Bormuth, J. R. "New Data on Readability." In *Elementary Reading Instruction: Selected Materials,* edited by Althea Berry, Thomas C. Barrett, and William R. Powell, pp. 168-76. Boston: Allyn & Bacon, 1969.

Brain, R. *Speech Disorders.* Washington, D. C.: Butterworth, 1961.

Brown, Sandra, editor. "A Hip Reader for Cool Cats." *Reading Newsreport* 4 (1970): 13-15.

————. "Where Computers Work Overtime." *Reading Newsreport* 4 (1970): 30-31.

Buchannon, C. D. *Programmed Reading.* Manchester, Missouri: Webster Publishing Co.; Sullivan Associates, 1966.

Buchannon, C. D., and Sullivan Associates. *Sullivan Programmed Readers.* New York: McGraw-Hill Book Co., 1963.

Bruininks, Robert H., and Clark, C. R. "Auditory and Visual Paired-Associate Learning in First-Grade Retarded and Nonretarded Children." *Journal of Mental Deficiency* 76 (1972): 561-67.

Bruner, C. C. "The Distar Reading Program." *Proceedings of the College Reading Association* 9 (1968): 59-67.

Carey, G. A. "A Comparison of Programmed and Standard Teacher-Prepared Material in the Teaching of Reading to Educably Mentally Retarded Children." *Dissertation Abstracts* (1968): 29-3488-A.

Caskey, Helen. "Guidelines for Teaching Comprehension." *The Reading Teacher* 23 (1970): 649-54; 669.

Cawley, J. F. "Reading Disability." In *Methods in Special Education,* edited by N. G. Haring and R. L. Schiefelbusch. New York: McGraw-Hill Book Co., 1967.

Cawley, J. F.; Goodstein, H. A.; and Burrow, W. H. *The Slow Learner and the Reading Problem.* Springfield, Illinois: Charles C. Thomas Co., 1972.

Cebulash, Mel. *American Adventures.* Englewood Cliffs, New Jersey: Prentice-Hall, Inc., 1970.

Cegelka, Patricia A., and Cegelka, Walter J. "A Review of Research: Reading and the Educable Mentally Handicapped." *Exceptional Children* 37 (1970): 187-208.

Clark, Hulda R. *Modern Reading.* Orange City, Florida: Humanitas Curriculum, 1967.

_____. *Teacher's Guide to Modern Reading.* Orange City, Florida: Humanitas Curriculum, 1967.

Clymer, Theodore. "The Barrett Taxonomy — Cognitive and Affective Dimensions of Reading Comprehension." In *Innovation and Change in Reading Instruction: Sixty-seventh Yearbook of the National Society for the Study of Education, Part II*, pp. 19-23. Chicago: University of Chicago, 1968.

Coleman, E. B. "Newsreport Interviewer." *Reading Newsreport* 4 (1970): 4-9.

Cushenberry, D. C. *Reading Improvement in the Elementary School.* West Nyack, New York: Parker Publishing Company, 1969.

Dale, E., and Chall, J. "A Formula for Predicting Readability." *Educational Research Bulletin* 27 (1948): 11-20.

Datta, Louis-Ellen. "Montessori and the Slow-Learning Child: Promise and Challenge." *Montessori and the Special Child,* edited by K. C. Orem, pp. 98-110. New York: G. A. Putnam Sons, 1969.

Davy, R. "An Adaptation of Progressive Choice-Method for Teaching Reading to the Retarded Child." *American Journal of Mental Deficiency* 67 (1962): 274-80.

Day, W. F., and Beach, B. R. "A Survey of the Research Literature Comparing the Visual and Auditory Presentation of Information." US Air Force Technical Report No. 5921, 1950.

Denholm, Richard, and Blank, Dale. *Mathematics Structure and Skills, Grades 7-9.* Chicago: Science Research Associates, 1972.

Dodds, William. "A Longitudinal Study of Two Beginning Reading Programs — Words in Color and Traditional Basal Readers." Doctoral dissertation, Case Western Reserve University, 1966.

Dunn, L. M. "Educable Mentally Retarded Children." In *Exceptional Children in the Schools,* edited by Lloyd M. Dunn. New York: Holt, Rinehart, & Winston, 1963.

Dunn, L. M., and Smith, J. O., editors. *Peabody Language Development Kit: Level #1.* Circle Pines, Minnesota: American Guidance Service, 1965.

Dunn, L. M., and Smith, J. O., editors. *Peabody Language Development Kit #3.* Circle Pines, Minnesota: American Guidance Service, 1967.

Dunn, L. M.; Horton, K. B.; and Smith, J. O. *Peabody Language Development Kit: Level #P.* Circle Pines, Minnesota: American Guidance Service, 1968.

Edwards, Thomas J. "The Progressive Choice Method." In *The Disabled Reader,* edited by John Mery and Gilbert Schiffman, p. 215-28. Baltimore: John Hopkins Press, 1966.

Ellson, D. G.; Barber, Larry; Engle, T. L.; and Kampworth, Leonard. "Programed Tutoring: A Teaching Aid and a Research Tool." *Reading Research Quarterly,* (1965): 77-127.

Engelmann, Siegfried. "Classroom Techniques: Teaching Reading to Children with Low Mental Age." *Education and Training of the Mentally Retarded* 2 (1967): 193-201.

Engelmann, Siegfried, and Bruner, E. C. *Distar Reading: An Instructional System.* Chicago: Science Research Associate, 1969.

_____. *Distar Library Series, Preschool-Grade 2.* Chicago: Science Research Associate, 1971.

Evans, R. A. "Use of Associative Clustering Technique in the Study of Reading Disability: Effects of Presentation Made." *American Journal of Mental Deficiency* 74 (1970): 765-70.

Fernald, Grace. *Remedial Techniques in Basic School Subjects.* New York: McGraw-Hill Book Co., 1943.

Fitzhugh, Kathleen, and Fitzhugh, Loren. *The Fitzhugh Plus Program.* Galen, Michigan: Allied Education Council.

Forsyth, Irene; Haggerty, Margaret; Patterson, Roberta; and Snow, Jack. Northridge, California: San Fernando Valley State College, 1971.

Frostig, M. "The Needs of Teachers for Specialized Information on Reading." In *The Teacher of Brain-Injured Children,* edited by W. M. Cruickshank. Syracuse, New York: Syracuse University Press, 1966.

Fry, Edward. "A Readability Formula That Saves Time." *Journal of Reading* 11 (1968): 513-16; 575-81.

Gates, A. I. *The Improvement of Reading,* 3rd ed. New York: The Macmillan Co., 1947.

Gattegno, Caleb. *Words in Color.* Chicago: Learning Materials, 1962.

Gillingham, A., and Stillman, B. *Remedial Work for Reading, Spelling and Penmanship.* New York: Hackett & Wilhelms, 1936.

_____. *Remedial Training for Children with Specific Disability in Reading, Spelling, and Penmanship,* 7th ed. Cambridge, Massachusetts: Education Publishing Service, 1965.

Goldberg, H. R., and Brumher, T. *New Rochester Reading Series.* Chicago: Science Research Associates.

Goldstein, L. S., and Gothin, L. G. "A Review of Research: Teaching Machines vs. Programmed Textbooks as Presentation Modes." *Journal of Programed Instruction* 1 (1963): 29-36.

Goodman, K. S. "Reading: A Psycholinguistic Guessing Game." *Journal of the Reading Specialist* 4 (1967): 126-35.

Goodman, K. S., and Fleming, James T. *Psycholinguistics and The Teaching of Reading.* Newark, Delaware: International Reading Association, 1969.

Greene, Francis, M. "Programed Instruction Techniques." In *International Review of Research in Mental Retardation,* vol. 2, edited by Norman R. Ellis, pp. 209-39. New York: Academic Press, 1966.

Guinet, Lynne. "Evaluation of Distar Materials in Three Junior Learning Assistance Classes." Report RR-71-16, Vancouver, British Columbia Board of School Trustees, July 1971.

Guralnick, M. J. "Alphabet Discrimination and Distinctive Features: Research Review and Educational Implication." *Journal of Learning Disabilities* 5 (1972): 428-34.

Hafner, L. F., and Karlin, Robert. "A Suggested Curriculum for Teaching Reading Skills to Youths Who Are Reluctant Readers." *Improving Reading in Secondary Schools: Selected Readings,* edited by L. Hafner, pp. 423-37. New York: The Macmillan Co., 1967.

Hammill, D., and Mattleman, M. "Programmed Reading Instruction in the Primary Grades: An Evaluation Study." *Elementary English* 46 (1969): 310-12.

Harris, Albert J. *How to Increase Reading Ability.* New York: David McKay Co., 1970.

Hatcher, Thomas. The Development of Comprehension Skills in Selected Basic Readers." Ph.D. dissertation, The Ohio State University Press, 1971.

Heckelman, R. G. "The Neurological Impress Method of Remedial Reading Instruction." *Academic Therapy* 4 (1969): 277-82.

_____. A Neurological Impress Method of Reading Instruction. Merced, California: Merced County Schools Office, 1962.

Hegge, T. G.; Kirk, S. A.; and Kirk, W. P. *Remedial Reading Drills.* Ann Arbor, Michigan: George Wohr, 1955.

Herman, W. L., Jr. An Analysis of the Activities and Verbal Behavior of Selected Fifth-Grade Social Studies Classes." *Journal of Educational Research* 60 (1967): 339-45.

Hill, Frank G. "A Comparison of the Effectiveness of Words in Color with the Basic Reading Program Used in the Washington Elementary School District." *Disseration Abstracts* 27 (1967): 3619A.

Hill, S. D., and Hecker, E. E. "Auditory and Visual Learning of Paired Associate Tack by Second-Grade Children." *Perceptual and Motor Skills* 23 (1966): 814.

Hillis, Viola. "The Multisensory Linguistic Approach: The Key to Language Problems?" *Reading Newsreport* 6 (1971): 18-26.

Hinds, Lillian R. "An Evaluation of Words in Color or Morphologico-Algebraic Approach to Teaching Reading to Functionally Illiterate Adults." Doctoral dissertation, Case Western University, 1966.

Hoffman Reading Achievement Program. Arcadia, California: Hoffman Information Systems, 1967.

Hofmeister, Alan. "Programmed Instruction: Revisited Implications for Educating the Retarded." *Education and Training of the Mentally Retarded* 6 (1971): 172-76.

————. "Programmed Reading with Severely Retarded: A Field Evaluation." Eugene, Oregon: Northwest Regional Special Educational Instructional Materials Center, 1968. Mimeographed.

————. "Selecting and Modifying Programmed Materials." *Teaching Exceptional Children* 2 (1969): 38-42.

Hollingsworth, P. M. "An Experiment with the Impress Method of Teaching Reading." *The Reading Teacher* 24 (1970): 112-14; 187.

Hunter, William F., and LaFollette, Pauline. *The Learning Skills Series: Arithmetic.* Manchester, Missouri: Webster Publishing Co., 1971.

Hyman, Ronald T. *Ways of Teaching.* Philadelphia: J. B. Lippincott Co., 1970.

Jensen, N. J., and King, E. M. "Effects of Different Kinds of Visual-Motor Discrimination Training on Learning to Read Words." *Journal of Educational Psychology* 61 (1970): 90-96.

Johnson, Doris, and Myklebust, Helmer. *Learning Disabilities.* New York: Grune & Stratton, 1967.

Johnson, G. O. *Education for the Slow Learners.* Englewood Cliffs, New Jersey: Prentice-Hall, Inc., 1963.

Johnson, M. S. "Tracing and Kinesthetic Techniques." In *The Disabled Reader,* edited by John Mory and Gilbert Schiffman, pp. 147-60. Baltimore: Johns Hopkins Press, 1966.

Jones, Kenneth. "Colors as an Aid to Visual Perception in Early Reading." *British Journal of Educational Psychology* 35 (February 1965): 21-27.

Jones, S. H. "Programmed Reading Report, So Far, So Good." *Nation's Schools* 28 (1966): 39-40.

Kaplan, Murray. "An Evaluation of the Effectiveness of Programmed Instruction in Elementary Reading with Mentally Retarded Adolescents in Junior High School." *Dissertation Abstracts* (1971): 32-5671-A.

Karnes, Merle B.; Teska, James A.; and Hodgins, Audrey S. "A Longitudinal Study of Disadvantaged Children Who Participated in Three Different Preschool Programs." Urbana, Illinois: Institute for Research on Exceptional Children, 1969.

Katz, P., and Deutch, M. "Modality of Stimulus Presentation in Serial Learning for Retarded and Normal Readers." *Perceptual and Motor Skills* 19 (1964): 627-33.

Kaufman, Maurice. *Words in Color for Intensive Remedial Instruction.* Boston: Northeastern University, 1972.

Kirk, Samuel A. "The Influence of Manual Training on the Learning of Simple Words in the Case of Subnormal Boys." *Journal of Educational Psychology* 24 (1933): 525-35.

Kline, C. L., and Lee, N. "A Transcultural Study of Dyslexia: Analysis of Reading Disabilities in 425 Chinese Children Simultaneously Learning to Read and Write in English and Chinese." *American Journal of Orthopsychiatry* 40 (1970): 2.

Koelsch, George. "Readability and Interests of Five Basal Reading Series with Retarded Students." *Exceptional Children* 35 (1969): 487-88.

Koenke, Karl. "Another Practical Note on Readability Formulas." *Journal of Reading* 15 (1971): 203-08.

Kottmeyer, William. *Teacher's Guide for Remedial Reading.* Manchester, Missouri: Webster Publishing Co., 1959.

The Language Master. Chicago: Bell & Howell Audio Visual Products Division, 1963.

Learning about Sounds and Letters: Ginn 360 Series. Arlington, Illinois: Ginn and Co., 1973.

Lent, James N. "Mimosa Cottage Experiment in Hope." *Psychology Today* 52 (1968): 51-58.

Linn, J. R., and Ryan, Thomas J. "The Multisensory-Motor Method of Teaching Reading." *Journal of Experimental Psychology* 36 (1968): 57-59.

Lockmiller, Pauline, and DiNello, Mario C. "Words in Color versus a Basal Reader Program with Retarded Readers in Grade 2." *Journal of Educational Research* 63 (1970): 330-34.

McCarthy, W., and Oliver, J. "Some Tactile-Kinesthetic Procedures for Teaching Reading to Slow-Learning Children." *Exceptional Children* 31 (1965): 419-21.

McCreary, P. L. "Software: The Problem of Construction." *Reading Newsreport* 4 (1970): 18-21.

McNeil, J. D. "Programmed Instruction versus Usual Classroom Procedures in Teaching Boys to Read." *American Educational Research Journal* 1 (1964): 113-19.

Malpass, Leslie F. "Programmed Instruction for Retarded Children." In *Mental Retardation, Apprasial, Education, and Rehabilitation,* edited by Alfred A. Baumeister, pp. 211-31. Chicago: Aldine Publishing Co., 1967.

Malpass, L.; Gilmore, A. S.; Hardy, M. W.; and Williams, C. A. "A Comparison of Two Automated Teaching Procedures for Retarded Children." Washington, D. C.: US Office of Education, 1963.

Malpass, L.; Hardy, M. W.; Gilmore, G. S.; and Williams, C. A. "Automated Instruction for Retarded Children." *American Journal of Mental Deficiency* 69 (1964): 405-12.

Mast Teaching System. Meadville, Pennsylvania: Keystone View Company, 1962.

Mendelsohn, M. "The Terminal Is the Best Friend I Know: Interview with M. Mendelsohn." *Reading Newsreport* 4 (1970): 32-37.

Monroe, M. *Children Who Cannot Read.* Chicago: University of Chicago Press, 1932.

Montessori, Maria. *Dr. Montessori's Own Handbook.* New York: Schocken Books, 1965.

_____. *The Montessori Method.* Cambridge: Robert Bently, 1964-65.

_____. *The Montessori Method.* New York: Stokes, 1912.

Moore, O. K. "Autoletic Responsive Environments and Exceptional Children." *The Special Child in Century 21,* edited by J. Hellmuth, pp. 87-138. Seattle, Washington: Special Child Publications, 1964.

Morris, J. "Teaching Children to Read." *Educational Research* 1 (1958): 38-39.

Myers, Patricia, and Hammill, Donald. *Methods of Learning Disorders.* New York: John Wiley & Sons, 1969.

Ofman, L., and Schaewitz, M. "The Kinesthetic Method in Remedial Reading." *Journal of Experimental Education* 31 (1963): 319-20.

Olson, David R. "Information Processing Limitations of Mentally Retarded Children." *American Journal of Mental Deficiency* 75 (1971): 478-86.

Open Court Kindergarten Program. LaSalle, Illinois: Open Court Publishing Co., 1970.

Open Court Reading Program. LaSalle, Illinois: Open Court Publishing Co., 1963.

Orem, R. C., editor. *A Montessori Handbook.* New York: G. P. Putnam, 1965.

Orton, June L. "The Orton Gillingham Approach." In *Disabled Reader,* edited by John Money and Gilbert Shiffman, pp. 119-45. Baltimore: Johns Hopkins Press, 1966.

Orton, Samuel T. *Reading, Writing, and Speech Problems in Children.* New York: W. W. Norton, 1937.

Parker, D. H. *SRA Reading Laboratories.* Chicago: Science Research Associates, 1961.

Pollack, C. *The Intersensory Reading Method.* New York: Book Lab, Inc., 1969.

Powers, R. B.; Sumner, W. A.; and Kearl, B. E. "A Recalculation of Four Readability Formulas." *Journal of Educational Psychology* 49 (1958): 99-105.

Rankin, E. F. "Cloze Procedure — A Survey of Research." *Yearbook of the Southwest Reading Conference* 14 (1965): 133-48.

Robins, Doris. *Special Education Guide to the Open Court Program.* LaSalle, Illinois: Open Court Publishing Co., 1970.

Rowland, Pleasant T. *Beginning to Read, Write, and Listen.* Boston: Boston Educational Research Company, 1971.

Ruddell, Robert S. "The Effect of Four Programs of Reading Instruction with Varying Emphasis on the Regularity of Grapheme-Phoneme Correspondences and the Relation of the Language Structure to the meaning on Adjustment on First Grade Reading." Report of Research Project #2699. Berkeley: University of California, 1965.

Schneyer, J. "Wesley Research, Classroom Verbal Instruction and Pupil Learning." *The Reading Teacher* 28 (1970): 369-71.

Science: A Process Approach. Arlington, Illinois: Xerox Corporation, 1967.

Scott, Foresman Reading Systems. Glenview, Illinois: Scott, Foresman and Co., 1971.

Shapiro, Alan: McCrea, Charles; and Beck, Vera. *America: Land of Change, Grade 6-8.* Chicago: Science Research Associates, 1970.

Shedd, C. L. "Ptolemy Rides Again or Dyslexia Doesn't Exist." *The Alabama Journal of Medical Science* 5 (1968): 481-503.

Shedd, C. L. "Some Exploratory Studies on the Clinical Management of Dyslexia." Universitys: University of Alabama, 1970.

Sitko, M.C. Input Organizational Strategies of EMR and Normal Ways in the Free Recall Verbal Learning." Doctoral dissertation, University of Michigan, 1970.

Sitko, M.C., et al. "The Relationship of Word-and-Sentence Associations of EMR Children to Reading Performances." Bloomington, Indiana: Indiana University Center for Innovation in Teaching the Handicapped School of Education, 1972.

Smith, Helen K. "The Responses of Good and Poor Readers when Asked to Read for Different Purposes." *Reading Research Quarterly* (1967): 53-83.

Spache, G.D. *Good Reading for Poor Readers.* Champaign, Illinois: Garrard Publishing Company, 1970.

_____. "A New Readability Formula for Primary-Grade Reading Materials." *Elementary School Journal* 53 (1953): 410-13.

_____. *Spache Readability Projects: Books for Slow Readers.* Chicago: Follett Library Book Company, 1969.

_____. *Spache Readability Projects: Correlation to Basal Readers.* Chicago: Follett Library Book Co., 1969.

_____. *Spache Readability Projects: Readability Level Catalog.* Chicago: Follett Library Book Company, 1969.

_____. *The Teaching of Reading.* Bloomington, Indiana: Phi Delta Kappa, Inc., 1972.

_____, *Toward Better Reading.* Champaign, Illinois: Garrard Publishing Co., 1963.

Stauffer, Russell G. *Teaching Reading as a Thinking Process.* New York: Harper & Row, Publishers, 1969.

Stuart, M.F. *Neuropsychological Insights into Teaching.* Palo Alto, California: Pacific Books, 1963.

M.W. Sullivan Reading Program. Palo Alto, California: Behavioral Research Laboratories, 1966.

Taba, Hilda; Levine, Samuel; and Freeman, F. Elsey. "Thinking in Elementary School Children." Cooperative Research Project No. 1574, US Department of Health, Education and Welfare Office of Educator. San Francisco: San Francisco State College, 1964.

Tansley, A.E., and Gulliford, A. *The Education of the Slow-Learning Child.* London: Routiledge & Kegan Printers, 1960.

Taylor, W.L. "Cloze Procedure: A New Tool for Measuring Readability," *Journalism Quarterly* 30 (1953): 415-33.

Williams, Robert T. "A Table for Rapid Determination of Revised Dale-Chall Readability Scores." *The Reading Teacher* 26 (1972): 158-68.

Williamson, Florence. *DISTAR Reading—Research and Experiment.* Urbana: University of Illinois, September 1970.

Wills, Martie. "Dovach's Machines Help Children Read." *American Education* 7 (1971): 3-8.

Witham, Anthony P. "The Index to Reading Material (Devices and Films for Improving Rate of Reading)" In *Reading on Reading,* edited by Alfred J. Binter, J. Deabal, and Leonard K. Kise, pp. 499-506. Scranton, Pennsylvania: International Textbook Co., 1969.

Woodcock, R. *The Peabody Chicago Detroit Reading Project—A Report of Second Year Results.* Nashville, Tennessee: George Peabody College, 1967.

Woodcock, R., and Clark, Charlotte L. *Peabody Rebus Reading Program.* Circle Pines, Minnesota: American Guidance Service, 1969.

Woolman, M. "The Effect of Varying the Number of Choices in the Identification of Very Similar Stimuli." *Dissertation Abstracts* 15 (1955): 1266.

_____. *Lift off to Reading.* Chicago: Science Research Associates, 1966.

_____. *The Progressive Choice Reading Program.* Washington, D.C.: Institute of Educational Research, 1962.

_____. *Reading in High Gear. Chicago:* Science Research Associates, 1965.

Zintz, Miles V. *The Reading Process: The Teacher and the Learner.* Dubuque, Iowa: William C. Brown Co., 1970.

NINE

Reading Related
Programs

There are many variables which have been considered to be related to reading achievement. Perceptual, neurological, and language disabilities are three of the most investigated such correlates of reading, and, consequently, a considerable number of programs have been developed in these areas. It is assumed that training in these areas will improve reading achievement; however, at the present time, the research concerning the effectiveness of such programs is inconclusive. This chapter presents a description of the nature of some of these programs and of related research on them.

VISUAL PERCEPTION PROGRAMS

Because research has indicated that many problem readers possess visual perception difficulties (see Chapter Three), several programs have been developed to ameliorate visual perception difficulties. These programs have been used as readiness exercises or as supplementary lessons with the intention of improving reading or academic achievement. However, while visual perception development and reading achievement may be related, the use of correlation studies to assume a cause-and-effect relationship may be fallacious

(Popp, 1967). In fact, studies have been conducted on the effectiveness of visual perception training and reading achievement (Arciszewski, 1967; Cohen, 1969) which have indicated that visual perception training does not influence reading achievement directly. A discussion of two visual perception programs — the Frostig-Horne Program and the Getman Program — as well as a listing of other visual perception programs is included in this section.

The Frostig-Horne Program in Visual Perception

This program (Frostig and Horne, 1964) was developed for use in conjunction with the *Developmental Test of Visual Perception* (Frostig, et al., 1964) (see Chapter Five for a discussion of the *DTVP*). The remedial program, which consists of 359 worksheet sets in the areas tested by the *DTVP* and a teacher's manual suggesting additional activities, was designed to be used with kindergarten and first-grade children as well as with other children who possess visual perception difficulties. The manual gives specific suggestions for the adaptation of the program for exceptional children and also suggests activities which should occur prior to workbook lessons in such areas as body image and schema.

Although Frostig (1967; 1969; 1972) recommends using various programs which match the strengths and weaknesses of children, she feels that the development of visual perception skills is extremely important to academic success. The use of a "comprehensive and integrated developmental readiness program,"[1] according to Frostig, can aid the child's progress in all phases of development.

The program has been used frequently with learning-disabled and retarded children in conjunction with reading programs. Some studies (Hammill and Wiederholt, 1972; Rosen, 1966) have indicated that the program may improve those visual perception skills most often as measured by the *DTVP*. Jacobs (1968) found the program to be more effective with culturally disadvantaged children, while Tyson (1963) found that the program was effective with cerebral palsied children.

A controversy still exists concerning the effectiveness of the Frostig-Horne program in developing reading achievement. Most

---

[1]Marianne Frostig and Phyllis Maslow, "Reading, Developmental Abilities, and the Problem of the Match," *Journal of Learning Disabilities* 2 (1969): 571-74.

of the research concerning the effectiveness of the program in influencing reading achievement of both normal and slow-learning children is not favorable (Allen, Dickman, and Haught, 1966; Bennett, 1968; Buckland, 1969; Buckland and Balow, 1973; Cohen, 1966; Hammill and Weiderholt, 1972; Jacobs, 1968; McBeath, 1966; Rosen, 1966). After reviewing the research, Myers and Hammill remarked:

> In summary, assessments of the Frostig-Horne training program differ, rendering additional research necessary in order to conclusively establish its efficacy. At present, the reactions of educators and researchers who have used the program vary widely regarding the effect of such training on the development of basic academic skills. Continued experimentation is recommended.[2]

We agree with authorities such as Cohen (1969) and Bateman (1969) who believe that children profit more from actual reading instruction than from the use of such visual perception programs as the Frostig-Horne. However, we do not mean to imply that visual perception training may not benefit some retarded children who possess severe visual perception problems. More research is needed before a definite conclusion can be reached.

G.N. Getman

In his work, G.N. Getman (1962) relates visuomotor skills and their development to academic performance. He cites five visual skills that are related to academic skills: eye movement skill; eye teaming skill (binocularity); eye-hand coordination skill; visual form perception, which includes visual imagery and visual memory; and refractive status (hyperopia, myopia, astigmatism, and problems of refraction) (Getman and Hendrickson, 1966).

According to Getman, visuomotor skills can be learned and teachers can aid children in the development of these skills. Getman and Hendrickson (1966) have suggested that visuomotor training be used in the classroom:

> Teachers can help children develop visuomotor skills and abilities. The teacher needs to become familiar with certain visual

---

[2]Patricia Myers and Donald Hammill, *Methods of Learning Disorders* (New York: John Wiley & Sons, 1969), p. 250.

training theories, procedures, and techniques, and to know the limitations within which improvements of these skills may be effected in the classroom and school environment.[3]

Getman has suggested that teachers refer to activities and procedures outlined by optometrists and educators for sources (e.g., *How to Develop Your Child's Intelligence*, 1962). One program based on Getman's theories is called *Developing Learning Readiness* and is available from McGraw-Hill.

Although Getman relates visuomotor skills to academic success, training in these skills may not transfer to reading achievement (Krippner, 1971), and the visual training techniques prescribed by many optometrists have been criticized by several authorities in reading and learning disorders (Krippner, 1971).

Additional Visual Perception Programs

There are many visual perception programs available which have not received as much attention as the ones already mentioned. One such program that has been used in some research studies is the *Winter Haven Program* (McQuarrie, 1967; Sutphin, 1964). This program includes training in the copying of geometric forms. Some researchers have related this training to academic success (Bosworth, 1967; DiMeo, 1967), although Kleim (1970) did not find it to be successful in eliminating visuomotor difficulties completely or obtaining significant gains in learning readiness scores.

Several other programs for visual perception training include *Visual-Motor Perception Teaching Materials* (Cheeves, 1972), and the *Fitzhugh Plus Program* (Fitzhugh and Fitzhugh, 1966).

AUDITORY PERCEPTION PROGRAMS

As stated in Chapter Three, auditory perception skills have been related to reading achievement by some authorities. For example according to Smith (1968), training in auditory perception or discrimination should be included in classroom programs for the retarded. There is some evidence to indicate that training in auditory

---

[3]G.N. Getman and Homer Henderickson, "The Needs of Teachers for Specialized Information and the Development of Visuomotor Skills in Relation to Academic Performance," in *The Teacher of Brain-Injured Children,* ed. W. Cruickshank (Syracuse, New York: Syracuse University Press, 1966), p. 165.

perception increases these perceptual skills (Smith, 1968); however, as with visual perception training, it is important that this auditory training relate to achievement in reading. In one study with retarded readers who were primarily from socially disadvantaged environments, Deutsch and Feldman (1966) found that auditory training did *not* influence the reading achievement of these children.

Some research indicates that knowledge of letter names and letter sounds is an important factor in reading achievement (Durrell, 1958). In addition, there may be prerequisite auditory perceptual skills to learning letter sounds, and training in these readiness skills may influence reading achievement. However, more research is needed in this area in order to draw any definite conclusions.

Recently, many programs in auditory perception have been developed, but, because they are all expensive, a teacher should study them very carefully before purchasing.

Programs, such as those in auditory discrimination, may not be beneficial to most educable retarded children if used in their entirety since a considerable amount of time is spent on the development of gross auditory skills (street sounds, animal sounds, etc.), and many children have acquired these skills by the time they have entered school. Because authorities are not in agreement about a hierarchy for the development of auditory perceptual skills, most programs sequence their introduction of these skills logically rather than empirically.

Auditory Discrimination in Depth

Auditory Discrimination in Depth (ADD) (Lindamood and Lindamood, 1969) is a two-month readiness or supplementary program in auditory perceptual skills for children and adults. The authors have suggested that the program may be beneficial for beginning preschool and kindergarten students, bilingual students, slow learners, students with learning disabilities, and students with language handicaps. The program may be used with individuals or small groups, although the manual does suggest the most effective group size for the lesson. The following purpose for this program has been stated by the authors:

> *Auditory Discrimination in Depth* is designed to teach beginning students, or below average students of any age, the basic

auditory perceptual skills they must have in order to read and spell correctly—the ability to decode and encode.[4]

The "basic auditory perceptual skills" taught in the program are:

An understanding of the basic concepts of the sound structure of our language

The ability to discriminate likenesses and differences between speech sounds (phonemes), individually and in sequence

Perception of the order of the sounds in sequences and the shifts and changes of sounds within patterns (syllables and words)

Judgment of the correspondence between oral (spoken) patterns and the graphic symbol (written) patterns which are used to represent them.[5]

The program is arranged according to four levels of auditory perceptual skills. Level One (gross level) introduces the student to environmental sounds and the association of these sounds to their sources. The second level (Oral-Aural Level) teaches the student auditory discrimination of speech sounds — consonants and vowels, using individual phonemes as well as syllable patterns. The third, Sound-Symbol, level teaches the student to associate the sound and the label (e.g. the grapheme *b* to the phoneme /b/), while at the Coding Level (encoding and decoding) the student begins to read and write. At this level, the student encodes sound patterns into graphic representations through the use of letter tiles. If the student is able to use the tiles successfully, he then writes the symbol that represents the sound. According to Lindamood and Lindamood, "Decoding is turning graphic patterns back into spoken patterns."[6] The student is taught to read the tiles and reading progresses from syllables (e.g. *ig* to sight words).

Materials for the program consist of an instructor's manual, a record for the pronunciation of phonemes, colored wooden blocks, letter symbol tiles, consonant and vowel symbol cards, felt squares, mouth-form flash cards, bingo master cards, and a filmstrip which

---

[4]Charles Lindamood and Patricia Lindamood, *Auditory Discrimination in Depth* (Boston: Teaching Resources, 1969), p. 12.

[5]*Ibid.*, p. 12.

[6]*Ibid.*, p. 83.

explains the program. Supplementary materials are suggested in the instructor's guide.

Several of the special techniques in the program include: oral-motor kinesthetic stimulation, association of sounds with their formation in the mouth, utilization of colored wooden blocks and felt squares to represent the sounds, and employment of a self-checking or monitoring system.

There is not a sufficient amount of information concerning the use of the *ADD* Program with retarded children at the present time. There are features of the program that may be of benefit to some retarded children. The program is more complete than many on the market and can be used as part of the reading and spelling program because of its presentation of the phoneme-grapheme correspondences. It is also relatively inexpensive. The *LAC* test (Linda-mood and Lindamood, 1971) may be used before placing children in the *ADD* program.

Audio-Presentation for Auditory Training

Several publishers have developed auditory perceptual lessons, many of which are relatively expensive, for record or tape presentations. Lessons in auditory discrimination, memory, closure, and following directions as well as other auditory skills are included in these lessons. These programs and materials allow for individual or small-group work without the aid of the teacher. Unfortunately, several limitations of these programs include the facts that many children with auditory perceptual problems have difficulty keeping pace with the tapes or records, the value of some of the contents are questionable in relation to transfer to reading achievement, and some programs may be beyond the budget of many school programs. Appendix Two lists several of these programs.

Informal Auditory Perception Lessons

Many of the lessons and materials found in commercial programs could be prepared by the teacher. Several reading and language arts texts give suggestions for lessons and games in auditory perception: *Principles and Practices of Teaching Reading* (Heilman, 1972); *Clinical Teaching: Methods of Instruction for the Retarded* (Smith, 1968); *Phonics in Proper Perspective* (Heilman, 1968); *Learning Disabilities: Educational Principles and Practices* (Johnson and Myklebust, 1967): and *The Remediation of Learning Disabilities* (Valett, 1967). Wiseman (1965) also gives suggestions for activities for auditory training as measured by the *ITPA* (Mc-Carthy, Kirk, and Kirk, 1968).

An important point to consider is that if the teacher is to use commercially prepared or teacher-made materials in the area of auditory perception, the closer the lesson is to actual reading the better the possibility of success (Myers and Hammill, 1969).

PERCEPTUAL-MOTOR PROGRAMS

Strauss and Lehtinen

Strauss (1939) distinguished between *endogenous* and *exogeneous retardates*. Endogenous cases involved a family where there was one or more mentally defectives although there was no evidence of brain injury or disease in the family. The term exogeneous referred to those whose medical history indicated disease or injury which may have caused injury to the brain. These latter cases are often referred to as brain injured or as possessing the *Strauss Syndrome.*

Because of brain injury involved, the psychological makeup of the exogeneous individual has been described by Strauss and Lehtinen (1947) as having the following deviations: disturbances in perception, disturbance in concept formation (thinking and reasoning), disturbances in language, and disturbance in emotional behavior.

In terms of behavior disorders, Strauss found the brain-injured child to be distractible, hyperactive, impulsive, and perseverative. Such behaviors naturally interfere with the educative process. Strauss turned to gestalt psychology to describe the perceptual difficulties the brain injured child possesses. In tests devised by Strauss and his coworkers, he found evidence that these children had difficulties with figure-ground relationships in their confused method of attacking perceptual problems. In observing their conceptual difficulties, he noticed that these children would group objects on the basis of details which were unessential to the problem and would concoct unrealistic explanations to explain their grouping. In addition, the children were easily sidetracked during the skill task. All of these characteristics have their parallels in the behavior of brain-injured adults (Strauss and Werner, 1942).

The education of the exogeneous retardate in reading by the Strauss and Lehtinen method has been explained by Bortner (1968). He has stated:

> Reading disability in brain-injured children is viewed as another manifestation of the more general disturbances of behavior and perception. Remedial training is therefore addressed

to these disturbances rather than showing any special concern for emotional conflicts, interests, or motivation. The latter are viewed as exacerbating rather than causative factors.

Those difficulties in visual perception which contribute to reading disability include: inability to distinguish similar letters; difficulty with word configurations that are similar because of form, or because they contain the same letters in different order, or because of similar prominent details; and inability to spatially sequence letters. When such difficulties are seen in reading, other more general visual-perceptual disturbances are usually found.

Clinical observations suggest that defective auditory perception is also implicated in reading disability. Difficulties are observed in differentiation of speech sounds, in establishing a phonic approach to new words, in appreciating auditory sequence or spatial organization of sounds, and in blending or synthesizing isolated sound units.

Opportunities for the expression of general disturbances such as disinhibition, distractibility, perseveration, and hyperactivity are always present and must therefore be considered in the planning of a given remedial procedure and in the structuring of the classroom environment itself. Since language development as a factor in reading readiness is not characteristically defective in brain-injured children, and since excellent resource material already exists for those children who do have difficulty in this area, emphasis is placed on perceptual activities. These include discrimination, spatial organization, figure-ground and part-whole relations. All of these abilities are involved in putting together jigsaw puzzle pieces. Puzzles are made by cutting pictures from magazines. Their complexity both in terms of content and number of pieces is easily controlled. Discrimination ability is utilized in matching geometric designs. Color cues are helpful in correcting errors on the more complex geometric designs. Quick exposures to designs with subsequent matching gives practice in the skill of perceiving a total visual entity as contrasted with part-details.

Exercises related directly to reading include those which deal with the perception of letters. Learning to discriminate the letter forms is facilitated by making sets of alphabet cards, sorting identical letters, and using color cues to overcome directional confusions. To further solidify recognition, letters may be cut into jigsaw puzzle parts to be reconstructed later.

Matching a word is a readiness experience. The selection of the match is initially made from among "Distractor" words that are quite different from the key word; the task is made progressively more difficult when the distractor words are made increasingly similar to the key word. It is not necessary for the child to know what the word means or how it is pronounced. Emphasis is simply on recognition.

Since distractibility may interfere with the process of reading sentences in a continuous manner and result in diverse, irrelevant behavior, aids which counter this tendency of the child to leave the field are encouraged. Cutting out separate sentences for pasting, and separating contiguous words from each other within a sentence by using bits of color are recommended. Use of markers and fingers for pointing is also helpful in preventing the child from rushing blindly ahead, and in emphasizing the foreground character of the word against the background of the page and other words.

Instruction in auditory perception is recommended as a means of helping the brain-injured child acquire a basic sight vocabulary. Many of these children do not spontaneously recognize the generalization that printed symbols may be equated with speech sounds. They benefit from further analysis of sounds and their relation to visual counterparts. Oral emphasis permits gradual recognition of isolated sound units occurring in words. This is supplemented with the activity of searching for pictures which contain given sounds. Sound blending is helped through the use of multiple-choice techniques. Pictures illustrating several blends are shown to the child. The teacher offers a multiple-choice of blend sounds from which the child matches to the appropriate picture. The emphasis here is on the recognition of the blend rather than its production. After the auditory discrimination is made, the visual symbol may be presented.

All of the exercises discussed in connection with both visual and auditory discrimination are illustrative of what may be termed an analytical approach as contrasted with a global approach. The former stresses part-whole relations; the latter stresses recognition and memory of totalities.

The stress on accurate visual and auditory perception is viewed as merely the necessary prelude to the eventual integration of these two modes of receiving information. The procedures discussed emphasize only the acquisition of reading skills since this is such a frequent area of deficit. More complex problems such as difficulties in comprehension are seen as reflecting damage to that area of the brain concerned with the thinking process. Or, the child may have skills, but he may be unable to relate the statements he reads to an external perceptual word. Reading ability, at this level, is helped indirectly through the enhancement of conceptual and perceptual adequacies.[7]

Kephart's Perceptual-Motor Approach

In his study of the area of perceptual motor handicaps, Kephart has been influenced greatly by Strauss. To Kephart, learning difficulties often are largely perceptual-motor in nature. Thus, the aim of remediation is improving perceptual-motor skills. In his book, *The Slow Learner in the Classroom* (1971), Kephart has emphasized perceptual-motor development rather than actual reading instruction.

Children with perceptual-motor handicaps include those with specific deficits resulting from injury to the motor area of the central nervous system as well as those whose perceptual motor performance is awkward or clumsy and lacks flexibility. These children also have difficulty with eye-hand coordination and tend to lack spatial orientation (Kephart, 1968).

Kephart believed that basic skills should be taught in their natural order of development. The first step is the development of motor *patterns*; these patterns take in broad spectrum of movements (e.g. locomotion) which includes walking, running, skipping, etc. and is thus more comprehensive than a motor *skill* such as walking. Motor patterns serve to permit extensive exploration of the environment. A combination of motor patterns result in motor *generalization*. Four such generalizations are basic to the educational process — balance, locomotion, contact, and receipt and propulsion. Balance and maintenance of posture refer to those activities by which the child maintains his relationship to gravity. Through awareness of this relationship, the development of an awareness of the dimensions of space are possible. By means of locomotion, the child is able to explore his environment and observe the relationships between objects. Through contact, the child manipulates objects by reaching for them, grasping them, and then releasing them to continue to the next object. Thus, he can observe relationships within objects. Receipt and propulsion is a two-way process in which, through receipt, the child makes contact with a movable object, and, by propulsion, moves the object himself (Kephart, 1966).

---

[7]Morton Bortner, editor, *Evaluation and Education of Children with Brain Damage* (Springfield, Illinois: Charles C. Thomas, Co., 1968), pp. 142-45. Reprinted by permission of the publisher.

As the child acquires motor information, he also comes into contact with perceptual information. When he combines the perceptual and motor information into a meaningful whole, perceptual-motor match occurs. Because the eyes are most important for the match to occur, ocular control is considered essential (Kephart, 1966).

According to Kephart, the teaching of a child with a perceptual-motor handicap often begins with developing motor patterns, for in many of these children, such patterns are inadequate. To teach balance and posture, the walking board, a piece of two-by-four ten feet long, suspended two inches from the floor, and the balance board are used. The child should learn to maintain his balance while walking forward, backward, and in a sideways direction. As the child develops these skills, variations in tasks are given.

The balance board is a platform sixteen by sixteen inches with a balance post which can be three, four, or five inches in height. The child first learns to balance using all three balance posts. Variations in tasks are then given, such as throwing objects from the balance board, or performing simple calisthenics on it (Kephart, 1971).

Locomotion is taught in order to provide a variety of locomotor skills and to increase the child's flexibility and variability. Therefore, exercises are provided in walking, running, jumping, crawling, skipping, and galloping. The teacher usually demonstrates these skills and the student attempts to imitate them (Kephart, 1968).

Contact skills are taught by giving the child objects (beginning with large objects in order to provide a larger visual target) which he can grasp. Exercises can be done to strengthen the grip and to aid release of the object.

In teaching receipt and propulsion, the teacher usually does receipt first. Objects are moved toward the child and he is required to intercept the movement. At first, he may simply trap objects between his legs, but later, he may be required to catch the object by extending his arms and legs. In propulsion, the child is required to exert force on a movable object and follow it as it moves. Later, he may throw objects and then throw at targets (Kephart, 1968).

In perceptual-motor match exercises, the child is required to control single acts, continuous activities, and sequential acts. In single acts, the child is required to identify a point in space and bring his body to it by a single motor act. In continuous activities, he may need to vary direction or speed in terms of the perceptual data introduced. Such activities involve simple tasks ranging from marking indiscriminately to drawing curved lines to copying. Sequential acts are a combination of single acts and continuous activities and involve manipulating concrete objects to a symbolic level as presented in workbooks. To insure ocular control, exercises can be given requiring visual fixation and ocular pursuit (Kephart, 1968).

Once the child has acquired the perceptual-motor skills, he is ready for more complex learning in form perception and concept formation.

Barsch's Movigenic Curriculum

Raymond H. Barsch believes "that a child's need to move is a constant and necessary variable in all learning"[8] and that learning should be sensori-motor perceptual process. Thus, he has developed a movigenic curriculum (Barsch, 1965) which accepts as its thesis that movement patterns lead to learning efficiency.

In this program, the child's coordination is a matter of co-ordinates. Barsch has indicated that there are three ordinates since the child moves vertically, horizontally, and on the depth axis and has used the term *triordination* to describe this fact. Each child develops his own unique set of triordinates within his gravitational field. For the child's triordinates to be efficient, alignment with his senses is necessary. Failure in this task will cause warping. Movement efficiency is necessary to allow the child comfortable and economic processes in learning; when movement is efficient, perception is efficient. Thus, Barsch emphasizes movement training to improve the alignment of the learner's triordinates and to achieve comfortable and economical movements in task performance.

The teacher must have three basic units of preparation. These include: the study of the developing organism (physiologic readiness, postural alignment, etc.), study of environmental design (learning environment — e.g., physical surroundings and design of materials), and the study of symbolic competency (language as comprehension) (Barsch, 1966).

Barsch's (1965) research regarding the movigenic curriculum is largely subjective; however, in 1966, Painter found that children performed with significantly higher skill on certain subtests of the *ITPA* after being enrolled in the movigenic curriculum.

---

[8]Ray H. Barsch, *A Movigenic Curriculum* (Madison, Wisconsin: Bureau for Handicapped Children, 1965), p. 183.

Research and Perceptual Motor Approaches

Perceptual motor deficits are often found among retarded children and children with reading disorders (Falik, 1969; Fisher, 1971), although all children who have perceptual difficulties do not necessarily have reading difficulties (Myers and Hammill, 1969). Also, there is some research to indicate that training in perceptual-motor skills will improve the specific skills trained (Fisher, 1971). However, training by means of perceptual-motor exercises, such as those suggested by Kephart, may not effect reading achievement (Balow, 1971; Falik, 1969). Therefore, although a relationship may exist between perceptual-motor abilities and reading achievement, there is currently no evidence to indicate that the relationship is one of cause-and-effect. In summarizing his review on the relationship between perceptual-motor development and reading achievement, Balow remarked:

> Since research on motor and perceptual programs for children with severe reading disability offers little support for the easy answers promulgated these days, a conclusion that perceptual-motor activities are desirable may be surprising. Although there is no body of experimental evidence supporting a direct effect of perceptual-motor activity on basic school skills, and it is clear that such activities are neither "cure-alls" for the general run of learning disabled pupils nor specific to any basic school skill, the case studies reported in the literature argue for the possibility that visual-motor programs *may* be a specific treatment for a few very unusual children. That, however, even if it were to be found true, is insufficient reason to argue the desirability of perceptual-motor activities for all pupils.[9]

NEURO-PHYSIOLOGICAL APPROACH

Doman-Delacato

The Doman-Delacato approach is based on neurological organization (Delacato, 1959; 1963; 1966). This organization assumes that ontogeny (individual development) recapitulates phylogeny (species development). Development proceeds in an orderly fashion and progresses to cortical hemispheric dominance (Delacato, 1963). Delacato has stated:

---

[9]Bruce Balow, "Perceptual-Motor Activities in the Treatment of Severe Reading Disability," *The Reading Teacher* 24 (1971):523

> This progression is an interdependent continuum; hence if a high level of development is unfunctioning or incomplete, such as in sleep or as a result of trauma, lower levels become operative and dominant (mid-brain sleep and higher cervical pathological reflexes). If a lower level is incomplete, all succeeding higher levels are affected both in relation to their height in the central nervous system and in relation to the chronology of their development.... If man does not follow this scheme he exhibits problems of mobility or communication.[10]

Thus, inadequate neurological organization can be considered in most cases to be the cause of mental retardation and learning problems. Reading problems are also receptive problems which result from faulty or incomplete neurological organization.

Neurological organization begins before birth and requires about eight years to be completed. At the birth of a child, the spinal cord and medulla, which operates on a reflexive basis, are generally the highest organized functions. By four months of age, mobility begins, placing the child on a level with certain other creatures (e.g., a fish). This mobility gradually proceeds to a neural organization of amphibians because of pons. At six months, neurological organization reaches the midbrain, which raises the child from the level of amphibians to that of land animals. Cross-pattern functioning (opposite hand and leg) then emerges. Ultimately, cortical dominance occurs. Thus, the "difference between man and animal is that man has cortical hemispheric dominance."[11] Because one hemisphere of the brain dominates the other, man develops a symbolic language.

As the child makes choices of sidedness, the culture must give him opportunities to develop complete unilaterality, a factor which results in onesidedness for handedness, footness, and eyedness (Delacato, 1959).

Treatment is based on the level of neurological organization the child has reached. McCarthy and McCarthy have stated:

> Thus a child whose organization has reached only the medulla ... would be programmed for organization at the next higher level by (a) allowing him the opportunity to use available reflex movements and (b) passively imposing those move-

---

[10]C.H. Delacato, *The Diagnosis and Treatment of Speech and Reading Problems* (Springfield, Illinois: Charles C. Thomas Co., 1963), pp. 4-5.

[11]C.H. Delacato, *Treatment and Prevention of Reading Problems* (Springfield, Illinois: Charles C. Thomas Co., 1959), p. 21.

ments on him if he is incapable of them. Similarly, treatment at any level of organization is aimed at reorganizing subsequent disorganized levels. In training at the level of cortical dominance, procedures are applied simultaneously, for what is being trained, in the words of Delacato, is not "a foot, an eye or a hand, but . . . a hemisphere of the brain. The retraining of one area alone cannot result in the establishment of hemispheric dominance". The first step, at this level, is the deletion of tonality (music, TV sound, etc.). . . . The retraining of sleep patterns is followed by training in footedness, handedness, and finally, writing. . . . A reexamination of the neurological reorganization precedes the actual instruction in reading. On satisfactory achievement of reorganization, instruction in reading commences.[12]

The Doman Delacato method of teaching reading requires the child to use large crayons, trace sandpaper letters, copy figures on a large chalkboard, and use the *Stereo-Reader*. The *Stereo-Reader* (distributed by Keystone View Co.) has a steroptic eyepiece facing a reading surface upon which visual training and reading materials can be employed. Thus, the *Stereo-Reader* is used for eye training. During the first and second grades, the main times when the reader is used, the eye training of *one* eye requires twenty minutes per day.

The Doman Delacato methods for reading are the following:

1. The child is introduced to words conceptually. The first words used are those which are derived from the child's experiences. The child reads *whole* words.
2. Contextual learning requires learning about words in relationship with other words in order to obtain sense from sentences.
3. Structural analysis consists of breaking up large words.
4. In phonics, consonants are taught first. As the consonants are being mastered, the student is introduced to vowels.

Thus, the child learns from conceptual wholes to phonics. All work in early reading is done orally. "All verbal and experiential discussion of early reading should be done aloud. Oral reading, however, should always be preceded by silent reading, and oral

---

[12]James J. McCarthy and Joan F. McCarthy, *Learning Disabilities* (Boston: Allyn & Bacon Co., 1969), pp. 53-54. Reprinted by permission of the publisher.

reading *should always be done in whispers.*"[13] In addition, reading instruction is accompanied by writing exercises using the same words, thereby providing the reinforcement necessary to establish cortical hemisphere dominance.

Research regarding the Doman Delacato approach is inconclusive. Kershner (1968), using two groups of trainable mentally retardates, pretested and post-tested them by using the "Creeping and Crawling Scale" adapted from the *Doman-Delacato Developmental Profile*, the *Kershner Dusewicz-Kershner Adaptation of the Vineland-Oseretsky Motor Developmental Tests (VOT)*, and the *Peabody Picture Vocabulary Test (PPVT)*. One group (experimental $n = 14$ received Doman Delacato procedures while the second group (control $n = 16$) received a program for balance, rhythm, coordination, and body image. His result indicated: (1) that creeping and crawling performance improves through creeping and crawling activities, (2) that recapitulation of early perceptual motor experiences may not be as Doman Delacato suggests, prerequisite to more sophisticated perceptual motor skills, (3) that no difference was indicated on *VOT* scores, and (4) that the *PPVT* showed the experimental group to be statistically favored. The author indicated that caution must be used in interpreting these results because of the small samples and the limitations of the research designs. However, the results do appear to support Delacato somewhat.

Robbins (1966) used three groups matched for age, intelligence, creeping, and laterality. Group one remained in the normal classroom setting; group two received the Delacato exercises, while group three was a nonspecific group. At the end of three months, no significant differences were found among the three groups in reading or arithmetic. In addition, lateralization and creeping were not beneficial. Thus, Robbins' results did not support the theory. O'Donnell and Eisenson (1969) also failed to find any significant achievement differences in reading performance or visual-motor integration after the use of the method with retarded readers.

Cruickshank (1968), in a position statement on the Doman-Delacato Method, pointed to the lack of controlled studies on the method. He indicated that: (1) improvements noted in the Doman-Delacato methods may be due to progress caused by maturation; (2) success or failure on the program depends upon the parents' following a strict regimen which requires them to sacrifice untold

---

[13]Delacato, *The Diagnosis and Treatment of Speech and Reading Problems*, p. 135.

time and energy; (3) acceptable evaluation of the program has not been made; and (4) individual reports have indicated that the program has not helped the patients.

LANGUAGE PROGRAMS AND TRAINING IN RELATION TO READING

Although "the relationship between facility in oral expression and reading achievement has not been clearly demonstrated by research,"[14] many language programs are used in conjunction with or prior to reading instruction. This is the case particularly in classes for the retarded because of the results of most research with culturally deprived and retarded children (see Chapter Three). However, language training with retarded children is in a very primitive stage at this time. One reason is the lack of adequate tests to isolate the language difficulties of the retarded (Dever, 1971); most of the language studies have dealt with the speech problems of the retarded rather than with language development and specific language characteristics (Sitko and Semmel, 1972). In relation to the language development of retarded children, Sitko and Semmel have stated:

> However, one comprehensive study of language development in retarded children demonstrated that language begins in the same manner in retardates as it does with nonretarded children. Later studies appeared to support the view that language development of the retarded seems to be slowed down, rather than being qualitatively different from that of nonretarded children.[15]

As was stated previously, language skills have been related to reading achievement, especially comprehension (Harris and Smith, 1972). If one views reading as a psycholinguistic process, reading and language are very closely related skills. Goodman (1969), a psycholinguist, feels that reading programs should be language centered.

---

[14]Samuel Weintraub, "What Research Says about Learning to Read," in *Coordinating Reading Instruction*, ed. Helen M. Robinson (Glenview, Illinois: Scott, Foresman and Co., 1971), p. 181.

[15]Merrill Sitko and Melvin Semmel, "Language and Language Behavior of the Mentally Retarded," in *The First Review of Special Education*, ed. Lester Mann and David Sabatino (Bloomington: Indiana University Center for Innovation in Teaching the Handicapped, 1973), p. 241.

Several language programs have been developed that serve as supplementary programs to the regular program or the primary area of skill developed in preschool or test-related programs.

Supplementary Language Programs

Peabody Language Development Kits (PLDK): One of the most often used language development programs in classrooms for the retarded is called the *Peabody Language Development Kits (PLDK)* (Dunn, Horton and Smith, 1968; Dunn and Smith, 1965, 1966, 1967). These programs, which are in kit form, have four different levels beginning with mental ages at the preschool level and extending through the primary grades. Materials in the kits consist of teacher's guides; large stimulus cards classified according to such concepts as clothes, color, and shape; large posters for use in oral discussion and memory lessons; puppets; magnetic tapes containing songs, folk tales etc.; *Teletalk (Kit #2)* for oral discussion; and colored chips that can be used for reinforcement. These materials are packed in a metal carrying case.

The teacher's manual gives very explicit suggestions and directions for lessons to be presented daily in hour-long group sessions. No reading or writing is required of the children. Presentations emphasize perception (e.g., auditory skills such as rhyming), conceptualization (e.g., time) and classification of concepts; and expression (e.g., descriptions of objects).

The kits have been used with educable retarded children, and according to Dunn and associates (1968), better results were obtained when the program was used over an extended period of time. In their study over a two and one-half year period with educable retarded children, they found that gains were significant in the areas of language and cognitive development, although they were not important in school achievement.

Although several authorities have found merit in the use of the kits, the program also has been criticized for not being characteristic of psycholinguistic principles (Rosenberg, 1970). The program has two particular limitations: There is no consideration of individual differences in language development; therefore, all children progress through the program at the same rate, and there are skills that are introduced without sequential follow-up (Latham, 1969).

Recently, perhaps because of the popularity of the *PLDK* and the interest in psycholinguistic development, several commercially produced language programs have been placed on the market. Some of these include: *Try: Experiences for Young Children* (Noble and Noble, 1967); *EDGE I* (D.C. Heath and Company, 1972); and *Early Learning Systems* (McGraw-Hill, 1971). Additional language programs are listed in Appendix Three.

Preschool Language Programs

Although most of the commercially prepared language programs are designed for skill development with very young children, there are several preschool programs that are more all-encompassing than the commercially produced materials.

Academic Preschool Program: This program was developed by Carl Bereiter and Siegfried Engelmann in 1966 for disadvantaged children. Bereiter and Engelmann consider language deprivation to be a chief characteristic of culturally deprived children and cited two special weaknesses of the language development of these children. Culturally deprived children view sentences as "giant words" that cannot be taken apart; therefore, they do not possess adequate knowledge of grammar and syntax. They described the second weakness as "a failure to master the use of structural words and inflections which are necessary for the expression and manipulation of logical relationships."[16] In describing teaching the culturally deprived child language skills Bereiter and Engelmann have stated:

> The problem for culturally deprived children is not so much learning to speak in sentences as learning to speak in sentences that are composed of discrete words.[17]

The Academic Preschool Program is highly structured with specific goals to be accomplished. Bereiter and Engelmann feel that specific programs must be established so that children can "catch up" on the skills necessary for success in school; thus, the preschool program is run much like programs in the grades with lessons planned and children working on basic language, reading, and arithmetic skills. Although classes last approximately fifteen minutes, the total program lasts for two hours each day. Children are given short breaks between classes for relaxation and play periods. Behavior is controlled by specific rewards and mild punishment.

---

[16]Carl Bereiter and Siegfried Engelmann, *Teaching Disadvantaged Children in the Preschool* (Englewood Cliffs, New Jersey: Prentice-Hall, Inc., 1966), p. 43.

[17]*Ibid.*, p. 43.

In language instruction, attempts are made to assure that the child is taught the minimum language skills necessary for processing concepts (Bereiter and Engelmann, 1966). Bereiter and Engelmann describe the basic language skills in the form of first-order and second-order statements. "This is a _____," and "This _____is_____" are examples of first-order and second-order statement forms respectively. In completed form, the example of the first-order or identity statement is, "This is an alligator," while the second-order statement would be "This ball is a football."[18]

Children also must learn to master such basic concepts as polar and non-polar. Polar concepts (e.g. opposites such as hot and cold), would be introduced through sentences. Non-polar concepts might be shared by the same members of an identity class ("This dog is brown") or by all members of an identity class ("This dog is an animal").

The program works on expanding sentences, labeling and classifying common objects, and formulating meaningful questions about relationships and properties of concepts. The basic statements, variations, and expansions are taught in systematic group lessons with the teacher making the initial response and the children in turn responding in the form of drill patterning.

The following is an example of the stereotyped procedure of the dialogues between the teacher and the children.

> a. Present an object and give the appropriate identity statement, "This is a ball."
> b. Follow the statement with a *yes-no* question. "Is this a ball?"
> c. Answer the question. "Yes, this is a ball."
> d. Repeat the question and encourage the children to answer it.
> e. Introduce *what* questions after the children have begun to respond adequately to the *yes-no* questions.[19]

Bereiter and Engelmann first developed this program in a class for fifteen deprived children assigned three teachers. At the end of nine months, Bereiter and Engelmann (1966a and 1966b) reported achievement scores ranging from first-grade to second-grade level, a mean gain of seven IQ points, and a mean gain of eighteen months on the *ITPA*.

---

[18]*Ibid.*, pp. 139-44.
[19]*Ibid.*, p. 140.

Since then, there have been several studies involving the use of *The Academic School Program* with young disadvantaged children. Several studies have found significant differences in favor of the program when compared to other language programs (Karnes, 1969; Miller, 1970; Rusk, 1969), although a few studies have shown no significant differences (Day, 1968; Dickie, 1968; Reidford and Berzonsky, 1967). Day did find significant differences in favor of the Bereiter-Engelmann program in the use of color and form words in descriptive language tasks and in the use of conceptual attributes though.

This program is controversial because of its directed teaching techniques because it demands three teachers for fifteen children. Both of these features are difficult for preschools to implement without highly competent personnel and an adequate staff (Nixon and Nixon, 1971). In addition, Spicker (1971) has given the following criticism of the Bereiter and Engelmann program:

> A preschool academic skill oriented program such as that developed by Bereiter and Engelmann tends to produce rote reading and arithmetic computation skills rather than improved reading comprehension and arithmetic reasoning skills.[20]

There have been other preschool programs that have helped children to achieve cognitive and language achievement (Hodges, McCandless, and Spicker, 1971; Weikart, 1969). A few considerations of these preschool intervention programs include: the age of the children for best progress, the duration of the intervention program, and the lasting results or effects of the program on later school achievement (Spicker, 1971). For a thorough discussion of *The Academic Preschool Program*, see *Teaching Disadvantaged Children in the Preschool* (Bereiter and Engelmann, 1966).

ITPA Language Training

This program may be used with preschoolers as well as older children (Hartman, 1966) with suggestions for activities that are based on the subtests of the *ITPA* discussed in Chapter Four. Three sources for suggested lessons are *Psycholinguistic Learning Disabilities: Diagnosis and Remediation* (Kirk and Kirk, 1971), *Aids to Psycholinguistic Teaching* (Bush and Giles, 1969), and "Classroom

---

[20]Howard H. Spicker, "Intellectual Development through Early Childhood Education," *Exceptional Children* 37 (1971): 635.

Procedure for Identifying and Remediating Language Problems" (Wiseman, 1965). Suggestions in such areas as auditory reception are similar to many of the exercises found in auditory perception programs. For auditory reception difficulties, such activities as training in discrimination of environmental sounds are suggested (Kirk and Kirk, 1972).

This program is one of the first attempts to teach language skills diagnostically. Children are tested on the *ITPA* prior to instruction and programs are established for individuals or groups of children in such areas as auditory decoding (Myers and Hammill, 1969). As was stated in Chapter Four, a teacher must be very cautious in planning diagnostic programs based upon the *ITPA* because of the lack of reliability of many of the subtests and the failure of the subtests as clearly separate entities. Also, as is the case with the Frostig-Horne program, training in the skills under discussion, while it may actually improve the performance of retarded children on the *ITPA* (Smith, 1962), may not transfer to academic achievement (Myers and Hammill, 1969). Nonetheless, programs such as those based upon the *ITPA* may encourage researchers to develop very effective diagnostically-based language programs which could relate to academic achievement.

SUMMARY

The language development of the retarded should be considered an important part of the reading program particularly because a child may benefit more from reading instruction if the materials are within his receptive vocabulary and commensurate with his grammatical structure. Errors a child makes in oral reading may be a clue to the language strategies the child is using (see Chapter Four), and this information may be of value in planning reading activities for the child. In addition, language skills cannot be separated from other activities and taught without consideration of the language skills which the child must utilize in all subjects, especially reading. The present authors agree with Cawley, Goodstein, and Burrow (1972) that reading instruction should be delayed if the child has an "immaturity" in language development. "Reading is a language process"[21] and should begin with the meaningful and the natural language of the child.

---

[21]Kenneth Goodman, "Reading: The Key Is in Children's Language," *The Reading Teacher* 25 (1972): 505-08.

Programs in reading for the retarded usually incorporate reading-related skills as well as direct skill development. The areas of perceptual, neurological, and language development are most often included in such programs. Although deficiencies in these skills have been found to exist among many retarded readers, the cause-and-effect relationship between these skills and reading achievement remains uncertain. For example, the influence of such programs as those developed by Frostig, Getman, and Kephart on reading success is not conclusive. Language programs for the retarded also have been developed, although, as with programs in the perceptual areas, these have not been related directly to reading achievement. Reading may be considered a perceptual and language process; however, the nature of the skills that should be included in the specific training programs requires further study.

REFERENCES

Allen, R.M.; Dickman, I.; and Haught, T. "A Pilot Study of the Immediate Effectiveness of the Frostig-Horne Training Program with Educable Retardates." *Exceptional Children* 31 (1966): 41.

Arciszewski, R.A. "A Pilot Study of the Effects of Visual Perception Training and Intensive Phonics Training on the Visual Perception and Reading Ability of First-Grade Pupils." Paper read at the 1967 annual meeting of the American Educational Research Association, February 1967, in New York.

Balow, Bruce. "Perceptual-Motor Activities in the Treatment of Severe Reading Disability." *The Reading Teacher* 24 (1971): 513-25; 542.

Barsch, Ray H. *A Movigenic Curriculum.* Madison, Wisconsin: Bureau for Handicapped Children, 1965.

_____. "Teacher Needs — Motor Training." In *The Teacher of Brain-Injured Children,* edited by William W. Cruickshank, pp. 183-95. Syracuse, New York: Syracuse University Press, 1966.

Bateman, Barbara. "Open Forum." *Journal of Learning Disabilities* 2 (1969): 16-17.

Bennett, R.M. "A Study of the Effects of a Visual Perception Training Program upon School Achievement, IQ, and Visual Perception." Doctoral dissertation, University of Tennessee, 1968.

Bereiter, Carl, and Engelmann, Seigfried. "Observations on the Use of Direct Instruction with Young Disadvantaged Children." *Journal of School Psychology* 4 (1966a): 55-62.

_____. *Teaching Disadvantaged Children in the Preschool.* Englewood, Cliffs, New Jersey: Prentice-Hall, Inc., 1966b.

Bortner, Morton, editor. *Evaluation and Education of Children with Brain Damage.* Springfield, Illinois: Charles C. Thomas Co., 1968.

Bosworth, M.A. "Prereading: Improvement of Visual-Motor Skills." Doctoral dissertation, University of Miami, 1967.

Buckland, Pearl. "The Effect of Visual Perception Training on Reading Achievement in Low Readiness First-Grade Pupils." Doctoral dissertation, University of Minnesota, 1969.

Buckland, Pearl, and Balow, Bruce. "The Effect of Visual Perception Training on Reading Achievement." *Exceptional Children* 39 (1973): 299-304.

Bush, W.J., and Giles, M.T. *Aids to Psycholinguistic Teaching.* Columbus, Ohio: Charles E. Merrill Publishing Co., 1969.

Cawley, J.; Goodstein, H.A.; and Burrow, W.H. *The Slow Learner and the Reading Problem.* Springfield, Illinois: Charles C. Thomas Co., 1972.

Cheves, R. *Visual-Motor Perception Teaching Materials.* Boston: Teaching Resources, 1972.

Cohen, R.I. "Remedial Training of First-Grade Children with Visual Perceptual Retardation." Doctoral dissertation, University of California at Los Angeles, 1966.

Cohen, S.A. "Studies in Visual Perception and Reading in Disadvantaged Children." *Journal of Learning Disabilities* 2 (1969): 498-503.

Cruickshank, W.M. "Position Statement on Doman-Delacato Method." *Exceptional Children* 34 (1968): 365-66.

Day, D.E. "The Effects of Different Language Instruction on the Use of Attributes by Prekindergarten Disadvantaged Children." Paper read at the American Educational Research Association Convention, February 1968, in Chicago.

Delacato, C.H. *The Diagnosis and Treatment of Speech and Reading Problems.* Springfield, Illinois: Charles C. Thomas Co., 1963.

_____. *The Treatment and Prevention of Reading Problems.* Springfield, Illinois: Charles C. Thomas Co., 1959.

Delacato, C.H., editor. *Neurological Organization and Reading Problems.* Springfield, Illinois: Charles C. Thomas Co., 1966.

Deutch, Cynthia P., and Feldman, Shirley C. "A Study of the Effectiveness of Training for Retarded Readers in the Auditory Skills underlying Reading." Title VII, Project Number 1124, Grant US Department of Health, Education, and Welfare Office of Education. New York: New York Medical College Institute for Developmental Studies, 1966.

Dever, Richard B. "The Use of Language by Mentally Retarded Children: A Review of the Literature." Technical Report Number 1.24. Bloomington, Indiana: Indiana University Center for Research and Development on the Improvement of Teaching Handicapped Children, 1971.

Dickie, Joyce P. "Effectiveness of Structural and Unstructural (Traditional) Methods of Language Training." Monograph of the Society for Research in Child Development, 1968.

Di Meo, R.P. "Visual-Motor Skills and Pretextural Behavior." Doctoral dissertation, University of Miami, 1967.

Dunn, L.M., and Smith, J.O., editor. *Peabody Language Development Kit: Level Number 1.* Circle Pines, Minnesota: American Guidance Service, 1965.

_____. *Peabody Language Development Kit: Level Number 2.* Circle Pines, Minnesota: American Guidance Service, 1966.

_____. *Peabody Language Development Kit: Level Number 3.* Circle Pines, Minnesota: American Guidance Service, 1967.

Dunn, L.M.; Horton, R.B.; and Smith, J.O. *Peabody Language Development Kit: Level P.* Circle Pines, Minnesota: American Guidance Service, 1968.

Dunn, L.M., et al. "Effectiveness of the *Peabody Language Development Kit* with Educable Mentally Retarded Children: A Report after Two and One-Half Years." *IMRID Papers and Reports #15.* Nashville, Tennessee: Peabody College, 1968.

Durrell, Donald D. "First-Grade Reading Success Study 1: A Summary." *Journal Of Education* 140 (1958): 2-6.

Falik, Louis H. "The Effects of Special Perceptual-Motor Training in Kindergarten on Reading and on Second-Grade Reading Performance." *Journal of Learning Disabilities* 2 (1969): 395-402.

Fisher, Kirk L. "Effects of Perceptual-Motor Training on the Educable Mentally Retarded." *Exceptional Children* 38 (1971): 264-66.

Fitzhugh, Kathleen, and Fitzhugh, Loren. *The Fitzhugh Plus Program.* Galien, Michigan: Allied Education Council, 1966.

Frostig, Marianne. "Education of Children with Learning Difficulties." *Educating Children with Learning Disabilities: Selected Readings,* edited by Edward C. Frierson and Walter B. Barbe, pp. 387-98. New York: Appleton-Century-Crofts, 1967.

_____. "Visual Perception, Integrative Functions, and Academic Learning." *Journal of Learning Disabilities* 5 (1972): 5-19.

Frostig, Marianne, and Horne, D. *The Frostig Program for the Development of Visual Perception.* Chicago: Follett Publishing Co., 1964.

Frostig, Marianne, and Maslow, Phyllis. "Reading, Developmental Abilities, and the Problem of Match." *Journal of Learning Disabilities* 2 (1969): 571-78.

Frostig, Marianne; Maslow, Phyllis; LeFever, W.; and Whittlesey, J.K.B. *The Marianne Frostig Development Test of Visual Perception, 1963 Standardization.* Palo Alto, California: Consulting Psychologist, 1964.

Getman, G.N. *How to Develop Your Child's Intelligence.* Luverne, Minnesota: Announcer Press, 1962.

Getman, G.N., and Hendrickson, Homer. "The Needs of Teachers for Specialized Information on the Development of Visuomotor Skills in Relation to Academic Performance." In *The Teacher of Brain-Injured Children,* edited by William Cruickshank, pp. 155-68. Syracuse, New York: Syracuse University Press, 1966.

Goodman, Kenneth. "The Linguistic Approach: Pro Challenger." In *Current Issues in Reading,* edited by N.B. Smith, pp. 268-76. Newark, Delaware: International Reading Association, 1969.

_____. "Reading: The Key Is in Children's Language." *The Reading Teacher* 25 (1972): 505-08.

Hammill, D.D., and Wierderholt, J.O. "Use of the Frostig-Horne Visual Perception Program as Reported in Researchlight." *The Reading Teacher* 25 (1972): 575.

Harris, Larry A., and Smith, Carl B. *Reading Instruction through Diagnostic Teaching.* New York: Holt, Rinehart, & Winston, 1972.

Hartman, A.S. "Preschool Diagnostic Language Programs." Harrisburg, Pennsylvania: Department of Public Education, 1966. Also in *Method for*

Learning Disorders, edited by Patricia Myers and Donald Hammill. New York: John Wiley & Sons, 1969.

Heilman, Arthur W. *Phonics in Proper Perspective*, 2d ed. Columbus, Ohio: Charles E. Merrill Publishing Co., 1968.

_____. *Principles and Practices of Teaching Reading,* 3rd ed. Columbus, Ohio: Charles E. Merrill Publishing Co., 1972.

Hodges, W.L.; McCandless, B.R.; and Spicker, H.H. *Diagnostic Teaching for Preschool Children*. Arlington, Virginia: The Council for Exceptional Children, 1971.

Jacobs, J.J. "An Evaluation of the Frostig Visual-Perceptual Training Program." *Journal of the Association for Supervision and Curriculum Development* 25 (1968): 332-40.

Johnson, Doris, and Myklebust, H.R. *Learning Disabilities: Educational Principles and Practices*. New York: Grune & Stratton, 1967.

Karnes, M.B. *Research and Development Program on Preschool Children*, volume 1. Final Report, Contract Number OE-6-10-235, United States Office of Education. Urbana: University of Illinois, 1969.

Keim, Richard P. "Visual-Motor Training, Readiness, and Intelligence of Kindergarten Children." *Journal of Learning Disabilities* 3 (1970): 256-59.

Kephart, Newell C. "The Needs of Teachers for Specialized Information on Perception." In *The Teacher of Brain-Injured Children*, edited by William Cruickshank. Syracuse, New York: Syracuse University Press, 1966.

_____. *The Slow Learner in the Classroom*, 2d ed. Columbus, Ohio: Charles E. Merrill Publishing Co., 1971.

_____. "Teaching the Child with a Perceptual-Motor Handicap." In *Evaluation and Education of Children with Brain Damage*, edited by Morton Bortner. Springfield, Illinois: Charles C. Thomas Co., 1968.

Kershner, John R. "Doman-Delacato's Theory on Neurological Organization Applied with Retarded Children." *Exceptional Children* 34 (1968): 441.

Kirk, Samuel, and Kirk, Winifred D. *Psycholinguistic Learning Disabilities: Diagnosis and Remediation*. Urbana: University of Illinois Press, 1971.

Kirk, Samuel; McCarthy, J.V.; and Kirk, Winifred. *Illinois Test of Psycholinguistic Abilities*, rev. ed. Urbana: University of Illinois Press, 1968.

Krippner, Stanley. "Research in Visual Training and Reading Disability." *Journal of Learning Disabilities* 4 (1971): 65-76.

Latham, L.C. "Classifying the Activities in the *PDLK* (Level 2) according to *ITPA* Subtests." Athens: University of Georgia, 1969. Mimeographed.

Lindamood, Charles, and Lindamood, Patricia. *Lindamood Auditory Conceptualization Test (LAC)*. Boston: Teaching Resources, 1971.

_____. *Auditory Discrimination in Depth*. Boston: Teaching Resources, 1969.

McBeath, P.M. "The Effectiveness of Three Reading Preparedness Programs for Perceptually Handicapped Kindergartners." Doctoral dissertation, Stanford University, 1966.

McCarthy, James J., and McCarthy, Joan F. *Learning Disabilities*. Boston: Allyn & Bacon, 1969.

McQuarrie, C.W. *A Perceptual Testing and Training Guide for Kindergarten Teachers*. Winter Haven, Florida: Lions Research Foundation, 1967.

Miller, Louise B. "Experimental Variation of Headstart Curricula: A Comparison of Current Approaches." Louisville, Kentucky: University of Louisville Psychology Department, 1970.

Myers, Patricia, and Hammill, Donald. *Methods of Learning Disorders.* New York: John Wiley & Sons, 1969.

Nixon, Ruth, and Nixon, Clifford. *Introduction to Early Childhood Education.* New York: Random House, 1971.

O'Donnell, Patrick, and Eisenson, Jon. "Delacato Training for Reading Achievement and Visual-Motor Integration." *Journal of Learning Disabilities* 2 (1969): 441-47.

Painter, G. "The Effects of a Rhythmic and Sensory Motor Activity on Perceptual Motor Spatial Abilities of Kindergarten Children." *Exceptional Children* 33 (1966): 113-19.

Popp, H.M. "The Measurement and Training of Visual Discrimination Skills Prior to Reading Instruction." *Journal of Experimental Education* 35 (1967): 15-26.

Reidford, P., and Berzonsky, M. "Field Test of an Academically Oriented Preschool Curriculum." Paper read at American Educational Research Association Convention, February 1967, in New York.

Robbins, M.P. "A Study of the Validity of Delacato's Theory of Neurological Organization." *Exceptional Children* 32 (1966): 517.

Rosen, C.W. "An Experimental Study of Visual Perceptual Training and Reading Achievement in First Grade." *Perceptual and Motor Skills* 22 (1966): 979-86.

Rosen, C.W., and Ohnmacht, F. "Perception, Readiness, and Reading Achievement in First Grade." In *Perception and Reading, Proceedings of the Twelfth Annual Convention of the International Reading Association,* edited by M.K. Smith 12 (1968): 33-38.

Rosenberg, S. "Problems of Language Development in the Retarded." In *Social-Cultural Aspects of Mental Retardation,* edited by A.C. Haywood, pp. 203-16. New York: Appleton-Century-Crofts, 1970.

Rusk, Bruce. "Field Test of the Bereiter-Engelmann Preschool Curriculum in a Six-Week Headstart Program." Paper read at American Educational Research Association Convention, February 1969, in Los Angeles.

Sitko, Merrill, and Semmel, M.I. "Language and Language Behavior of the Mentally Retarded." In *The First Review of Special Education,* vol. 1, edited by Lester Mann and David Sabatino, pp. 203-59. Bloomington: Indiana University Center for Innovation in Teaching the Handicapped, 1973.

_____. "Language and Language Behavior of the Mentally Retarded." Occasional Paper 1. Bloomington: Indiana University Center for Innovation in Teaching the Handicapped, 1972.

Smith, J.C. *Affects of a Group Language Development Program upon the Psycholinguistic Abilities of Educable Mental Retardates.* Special Education Research Monographs, Number 1. Nashville, Tennessee: Peabody College, 1962.

Smith, R.M. *Clinical Teaching: Method of Instruction for the Retarded.* New York: McGraw-Hill Book Co., 1968.

Spicker, Howard H. "Intellectual Development through Early Childhood Education." *Exceptional Children* 37 (1971): 629-40.

Strauss, A.A. "Topology in Mental Deficiency: Its Clinical, Psychological, and Educational Implications." *Proceedings of the American Association of Mental Deficiency* 44 (1939): 85-90.

Strauss, A.A., and Lehtinen, L.F. *Psychology and Education of the Brain-Injured Child.* New York: Grune & Stratton, 1947.

Strauss, A.A., and Werner, H. "Disorders of Conceptual Thinking in the Brain-Injured Child." *Journal of Nervous and Mental Disorders* 96 (1942): 153-72.

Sutphin, E.C. *Perceptual Testing-Training Handbook for First-Grade Teachers.* Winter Haven, Florida: Lions Research Foundation, 1967.

Tyson, M.C. "Pilot Study of Remedial Visuo-Motor Training." *Special Education* 52 (1968): 22-25.

Valett, Robert E. *The Remediation of Learning Disabilities.* Palo Alto, California: Fearon Publishers, 1967.

Weikart, D.P. "Comparative Study of Three Preschool Curricula." Paper read at the biennial meeting of the Society for Research in Child Development, March 1969, at Santa Monica, California.

Weintraub, Samuel. "What Research Says about Learning to Read." In *Coordinating Reading Instruction,* edited by Helen M. Robinson, pp. 180-201. Glenview, Illinois: Scott, Foresman and Co., 1971.

Wiseman, D.E. "A Classroom Procedure for Identifying and Remediating Language Problems." *Mental Retardation* 3 (1965): 20-24.

TEN

Application of
Reading Approaches

In implementing methods and materials in instructional settings, the teacher may be concerned initially with finding a program that meets the needs of the entire group. However, as he begins his program, he may discover that no matter how "homogeneous" his particular group or groups of children may seem to be, individual differences still exist. In addition, strengths and weaknesses in reading performance may vary within one child. Thus, the special education teacher, as well as the regular classroom teacher, has the task of attempting to individualize instruction within group settings. Unfortunately, little has been written that will aid the teacher with this procedure. Many texts give examples for the development of reading skills, and some list actual exercises or lessons that may be used by the teacher. Yet caution must be exercised that this process does not become one of merely adding suggestions to the teacher's "bag of tricks" or "book of recipes."

In the process of selecting materials or techniques for group or individual instruction, the teacher also will discover the availability of a variety of reading programs, methods, and materials, and since so many programs are being developed, it is difficult for the teacher to keep abreast of all of them. Thus, more important than just a *knowledge* of these programs is the *ability* of the teacher to *adapt any material or method* to the specific needs of the child and to monitor the child's progress or achievement as the result of such instruction. This skill requires that the teacher view instruction as the problem-solving process as outlined in Chapter Six. In an inquiry or problem-solving approach, the matching of materials to the needs of children allows the teacher to evaluate constantly the efficacy of materials or approaches implemented.

In order to aid the teacher with the matching of materials and/or methods to the needs of children, much of this chapter will follow a problem-solving approach. A simulated class of exceptional children will be presented accompanied by suggestions for the steps of diagnosing, prescribing, and managing reading programs for these children. But before the presentation of instructional strategies for a group of exceptional children, it is necessary to discuss such issues as the administrative placement of educable retarded children, learning management techniques, and diagnostic-prescriptive procedures.

EDUCATIONAL PLACEMENT

A considerable amount of the literature on exceptional children is devoted to the discussion of settings or placement for educable retarded children (see Chapter One). Discussion of the programs established for educable retarded children is complicated because the programs vary from state to state or district to district depending upon differing philosophies and/or funds. For example, retarded children may be in regular classes in one district or state merely because the area's lack of facilities or money dictates regular class placement. Another district or state may feel that regular classroom placement is more beneficial for educably retarded children, if special personnel are hired to aid classroom teachers with programming for these children. In still another area, special services for retarded children may be in the form of resource rooms for instruction in reading and math, paraprofessional tutors, or media and methods consultants who work directly with regular class teachers as well as other special service personnel.

Regardless of the nature of the setting or placement, some professional person must be responsible for the instructional strategies to be implemented. Ultimately, after diagnosis, the responsibility is placed upon the shoulders of the person who is working directly with the child. In most instances, this is the special or regular class teacher. Whether or not an educable retarded child is to benefit from regular or special class placement, depends, in many cases, upon the nature of the instruction offered within the setting or placement. If a regular classroom teacher attempts to meet the needs of all children in his class, he will not reject a "slow" child on the basis that the child "is not able to keep up" with the rest of the children. Also, if a child is "placed" in a special class, his individual strengths and weaknesses should continue to be considered. Too often, children in special classes are considered to be a homogeneous group.

The simulated classroom in this chapter is within the setting of a special class placement, not because the authors feel special class placement is the solution for educable retarded children, but because an effort is made in this case to emphasize that children who are labeled as retarded possess a wide range of characteristics. Most, if not all, the strategies suggested in this chapter can be implemented in regular as well as special classrooms.

MANAGEMENT OF LEARNING ENVIRONMENTS

Methods of reading instruction may vary according to the management of the learning environment in the classroom or the total school structure. Various techniques or philosophies for motivating and structuring children's learning are being employed in regular and special class placements. The ones to be discussed in this section are: the engineered classroom, programmed classrooms, precision teaching, stimulus controlled environments, nongraded programs, individualized instruction, and the open-space concept or open-concept programs. Various techniques of behavior management such as behavior modification, are included within these environments.

Engineered Classroom

The *engineered classroom* (Hewett, 1963) was designed initially for management of emotionally disturbed children and was based upon classical operant conditioning devices and the development of specific tasks or goals. Hewett explains the term "engineer" in the following way:

> ... The teacher is urged to determine "what" the child's deficits are according to the developmental sequence of educational goals and then "engineer" a successful program of remediation through manipulation of the three sides of the learning triangle — task, reward, and structure. It is hypothesized that

a natural consequence of such an approach will be the improvement of psychological and perceptual-motor difficulties. And it will engage the teacher in the role of learning specialist rather than educational therapist or diagnostician — a role far more consistent with the teacher's preparation and one which no other professional person is as well qualified to fulfill in the classroom.[1]

The engineered classroom focuses on what Hewett terms the "learning triangle"; this "triangle" consists of tasks, rewards, and structure. Hewett (1964) also has formulated a hierarchy of educational tasks or goals: the attention, response, order, exploratory, social, mastery, and achievement tasks or goals. A learning task is "any activity, lesson, or assignment given the child which is directed toward assisting him in achieving one or more goals on the developmental sequence."[2] The developmental goals move from a very low level (i.e., merely attending to a task) to a high level of achievement. At the highest level, the child becomes involved in educational tasks in the classroom and moves from attending to responding and then ordering (e.g. following directions). Higher levels involve the child's learning through exploring his environment, learning in groups, mastering tasks, and desiring to learn or master other educational tasks or achievement. A hierarchy of tasks allows the teacher to place emphasis on discrete learning tasks and to place children at "appropriate task levels."

Another side of the learning triangle is reward. Hewett (1968) has defined reward as:

> . . . a positive consequence which tends to maintain or increase the strength or frequency of behavior associated with accomplishing tasks related to the achievement of educational goals on the developmental sequence.[3]

Rewards may be in the form of check marks which can be exchanged for tangible items such as candy or toys. Check marks are administered every fifteen minutes during lessons.

The last side of the triangle is structure, the control by the teacher in the learning environment. The teacher decides what tasks should be learned by the child, when he should learn them (the schedule) and where the learning should be done (the design of the

---

[1]Frank Hewett, *The Emotionally Disturbed Child in the Classroom* (Boston: Allyn & Bacon, 1968), p. 240.
[2]*Ibid.*, p. 61.
[3]*Ibid.*, p. 65.

room). Other decisions made by the teacher concern how the child will accomplish the task and to what level of mastery. Hewett has designated a precise schedule for the class setting and the design or order of the classroom. For example, areas should be assigned for various levels, such as the exploratory center for the exploratory and social levels; the order center for the attention, responses, and order levels; and the mastery center for the mastery and achievement levels.

Within this environment, academic skills such as reading are taught. One of the reading programs discussed by Hewett (1968) is similar to that developed by Birnbrauer, Bijou, Wolf, and Kiddler (1965), the *Edmark Program* as it is known commercially. This program is based upon principles of programmed instruction. Discrimination exercises in visual and auditory perception are used. These discrimination tasks are closely related to the actual reading task (e.g. visual discrimination of words). Reinforcement, both verbal and tangible, is used for correct responses. Children learn to read stories from basal readers, and during the exploratory period, the teacher reads stories to the children. Other materials and procedures in teaching reading are also included.

According to Hewett (1971), the engineered classroom has the disadvantage of being a self-contained unit without plans to integrate the child into a regular classroom. Because of this limitation, Hewett has developed *The Madison Plan* in which the child is moved along a continuum toward behavior appropriate for regular class placement. The levels are determined according to academic readiness: Preacademic I, Preacademic II, Academic I and II. Preacademic I is the engineered classroom model while Academic II is the regular class. The intervening stages work gradually toward the goal of regular class placement. In these programs a variety of reading materials and methods, including programmed instruction, reading kits, language experience, and the Fernald method are employed. For a thorough discussion of the engineered classroom and the reading programs used within this environment, see *The Emotionally Disturbed Child in the Classroom* (Hewett, 1968).

Programmed Classroom

One of the first models for a programmed classroom was designed by Bijou, et al. (1966) as part of the Rainier School Project for institutionalized retardates. Various activities were conducted in the classroom, and as in an engineered classroom, the floor plan reflected these activities. (Hewett's classroom design, in fact, and activities were influenced by this program.) Individual study cells equipped with teaching machines and materials, tables for writing exercises, large work tables, and a time-out room, which was used for the removal of a child from disruptive situations, were all part of the classroom facilities. There was a small teacher-pupil ratio, and motivational systems, such as the check-mark system, were used. As in the engineered classroom, the principles of operant and classical conditioning were employed. The reading program was programmed (see Chapter Seven for a discussion of programmed reading and the Edmark Reading Program).

A similar program was developed by Haring and Phillips (1962) for emotionally disturbed children. In this classroom, activities were highly structured and individualized. Isolation booths were provided, and rewards for achievement were used. Haring and Phillips reported significant gains in academic achievement with this highly structured program compared to the more traditional classroom program. Haring and Hauch (1969) have also used behavior modification techniques for improvement of reading skills.

Besides the common characteristic of structure, these programs possess the common feature of controlling behaviors through some form of behavior modification. For a thorough discussion of operant conditioning and behavior modification techniques, see Skinner (1953, 1963), Hewett (1968), Ullman and Krasner (1965), and Bandura (1969). Although many studies have reported significant academic achievement of exceptional children through the use of behavior modification techniques, it is not without its limitations. Macmillan and Forness (1970) have discussed some of these limitations:

> In conclusion, the behavior modification strategy has tremendous potential for work with atypical children. Its use with these children is promising; however, its misuse could be terrifying. It is not a panacea. It gives no direction in determining educational goals; it reduces constructs of learning, motivation, and reinforcement to simplistic terms on occasion. To the unsophisticated practitioner, it may be blinding to broader frames of reference regarding the constructs listed above. Furthermore, it may preclude children from learning how to learn and thus becoming independent of teachers as such — a major goal of education.[4]

---

[4]Donald MacMillan and Steven Forness, "Behavior Modification: Limitations and Liabilities," *Exceptional Children* 37 (1970): 296.

Although most of the reading methods used within the framework of such programs are programmed text or highly structured, this in no way signifies that these programs meet the needs of every child in the class. Most often, the individualization is a matter of pacing rather than presentation.

Since many of these programs are highly skill-oriented—especially in the area of word attack—this approach may force the teacher to view reading instruction in a simplistic manner. The attempt to isolate educational tasks or goals so that instruction may be monitored and so that children may feel success during instruction are elements of these programs which could benefit any instructional system employed.

Precision Teaching

The term *precision teaching* was first used by Ogden Lindsley in the middle 1960s. The principles for precision teaching were founded upon those formulated by B.F. Skinner. The approach is "a system of education which carefully evaluates its own methods through the framework of science and makes corrections based on data rather than fiction.[5]

As its name suggests, precision teaching emphasizes precision and deals with behaviors that are observable. It is a system of continuous recording of behaviors that have been pinpointed. The assumption is made that before a teacher can truly individualize instruction, he must be able to observe the child and record accurately pertinent information concerning the child's behavior. The classroom is viewed as an educational laboratory where the teacher constantly is evaluating the effectiveness of educational materials and teaching techniques (Meacham and Wiesen, 1970). Modifications of curriculum and teacher-pupil interaction may be established on the basis of the findings of careful observations.

One of the first steps in pinpointing behavior is establishing a baseline or "initial" example of behavior. Recorded behavior is usually in chart form and may be done by the teacher, the child, or an outside observer. If the teacher has an idea of the initial behavior, he can monitor changes in behavior which occur as a result of modification in methods, behavior management, and other variables.

---

[5]Merle L. Meacham and Allen E. Wiesen, *Changing Classroom Behavior: A Manual for Precision Teaching* (Scranton, Pennsylvania: International Textbook Co., 1970), p. 3.

Precision teaching may be incorporated into existing teaching methods, and has been used with both emotionally disturbed (Haring and Kinzelmann, 1966) and retarded children (Lindsley, 1971). According to Haring and Kinzelmann, this system could serve as a model for special education in the future.

Stimulus Controlled Environments

Management of the environment in such a manner as to control the amount of stimuli presented was employed originally with brain-injured children (Strauss and Lehtinen, 1947, Cruickshank, 1961). The setting of the classroom was designed to reduce the distractibility which was considered to be a characteristic of brain-injured children. The "therapeutic educational environment" was planned initially to counteract as much as possible the general organic disturbances of behavior and attention."[6] In order to establish this environment, class size was small; materials on the walls were absent; and children were not seated closely together. Strauss and Lehtinen recommended that classes be on the second floor of the school building, if possible, in order to reduce visual and auditory stimuli. The lower quarters of the windows also were covered, and teachers were encouraged to refrain from wearing brightly colored clothes or jewelry. The environment was labeled "therapeutic" because it was not to be considered permanent. Instead, it was established in order to teach the child the necessary skills that would enable him to return to the regular classroom environment.

Along the same lines, Cruickshank (1961) felt that a teaching environment should reduce auditory and visual stimulation as well as space. The limited space should be in the form of small cubicles for each child. He suggested that the furniture, woodwork, and the floor in these cubicles be similar in color, that the windows be opaque, and that the room be treated acoustically in order to reduce sound.

In the environment established by Strauss and Lehtinen, the teacher should avoid the presentation of materials containing many distractions, (e.g. workbooks with many pictures or exercises on the same page). The materials should be presented in some form that would not allow one exercise or task to interfere with another one.

---

[6]A.A. Strauss and L.F. Lehtinen, *Psychopathology and Education of the Brain-Injured Child* (New York: Grune & Stratton, 1947), p. 131.

On the other hand, Cruickshank suggested using materials that attracted the child's attention (e.g. color for letters).

Both environments structured the child's daily lessons or subjects and allowed for some group activity. However, Cruickshank recommended that children be isolated most of the time. For a discussion of reading methods within these programs, see Chapter Nine and *A Teaching Method for the Brain-injured and Hyperactive Children* (Cruickshank, et al., 1961).

Although Strauss and Lehtinen and Cruickshank reported that a controlled environment and modified behavior aided in improving academic achievement, several researchers have found that background distractions may not affect brain-injured children as much as was assumed by Strauss, Lehtinen, and Cruickshank (Burnette, 1962; Carter and Diaz, 1971; Spradlin, Cromwell, and Foshee, 1960). Other studies have found that cubicles do not increase academic achievement significantly (Cruickshank et al., 1961; Rost and Charles, 1967; Shores and Haubrick, 1969), although they may increase attending behaviors. Shores and Haubrick (1969) concluded that attending behavior and academic achievement may not be closely related and that other variables besides attention contribute to academic success. They suggest that cubicles may be of the most benefit in the early stages of working with hyperactive children in order to increase attention to the task.

Reducing the stimuli or structuring the child's environment should be a matter of recognizing individual differences rather than making a decision for an entire group of children. In discussing the attending behavior of retarded children, Turnure has stated: "Also, individual differences in strategies of attention deployment are a distinct possibility with the retarded, just as they are with normal children."[7] The present authors would agree with this statement; although we realize that some children can not work in a stimulating environment, this is not true of all retarded children.

Nongraded Programs

The nongraded school is an attempt to completely alter the progression of children through school by grades (Goodlad and Anderson, 1963). Although the use of grading for grouping children is one

---

[7]James Turnure, "Distractibility in the Mentally Retarded: Negative Evidence for an Orienting Inadequacy," *Exceptional Children* 37 (1970): 185.

way of controlling vertical progress of students, Goodlad (1966) has explained nongrading in terms of rearranging vertical organization. They have stated:

> Nongrading is an arrangement in which grade levels are removed from some or all classes. When grade levels are removed from kindergarten and the first three grades, the arrangement is known as the nongraded primary unit. A similar vertical arrangement for the customary four, five, and six is a nongraded intermediate unit.[8]

According to Goodlad (1966), nongrading is a means by which instructional provisions can be made for individuals in group environments; however, meeting this purpose requires more than merely removing grade levels. Procedures for allowing children to progress are most often based upon the reading level of the child. In most cases, reading skills are placed in a logical sequence, and children progress according to their achievement in these designated skills. Progress is reported by means of parent conferences or written reports rather than by grades or report cards.

If a child moves at his own pace, he may finish the primary or intermediate unit in fewer than the usual number of years (e.g. the child may complete the same work faster than children who spend three years in the primary grades in the traditional vertical organization).

Another feature that is usually included in nongraded programs, although it is not essential, is team-teaching. Goodlad (1966) has classified team-teaching as a means of horizontal organization in the school program and designated the following characteristics as important in team-teaching:

> (1) A hierarchy of personnel-team leader, master teacher, auxiliary teacher, teacher aide, intern teacher, clerk and so forth; (2) A delineation of staff function based on differences in preparation, personnel interests, and so on, or on the kinds of learning activities planned; (3) flexibility in grouping embracing all the students under supervision of a team.[9]

---

[8]John I. Goodlad and Robert Anderson, *The Nongraded Elementary Schools*, rev. ed. (New York: Harcourt, Brace, Jovanovich, 1963), p. 23.

[9]John I. Goodland, *School, Curriculum, and the Individual* (Waltham, Massachusetts: Blaisdell Publishing Co., 1966), pp. 25-26.

The number of members on a team varies; however, the teacher-pupil ratio remains the same as in traditional programs. Members of a team may possess varied interests and skills which may be used effectively in planning instruction. One member of the team may be responsible for a large group of children in such a situation as a lecture presentation, while other members are free to plan. Large-group and small-group instruction is provided by the team.

Attempting to measure the effectiveness of nongraded programs compared to traditional ones is difficult because of problems in research design. It is an arduous task to isolate clearly nongraded programs from graded ones because many teachers in "nongraded" programs still retain traditional practices, while many regular class teachers incorporate principles used in nongraded programs (Goodlad, 1966) in their classrooms.

Dreeben (1970) has cited several problems involved in the nongraded school concept. One is the lack of clarity concerning how many variations in levels of achievement the program is able to accommodate. The wider the range in abilities, the more difficult it is to decide how long children should remain in a given level. For example, a very bright child may finish the "first six years" in a very short time. Secondly, the plan may still possess boundaries (i.e., levels or tasks that must be mastered in order for the progression of the child to take place). Dreeben feels that the nongraded program may be beneficial to the average child yet still not meet the needs of the bright or dull child. On the other hand, Hillson (1965) has stated that the nongraded program may aid the slower child in giving him more time to attain concepts.

Approaches for reading in the nongraded program are no different than those in traditional programs; however, because progress is based most often upon reading level, some schools attempt to outline carefully the reading skills that are thought to be necessary for academic achievement.

Multiage Grouping: A grouping of children similar to the nongraded program is multi-age grouping. Hetland (1969) has defined this organizational structure:

> The multiaged organization is a plan whereby equal numbers of six, seven, and eight year olds are included in primary multiaged classes. Furthermore, an attempt is made to have each age group of children be a representative sample of the abilities and

achievements of the entire school population of that particular age (p. 13).

According to Hetland, proponents of multiage grouping do not establish sequences that the child must follow as in the nongraded program. Instead, teachers aid the child in developing individualized, sequential programs in which the child stays with the same teacher for three years. Emphasis is placed upon socialization and learning across ages (Mitchell and Zoffness, 1971). In many multiaged classes, children learn from each each other through the practice of cross-age or peer teaching. In most multiaged programs, reading is individualized, and small groups are established for the development of specific reading skills (Hetland, 1969).

Individualized Instruction

Individualization of instruction was attempted in the United States as early as 1913 (Keith, Blake, and Tiedt, 1968), and the Winnetka, Illinois School District implemented the plan in its schools in 1919. Units of instruction in basic academic instruction were developed, and children moved at their own pace through these units. Because of the reported success of these programs, other similar programs such as the Dalton Plan (Parkhurst, 1924), were established.

Although the development of individualized instruction emerged in the early 1900s, it did not become prominent as a means of organizing instruction until the 1960s. Many of the more recent programs emphasize pacing as the chief means of individualization. In order to accomplish this task, these programs utilize programmed instruction and/or computer-assisted instruction (Howes, 1970). The employment of a large variety of materials in order to accommodate a wide range of interests, levels, and learning styles is a feature of many individualized programs.

Self-direction and independence are skills encouraged in some individualized instruction programs. The teacher is considered to be a facilitator of knowledge through the careful arrangement of materials and equipment rather than an imparter of knowledge (Veatch, 1970).

Some programs have been planned carefully and used by the entire elementary and/or secondary program in a school system. Two of these are *Individually Prescribed Instruction (IPI)* developed by the Learning Research and Development Center of the

University of Pittsburgh during 1963 and 1964 and *Project Plan* developed by the American Institutes for Research, Westinghouse Learning Corporation. Both of these programs include the use of placement tests, specific learning objectives, prepared units of instruction, programmed materials, and audio-visual equipment such as tape recorders and film loops. *Project Plan* monitors the child's progress through the use of a computer, while *IPI* utilizes teacher's aides for checking progress. Group instruction is employed in both of these programs.

In individualized programs, reading instruction most often occurs in the form of programmed reading, computer-assisted instruction, or the utilization of a wide variety of reading materials and techniques. Specific objectives are written for children, and progress is carefully monitored.

Silberman (1970) has criticized individualized programs, specifically *IPI*. According to him, limitations are: the setting of goals for children without allowing choices; individualization through pacing only; and forcing children to take passive rather than an active role in learning.

Individualization of instruction or treatment is not new to the field of special education. In fact, many special-education texts suggest that the special teacher consider his class as "a collection of individuals each with particular characteristics and needs."[10] Some special education programs utilize systems such as *IPI*, and the aim of most educational programs is the individualization of instruction. However, this utilization requires a considerable amount of planning and, in most cases, expense. According to Southworth (1972), if a teacher attempts to individualize instruction, he must be competent in such areas as specifying learning goals, assessing pupil achievement, planning programs, guiding children in learning tasks, utilizing behavior management techniques, and working with professional peers in instructional planning.

The Open-Space Concept

Open education, the open classroom, informal education, and the integrated day are all terms for a form of education which has its origins in the British Infant School. After the introduction of open

---

[10]A.E. Tansley and R. Gulliford, *The Education of Slow-Learning Children* (London: Routledge and Kegan Paul, 1960), p. 90.

education into American schools during the 1960s, numerous interpretations of what it entails began to appear. According to Gross and Gross (1972), there are several unique principles involved in open education:

> There are four operating principles of the open classroom. First, the room itself is decentralized; an open flexible space divided into functional areas, rather than one fixed, homogeneous unit. Second, the children are free for much of the time to explore this room, individually or in groups, and to choose their own activities. Third, the environment is rich in learning resources, including plenty of concrete materials, as well as books and other media. Fourth, the teacher and the aides work most of the time with individual children of two or three, hardly ever presenting the same material to the class as a whole.[11]

Other characteristics of open education include: the use of contract commitment methods, individualized instruction, self-direction in learning, use of an effective learning environment which is conducive for motivation to learn, and daily logs or records on each child's progress (Hertzberg and Stone, 1971).

Although the word "open" may suggest permissiveness or lack of structure, this is a misconception (Richman, 1972). Children are encouraged to accept responsibility for their learning, and the teacher spends much of his time planning for the needs of children. One reason such programs *appear* "unstructured" is that children are moving about in various areas and engaging in different activities at different times of the day. Because of such diversity, a casual observer of this activity may have difficulty in determining what each child is actually doing.

Many school systems have adopted the open-classroom concept. Although the concept may be transferred to a self-contained classroom, numerous districts are constructing "open-space" structures which allow for large-group, small-group, and individualized instruction. These schools have very few internal walls, and children may move across several areas. Various elements of nongraded instruction are employed within this system.

One of the chief criticisms of the use of open education with educable retarded children is the lack of "structure" and the "free-

---

[11]Beatrice Gross and Ronald Gross, "British Infant Schools—American Style," in *Will the Real Teacher Please Stand Up?*, ed. Mary Geer and Bonnie Rubinstein (Pacific Palisades, California: Goodyear Publishing Co., 1972), p. 85.

dom of choice" children are allowed. On the other hand, open class-room has been recommended as being an "environment where problems are more manageable."[12] Nonetheless, we suggest that some problem children need more direct guidance from the teacher.

In one study with a small group of exceptional children (poor achievers as identified by standardized tests and poor socially ad-justed children as rated by teachers and peers), Bartel (1972) found that these same children were able to engage in academic activities in the open classroom. Although the time these children were involved in academics was slightly less than half of their total time in the class, according to Bartel, the time spent in academics in the traditional classroom is not much more.

In comparing the least "benefiting" children with the more suc-cessful ones, Bartel found that these children spent less time in academics and more time in peer interaction involving non-academic activities. As an important conclusion drawn from her study, Bartel emphasized that the academically-oriented children spent more time with their peers in academically-oriented activities, while chil-dren who were less successful spent less time with their peers in academically-oriented activities.

The present authors have employed open education with re-tarded children and have observed that some children are able to accept responsibility for their learning while others appear completely lost in the setting. Again, as with *all* approaches or organizational structures, reactions depend upon the individual characteristics of the child. If a teacher chooses to develop an open-concept program with retarded children, he must allow for mod-ifications for some children who cannot entirely adapt to such an environment. For further discussion of open education, see Hertz-berg and Stone *Schools are for Children* (1971) and Rathbone *Open Education: Selected Readings* (1970).

DIAGNOSTIC-PRESCRIPTIVE TEACHING

An approach to teaching which has received considerable attention in special education is the diagnostic-prescriptive approach. As with such programs as the nongraded and individualized, this approach concerns itself with the needs of the individual. An impetus to the diagnostic-prescriptive approach is the realization by educators that

---

[12]Alvin Hertzberg and Edward F. Stone, *Schools Are for Children* (New York: Schocken Books, 1971), p. 214.

children's abilities vary even though groups may appear to be homogeneous and that children vary in abilities within themselves.

Many of the characteristics of this approach are the result of diagnostic processes in the field of learning disabilities. Bateman (1967) has suggested that the approaches employed in the area of learning disabilities be extended to mental retardation. Bateman (1967) has designated some of these features as:

> ... individual appraisal of patterns of cognitive abilities, to a reexamination of a philosophy of teaching through strengths or weaknesses, and to the need for direct teaching of the process of thinking rather than the products of someone else's thinking.[13]

In relating prescriptive teaching to the handicapped, Peter (1965) has stated: "Prescriptive teaching for the handicapped child consists of those modifications of instruction and other school variables which are based upon individual diagnosis in the direction of assisting the child's learning.[14]

Diagnostic-prescriptive procedures have not been established conclusively as effective means of instruction (Bateman, 1970). Many of the test-related programs, such as those based upon the *ITPA* and the *DTVP*, have had little substantial research concerning their effectiveness in academic areas such as reading (see Chapter Nine).

Two limitations of the diagnostic-prescriptive procedure are that conclusions may be drawn after only a few hours of testing and that programs are established, in some cases, upon the basis of these tests without adequate evaluation of their on-going usefulness.

In order for the diagnostic-prescriptive approach to be of any benefit, the teacher or the specialist must develop a process of diagnosing formally and informally and prescribing programs which can be modified easily. This problem-solving approach is the heart of the diagnostic-prescriptive approach.

The movement toward individual rather than group treatment requires much planning on the part of the professionals involved. As this approach emerges, special educators will become more concerned with its effectiveness, although there have been some attempts to analyze statistically the effects of individual treatment

---

[13]Barbara Bateman, "Implications of a Learning Disability Approach for Teaching Educable Retardates," *Mental Retardation* 5 (1967): 25.

[14]Lawrence Peter, *Prescriptive Teaching* (New York: McGraw-Hill Book Co., 1965), p. 1.

already (Blackman, 1972). Regardless of the concern of statistical treatment, most teachers have always questioned the efficacy of techniques or methods used with individual children. Many of the techniques developed in diagnostic teaching which encompass observational systems, specific objectives, and evaluation techniques can aid the teacher in establishing effective programs.

In addition, successful programming requires the ability to manage individuals in group settings. Although technological aids and programmed instruction have assisted in individualizing instruction, teachers will be working with groups of children during much of the school day. It is not necessary to consider one-to-one instruction as the only alternative in meeting children's specific needs. How to use a problem-solving approach both to manage groups of children and to match appropriate instructional strategies to individual children is the focus of the remainder of this chapter.

APPLICATION OF
DIAGNOSTIC-PRESCRIPTIVE TECHNIQUES

Description of the Class

Most often, when a teacher confronts his class for the first time, he possesses little information about the children which will be beneficial in developing reading programs. Few teachers are fortunate enough to obtain complete diagnostic reports and suggestions for instruction prior to the beginning of the term. In addition, in most cases, no matter how thorough previous diagnosis may have been, the teacher finds that he still needs additional information or examples of the children's performance. It also has been the experience of the present authors that while clinical diagnosis may have been very explicit, some of the information inevitably is incorrect because of the variability of children's performance from day to day, the artificiality of testing situations, and the nature of the instruments—especially standardized ones.

The perusal of existing records of children before a term begins has been criticized by some educators. On this subject, Kohl (1969) has stated:

> When the teacher meets his class on the first day of the school year, he is armed with all of this "professional" knowledge. Anticipating a dull class, for example, a teacher may have spent several weeks preparing simple exercises to keep his students busy. On the other hand, faced with the prospect of teach-

ing a bright class, he may have found a new and challenging textbook or devised some ingenious scientific experiments.

If the record cards indicate that several pupils are particularly troublesome or, what is more threatening, "disturbed," the teacher will single them out as soon as they enter the room and treat them differently from the other pupils. He may do the same with bright students or ones rumored to be wise, funny, lazy, violent, scheming, deceitful.... The students will sense this and act in the manner expected of them. Thus the teacher traps both himself and his pupils into repeating patterns that have been set for years.[15]

We agree with Kohl that many of the teachers who read cumulative files prior to meeting their classes establish expectations of children's academic and behavioral performance. We have observed teachers who place IQ scores next to the child's name in the roll books. However, if a teacher believes in a problem-solving approach, he will not "jump to conclusions" based upon the insufficient information in the cumulative files. These prior recordings should be considered tentative rather than definite. Still, many teachers prefer not to read the files prior to meeting the children, although an observant teacher may benefit from such a practice. This issue may be a matter of individual preference rather than one that requires that a firm policy be established.

In order that the diagnostic-prescriptive techniques be discussed, information about a group of hypothetical children is presented beginning on page 299 in the form of records. These children's characteristics are compilations of those observed by the present authors in their work with exceptional children. These children are not considered to be typical of all children who are "labeled" retarded though. They are simply presentations of data usually found in cumulative folders by the teacher so that the teacher can see the data as he would initially see information about his own class.

The Classroom Program

The cumulative files may be helpful in providing information in such areas as attendance, physical disabilities, and past academic

---

[15]Herbert Kohl, *The Open Classroom* (New York: Random House, 1969), pp. 18-19. Reprinted with permission from *The New York Review of Books.* Copyright © 1969 by Herbert Kohl.

Name _Marshall_ Age _9_ Years _4_ Months___

Grade _Special Class_

School_____

Attendance Record

1	2 (SC)	3 (SC)	4	5	6	Total Days (180)
	170	158	160			SC Special Class

Achievement (Grades)

(Grade)	1	2 (SC)	3 (SC)	4		6
Reading	U-	P	P			
Math	U-	P	P			
Spelling						
Writing	U-	P	P			
Social Studies						
Science						
Music	S	P	P			
Art	S	P	P			
Health						
Physical Education						
Conduct	S	S	S			

U — Unsatisfactory   P — Progressing
S — Satisfactory   NP — Not Progressing
O — Outstanding

Achievement Test

Grades		Names of Tests	Age	Score
	1	Readiness	6	Letter Rating E
	2			
	3			
	4			
	5			
	6			

Ability (Test Scores)

Grade		Name of Test	Age	Score
	1	Individual I.Q.	7	65
	2			
	3			
	4			
	5			
	6			

Family Background

Father's Name _Charles_

Mother's Name _Rachel_

Address_____

Telephone_____

Occupation: Father _lawyer_

Occupation: Mother_____

Siblings:

Name	Age
Joseph	14
Mark	13
Dennis	10

Health Record: _Absent quite often due to cold and flu (ear infection)_

Teacher's Comments:

Grade 1: _Marshall is very quiet. He tries hard._

Grade 2: _Marshall's mind seems_ SC _to wander. He does not express himself._

Grade 3: SC _He has problem remembering his letters and words_

Grade 4:

Grade 5:

Grade 6:

299

Name **Harry**   Age **7** Years **2** Months

Grade **Special Class**

School _____

Attendance Record

	1	2	3	4	5	6	Total Days (180)
45							*Entered at end 4 year*

Achievement (Grades)

(Grade)	1	2	3	4		6
Reading	U					
Math	U					
Spelling						
Writing	U					
Social Studies						
Science						
Music	U					
Art	S					
Health						
Physical Education						
Conduct	U					

U — Unsatisfactory   P — Progressing
S — Satisfactory   NP — Not Progressing
O — Outstanding

Achievement Test

Grades	Names of Tests	Age	Score
1			
2			
3			
4			
5			
6			

Ability (Test Scores)

Grade	Name of Test	Age	Score
1	*Individual I.Q.*	7	72
2			
3			
4			
5			
6			

Family Background

Father's Name **George (foster)**

Mother's Name **Patricia**

Address _____

Telephone _____

Occupation: Father **Store Manager**

Occupation: Mother **Secretary**

Siblings: **name**   **age**

     Sharon   **8**

     Henry   **7**

Health Record:

Teacher's Comments:

Grade 1: *Harry is a very hyperactive and socially "immature" child.*   Grade 4:

Grade 2:   Grade 5:

Grade 3:   Grade 6:

ame _Robert_____ Age _8_ Years _0_ Months_____

ade _Special Class_____

hool_____

Attendance Record								
	1	2(1)3	4	5	6	Total Days	(180)	
	'78 '76							

Achievement (Grades)

(Grade)	1	2	3	4		6
eading	U	U				
ath	U	U				
pelling						
riting	U	U				
ocial Studies						
cience						
usic	S	S				
rt	S	S				
ealth						
hysical Education						
onduct	U	U				

— Unsatisfactory   P — Progressing
— Satisfactory   NP — Not Progressing
— Outstanding

Ability (Test Scores)

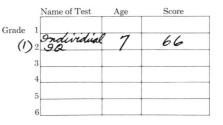

	Name of Test	Age	Score
Grade 1			
(1) 2	Individual 92	7	66
3			
4			
5			
6			

Achievement Test

	Names of Tests	Age	Score
rades 1	Readiness	6	Letter Rating-E
2			
3			
4			
5			
6			

Family Background

Father's Name _Joseph_____
Mother's Name _Shirley_____
Address_____
Telephone_____
Occupation: Father _Painter (ill unemployed)_
Occupation: Mother _Housewife_____

Siblings: Name _____ Age
_John_____ 6

ealth Record:

eacher's Comments:

rade 1: _Very active child. Short attention span. Problems in math and reading._   Grade 4:

rade 2: _Not progressing — very slow._   Grade 5:

rade 3:   Grade 6:

301

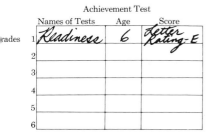
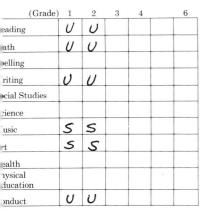

Name __Paul__ Age _10_ Years _10_ Months

Grade __Special Class__

School _____

Achievement (Grades)

(Grade)	1	2	3	4		6
Reading	U	U	D–	NP		
Math	U	U	D–	NP		
Spelling						
Writing	U	U	D	P		
Social Studies						
Science						
Music	U	U	D	NP		
Art	S	S	B	P		
Health						
Physical Education						
Conduct	S	S	S	S		

U — Unsatisfactory   P — Progressing
S — Satisfactory   NP — Not Progressing
O — Outstanding

Ability (Test Scores)

	Name of Test	Age	Score
Grade 1			
(1) 2	Group Intelligence	7	60
(2) 3	Individual Intelligence	9	64
4			
5			
6			

Achievement Test

	Names of Tests	Age	Score
Grades 1	Readiness	6	Letter Rating – C
(1) 2	Achievement	8	(R)–1.9 (M) 1.8 A–1.6
(2) 3	Achievement	9	R–1.8 M–1.7 A–1.7
4			
5			
6			

Family Background

Father's Name __Frank__

Mother's Name __Hariett__

Address _____

Telephone _____

Occupation: Father __Factory worker__

Occupation: Mother __Housewife__

Siblings:
Name	Age
Janet	15
Howard	13
Jean	6

Health Record: _A conductive hearing loss. He is very susceptible to ear infections. Ill quite often._

Teacher's Comments:

Grade 1: _Paul is ill quite often. He is not doing well in reading, etc._

Grade 4: SC _Very poor in reading and math._

Grade 2: ONE _Speech is very poor._

Grade 5:

Grade 3: TWO _Very cooperative and pleasant. Speech is a problem!_

Grade 6:

302

Name **Dara**   Age **8** Years **4** Months

Grade **Special Class**

School _____

Attendance Record							
1	2	3	4	5	6	Total Days	(180)
175	173						

Achievement (Grades)

(Grade)	1	2 (3c) 3	4		6
Reading	U	NP			
Math	U+	P			
Spelling					
Writing	S	P			
Social Studies					
Science					
Music	S	P			
Art	S	P			
Health					
Physical Education					
Conduct	S	S			

U — Unsatisfactory   P — Progressing
S — Satisfactory   NP — Not Progressing
O — Outstanding

Ability (Test Scores)

Grade		Name of Test	Age	Score
	1	Individual IQ	7	75
	2			
	3			
	4			
	5			
	6			

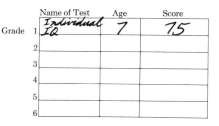

Family Background

Father's Name **Thomas**

Mother's Name **Evelyn**

Address _____

Telephone _____

Occupation: Father **Teacher**

Occupation: Mother **Secretary**

Siblings: Name   Age

     Mike   **6**

Achievement Test

Grades		Names of Tests	Age	Score
	1	Readiness	6	Letter Rating - E
	2	Achievement	7	R-1.8 M-1.6 A-1.7
	3			
	4			
	5			
	6			

R - reading   M - math   A - average

Health Record:

Teacher's Comments:

Grade 1: *A very pleasant and quiet child. (Reading problems)*

Grade 2: *Dara seems to have*
SC *perceptual problems in reading.*

Grade 3:

Grade 4:

Grade 5:

Grade 6:

Name	Dennis	Age 10 Years 3 Months	Attendance Record

Grade	Special Class

School _____

	1	2	3	4	5	6	Total Days (180)
	'75	'78	'76				

Achievement (Grades)

(Grade)	1	2	3	4		6
Reading	U	U	U			
Math	U	U	U			
Spelling						
Writing	S	S	S			
Social Studies						
Science						
Music	S	S	S			
Art	S	S	S			
Health						
Physical Education						
Conduct	U-	U-	U-			

U — Unsatisfactory   P — Progressing
S — Satisfactory   NP — Not Progressing
O — Outstanding

Achievement Test

	Names of Tests	Age	Score
Grades 1	Readiness	6	Letter rating C
2	Achievement	8	R (1.5) M (1.8) A (1.7)
3			
4			
5			
6			

R-Reading   M-Math   A-Average

Health Record:

Ability (Test Scores)

	Name of Test	Age	Score
Grade 1	Group IQ	7	80
2			
3	Individual IQ	9	79
4			
5			
6			

Family Background

Father's Name _Vernon_
Mother's Name _Sylvia_
Address _____
Telephone _____
Occupation: Father _Salesman_
Occupation: Mother _Cook (at school)_

Siblings:	Name	Age
	Ray	6

Teacher's Comments:

Grade 1: Dennis is a very hyperactive child.

Grade 2: A behavior problem.

Grade 3: Many learning problems very hyperactive (needs structure).

Grade 4:

Grade 5:

Grade 6:

304

Name _Joyce_ Age _9_ Years _3_ Months

Grade _Special Class_

School _____

Achievement (Grades)

(Grade)	1	2(1)	3(2)4		6
Reading	U	U	C-		
Math	U	U	C-		
Spelling					
Writing	U	S	C		
Social Studies					
Science					
Music	S	S	B		
Art	S	S	B		
Health					
Physical Education					
Conduct	S	S	S		

U — Unsatisfactory   P — Progressing
S — Satisfactory   NP — Not Progressing
O — Outstanding

Ability (Test Scores)

	Name of Test	Age	Score
Grade 1			
2	Individual I.Q.	9	76
3			
4			
5			
6			

Family Background

Father's Name _John_

Mother's Name _Helen_

Address _____

Telephone _____

Occupation: Father _Construction_

Occupation: Mother _Housewife_

Siblings: Name _Matthew_   Age _7_

Achievement Test

	Names of Tests	Age	Score
Grades 1	Readiness	6	Letter rating E
2	Achievement	7	1.3 (R) 1.1 (M) / 1.7 (R) 1.8 M 1.8 a
3			
4			
5			
6			

R-reading m-math a-average

Health Record:

Teacher's Comments:

Grade 1: _Joyce tends to be a tattle tale. She is a very poor reader._   Grade 4:

Grade 2 ONE: _She does not complete her work._   Grade 5:

Grade 3 TWO: _She is very unattentive. Mind wanders._   Grade 6:

Name **George** Age **7** Years **10** Months

Grade **Special Class**

School _____

Achievement (Grades)

(Grade)	1	2 (SC)	3	4		6
Reading	U	NP				
Math	U	NP				
Spelling		NP				
Writing	U	P				
Social Studies						
Science						
Music	S	S				
Art	S	S				
Health						
Physical Education						
Conduct	S	S				

U — Unsatisfactory   P — Progressing
S — Satisfactory   NP — Not Progressing
O — Outstanding

Achievement Test

Grades		Names of Tests	Age	Score
	1	Readiness	6	Rating
	2			
	3			
	4			
	5			
	6			

Ability (Test Scores)

Grade		Name of Test	Age	Score
	1	Individual IQ	6	68
	2			
	3			
	4			
	5			
	6			

Family Background

Father's Name **Raymond**

Mother's Name **Stella**

Address _____

Telephone _____

Occupation: Father **Handyman**

Occupation: Mother **Housewife**

Siblings:	name	age
		12
		11
		10
		7

Health Record:

Teacher's Comments:

Grade 1: Short attention-span. Quiet. Needs extra help.

Grade 2: Learning alphabet and (SC) colors. Short attention span.

Grade 3:

Grade 4:

Grade 5:

Grade 6:

Name __Janet__ Age _8_ Years _2_ Months

Grade __Special Class__

School _____

	1	2 (1) 3	4	5	6	Total Days (180)
	17 8	7 5				

Attendance Record

Achievement (Grades)

(Grade)	1	2 (1) 3	4		6
Reading	U	U-			
Math	U	U-			
Spelling					
Writing	S	S-			
Social Studies					
Science					
Music	S	S			
Art	S	S			
Health					
Physical Education					
Conduct	S	S			

U — Unsatisfactory   P — Progressing
S — Satisfactory   NP — Not Progressing
O — Outstanding

Achievement Test

	Names of Tests	Age	Score
Grades 1	Readiness	6	Letter Rating-D
2	Achievement	8	R-1.5 M-1.8 A-1.6
3			
4			
5			
6			

R-reading M-math A-average

Health Record: _Allergies_

Ability (Test Scores)

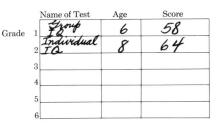

	Name of Test	Age	Score
Grade 1	Group IQ	6	58
2	Individual IQ	8	64
3			
4			
5			
6			

Family Background

Father's Name __Benjamin__

Mother's Name __Jewel__

Address _____

Telephone _____

Occupation: Father __Carpenter__

Occupation: Mother __Clerk__

Siblings: _____

_____

_____

_____

Teacher's Comments:

Grade 1: _Janet "tries." Has a speech problem (articulation)._   Grade 4:

Grade ~~2~~ _Immature._
One   Grade 5:

Grade 3:   Grade 6:

Name **Roger**   Age **11** Years **11** Months

Grade **Special Class**

School _____

Achievement (Grades)

(Grade)	1	2(1)	3(2)	4 (2)	5(sc)6
Reading	U	U	D-	D-	NP
Math	U	U	D-	D-	NP
Spelling					
Writing	U	U	D-	D-	NP
Social Studies					
Science					
Music	S	S	C	C	P
Art	S	S	C	C	P
Health					
Physical Education					
Conduct	U	U	U	U	U

U — Unsatisfactory   P — Progressing
S — Satisfactory   NP — Not Progressing
O — Outstanding

Ability (Test Scores)

		Name of Test	Age	Score
Grade	1	Group IQ	6	50
(1)	2			
(2)	3			
(2)	4	Individual IQ	10	62
	5			
	6			

Achievement Test

	Names of Tests	Age	Score
Grades 1	Readiness	6	Letter rating E
(1) 2	Achievement	7	R-1.5 M-1.6 A-1.5
(2) 3	Achievement	8	R-1.8 M-.16 A-1.6
4			
5			
6			

R-reading   M-math   A-average

Health Record:

Family Background

Father's Name **Merle**

Mother's Name **Billy Jean**

Address _____

Telephone _____

Occupation: Father **Janitor**

Occupation: Mother **Housewife**

Siblings:

Name	Age
Joan	6
Mary	7
Eddie	9
Jesse	10

Teacher's Comments:

Grade 1: Roger is very aggressive toward other children. He does not like group activities.

Grade 2 one: Roger picks at other children — very poor in subjects.

Grade 3 two: Roger fights with other children.

Grade 4 two: Roger doesn't complete his work. Very slow.

Grade 5: Special class. Roger doesn't respond well to adults.

Grade 6: He is very clumsy and poorly coordinated.

Name_ _Loretta_ Age _10_ Years _2_ Months_

Grade_ _Special Class_

School_____

	1	2	2+3	5	6	Total Days (180)
	65	54	55 6			Special Class

Achievement (Grades)

(Grade)	1	2 (1)	3 (2)	4 (SC)	6
Reading	U	U	D-	NP	
Math	U	U	D	NP	
Spelling			D	P	
Writing	U	U	C	P	
Social Studies			C	P	
Science			C	P	
Music	S	S	S	P	
Art	S	S	S	P	
Health					
Physical Education					
Conduct	S	S	S	S	

U — Unsatisfactory   P — Progressing
S — Satisfactory   NP — Not Progressing
O — Outstanding

Ability (Test Scores)

		Name of Test	Age	Score
Grade	1			
	2	Group IQ	8	83
SC	3	Individual IQ	9	73
	4			
	5			
	6			

Achievement Test

	Names of Tests	Age	Score
Grades 1	Readiness	6	Letter Rating-D
2	Achievement	7	1.3-r 1.1 m 1.1-a
3	Achievement	8	1.5-r 1.6 m 1.5-a
4			
5			
6			

r - reading   m - math   a - average

Family Background

Father's Name _James_

Mother's Name _Susan_

Address_____

Telephone_____

Occupation: Father _Bus Driver_

Occupation: Mother _Housewife_

Siblings: Name	Age
Sharon	14
James	12
Elizabeth	8
John	7

Health Record: No special problems

Teacher's Comments:

Grade 1: Loretta is a very shy child. She is not progressing in subjects.

Grade 2: Loretta seems to be standing still in reading and math.

Grade 3: Loretta is afraid of adults. Very shy and slow in subjects.

Grade three: Loretta does not like to read and is progressing in some subjects.

Grade 5:

Grade 6:

309

Name **Tom** Age **11** Years **3** Months

Grade **Special Class**

School _____

Attendance Record						
1	2(1)	(2)	60	60	Total Days (180)	
'64	'65	'60	'63	'73	Special Class	

Achievement (Grades)

(Grade)	1	2(1)	2(2)	4(sc)	5(sc)	6
Reading	U	U	D-	P	P	
Math	U	U	D-	P	P	
Spelling						
Writing	S-	S	C	P	P	
Social Studies						
Science						
Music	S	S	C	P	P	
Art	S	S	C	P	P	
Health						
Physical Education						
Conduct	U	U	U	U	U	

U — Unsatisfactory   P — Progressing
S — Satisfactory   NP — Not Progressing
O — Outstanding

Ability (Test Scores)

	Name of Test	Age	Score
Grade 1			
(1) 2	Individual IQ	8	74
3			
4			
5			
6			

Achievement Test

	Names of Tests	Age	Score
Grades 1	Readiness	6	Letter rating - D
(1) 2	Achievement	6	r-1.1 a-1.0 m-1.3
(2) 3	Achievement	8	r-1.5 a-1.3 m-1.4
4			
5			
6			

r - reading   m - math   a - average

Health Record:

Family Background

Father's Name **Harvey**

Mother's Name **Mary**

Address _____

Telephone _____

Occupation: Father **Delivery Man**

Occupation: Mother **Housewife**

Siblings: Name   Age
   Paul   8

Teacher's Comments:

Grade 1: Tom is very hyperactive. He reverses letters and has "Perceptual Problems."

Grade 2: Reading is a problem for me Tom. A very aggressive child.

Grade 2 Two: Likes to hit, fight, and kick. Not progressing.

Grade 4 (sc): Tom likes school—slightly hyperactive.

Grade 5 (sc): Has perceptual problems.

Grade 6:

performance, but, as was stated previously, the teacher should not draw conclusions simply as the result of reading these files. Establishing programs and grouping children should not be done on the basis of cumulative file data. Instead, before a teacher is able to determine the needs of children, he must spend some time in initial diagnosis and observation. Although many teachers feel that time does not allow them to do this, a teacher should be able to provide activities that allow him to garner pertinent information concerning the characteristics of the children if he plans carefully. If he has an aide, he may enlist that person's help in developing materials and working with the children. Also, many of the usual activities that teachers perform can be done by the children.

The Beginning Program: If the teacher does not place children in groups initially, he must plan activities that will yield diagnostic information about the children in a group. To do this, before the children arrive, the teacher could place materials that may be of interest to the children about the room. Free time should be allowed so that the children have time to explore their environment. Some of these materials could be: a tape recorder (preferably with headphone sets); a record player (preferably with headphone sets) and accompanied by various types of recordings (e.g., music, stories, fairy tales, poetry); a *Language Master; a Tutorgram;* reading kits on various levels; puppets; books; puzzles; magazines on various topics; toys; paper and pencil; art supplies; word games (Garrard Press publishes the Dolch Word games); and crossword puzzles.[16]

In addition to placing various materials around the room, the teacher can establish interest centers in the corners of the room. Interest centers for science, mathematics, writing, and other areas could be developed. As the children learn to use these centers, they may want to establish their own centers. In order to give the reader a "flavor" of what might be placed in an interest center, the following materials could be included for a science center: magnifying glasses; plants; an ant farm; magnets and materials that may or may not be attracted; litmus paper; picture books on such topics as dinosaurs, plants, and animals (some teachers find old science books and place stories from them in attractive covers); a thermometer; a barometer; a microscope; aquariums; live animals (e.g., guinea pigs); binoculars.

---

[16]Materials listed are found in various parts of the book and the appendices.

Gathering Information: As children are free to move in these areas
of the room, the teacher should observe each child carefully. It is
very helpful if the teacher keeps a record of what he observes during
these sessions. The following comments are the teacher's initial
observations of the hypothetical class:

> 9/2 — Loretta appears very sulky. She does not participate in
> activities with the other children. However, she has made
> friends with Dara.

> 9/2 — Roger is very quiet and seldom responds verbally. He
> likes the tape recorder. He tends to antagonize the other chil-
> dren. He takes things from others and lies about the things he
> had done.

> 9/2 — Robert likes rocks. He brought an arrowhead to school
> today and said he would bring in rocks that he likes in order to
> show the class.

> 9/2 — Tom seems to be able to work independently with min-
> imal directions or support. He maintains his interest for a long
> period of time. He loves the tape recorder.

> 9/2 — Dara appears very patient and cooperative.

> 9/2 — George is very quiet and pleasant.

> 9/2 — Marshall is becoming rather aggressive. He is friends
> with Tom.

> 9/2 — Paul has "slurred" speech. I talked softly to him, and he
> was able to hear me. He plays aggressively and expresses no
> interest in suggested activities, although he may join in later.

> 9/2 — Dennis has carefully explored the room. He has made
> friends with Dara. He likes the tape recorder and the puppets.

> 9/2 — Harry "whines" a great deal. He likes to fight with the
> other children. He is very negative and seems to try to get at-
> tention and physical contact by acting as if he does not want it.

> 9/2 — Joyce pouts a great deal. She fusses when she does not
> get her way with other children.

> 9/2 — Janet has made friends with all of the girls. She "bab-
> bles" all the time.

As the teacher records his impressions of the children, he will
discover many of their interests and personality traits. Although the
teacher may want to record these interests on an interest inventory
such as the one found in Chapter Eight, this should be done grad-

ually. Asking the child all the questions that appear on an inventory is an artificial manner of learning about the children. Most children will not respond to such questioning until they are well acquainted with the teacher. A more effective manner of obtaining information about the children's interests is to observe them as they talk with their peers and to engage in conversation with each child during the day or week.

Seeking Pertinent Information: In gathering information about children's needs, the teacher must establish clearly what he should know about the children in order to develop programs for them. For example, what information is vital for effective programming in reading? The answer to such a question depends upon the teacher's definition or philosophy of reading. If a teacher feels that correlates of reading are important, he may seek such characteristics about the children as their strengths and weaknesses in auditory perception. Thus, in establishing a process for obtaining information about children, the present authors cannot avoid suggesting examples that reflect a philosophy of teaching reading. This philosophy, of course, will not be the same as all other educators who work with exceptional children. However, the *process* for obtaining the information may be of use to any teacher, regardless of his biases.

The teacher will, of course, need to obtain *expressive information*. As the children become familiar with the environment, the teacher and the children may begin to express themselves to others. A teacher may obtain valuable data from such expressions. If the teacher provides opportunities for group discussions and also listens to children converse among each other, he will learn a great deal about the children's language, background experiences and interests.

The following are examples of conversations of the children and some interpretations by the teacher:

9/8 — Roger does not respond often verbally. When I ask him a question, he shakes his head "yes" or "no."

9/12 — In a group discussion this morning, the children were discussing what they did with their families over the week-end. In the middle of the conversation, Harry raised his hand and remarked to the group, "Have you ever noticed that potato chips are brown on the edge and a little green?". (I have noticed several times that his mind wanders. Also, because he is in a new foster placement, he may not be interested in discussing family activities.)

9/13 — Janet has a slight "articulation" problem. However, this does not keep her from talking. She talks quite frequently to her friends and to me. She likes to "pretend" when playing with her friends. She has a tendency to "ramble." She also has problems formulating sentences. Sometimes, she seems to be grasping for words.

9/14 — Loretta told me today that she is beginning to like the class.

9/14 — I overheard Paul talking "through the use of a puppet" today. I sat down to listen. He was talking about the farm and how he likes to play in the woods and in the barn. His speech is very slurred, but I am able to understand him quite well. (I must note this as an interest on which to capitalize.)

Many children like to express themselves in writing, and the teacher can use this writing to gather information relating to all aspects of language arts. The following are comments made by the teacher about the children's written expression and examples of their work.

9/8 — George has been spending a great deal of time at the writing corner. He enjoys writing stories and reading them to the group or to me. An example of his writing is included.

Figure 14

"My dog plays with the puppies. My brother feeds the dogs."

9/10 — Many of the children have attempted to write. Dara started a "post office." Each child has a "mail box" at his/her desk and the children deliver notes. Dara also gave mailboxes to me and the aide. I have noticed several children such as Dara, George, and Roger rotate letters and reverse letters and words. Dara wrote "god" for "dog." I asked her to read the sentence to me. She read it as "dog." Many of the children have not attempted to write sentences (e.g., Harry). If they send letters, they usually draw a picture and place their name at the bottom or copy words from around the room. Some of the children (e.g., Tom) are unable to write all the letters of the alphabet or to recognize them.

Planning for Grouping and Obtaining Data: Planning is the *key* to gathering specific information about the reading skills of the children. In accomplishing such planning, the teacher may establish groups according to interests, skills, or levels of reading. For example, after the teacher places books of varying difficulty about the room, he may ask what children would like to share with the other children, the teacher, or an aide as well as what they have read in these books.

During the beginning of the reading program, interest groups (e.g., about animals) could be formed. While some children are working on their interest groups—reading books, writing stories, listening to records, viewing filmstrips in a corner of the room, or drawing pictures—another group might be working with the teacher or an aide (if the teacher has one). Some children could be working individually on such activities as sentence reading on the *Language Master*.

All of these activities appear simple to plan; however, many teachers fail to achieve success in such planning. Harris and Smith (1972) have emphasized that before grouping can be successful, children must be able to work independently and "clear and concise goals must be established for children working independently."[17] On this topic, they also have remarked:

> The teacher who wants only to keep children busy cannot be effective with a grouped approach to instruction. A healthier attitude toward independent work gives real emphasis to these activities. One of the major goals of reading instruction is making each child an independent reader, one who sets purposes for himself, organizes his resources, and carries a task through to completion. Only by carefully planning and conducting independent activities as an important aspect of the reading program can this goal be realized.[18]

---

[17]Larry A. Harris and Carl B. Smith, *Reading Instruction through Diagnostic Teaching* (New York: Holt, Rinehart, & Winston, 1972), p. 91.
[18]*Ibid.*, pp. 96-97.

In the simulated class, some of the children (e.g., Tom) are able to work independently. Others cannot. Initially, then, activities that are very meaningful must be found for children who have problems working independently, often because many of the tasks are too difficult. An analysis of these tasks may help the teacher find activities on which the children can work successfully. Again, this is not as simple a task as it seems, especially with some children who *appear* to be distractible and to have short attention spans. Many of the behaviors that teachers describe, such as "short attention spans," may actually result from the nature of the tasks rather than the characteristics of the child. All of these characteristics should be viewed in terms of the child rather than in terms of "types" of children.

The following observations concerning work skills were made by the teacher over a several-week span. Therefore, the teacher's means of dealing with the situation may be included.

10/11 — George is very pleased with his stories and words he learns. Sometimes it is difficult to make him complete a task without being distracted easily, but he is also proud of what he completes.

10/25 — George is doing his work very well. He gets stars for the completion of ten tasks immediately after the task is finished. This has helped to motivate him. However, he is still eager to get off task if rewards aren't constant. I must carefully analyze what type of tasks he attends to the most.

11/15 — George has been given more structure. He is given independent work which he must finish before he can do other things of his choice. This has helped him complete his tasks. His attention span has increased a great deal and in small groups he works very well.

11/15 — Dennis has little interest in reading. He does not like group activities. I feel that his reading level is high, however.

9/28 — Paul enjoys puzzles. He will spend two or three days working on a task. He is very cooperative and sticks to tasks diligently. He is somewhat of a loner and will not often work with the group.

10/18 — Paul will join the group if he is able to do something successfully, such as work the puppets in a puppet show.

10/3 — Marshall is motivated easily to work on his own if he can succeed. He is very proud of the new things he learns. In doing cursive writing, he was so delighted with his progress that he asked for more exercises.

10/2 — Harry requires a great deal of my time. He is constantly seeking attention. He asks for help or approval of practically everything he does.

9/28 — Roger is rather resistant in doing his assignments.

9/30 — I think that most of the time Roger is reluctant to work for fear of failure.

10/1 — Most often, Roger refuses to join a group. If a task becomes hard for him, he leaves the group. Many times he will be aggressive toward other children when tasks become harder.

10/15 — Roger is very aggressive sometimes. He still refuses to read, especially in a group.

10/25 — Roger has been placed on a "management" schedule for fighting and bothering other children. His behavior is improving some.

10/30 — Roger's behavior has improved a great deal. He has also been completing work. His peers are beginning to accept him. I've found it better to concentrate on materials for motivating him. We read *The Bus Ride*,[19] and he would not respond for the first few pages. However, he began reading after the first few pages and enjoyed it. (Other techniques used with Roger will be discussed later in this chapter.)

Cross-age or peer teaching: In planning for grouping, the teacher may not be able to cope with all the groups as successfully if he does not have an aide. However, children can help to accomplish much of the teaching themselves. Peer or cross-age teaching has been used very successfully in many classrooms. Cross-age teaching is very beneficial to both children involved. In discussing cross-age teaching, Greer (1972) has stated:

> Cross-age associations through these activities can result in marked changes in interpersonal relations among children involved. Older children have an opportunity to see younger ones in a different perspective as they share emotional experiences through reading content.[20]

---

[19]From Scott-Foresman Reading Systems (see Appendix Two).
[20]Margaret Greer, "Affective Growth through Reading," *The Reading Teacher* 25 (1972): 339-40.

The comments from the teacher concerning cross-age and peer teaching in this simulated class include the following:

11/1 — Began cross-age teaching yesterday. Kids were very excited! They worked hard on their lessons.

11/2 — Loretta has responded well to peer teaching, and she eagerly takes initiative. She is very concerned about what takes place when she teaches. She reads her instructions in the manual as well as reading for other children. At the first of the term, she stated that she hated to read.

11/5 — Joyce is usually very pouty and defiant. She refuses to do much of her work occasionally. She is also very suspicious of others. However, she has been tutoring Harry on such skills as letter recognition. She is very excited about helping him.

11/6 — Janet enjoys tutoring some of the younger children because it is like "playing school."

11/24 — Loretta has been helping Dara with her reading. They chose some readers that Dara might read. They both agreed that the reading "looked hard." Dara said she *could learn* to read the stories. Loretta asked me for a teacher's manual.

Diagnosis in Reading: All of the activities and procedures listed previously are suggestions that a teacher might use in organizational structure. But as the teacher becomes more familiar with the children, he must begin to seek more specific information about their performance in reading, and this becomes time-consuming. Therefore, the teacher must plan carefully for this type of analysis. Many inventories, such as the one developed by Valett (1968), are quite helpful to the teacher. In addition, there are several taxonomies [e.g. Barrett's reported in (Clymer, 1968)] and checklists such as the one developed by Guszak (1971). In using a task-analysis approach, the teacher must be aware of the limitations of such aids (see Chapter Four on diagnosis). However, such an approach is very beneficial in gathering specific information. For example, if the teacher notes that some of the children are not able to recognize all of the letters of the alphabet, he should list the specific letters.

In developing strategies for diagnosing children's reading, the teacher may continue with recording his observations before formal or informal tests are given. A teacher should have explicit reasons for administering tests rather than giving them merely for the "sake of testing." Careful observation of children's behavior while reading allows the teacher to establish hypotheses that can be checked through formal or informal testings or diagnostic teaching lessons.

The following are such observations by the teacher:

9/15 — Dennis — I noticed today that Dennis was attempting to "sound out" every word as he read the directions to a game.

9/20 — I did not think that Paul could read at all. Today I noticed that he was reading the names of the class from the list of birthdays.

9/20 — Several of the children were reading a story into the tape recorder. Tom would not read. However, I noticed later in the day he was sitting reading a book.

9/22 — I have noticed that Dara does not attempt to "say" a word that she does not know immediately. She does this while reading sentences as well as isolated words.

10/15 — Today we were working on a short experience story. I was transcribing many of the words for Joyce. When she attemped to read some of the sentences back to me, she spent a great deal of time "sounding out" each letter. This did not help her in pronouncing the word.

10/15 — In dictating a word for Marshall today, I noticed that he did not know how to write the letters *z* and *w*. I asked him to name the letters on a poster in the room. He did not know the letters *f*, *l*, *q*, *z*, and *y*. Many of the children do not seem to be able to write the letters or read them. We worked on some of the letters by having him say them to me.

10/16 — I asked Marshall to name the letters we worked on the day before. He forgot two out of the three.

10/16 — I noticed that Janet has problems following simple written directions. She can read all the words fluently; however, she is not able to carry through on the task asked of her in the directions.

10/16 — Roger still refuses to read with a group of children.

10/18 — Harry does not appear to be able to read at all. He pays little attention to reading materials. I noted today that he attempted to copy something that was on the board. His copying did not at all resemble the original words.

10/18 — Dennis is extremely hyperactive in group activities. He does not attempt to read. He enjoys the tape recorder and the puppets. Today Dara, Loretta, and Tom wrote a play for the puppets (with my help on some of the spelling). They asked Dennis to be one of the characters. He had *no* problem reading any of the words.

10/20 — Robert is constantly picking up books and then return-ing them immediately to the shelf. He has problems working in a group, especially when any reading is being done. If he tries to read, most of the children tell him all of the words.

10/20 — At first, Loretta was very hesitant to read. Now she enjoys reading and likes to go to the library to select books.

A variation of reading problems and styles exists in this class-room, as it does in most classrooms. In order to acknowledge all the individual differences in this classroom, the teacher needs to possess as much information as possible. After observing the children in many situations, he may be more able to establish hypotheses.

Testing out these hypotheses is the next step in diagnostic teaching. For example, he may want to test many of the children in-dividually on such instruments as an individual diagnostic reading test or an Informal Reading Inventory. Most often, a teacher is not able to do this type of testing at the very beginning of the term because of the inability of the children to work in groups and/or independently. Consequently, many teachers may want to refer a child to a resource teacher or a reading specialist for individual test-ing. However, if at all possible, the person who is *directly* involved with the children should do the testing, and this is usually the teacher, although if an aide is available, he may be able to do some simple testing (e.g. checking letter recognition).

Because there are many limitations to individual diagnostic reading tests, such as their analysis of oral reading errors and their lack of adequately testing comprehension (see Chapter Four on Diagnosis), the teacher (or specialists) may want to consider the *Reading Miscue Inventory* on page 111. If a teacher is to analyze the oral reading of children, the "miscues" should be analyzed care-fully. The manual for the *Reading Miscue Inventory* gives directions for interpreting miscues. For example, from the results of the *RMI*, the teacher was able to ascertain that Joyce attended to specific graphemic/sound relationships regardless of context or meaning. Her strategies in reading were limited to utilizing cues within the words, especially phonemic/graphemic cues which did not aid her in comprehending the material. As a result, the teacher could be sure that he must be encouraged to minimize the use of such cues and learn to substitute meaningful words instead (Goodman and Burke, 1972).

Although children such as Loretta, Tom, Janet, Dennis, Joyce, and Dara read well enough to be tested on individual diagnostic reading tests, others such as Roger, Robert, George, Harry, Paul, and Marshall do not respond to paragraph reading.

Diagnostic Teaching Lessons:　The teacher can devise diagnostic teaching lessons for individuals or the group in most areas of reading. As was stated previously, much of the diagnosis depends upon the teacher's definition or philosophy of reading. In testing for correlates of reading, the teacher must realize that although certain perceptual skills correlate with reading, there may not be a cause-and-effect relationship between those skills and reading achievement.

Because several of the children were not able to respond to paragraph meaning, the teacher may want to test various assumed reading skills. The following are examples of diagnostic teaching lessons that a teacher may develop:

Subject: Visual Discrimination of Words. (This lesson is for Harry, Robert, and George.)

  I. Objective: Given the words *now-won, on-no, was-saw* in column form, the child will match each word correctly.

 II. Analysis of task presentation.
    A. Manner of Presentation: Visual (words) and Auditory (directions)
    B. Content:

was	on
no	now
on	saw
now	no
won	was
saw	won

    C. Environment: Structured group setting — one to three

III. Analysis of pupil performance.

    A. Modality: Visual/motor

    B. Process: Association

    C. Level of Response: Discrimination

D. Affective Response: All the children responding well to the task

IV. Remarks — Harry matched *saw* to *was* and *on* to *no.* The other children had no problems.

Subject: Auditory Perception — Discrimination of Minimal Word Pairs. (Lesson is for Paul.)

I. Objective: Given the pictures of the words such as *fish-dish,* the child will correctly select pictures to match the words spoken by the teacher. (The words were presented previously in order to determine if they were in the child's receptive vocabulary.)

II. Analysis of task presentation.

A. Manner of presentation: visual and auditory

B. Content: Picture cards representing fish, dish, cat, rat, hat, bat, car, star, rug, and mug

C. Environment: Structured one-to-one

III. Analysis of pupil performance.

A. Modality: Intersensory — Visual (picture interpretation), Auditory/motor — Must hold up cards

B. Process: Association

C. Level of Response: Discrimination

D. Affective Response: Hesitant at first

IV. Remarks: Paul missed *cat-rat, rug-mug,* and *hat-bat.*

Subject: Sentence Reading or Anticipating Words. (Lesson is for Janet.)

I. Objective: Given a sentence with one word missing, the child will insert a meaningful word.

II. Analysis of task presentation.

   A. Manner of presentation: Visual and auditory

   B. Content: The boy and his _____ ran up the hill

   C. Environment: One-to-one

III. Analysis of pupil performance

   A. Modality: Visual/auditory

   B. Process: Expressive

   C. Level of Response: — Strategy or problem-solving

   D. Affective Response: Janet became very frustrated with this task.

IV. Remarks: Janet had problems with this seemingly simple task. I had to give her an example (dog) before she could perform the task. However, every response was an animal. I think she was cueing on my answer rather than the sentence meaning. This same lesson was given to Dara who had no problems. She enjoyed the exercise. I have noticed that Dara does not attempt a word that she doesn't know immediately. I thinks she thinks reading is a process whereby one "strings together words that have been memorized."

If the teacher files his diagnostic teaching lessons, he may use them with other children when necessary. The information obtained from these lessons may help pinpoint some of the difficulties children are having. The lessons should be designed for the analysis of specific tasks. So often, a teacher will conclude that a child has a particular problem without breaking down the tasks. For example, in order to test auditory perception of initial consonants, a teacher may ask the child to write the letter that represents the sound at the beginning of the word. If the child is able to do this task successfully, the teacher may conclude that the child associates the sound with the letter. However, if he is unable to complete this task, the teacher is not able to conclude that the child does not perceive the sound because other factors are involved, such as the child's ability to write the letters. The child may "hear the sound" but not be able to associate it to a grapheme representation. Therefore, the task must be broken down into more discrete units or steps.

Much of the information the teacher needs may be found through the use of diagnostic teaching or diagnostic teaching lessons. One distinct advantage of the teacher's writing the lessons is that he has a specific objective for testing in mind. However, he may do the same with formal tests. Still, no formal test should be administered by the teacher unless he has specific objectives or reasons for giving the test.

Developing Tentative Programs: After the teacher has observed the children and completed some types of diagnostic procedures, he may establish tentative programs on the basis of his findings. No program should be established for a child without its constantly being checked for its effectiveness. The present authors have recommended programs that would appear to work for a child, only to see them fail immediately, although another child may be using the same materials and doing very well. One characteristic for all good programs for children is that any exercises to be used should be related to the goal of comprehension. On this point, Goodman (1972) has stated:

> Teaching and learning in reading must always be centered in comprehension. The importance of any particular letters and words in a sequence can be determined only in relationship to the message the whole sequence is conveying.[21]

Reading should be related to meaningful experiences of the children. The teacher should encourage children to read for various reasons rather than teaching "isolated" reading skills. In order to accomplish this task, he must be a "facilitator of learning"[22] instead of a teacher of reading.

In developing programs for the children, the teacher must consider as many variables as possible. It may appear that all children in the class would be "turned on" to certain programs such as language experience. Unfortunately, due to such factors as past experiences, motivation, attention to the task and so forth, not all children enjoy the same programs. The following are illustrations of the instructional strategies designed for the simulated classroom:

---

[21]Kenneth Goodman, "Reading: The Key Is in Children's Languages," *The Reading Teacher* 25 (1972): 508.

[22]*Ibid.*, p. 508.

10/15 — From the beginning of the term, George enjoyed writing stories and reading them to the group. I have decided to continue the language experience approach with him. Because his written expression in terms of spelling is so poor (see 9/8), he tells his story into the tape recorder. I, my aide, or Loretta transcribes these stories for him. Most often, he likes to recopy them and illustrate them. Many have been "bound" and placed on the table at the reading corner. He likes to read his stories to the other children. Some have been the scripts for puppet shows. He also keeps a word file and uses the words to make new sentences. He is working on writing his alphabet and spelling words as well as learning to read. He enjoys reading simple library books also.

10/12 — Loretta is really beginning to enjoy reading. Cross-age teaching has given her a great deal of confidence. She is reading in the *Scott, Foresman Reading Systems* as well as in many high-interest low-vocabulary books such as the *Dolch Books*. She also enjoys writing stories and reading them. Finding interesting books for her seems to be the only problem. I have been having conferences with her about what she is reading and keeping a file on her progress. She has some problems in following lengthy directions. I have noticed that she is overcoming this problem to some degree because she must read directions for lessons in her sessions with Harry and Dara.

10/12 — Dennis was very hyperactive at the beginning of the term. I have had to set up limits and "boundaries" for him and help *him* structure his work. On diagnostic tests, for example, auditory measures such as the *LAC,* he has some blending problems. His auditory memory span appears to be short. That may be due to distractibility. All of these problems do not seem to hinder his reading. He and Loretta are two of the better readers in the room. The main problem is finding interesting reading materials. He enjoys high-interest low-vocabulary materials such as the *Jim Forest Series* (Field Educational Publications, Inc.). Occasionally, he likes to write stories. He does not like to keep card files. I have used phrases and sentences that Dennis reads when flashed so that he may discontinue "sounding out" all letters.

10/5 — Marshall appears to have a visual memory problem. He dislikes adding word after word to a file. He attempts to memorize the words and becomes frustrated when reading sentences. We have been using a combined Fernald-Ashton-Warner-language experience approach. This helps him remember the words. Comprehension is heightened because he writes or tells many stories that are highly interesting to him. Many of these center around cars and trucks.

10/12 — Paul has been a real problem in terms of reading. I have tried several visual approaches with him. (He has severe auditory problems). He has lacked interest in any of them. I don't think he sees any reason for reading.

10/5 — Most of Roger's problem has been motivational. His reading skills are extremely limited. His sentence recognition is very low. He seldom attempts to read. I have been reading with him stories from several reading programs. He has been hard to test. Many times he refuses to respond. From observation and some diagnostic teaching lessons, he appears to possess some memory and perceptual difficulties. His behavior is improving, however. I must keep trying with his reading.

10/16 — Harry is a challenge. He is far behind the ability of the other children in beginning reading. He is very distractible and whines when he doesn't want to do his work. However, he is progressing in social skills. Also, lately he has expressed a desire to read and write. He likes to take home examples of his work to his foster parents. I have used this as motivation. He dictates simple messages to me and he then carries them home. We have been collecting some of these in a book. He enjoys filling in missing words in short sentences such as "I ate _____." I have noticed that he loves food. We have written stories about going to the ice cream store, etc. He appears to have some visual discrimination problems. He has some problem in copying sentences also. Sessions must be extremely short and simple. He also likes the *Language Master*. I have been placing sentences and parts of sentences about such topics as food on the blank cards. Sometimes he will work at the language master for thirty to forty-five minutes. He also likes to "type." Sometimes he can spell words. I will try to encourage this. Janet helps Harry with some skills.

10/12 — Dara has some fear of sentence reading. She has memorized words and uses no strategies unless blanks are used (see diagnostic teaching lesson). I have tried to get her to use this ability with words that are present. We have been reading riddles, nursery rhymes, and familiar stories. I try to encourage her to "guess." She has some fear of failure. Tutoring Harry has helped her gain some self-confidence. Loretta helps her in her reading also.

10/15 — Joyce spends most of her time in reading, laboriously "sounding out" words. This does not help her at all. She also has a serious blending problem. She will sound out /c/ /a/ /t/

and then guess with such words as *at, rat,* or *sat.* It will be some time before she is able to learn beneficial strategies. Evidently, in the past, she has been taught to sound out every letter. She knows all of her letters. I must encourage sentence and phrase reading. I have placed sentences on the Language Master. She plays them and then repeats what she hears. All of the sentences are meaningful ones to her. Joyce's pouting and aggressive behaviors are also a deterrent to her learning to read.

10/16 — Robert displayed interests at the beginning of the term. I have used some of these interests (e.g. rocks) in helping him write books for the reading table. His word recognition and sentence reading is very low. He becomes very frustrated if he is asked to write anything. His writing skills are extremely poor. He "hates" to trace. He is embarrassed if anyone sees him tracing over words. He idolizes Dennis; therefore, I have asked Dennis to help Robert with his reading. He does respond well to praise, especially to the comments on his books. He is becoming more creative in his stories and his play with other children.

10/12 — Tom is able to work independently. However, sometimes he is very bossy and boisterous. He is interested in many types of books and loves to select his own books to read. He does not like to read with the group for very long. He also does not like to read from many basal series. He enjoys very short stories. I have used some of the stories from the *SRA* kits. He is usually able to determine if a story or book is too difficult for him. We have conferences about what he reads. He sometimes enjoys reading the other children's books or stories and he likes to read poetry also. He has some problems in comprehending inferential questions and tends to take everything literally. I have noticed this in all areas. He is very concrete and is sometimes easily confused. I am treating it as more than a reading comprehension problem. He has no problem comprehending material that is meaningful to him, but he appears to be lacking in many experiences. I have encouraged him to write stories. We work on comprehensional strategies from these stories. I have used riddles for the development of inference skills. This is a very difficult area to teach.

10/15 — Janet can "read" very fluently. However, she remembers little of what she reads. She has been able to read as high as Level Five paragraphs in an individual diagnostic reading test. However, she does not appear to "comprehend" what she reads. Therefore, she has problems in following directions and reading in the content areas. I have noticed that she has problems in word meaning and in generalization. For example, a dog in one story was named "Spot." She remarked that this was not possible because her dog is named "Spot." She is constantly rambling about something and much of what she says is not logical. She does like to pretend. I could try some role-playing. I feel she has a language or reasoning problem that may require the services of a speech therapist, as with Paul. She also has a slight "articulation problem." We have been working on time and writing simple sentences about the days of the week and so forth. We dramatize many of the stories she reads as well. Also, I have tried to give her purposes for everything she reads. All stories have been as meaningful as possible. I have also used filmstrips about animals and so forth. In order that she may narrate the story, I blank out the words by not completely exposing the frame.

Not every program is going to be a success immediately. Many times the teacher must "field" problems as they arise (Hammill, 1971). A search for what seems to work for every child must be continual. The following comments by the teacher demonstrate programs that appear to be working with Paul and Roger.

11/30 — Paul has been working in the *Edmark Program* (see Chapter Five). He went through the beginning stages with no difficulty at all. He is now doing sentence reading and is very excited. He goes about the room reading what he has learned to everyone. He looks for the new words in other books. For the first time, he seems to realize that reading means something. I hope there is transfer to other reading materials. The program is designed in such a way that an aide or untrained person can be engaged to work with the child. Junior high students have been helping. Paul likes the attention also.

11/25 — Roger has been receiving extra attention in reading. We have been using objects such as candy and writing lessons about them. For example, he describes the object: "The candy is green." The sentences are written down. Roger is encouraged to think of as many descriptive statements as possible. He is very good at this. After the sentences are written, he enjoys copying them and making cards for a word file. A "token/reward system" was used as a crutch at first. I think that most of the success comes from the fact that he feels special and that the sentences were his own. He has an extreme fear of failure and reading groups. Lately he has been asking the other children to join him in writing sentences.

The programs established for this class were not all of the possible ones that could have been used. Many educators may have desired to use other types of reading experiences with these children. Readers are encouraged to use their problem-solving skills in designing programs for these hypothetical cases. Although the teacher in these examples had established programs by the second month of school, he would consider these programs to be tentative other than final.

SUMMARY

In attempting to present the reader with suggestions concerning classroom application of diagnostic-prescriptive techniques, different types of classroom arrangements, environments, and groupings were discussed initially. The present authors chose to simulate a class of special children in order to demonstrate the use of a problem-solving approach to diagnostic teaching. Examples of educational strategies were suggested.

REFERENCES

Bandera, A. *Principles of Behavior Modification.* New York: Holt, Rinehart, & Winston, 1969.

Bartel, Nettie. *The Philadelphia Open-Classroom Project.* Bloomington: Indiana University School of Education Center for Innovation in Teaching the Handicapped, 1972.

Bateman, Barbara. "Implications of a Learning Disability Approach for Teaching Educable Retardates." *Mental Retardation* 5 (1967): 23-25.

_____. "The Role of Individual Diagnosis in Remedial Planning for Reading Disorders." *Reading Forum, NINDS Monograph Number 11.* Bethesda, Maryland: National Institute of Neurological Diseases and Strokes Public Health Service, National Institute of Health, US Department of Health, Education, and Welfare, 1970.

Bijou, Sidney, et al. "Programmed Instruction as an Approach to Teaching of Reading, Writing, and Arithmetic to Retarded Children." *The Psychological Record* 16 (1966): 505-22.

Birnbrauer, J.; Bijou, S.; Wolf, M.; and Kiddler, J. "Programmed Instruction in the Classroom." In *Case Studies in Behavior Modification*, edited by L. Ullman and L. Krasner. New York: Holt, Rinehart, & Winston, 1965.

Blackman, Leonard. "Research and the Classroom: Mohammed and the Mountain Revisited." *Exceptional Children* 39 (1972): 181-90.

Blum, Evelyn R. "The Madison Plan as an Alternative to Special-Class Placement: An Interview with Frank Hewett." *Education and Training of the Mentally Retarded* 6 (1971): 329-42.

Burnette, E. "Influence of Classroom Environment on Word Learning of Retarded with High and Low Activity Levels." Doctoral dissertation, Peabody College, 1962.

Carter, John L., and Diaz, Angelo. "Effects of Visual and Auditory Background on Reading Test Performance." *Exceptional Children* 38 (1971): 43-50.

Clymer, Theodore. "The Barrett Taxonomy — Cognitive and Affective Dimensions of Reading Comprehension." In *Innovation and Change in Reading Instruction, Sixty-seventh Yearbook of the National Society for the Study of Education, Part K*, edited by Helen M. Robinson, pp. 19-23. Chicago: University of Chicago Press, 1968.

Cruickshank, W.; Bentzen, F.; Ratzeburg, F.; and Tarnhauser, M. *A Teaching Methodology for Brain-Injured and Hyperactive Children*. Syracuse, New York: Syracuse University Press, 1961.

Dreeben, Robert. *The Nature of Teaching: Schools and the Work of Teachers*. Glenview, Illinois: Scott, Foresman, and Co., 1970.

Goodlad, John I. *School, Curriculum, and the Individual*. Waltham, Massachusetts: Blaisdell Publishing Co., 1966.

Goodlad, John I., and Anderson, Robert. *The Nongraded Elementary Schools*, rev. ed. New York: Harcourt, Brace, Jovanovich, 1963.

Goodman, Kenneth. "Reading: The Key Is in Children's Languages." *The Reading Teacher* 25 (1972): 505-08.

Goodman, Yetta M., and Burke, Carolyn. *Reading Miscue Inventory: Manual Procedures for Diagnosis and Evaluation*. London: The Macmillan Co., 1972.

Greer, Margaret. "Affective Growth through Reading." *The Reading Teacher* 25 (1972): 336-41.

Gross, Beatrice, and Gross, Ronald. "British Infant Schools — American Style." In *Will the Real Teacher Please Stand Up?* edited by Mary Greer and Bonnie Rubinstein, pp. 85-90. Pacific Palisades, California: Goodyear Publishing Co., 1972.

Guszak, Frank. *The Reading Checklist and Reading Checksheet*. Austin, Texas: Educational Program Development, 1971.

Hammill, Donald. "Evaluating Children for Instructional Purposes." *Academic Therapy* 4 (1971): 341-53.

Haring, Norris, and Hauch, Mary Ann. "Improving Learning Conditions in the Establishment of Reading Skills with Disabled Readers." *Exceptional Children* 35 (1969): 341-52.

Haring, Norris, and Kinzelmann, H. "The Finer Focus of Therapeutic Behavior Management." In *Educational Therapy*. Seattle, Washington: Bernie Straub, 1966.

Haring, Norris and Phillips, E. Lakew. *Educating Emotionally Disturbed Children*. New York: McGraw-Hill Book Co., 1962.

Harris, Larry A., and Smith, Carl B. *Reading Instruction through Diagnostic Teaching*. New York: Holt, Rinehart, & Winston, 1972.

Hertzberg, Alvin, and Stone, Edward F. *Schools Are for Children.* New York: Schocken-Books, 1971.

Hetland, Melvin. *Organizations for Individualizing: Individualizing Instruction Extension Service.* Chicago: Science Research Associates, 1969.

Hewett, Frank. *The Emotionally Disturbed Child in the Classroom.* Boston: Allyn & Bacon, 1968.

_____. "A Hierarchy of Educational Tasks for Children with Learning Disorders." *Exceptional Children* 31 (1964): 207-14.

Hillson, Maurice. "Nongraded Schools: Organizational Design for Elementary Education." In *Change and Innovation in Elementary School Organization: Selected Readings,* edited by Maurie Hillson, pp. 309-23. New York: Holt, Rinehart, & Winston, 1965.

Howes, Virgil M. "Individualized Instruction: Form and Structure." In *Individualization of Instruction: A Teaching Strategy,* edited by Virgil M. Howes. New York: The Macmillan Co., 1970.

Individually Prescribed Instruction. Pittsburgh, Pennsylvania Research for Better Schools, Inc. and the Learning Research and Development Center, undated.

Keith, Lowell; Blake, Paul; and Tiedt, Sidney. *Contemporary Curriculum in the Elementary School.* New York: Harper & Row, Publishers, 1968.

Kohl, Herbert. *The Open Classroom.* New York: Random House, 1969.

MacMillan, Donald, and Forness, Steven. "Behavior Modification: Limitations and Liabilities." *Exceptional Children* 37 (1970): 291-97.

Meacham, Merle L., and Wiesen, Allen E. *Changing Classroom Behavior: A Manual for Precision Teaching.* Scranton, Pennsylvania: International Textbook Company, 1970.

Mitchell, Joy, and Zoffness, Richard. "Multi-age Classroom." *Grade Teacher* 88 (1971): 55-61.

Peter, Lawrence. *Prescriptive Teaching.* New York: McGraw-Hill Book Co., 1965.

"Precision Teaching in Perspective: An interview with Ogden Lindsley." *Teaching Exceptional Children* 3 (1971): 114-19.

Rathbone, Charles. *Open Education: Selected Readings.* New York: Citation Press, 1970.

Richman, Vivian. "Open Education: Notes on Implementation." *Grade Teacher* 89 (1972): 67-68; 70-72.

Rost, K.J.; and Charles, D.C. "Academic Achievement of Brain-Injured and Hyperactive Children in Isolation." *Exceptional Children* 34 (1967): 125-26.

Shores, Richard, and Haubrick, Paul A. "Effect of Cubicles in Educating Emotionally Disturbed Children." *Exceptional Children* 36 (1969): 21-24.

Silberman, Charles. *Crisis in the Classroom.* New York: Random House, 1970.

Skinner, B.F. "Operant Behavior." *American Psychologist* 18 (1963): 505-15.

_____. *Science and Human Behavior.* New York: The Macmillan Co., 1953.

Southworth, Horton C. "A Model of Teacher Training for Individualization of Instruction." In *Perspectives in Individualized Learning,* edited by Robert H. Weisgerber, pp. 249-58. Palo Alto, California: American Institute for Research, 1972.

Spradlin, J.E.; Cromwell, R.L.; and Fosher, J.G. "Studies in Activity Level III—Auditory Stimulating." *American Journal of Mental Deficiency* 64 (1960): 754-57.

Strauss, A.A., and Lehtinen, L.F. *Psychopathology and Education of the Brain-Injured Child.* New York: Grune & Stratton, 1947.

Tansley, A.E., and Gulliford, R. *The Education of Slow-Learning Children.* London: Routledge and Kegan Paul, 1960.

Turnure, James. "Distractibility in the Mentally Retarded: Negative Evidence for an Orienting Inadequacy." *Exceptional Children* 37 (1970): 181-86.

Ullmann, L., and Krasner, L. *Case Studies in Behavior Modification.* New York: Holt, Rinehart, & Winston, 1965.

Valett, Robert. *A Psychoeducational Inventory of Basic Learning Abilities.* Palo Alto, California: Fearon Publishers, 1968.

Veatch, Jeannette. "Individualizing: in Individualization of Instruction." In *A Teaching Strategy*, edited by Virgil M. Howes, pp. 90-99. New York: The Macmillan Co., 1970.

High Interest-Low Vocabulary Materials

The Action Library 1
Scholastic Magazine and Book Service
Reading Level: 2.0-2.4

American Ace Books
Garrard Publishing Co.
Reading Level: 4

Basic Vocabulary Series
Garrard Publishing Co.
Reading Level: 3

Breakthrough Series
Allyn & Bacon, Inc.
Reading Level: 6

Checkered Flag Series
Field Educational Enterprises
Reading Level: 2

Citizens All Series
Mafex Associates, Inc.
Reading Level: 1-3

Cowboy Sam Series
Benefic Press
Reading Level: 2-3

Creative People Books
Garrard Publishing Co.
Reading Level: 5

*Creative People in the Arts
    and Sciences*
Garrard Publishing Co.
Reading Level: 5

Defenders of Freedom
Garrard Publishing Co.
Reading Level: 5

Discovering Books
Garrard Publishing Co.
Reading Level: 3

Folklore of the World Series
Garrard Publishing Co.
Reading Level: 3

+4 Reading Booster
Webster Publishing Division of
    McGraw-Hill
Reading Level: Middle grades
    below Grade 4

The Frontiers of America Books
Children's Press, Inc.
Reading Level: 4

High-Interest Easy to Read Books
Follett Publishing Co.
Reading Level: PP-3

The Hip Reader
Book-Lab, Inc.
Reading Level: Beginning to
    600 Words

Jim Forest Readers
Field Educational Enterprises
Reading Level: 2-3

Junior Everyreader Series
Webster Publishing Division of
    McGraw-Hill
Reading Level: 3 and 4

Know Your World (Newspaper Form)
Xerox Education Publications
Reading Level: 3-5

Legends and Folktales
Garrard Publishing Co.
Reading Level: 4

The Magpie Series
Mafex Associates, Inc.
Reading Level: 1-3

Morgan Bay Mystery Series
Harr Wagner
Reading Level: 3.0-3.5

*Morrow's High Interest/Easy
  Reading Books*
William Morrow & Co., Inc.
Reading Level: 1-8

Pacemaker Series
Fearon Publishers
Reading Level: 2.0-3.6

People Profiles
Teaching Resources, Inc.
Reading Level: 3.0-3.5

Pleasure Reading Series
Garrard Publishing Co.
Reading Level: 3

Reading Attainment Series
Grolier Educational Corp.
Reading Level: 3-4

Reading Essentials Series
Steck-Vaughn Co.
Reading Level: 1-8

Reading for Concepts
  (for Skill Development)
McGraw-Hill Book Co.
Reading Level: 3-12

Reading Laboratory Series
Science Research Associates
Reading Level: 1-12

SRA Pilot Library Series
Science Research Associates
Reading Level: 2-12

Stories for Teenagers
Globe Book Co., Inc.
Reading Level: 6

Teen-Age Tales
D.C. Heath & Co.
Reading Level: 5-6

*Young Adult Sequential Reading
    Action Program*
Book Lab, Inc.
Reading Level: 6

Occupational Education
and Work Study

A distinguishing characteristic of many curriculums for the exceptional and disadvantaged is an emphasis upon occupational information and work study. Initiated generally at primary age and grade levels, the program becomes increasingly specific at the secondary level. The program differs sharply from college-bound curriculum, in that occupational courses of study focus upon unskilled and semiskilled jobs.

Instructional material presented in this chapter include books, worktexts, resource units, practice materials, audiovisual aids, and a variety of teacher resources. Only a sampling of such suggested sources could be included. New materials are appearing on the market each year. A preferred approach to this area of the curriculum would provide for the development of local materials allowing for a specificity not possible in commercial sources. This is especially true in the work study phase of the program, in which local work stations are used and motivation is high.

In addition to the sources suggested, other materials relating to occupational education may be located in all other chapters of this handbook.

Appendix Two is reprinted from *Instructional Resources for Teachers of the Culturally Disadvantaged and Exceptional Child* by Robert M. Anderson, Robert Hemenway, and Janet Anderson (Springfield, Illinois: Charles C. Thomas Co., 1971), pp. 195-207, Chapter 10, by permission of Robert M. Anderson.

BOOKS AND WORKTEXTS

Accent Education Series	manual and workbook
Dare and Wolfe	12-adult
Follett	3-4

High interest instructor's books and text booklets used as resource materials in special education programs and with culturally disadvantaged students. Individual titles are *You and They, You Are Heredity and Environment, Taking Stock, You and Your Needs, Getting That Job, You and Your Occupation, Keeping That Job, You and Your Pay, Paycheck, Retail Sales Clerk — Yardgoods, Just Married, Containers, On Your Own,* and *Family of Five.* $0.69—$1.50 each.

Campus Work Experience	
Teenagers Prepare For Work	worktexts
Carson and Daly	14-21
Allyn & Bacon	9-12

Keyed to school work experiences as custodian's assistant and cafeteria helper. Book One of *Teenagers Prepare For Work* covers employment in factories, messenger service, food trades, dish-washing-machine operation, baby-sitting, and service stations. Book Two includes getting and holding a job, spending, income, application forms, and other topics. For use in prevocational training programs at the high school level. $2.25 each.

Employment Phase	text, aids
Matyas, Sofish, and others	12-18
Mafex	4

Designed for junior and senior high school low-achieving culturally disadvantaged and special education students. Employment Phase One of the Target Series may be used as a basic course in work adjustment programs. Includes a student text, activity book, eight classroom-size posters, and a teacher's guide. The text, *Pete Saves the Day,* concentrates on providing information common to all jobs and includes self-evaluation, interviews, seniority, unions, and getting along with others on the job. Student activity book contains two high-interest stories, a general information section and worksheets with application blanks and pay deduction forms. $0.50—$3.00.

Family Life	text and workbook
Prevo	14-adult
Frank E. Richards	4

Discusses problems and experiences of young married couple who are graduates of a special class. Includes finding an apartment, buying furniture, budgeting, out of work, job at the bakery, bringing up children, and others. Paperback book, $2.00. Fabrikoid bound, $4.75. Workbook, $1.25.

Finding Your Job, Units 1A-6	units, workbook
Company	13-adult
Finney	2-4

Designed for students in special classes and others in which the occupational level will be unskilled or semiskilled. Each of six units contains five volumes with twelve monograph briefs per volume. Each brief contains information about a specific job and includes kind of jobs, pay, history of the job, working hours, schooling needed, positive and negative aspects of the job, vocabulary, and additional outside resources. $20.50 per unit. Workbook relates generally to the units and contains an assortment of exercises. Student selects his preferred occupation from the units and relates exercises in the workbook to his choice. Should be routinely available to secondary special education programs. Workbook, $1.50.

Foundations of Citizenship	books
Shawn	15-adult
Frank E. Richards	4

Social adjustment books emphasizing areas of occupational education. Contains material on the family, the community, jobs and how to get them, how to hold them, spending, saving, taxes, social security, recreation and leisure time, occupational word lists and spelling word lists based on mental-age levels. Designed for special classes, guidance, and the disadvantaged. $3.75 each.

Getting Along Series	worktexts
Mooney	14-adult
Frank E. Richards	2-4

Five, soft cover worktexts appropriate for special education classes, adult programs, and slow learning tracks at the secondary level. Each chapter includes sections on spelling words, word study, discussion, exercises, projects, and a comprehension test. Individual titles are *After School Is Out, Al Looks for A Job, A Job at Last, Money in the Pocket,* and *From Tires to Teeth.* $1.25 each.

Getting Ready for Payday	worktexts
Hudson and Weaver	14-adult
Frank E. Richards	4

Three books dealing with checking accounts, savings accounts, and planning ahead. Designed for special classes, culturally disadvantaged, and adult basic education. $1.00 each. Set of three, $2.50.

Happy Housekeepers worktext
Prevo 14-adult
Frank E. Richards 4

Experiences of two girls working as domestics in three different house-holds. For special classes, culturally disadvantaged, and adult basic education. $1.35.

Help Yourself to a Job, Parts I and II workbooks
Dogin 13-adult
Finney 2-4

Two workbooks designed for special education classes. Part I presents lessons and exercises related to getting a job. Part II presents lessons and exercises discussing the difference between skilled, semiskilled, and unskilled work, as well as information related to occupational forms, e.g. social security. 70 pp., $1.50 each.

How to Get a Job booklet, manual
Fraenkel 14-adult
President's Committee on Employment 8-12
of the Handicapped

Designed as a guide for physically and mentally handicapped job seekers. Explains appropriate way to choosing the right kind of work, looking for a job, interviewing, and starting work. Good grooming tips are emphasized and checklists for the job seeker are provided. Teacher's manual provides many suggestions for a classroom prevocational train-ing program. May also be used with culturally disadvantaged. Free.

How to Hold Your Job workbook
Fudell and Peck 13-16
John Day 2

Frequently recommended for occupational education classes at the sec-ondary level and for special education classes. Appropriate for a full year of work. Manual complements workbook and emphasizes work values and attitudes rather than specific job skills. Workbook, $2.50. Manual, $6.45.

I Want a Job worktext
Hudson and Weaver 14-adult
Frank E. Richards 4

Presents forms and procedures essential for job applications. Designed for special classes, culturally disadvantaged, and adult basic education. $1.20.

Jerry Works in a Service Station book, manual
Wade 13-18
Fearon 3

Divided into ten chapters relating the story of a high school graduate who begins work in a service station. Interesting exercises on vocational materials and language-arts skills follow each chapter. Appropriate for junior and senior high EMH. $1.50.

Jobs in Your Future worktext
Company 13-18
Scholastic 4-5

Forty lessons written for the slow-learning student. Short stories present job-hunting situations, practice exercises including filling out application forms, social security forms, and others. $0.75.

New Rochester Occupational Reading books, workbooks
Series 12-18
Goldberg and Brumber 2-5
Science Research Associates

Basic text for use in secondary special education classes and programs for the slow learner in occupational education classes. Content provides three different achievement levels. Workbooks and teacher's guide available for each of the texts. $1.00—$5.30.

Off to Work book, workbook
Voelker and Pritchard 10-18
Stanwix House 2-4

Parallel reader of the Functional Basic Reading Series. Has been used as a basic text in occupational education courses in special education classes and for slow-learning children in slow-track programs. Available in three levels of difficulty, grades two through four. Manuals available. $0.85—$4.00.

On the Job worktext
Hudson and Weaver 14-adult
Frank E. Richards 4

Sequel to *I Want a Job*. Designed for special education classes, culturally disadvantaged and adult basic education. $1.20.

Preparing for Job Success workbook, manual
Peal 12-15
Houston Independent School District 7-9

Prevocational reading workbook for junior high mentally retarded. Covers health and grooming, courtesy, and handling money. Teacher's manual available. 157 pp. Other resource units from this school system are *Building Maintenance, Motor Vehicle Maintenance, Building Trades, Learning About Jobs, Parking System,* and *Food Trades.* Highly recommended for use in secondary work-experience programs for the retarded.

Scholastic Scope	news magazine
Company	13-18
Scholastic	4-6

Published weekly for poorly motivated teenagers, poor readers, disadvantaged students. Current news, personal and job guidance are emphasized. Teacher's edition offers detailed lesson plans, student activities, and two transparency masters. $1.65 each.

Soft-cover Adult Library Books	books
Knott and Dubnick	12-adult
Steck-Vaughn	4-6

Two occupational education books of high interest and low vocabulary, originally designed for basic adult-education courses. May be used in secondary education programs for slow learners and in special education programs. Titles and grade levels are *They Work and Serve* (four and five), and *A Job for You* (five and six). $1.24 each.

Turner Career Guidance Series	booklet
Turner	14-adult
Follett	4-6

Six booklets appropriate for secondary school special education programs and slow learners in occupational education classes. Titles are *Wanting a Job, Training for a Job, Starting a Job, Looking for a Job, Holding a Job,* and *Changing a Job.* Teacher's guide available. $0.84 each.

Turner Livingston Reading Series	worktexts
Turner and Abramowitz	13-18
Follett	5-6

Six worktexts for the culturally deprived adolescent, slow learner, remedial-reading classes, adjustment classes, and others. Stories include comprehension and skill development activities. Teacher's manual available. Individual titles are *The Person You Are, The Money You Spend, The Family You Belong To, The Jobs You Get, the Friends You Make,* and *The Town You Live In.* $0.84 each.

Unemployed Uglies	book, workpads
Howard	14-adult
Frank E. Richards	4

A course on what not to do on the job. Includes teacher's instruction book with twenty cartoons, twenty pads of twenty cartoons and jingles. Designed for use with special classes, guidance, and the disadvantaged. $29.75.

Vocational Reading Series	worktext
Lerner and Moller	12-adult
Follett	4-6

For use in any class where students are working below grade level. Each of four texts features a high-interest story with appropriate student activity pages. Teacher's guides and answer keys available. Stories about beauticians, auto mechanic, practical nurse, butcher, baker, chef, department-store workers, and office worker. $0.87—$1.26.

What Job for Me	booklets
Anton, Appleton, and others	14-adult
McGraw-Hill	4

Series of illustrated, dramatic short stories about noncollege-educated people and the jobs they do. Fact sheet provides information on responsibilities and duties of each job, educational and training prerequisites, places to look for such employment, hours of work, pay scales, physical demands, and future opportunities. Social skills are emphasized. Correlated sound filmstrips are being prepared to provide the student with an additional learning aid. $1.20 each.

World of Work Series	books
Bohn and Wool	14-adult
Curriculum Research Press	3

Topics selected to provide understanding of work world. Two texts, *Your Job and Success* and *You and Success,* include practice lessons, unit tests, and teacher's edition. $2.60 each.

AIDS

Fifty-four Functional Words	kit
Van Ness and Bergwall	12-16
Wasp Filmstrips	3-6

Self-contained kit of teaching materials designed to teach fifty-four words in the categories of safety, direction, and places. Includes fifty-four flash cards with textured words, nine filmstrips, a sixty-four page workbook, and a teacher's guide. Words are taught using a combination of the picture word, kinesthetic, and tracing methods. Recommended for use with exceptional children. $68.00.

Grooming for Boys Filmstrip Series	filmstrips
Not Stated	12-18
McGraw-Hill	**7-9**

Stresses the importance of appearance in business and social situations. Discusses grooming and conduct when applying for a job. Titles are *Clean as a Whistle, Fit as a Fiddle, Time to Attire,* and *Strictly Business.* Set of four, $24.50. $6.75 each.

Laundry Workers	film
Not stated	12-18
Captioned Films for the Handicapped	4

Depicts a modern, semiautomated laundry and dry cleaning plant employing largely unskilled workers. Source of general information to students studying the world of work in service industries. Fifteen minutes. Price not stated.

Occupational Education	filmstrips
Not stated	14-adult
Eye Gate	2-4

Nine color filmstrips designed for older educable mentally retarded students and highly recommended. Individual titles are *The Job Interview, Stocker in a Super Market, The Waitress, Fixing a Flat Tire, How to Use a Checkbook, The Variety Store, The School Cafeteria Worker, The Nurses Aid,* and *The Gas Station Attendant.* Teacher's manual included. $39.00.

Occupational Education Materials for	pictures
the Mentally Retarded	12-18
Company	1-3
Occupation Education Materials	

Functional pictures on heavy paper may be used in experience units. Two sets of twelve pictures each available. Includes self-care skills, duties in the home, communication, preparing for and getting a job.

TEACHER RESOURCES

A Functional Core Vocabulary for Slow	list
Learners	14-18
Borreca	2-6
Harris Country Center	

Originally published in the *American Journal of Mental Deficiency,* this reprint is an extensive listing of functional basic-vocabulary words. Classifications are standard, core, and vocational. 28 pp., $1.00.

Guide to Jobs for the Mentally Retarded	book
Peterson and Jones	12-adult
American Institute for Research	2-6

Provides comprehensive job information appropriate for EMH. Information includes school and community work training, workshops, job analysis, evaluation, and placement. An excellent reference for planners of work-experience programs. $5.00.

Handbook of Job Facts	book
Murphy	12-18
Science Research Associates	4-12

Provides information on over two hundred occupations. A must for developing occupational information curriculum and presenting job descriptions. $3.96.

A High School Work Study Program for	book
Mentally Subnormal Students	14-18
Kolstoe and Frey	2-6
Southern Illinois University Press	

Hard-cover book presents the high school curriculum for the EMR in depth. Emphasis is on work-study programs, curricular needs, course of study, and sheltered workshops. Also helpful are extensive listings of job-analysis and work-experience forms. $5.00.

Occupational Information in the	book
Elementary School	7-18
Norris	1-12
Science Research Associates	

Although written for the elementary school teacher, this professional book is helpful for teachers of exceptional children in developing occupational education programs. Practical outlines, techniques, and examples are presented for offering occupational information. $4.95.

Social Skills for Living and Learning	curriculum guide
Neuber	adult
Penn State University	professional

Based on work initiated by Hungerford in New York City. Arranged in four stages to include basic EMH levels. Each stage is assumed to cover from three to four years of growth. Material is further divided in four levels—primary, the immediate community; intermediate, the widening community; junior high, the world of work through school job training, homemaking, family living, and community membership; senior high, the world of work through community job training, homemaking, family living, and citizenship. 225 pp., $2.00.

Instructional
Materials

DEVELOPMENTAL READING SERIES*

> *Basic Reading System*
> J.B. Lippincott Co.
>
> *Bookmark Reading Program*
> (nonfiction materials)
> Harcourt Brace Jovanovich
>
> *Design for Reading*
> Harper & Row, Publishers
>
> *Holt Basic Reading System*
> Holt, Rinehart & Winston, Inc.
>
> *Houghton Mifflin Reading Program*
> Houghton Mifflin Co.
>
> *Harper & Row Linguistic Readers*
> Harper & Row, Publishers
>
> *The Linguistic Readers*
> Benziger, Inc.
>
> *Macmillan Reading Program*
> The Macmillan Co.

---

*The developmental reading programs emphasize various methods or skills. The teacher should consult each publisher's brochures for information.

Merrill Linguistic Readers
Charles E. Merrill Publishing Co.

Miami Linguistic Readers
D.C. Heath & Co.

Open Court Reading Program
Open Court Publishing Co.

Palo Alto Reading Program:
    Sequential Steps in Reading
    (linguistically based)
Harcourt Brace Jovanovich

Patterns, Sounds, and Meaning
    (linguistic)
Allyn & Bacon, Inc.

Reading Essentials Series
Steck-Vaughn Co.

The Read System
American Book Co.

Reading System
American Book Co.

Scott, Foresman Reading Systems
Scott, Foresman and Co.

Sheldon Basic Reading Series
    (linguistically based)
Allyn & Bacon, Inc.

SRA Reading Program, Revised
Science Research Associates

Structural Reading (K-3)
Random House

The Young America Basic Reading
    Program (content materials)
Lyons & Carnahan

PROGRAMMED READING MATERIALS

Edmark (not entirely self-
    instructional)
Edmark Associates

Peabody Rebus
American Guidance Associates

Program Reading Systems
Webster Publishing Division of
McGraw-Hill

Sullivan Remedial Reading Program
Behavioral Research Laboratory

MULTISENSORY MATERIALS*

Alpha Chest
Age Stein and Co.

Alphabet Motor Activities
Catalogue Number 206 (book and
    tape)
Developmental Learning Materials

Audio-Reading Tutor
Department GTM
Reader's Digest Services, Inc.

Beginning to Read, Write, and Listen
    (multisensory program between
    readiness and actual reading—work-
    books and cassettes)
J.B. Lippincott and Co.

First Experiences (letters and sounds)
McGraw-Hill Book Co./Early
    Learning

Instructo Kinesthetic Alphabet Cards
Instructo Corp.

Learning about Sounds and Letters
Ginn & Co.

Learn to Write Cursive Letters
Milton Bradley Co.

Learn to Write Manuscript Letters
Milton Bradley Co.

Lok-Letters
Mafex Associates, Inc.

Luxor Learning Letters
J.C. Coffey Co.

Multi-Modality Units
Milton Bradley Co.

Multisensory Letters and Numerals
Ideal School Supply Co.

Touch Flash Folds
Touch, Inc.

*Vowel Sounds/ A Self-Instructional
    Modalities Approach*
Milton Bradley Co.

---

*For other multisensory materials, see Chapter Eight.

PHONICS PROGRAMS

Alpha One (multisensory)
New Dimensions in Education, Inc.

Breaking the Sound Barrier
The Macmillan Co.

Building Reading Skills (workbook)
McCormick-Mathers Publishing Co.

*Durrell-Murphy Phonics Practice
    Program*
Harcourt Brace Jovanovich

*The Efi Patterns in Phonics: A
    Decoding Approach (EFI Audio
    Flashcard Program)*
Electronic Future, Inc.

Eye and Ear Fun (workbook)
Webster Publishing Division of
    McGraw-Hill

Get Set Games
Houghton Mifflin Co.

Learning to Read with Phonics
Teaching Aids Institute

Listen-Look-Learn
Ideal School Supply Co.

Phonics (records)
Bowmar

Phonics Is Fun Program
Modern Curriculum Press
Level: Grades 1-3

Phonics Skilltext
Charles E. Merrill Publishing Co.

Phonetic Keys to Reading
Economy Co.
Level: Grades 1-4

Phonics Practice Program
Harcourt Brace Jovanovich

Phonics We Use Learning Game Kit
Lyons & Carnahan

Phonics We Use (workbooks)
Lyons & Carnahan

Reading with Phonics (Hay-Wingo)
J.B. Lippincott & Co.

Sound Foundations Program (spelling
    series)

Developing Learning Materials

Speech to Print Phonics, 2d ed.
Harcourt Brace Jovanovich

Target Series
Field Educational Enterprises

*Wenkart Phonic Readers and
    Workbooks*
Wenkart Publishing Co.

PROGRAMS AND MATERIALS FOR AUDITORY PERCEPTION

Action-Reading (includes active
    participation by students)
Allyn & Bacon, Inc.

Auditory Discrimination in Depth
Teaching Resources, Inc.

Auditory Perception Training (APT)
    (auditory memory, auditory motor,
    auditory discrimination, and
    auditory imagery)
Development Learning Materials

Becoming a Learner (also includes
    language development)
Charles E. Merrill Publishing Co.

*The Goldman-Lynch Sounds and
    Symbols Development Kit*
Harcourt Brace Jovanovich

The Look, Listen, and Learn Series
Millikin Publishing Co.
>   *It's Fun to Listen* (auditory
>   discrimination)
>   *It's More Fun to Listen* (place
>   relationships)
>   *It's More Fun to Rhyme*
>   (rhyming words)

Rhyming (liquid duplicating masters
    and transparencies)
Continental Press, Inc.

*Target Red: Auditory-Visual
    Discrimination Kit*
Field Educational Publications, Inc.

Vowel Sounds and Consonant Sounds
Milton Bradley Co.

READING KITS FOR INDIVIDUALIZED INSTRUCTION

The Creative Reading Program
Harper & Row, Publishers
Level: Grades K-3

Individualized Reading
Scholastic Magazine and Book
    Services

Personalized Reading Center
Xerox Education Group
Level: Grades 4-6

Random House Reading Program
    (orange)
Random House

Reading Attainment System
Grolier Educational Corp.

SRA Reading Laboratories
Science Research Associates, Inc.

Yearling Individualized Reading
    Program
Noble & Noble, Publishers

CRITERION READING (PERFORMANCE OBJECTIVES)

Criterion Reading (Diagnostic
    Reading Profile) *
Random House

Fountain Valley System
Zweig Associates

Programed Reading (criterion-
    referenced tests)
Webster Publishing Division of
    McGraw-Hill

Read On *
Random House

The Read System (803 objectives for
    entire series)
American Book Co.

READING COMPREHENSION

Barnell-Loft Specific Skill
Barnell-Loft
Level: Grades 1-6

---

*Both Random House assessment programs correlate with basal and remedial series.

Detecting the Sequence (beginning
   readers)
Barnell-Loft

Macmillan Reading Spectrum
The Macmillan Co.

New Goals in Reading
Steck-Vaughn Co.
Level: Grades 3-6

New Practice Readers
Webster Publishing Division of
   McGraw-Hill
Level: Grades 2-8

Reading-Thinking Skills
Continental Press, Inc.
Level: Grades PP-6

VISUAL PERCEPTION MATERIALS

Come and Play
Steck-Vaughn Co.
Creative Playthings
   (three-dimensional materials)
Creative Playthings, Inc.

Developing Learning Readiness
   (visual-motor-tactile skills)
Webster Publishing Co.

Dubnoff School Program
Teaching Resources, Inc.

EDL Tachistoscopic Programs (visual
   perception and visual memory)
EDL/McGraw-Hill Book Co.

Fitzhugh Plus Program (programmed
   perceptual training in shape
   matching; shape completion, shape
   analysis, and sequencing; letter
   discrimination)
Allied Education Council

*Frostig Developmental Visual
   Perception Program*
Follett Educational Corp.

Large and Small Parquetry Designs
   (materials on eye-hand coordination, spatial relationships, etc.)
Developmental Learning Materials

Magic Squares (games designed for discrimination of letters)
Educators Publishing Service, Inc.

Manual of Primary Perceptual Training
Mafex Associates, Inc.

Michigan Tracking Program (visual discrimination)
Mafex Associates, Inc.

O'Hare Starite Programs (self-correcting training in shape matching, hand/cuscle coordination, size variations, visual/motor memory, rotation of shapes, left-to-right eye movement, letter discrimination)
Allied Education Council

The Parkinson Program for Special Children
Follett Education Corp.

Pathway School Program (coordination of arm, hand, eye dexterity; and of controlled rhythmic movement)
Teaching Resources, Inc.

Perceptual Skills (training materials on form, color, size, spatial relationships, and figure/ground discrimination)
Teaching Resources, Inc.

A Perceptual Testing and Training Handbook for First-Grade Teachers (visual motor integration templates)
Winter Haven Lions Research Foundation, Inc.

Ruth Cheeves Program
Teaching Resources, Inc.

Sequential Programmed Learning (shapes and forms)
Mafex Associates, Inc.

Silver Burdett Visual Learning Projectuals
Silver Burdett Co.

Try-Experience for Young Children
Noble & Noble, Publishers

Visual Motor Skills Materials (matching objects, copying shapes, identifying objects in pictures, etc.)
Dick Blick/Ideal Early Learning

Working with Word Patterns
Steck-Vaughn Co.

LANGUAGE PROGRAMS

Becoming a Learner
Charles E. Merrill Publishing Co.

Early Learning Systems
EDL/McGraw-Hill Book Co.

Edge I
D.C. Heath & Co.

Efi Special Language Programs
Electronic Future, Inc.

Language/Communication Program
Bowmar

Language Experiences in Early Childhood
Encyclopedia Britannica Educational Corporation

Language Experiences in Reading
Encyclopedia Britannica Educational Corporation

Peabody Language Development Kits
American Guidance Services

Try Experiences
Noble & Noble, Publishers

TECHNOLOGICAL AIDS

Audiotronics Tutorette (similar to *Language Master*)
Audiotronics

Bell & Howell Language Master
Bell & Howell

EDL Listen-Look-Learn System (combines reading skills programs and machines such as *Controlled Reader* and *Tach-X*)
EDL/McGraw-Hill Book Co.

Efi Audio Flashcard System
Electronics Future, Inc.

Hoffman Reading System
Hoffman Information Systems

Mast Teaching System
Keystone Viewing Co.

Phono-Viewer Programs (film/slide
  based upon the Sesame Street
  alphabet)
General Learning Corp.

Read On Series
ACI Films, Inc.

Starting to Read Series
ACI Films, Inc.

System 80 (self-instructional training in phonics and sight vocabulary)
Borg-Warner Educational Systems

TTC Magnetic Cards
Teaching Technology Corp.

Tutorgram
Enrichment Corp. of America, Inc.

APPENDIX FOUR

Publishers

Academic Therapy Publications
1543 Fifth Avenue
San Rafael, California 94901

ACI Films, Inc.
35 West 45th Street
New York, New York 10036

Age Stein and Co.
Seattle, Washington 48105

Allied Education Council
P.O. Box 78
Galien, Michigan 49113

Allyn & Bacon, Inc.
470 Atlantic Avenue
Boston, Massachusetts 02210

American Book Co.
450 West 33rd Street
New York, New York 10001

American Guidance Associates
1526 Gilpin Avenue
Wilmington, Delaware 19706

American Guidance Service, Inc.
Publishers' Building
Circle Pines, Minnesota 55014

Appleton-Century-Crofts
440 Park Avenue South
New York, New York 10016

Barnell-Loft
111 South Centre Avenue
Rockville Centre, New York 11571

Behavioral Research Laboratories
P.O. Box 577
Palo Alto, California 94302

Bell & Howell
7100 McCormick Road
Chicago, Illinois 60645

Benefic Press
10300 West Roosevelt Road
Westchester, Illinois 60153

Benzinger, Inc.
8701 Wilshire Boulevard
Beverly Hills, California 90211

Book-Lab, Inc.
1449 37th Street
Brooklyn, New York 11218

Borg-Warner Educational Systems
7450 North Natchez Avenue
Niles, Illinois 60648

Bowmar
622 Rodier Drive
Glendale, California 91201

Children's Press, Inc.
1224 West Van Buren Street
Chicago, Illinois 60607

J.C. Coffey Co., Inc.
104 Lake View Avenue
Waukegan, Illinois 60085

Continental Press, Inc.
Elizabethtown, Pennsylvania 17022

Creative Playthings, Inc.
Edinburg Road
Cranbury, New Jersey 08540

Developmental Learning Materials
3505 North Ashland Avenue
Chicago, Illinois 60657

Dick Blick Co.
P.O. Box 1269
Galesburg, Illinois 61405

Economy Co.
1901 North Walnut Avenue
Oklahoma City, Oklahoma 73105

Edmark Association
655 South Orcas Street
Seattle, Washington 98108

Educational Developmental
  Laboratories
284 Pulaski Street
Huntington, New York 11744

Educator's Publishing Service
75 Moulton Street
Cambridge, Massachusetts 02138

Electronic Future, Inc.
57 Dodge Avenue
North Haven, Connecticut 06473

Encyclopedia Britannica Educational
  Corp.
425 North Michigan Avenue
Chicago, Illinois 60611

Enrichment Reading Corp. of
  America, Inc.
Iron Ridge, Wisconsin 53035

Essay Press
Box 5
Planetarium Station
New York, New York 10024

Fearon Publishers
2165 Park Boulevard
Palo Alto, California 94306

Field Educational Publications, Inc.
609 Mission Street
San Francisco, California 94105

Follett Educational Corp.
1010 West Washington Boulevard
Chicago, Illinois 60607

Garrard Publishing Co.
1607 North Market Street
Champaign, Illinois 61820

General Learning Corp.
250 James Street
Morristown, New Jersey 07960

Ginn & Co.
191 Spring Street
Lexington, Massachusetts 02173

Globe Book Co., Inc.
175 Fifth Avenue
New York, New York 10010

Grolier Educational Corp.
845 Third Avenue
New York, New York 10022

Grune & Stratton, Inc.
757 Third Avenue
New York, New York 10017

Harcourt Brace Jovanovich, Inc.
757 Third Avenue
New York, New York 10017

Harper & Row, Publishers
49 East 33rd Street
New York, New York 10016

Harr Wagner
609 Mission Street
San Francisco, California 94105

D.C. Heath & Co.
125 Spring Street
Lexington, Massachusets 02173

Hoffman Information Systems, Inc.
5632 Peck Road
Arcadia, California 91006

Holt, Reinhart & Winston, Inc.
383 Madison Avenue
New York, New York 10017

Houghton Mifflin Co.
110 Tremont Street
Boston, Massachusetts 02107

Ideal School Supply Co.
11000 South Lavergre
Oak Lawn, Illinois 60453

Initial Teaching Alphabet (i/t/a)
   Publications, Inc.
6 East 43rd Street
New York, New York 10017

Instructo Corp.
200 Cedar Hollow Road
Paoli, Pennsylvania 19301

Keystone View Co.
Meadville, Pennsylvania 16335

Laidlaw Brothers
Thatcher & Madison Streets
River Forest, Illinois 60305

J.B. Lippincott Co.
East Washington Square
Philadelphia, Pennsylvania 19105

Lyons & Carnahan
407 East 25th Street
Chicago, Illinois 60616

The Macmillan Co.
866 Third Avenue
New York, New York 10022

Mafex Associates, Inc.
111 Barron Avenue
Johnstown, Pennsylvania 15906

McCormick-Mathers Publishing
Co., Inc.
450 West 33rd Street
New York, New York 10001

McGraw-Hill Book Co.
330 West 42nd Street
New York, New York 10036

Charles E. Merrill Publishing Co.
1300 Alum Creek Drive
Columbus, Ohio 43216

Milton Bradley Co.
74 Park Street
Springfield, Massachusetts 01101

Modern Curriculum Press
13900 Prospect Road
Cleveland, Ohio 44136

William Morrow & Co., Inc.
425 Park Avenue South
New York, New York 10016

New Dimensions in Education, Inc.
Long Island House
Jericho, New York 11753

Noble & Noble, Publishers
750 Third Avenue
New York, New York 10017

Open Court Publishing Co.
Box 599
LaSalle, Illinois 61301

Phonovisual Products
P.O. Box 5625
Washington, D.C. 20016

Prentice-Hall, Inc.
Englewood Cliffs, New Jersey 07632

Random House
201 East 50th Street
New York, New York 10022

Reader's Digest Services
Pleasantville, New York 10570

Scholastic Magazine and Book
   Services
50 West 44th Street
New York, New York 10036

Science Research Associates
259 East Erie Street
Chicago, Illinois 60611

Scott, Foresman & Co.
1900 East Lake Avenue
Glenview, Illinois 60025

Silver Burdett Co.
Park Avenue & Columbia Roads
Morristown, New Jersey 07960

Steck-Vaughn Co.
P.O. Box 2028
Austin, Texas 78767

Teaching Aids
159 West Kinzie Street
Chicago, Illinois 60610

Teacher Resources
100 Boylston Street
Boston, Massachusetts 02116

Touch, Inc.
P.O. Box 5385
Reno, Nevada 89503

University of Chicago Press
5750 Ellis Avenue
Chicago, Illinois 60637

University of Illinois Press
Urbana, Illinois 61801

Webster Publishing Division of
   McGraw-Hill Book Co.
Manchester Road
Manchester, Missouri 63011

Wenkart Publishing Co.
4 Shady Hill Square
Cambridge, Massachusetts 02138

Winter Haven Lions Research
  Foundation, Inc.
Box 1112
Winter Haven, Florida 33880

Xerox Education Group
1200 High Ridge Road
Stamford, Connecticut 06903

Xerox Education Publications
55 High Street
Middletown, Connecticut 06457

Zweig Associates
20800 Beach Boulevard
Huntington Beach, California 92648

Index

AUTHOR INDEX

SUBJECT INDEX